D1369868

DS
340
V34

STAMFORD BRANCH LIBRARY

UNIVERSITY OF CONNECTICUT

SCOFIELDTOWN ROAD

STAMFORD, CT 06903

UCONN STAMFORD

a34012 022468081b

DEMCO

149

Politics of the Indian Ocean Region

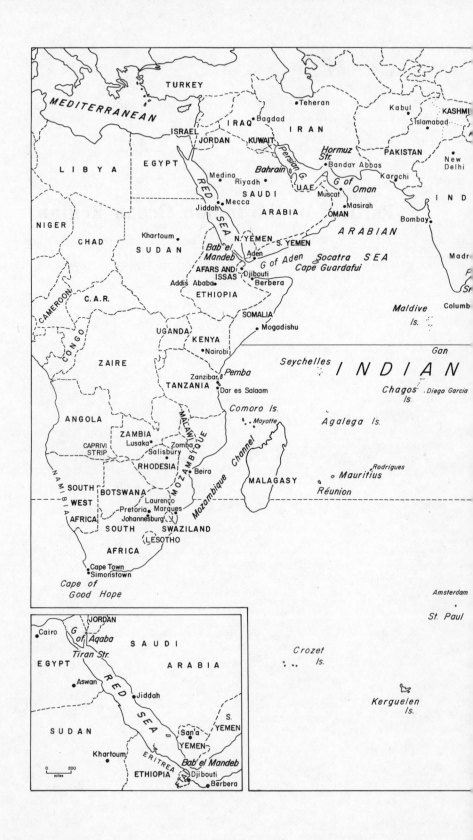

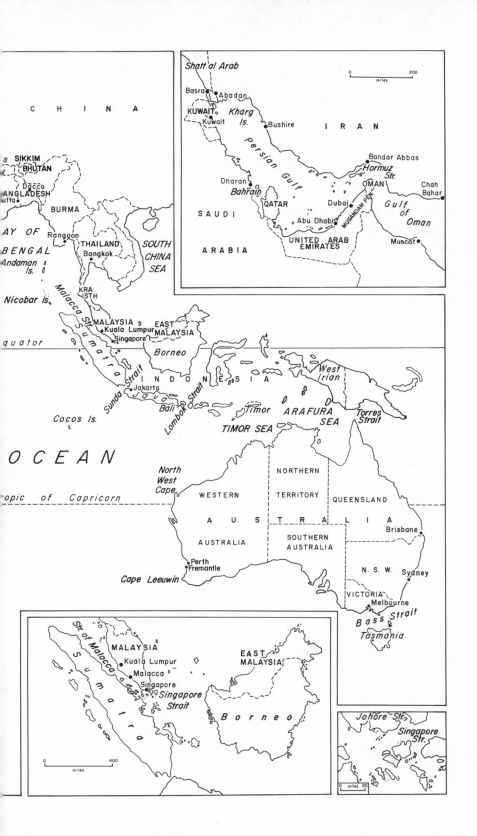

A false balance is abomination to the Lord; but a just weight is his delight.

Proverbs

Politics of the Indian Ocean Region

The Balances of Power

Ferenc A. Váli

Stamford Branch Library
University of Connecticut
Scofieldtown Road
Stamford, Conn. 06903

THE FREE PRESS
A Division of Macmillan Publishing Co., Inc.
NEW YORK

Collier Macmillan Publishers
LONDON

DS
340
V34

Copyright © 1976 by The Free Press
A Division of Macmillan Publishing Co., Inc.

All rights reserved. No part of this book may be reproduced
or transmitted in any form or by any means, electronic or
mechanical, including photocopying, recording, or by any
information storage and retrieval system, without permission
in writing from the Publisher.

The Free Press
A Division of Macmillan Publishing Co., Inc.
866 Third Avenue, New York, N.Y. 10022

Collier Macmillan Canada, Ltd.

Library of Congress Catalog Card Number: 76-8148

Printed in the United States of America

printing number

1 2 3 4 5 6 7 8 9 10

Library of Congress Cataloging in Publication Data

Váli, Ferenc Albert
    Politics of the Indian Ocean region.

    Includes bibliographies and index.
    1. Indian Ocean region--Politics and government.
I. Title.
DS340.V34   320.9'165   76-8148
ISBN 0-02-933080-7

Poetic lines from Hilaire Belloc, *Complete Verse* (London:
Gerald Duckworth & Co. Ltd., 1970), p. 117. Reprinted by
permission of the publishers. (*See page 88.*)

Contents

About the Author   x

Acknowledgments   xi

Introduction   xiii

1. Historical Survey   1

Introduction
Culture and Power before the Portuguese
Portuguese Monopolism in the Indies
Dutch, British, and French Rivalry
Britain Conquers India
Pax Britannica over the Indian Ocean
World War I and World War II

2. Geography and Geopolitics   24

The Geographic Setting
Divisions of the Indian Ocean Region
The Geopolitical Setting
Is the Indian Ocean Region a Geopolitical Unit?
Physical Geographic Unity?
Historical Legacy
Geostrategic Considerations

3. Balance of Power in the Indian Ocean   44

Power Balance and Power Vacuum
Local Balances of Power
Role of Nonregional Powers
Nonregional Powers and Their Bases
Alternative to Power Balance? The Zone of Peace Move

4. The Southeast   65

Australia
Indonesia

Malaysia
Singapore
The Malacca and Singapore Straits
Thailand

5. **Subcontinent India and its Neighbors**   88

India
Pakistan
Bangladesh
Sri Lanka
The Maldives
The Himalayan States: Nepal, Bhutan, and Sikkim
Burma
Afghanistan

6. **Countries of the Persian Gulf**   111

Iran
Iraq
Kuwait
Saudi Arabia
Bahrain and Qatar
United Arab Emirates
Oman
The Strait of Hormuz

7. **The Horn of Africa and the Red Sea Countries**   128

Ethiopia
Somalia
French Territory of Afars and Issas
The Strait of Bab el Mandeb
People's Republic of Southern Yemen
Yemen Arab Republic
Sudan
Egypt, Israel, Jordan, and Saudi Arabia
Kenya

8. **The Southwest**   144

Republic of South Africa
Botswana, Lesotho, and Swaziland
Rhodesia
Mozambique
Zambia
Malawi
Tanzania

Malagasy Republic
The Seychelles, the Comoros, and Réunion
Mauritius

9. **The Strategic Triangle: U.S.A., U.S.S.R., and China**   **171**

American Presence
Soviet Presence
Soviet Interest
American Interest
Rivalry or Coexistence
China and the Indian Ocean

10. **Residual Colonials and the Principal Outsider:**
    Britain, France, Portugal, and Japan   **199**

British Interest in the Indian Ocean
French Interest in the Indian Ocean
The End of Portugal's Indian Ocean Empire
Japan's Interest in the Indian Ocean

11. **Oil, Shipping, and the Law of the Sea**   **210**

The Oil-rich and the Oil-poor Countries
Oil and the Balance of Power
Shipping and Its Protection
Territorial Waters and Straits
The Archipelago Concept
The Continental Shelf and Resource Jurisdiction

12. **The Weight of Balances**   **230**

The Role of Superpowers
Regional Powers, Great and Small
Neutralization and Denuclearization
The Indian Ocean and the Central Balance of Power

Appendix 1. Littoral and Hinterland States of the Indian   **247**
           Ocean Region

Appendix 2. Coastline Measurements of the Indian Ocean   **263**
           Littoral States

Appendix 3. Principal Straits and Channels in the Indian   **265**
           Ocean Region

Index   **267**

About the Author

Ferenc A. Váli was born in Budapest, Hungary, in 1905. He received his Doctor Juris degree at the University of Budapest in 1927, and his Ph.D. in political science at the University of London in 1932. Before World War II he engaged in an international legal practice, and from 1935 was on the Law and Political Science faculty of the University of Budapest. He published several books in Hungarian and German. During World War II the Hungarian government sent him to Turkey on a confidential mission to make contact with the Allied Powers. In Turkey from 1943 to 1946 he lectured at the University of Istanbul.

Returning to Hungary in 1946, he served as international law adviser to the Hungarian Ministry of Finance and taught again at the University of Budapest, until he was banned from both the faculty and the ministry when the Communists finally took over in early 1949. In 1951 his Western connections led to his arrest and condemnation to fifteen years of imprisonment. He was, however, released at the time of the revolution of 1956.

When the revolution was crushed by the Soviet intervention in November 1956, Professor Váli and his wife escaped from Hungary to Austria. They spent one year in London, Paris, and The Hague on a Rockefeller Foundation fellowship, and entered the United States at the end of 1957. From 1958 to 1961, Dr. Váli was a Research Associate at the Harvard Center for International Affairs. Since September 1961 he has taught at the University of Massachusetts at Amherst as Professor of Political Science.

After his arrival in the United States (where he became a citizen in 1963), Professor Váli published several books and articles on international politics. Among his books, *Servitudes of International Law: Rights in Foreign Territory* is the standard work on that subject. At Harvard he wrote *Rift and Revolt in Hungary: Nationalism versus Communism*. In 1967, pursuant to research in Germany, he published *The Quest for a United Germany*. Taking advantage of his knowledge on Turkey, he wrote *Bridge across the Bosporus: The Foreign Policy of Turkey* and *The Turkish Straits and NATO*.

This last study led Professor Váli to become interested in the political and strategic questions of the Indian Ocean region, where Soviet naval presence added to the already existing instabilities. His research on these multifarious problems was conducted in this country, in European capitals, and finally in the states around the periphery of the Indian Ocean itself. The results of his four-year study, including his interviews with knowledgeable persons in the interested countries, are laid down in this volume.

Acknowledgments

Library research on this project started in 1972. In the summer of 1973 I spent several months in London, Paris, Bonn, and Lisbon interviewing scholars, diplomats, and journalists on the questions of the Indian Ocean region. During the first six months of 1974 I traveled in the "target area." I visited the countries around the periphery of the Indian Ocean, from Australia to South Africa, interviewing foreign ministry officials, scholars, members of the diplomatic corps, and publicists. Without the benefit of these direct sources of information, it would not have been possible to develop ideas and express views on the multifarious questions of the region to the extent I hope to have achieved. A grant awarded by the U.S. Naval War College and two grants by the Earhart Foundation enabled me to travel into these distant lands.

I owe a primary debt to those who assisted me in implementing my project: to Professor Richard R. Baxter, Professor Robert R. Bowie, and Mr. Benjamin H. Brown—all of Harvard University; to Professor Zbigniew K. Brzezinski of Columbia University; to Mr. John C. Campbell of the Council on Foreign Relations; to Dr. Henry A. Kissinger; to Mr. E. Michael Rose, former British ambassador in Zaire; and to Mr. Jonathan D. Stoddard, Director of the Office of International Security Operations, Department of State.

Professor James E. King of the Naval War College and Mr. Richard A. Ware, President of the Earhart Foundation, showed particular interest in my work. I am also indebted to Professor King for having read my manuscript and provided me with valuable comments and well-deserved criticism.

In addition to the advice and help I received from members of United States diplomatic missions throughout my travels, I was fortunate enough to receive similar assistance from British and West German diplomats. For this help I owe thanks to former ambassador Sir A. Duncan Wilson and Messrs. Iain Sutherland and George B. Chalmers—all of the British Foreign and Commonwealth Office, as well as to Ambassador Klaus Curtius of the Foreign Office of the Federal Republic of Germany.

It would be neither possible nor permissible for me to list the names of all scholars, publicists, members of the diplomatic corps, and other government functionaries of many countries who allowed themselves to be interviewed. Still, I feel obligated to mention a few of them: Mrs. Virginia Adloff and Mr. Richard Adloff, writers on Madagascar and Djibouti; Professors Hedley Bull, T. B. Millar, and Robert J. O'Neill of the Australian National University; U.S. Ambassadors Christopher Van Hollen, Sri Lanka, and Edwin M. Cronk, Singapore; Mr. K.

Subrahmanyam, Director of the Institute for Defense Studies and Analyses, New Delhi; Mr. A. Paul Fabian of the British High Commission, New Delhi; Mr. R. H. Ellingworth, Political Counselor, British Embassy, Tehran; Mr. Peter Sebastian, Political Counselor, U.S. Embassy, Addis Ababa; and Mr. D. Burrenchobay, Permanent Secretary to the Office of the Prime Minister, Mauritius.

I also owe thanks to the Research Council, University of Massachusetts at Amherst, and to colleagues in that university: Professors Edward E. Feith, J. Henry Korson, Karl W. Ryavec, Anwar H. Syed, and Howard J. Wiarda. Finally, I wish to express my sincere gratitude to my former student Professor John F. Kikoski for his invaluable help.

I am indebted to Professor Terence Burke and Mrs. Robin S. Mooney for having prepared the map of the Indian Ocean region. Mrs. Doris Holden did, as on previous occasions, an excellent job in typing the manuscript in its final form.

FERENC A. VÁLI

Introduction

When Columbus set out in 1492 to reach fabulous India by sailing westward, he was aware of the sphericity of the earth; but he still believed in the Ptolemaic concept of one "Ocean Sea." However, the Portuguese soon knew better: Vasco da Gama and his successors recognized the separate existence of the semicircular "great sea of India," and attempted to control it by occupying its "choke-points" of entry.

Domination over most of the territories around this ocean, as distinguished from the supremacy over the waters themselves, was achieved by Britain at a time when most of the nations of the New World had ended their subordination to their European colonial rulers. Only some 150 years later did the peoples of the Indian Ocean region regain their independence.

British control over these waters and most of the littoral of this ocean brought order and peace and excluded them from the ambitions of other great powers. No wonder that the successive abandonment of the United Kingdom's commitments created an entirely new situation in this oceanic region which upset the former power balances and unleashed potential crises of local and global significance.

The near-endemic instabilities of the region—more acute in some parts and less in others—have focused recent interest on the area. Whether these hazards are prompted by the interference of governments exogenous to the region, as maintained by some local spokesmen, or stem from indigenous causes is difficult to determine because of the evident interactions between regional conflicts and the rivalries of outside powers. In this context, it also should be noted that the regional powers' perceptions of their own individual problems and the collective problems of their region often differ significantly from the perceptions held by nonregional powers.

Since the British have abandoned their almost monopolistic control over the region and its waters, no other naval power has attempted to establish an overall naval supremacy. American interests appear to be limited, especially when compared to those in the Atlantic and Pacific. However, increased Soviet naval presence has raised agonizing questions as to its objectives, nature, and future scale.

While the British withdrawal continued, interest in the Indian Ocean increased. Some legislative bodies (the Subcommittee on National Security Policy of the Committee on Foreign Affairs of the US House of Representatives in

1971; the Joint Committee on Foreign Affairs of the Australian Parliament in 1970-71) made inquiries on the political and security problems of the Indian Ocean and published their findings. Some scholarly institutions (the Center for Strategic and International Studies, Georgetown University, in March 1971; the Department of Extra-Mural Studies, University of Southampton [England] in 1971; the Disarmament Studies Division of the School of International Studies, Jawaharlal Nehru University, New Delhi, in 1974; the Institute for International Political and Economic Studies, Tehran, in 1975) also held conferences dealing with these questions and edited collective publications written by the participants.

However, in the view of this writer, it also seems useful to examine the problems of the Indian Ocean region from a synoptic point of view. Important general themes both theoretical and practical, such as the geopolitical or geostrategic unity of the region, the alleged "vacuum" created by the British pull-out, and the question of the nature of strategic "bases," should not thus escape attention. A single conspectus will be able to concentrate comparatively on the attitudes and views of regional powers and on the often cited local conflicts of the area and their impact on nonregional powers. Economic (e.g., oil), navigational, and international legal questions of the region and their impact on local and global politics also have to be examined.

All these problems demand to be analyzed in the comprehensive yet singular context in which the balancing and counterbalancing geopolitical contingencies are duly weighed. The region is vast, and therefore unwarranted generalizations concerning its relative political and strategic significance are to be avoided. Nevertheless, its problems should be viewed both in the context of the global balance of power and in regard to more restricted local power relations. This attempt is made in this study.

The first chapter seeks to provide the indispensable historical background for subsequent investigations. Chapters 2 and 3 examine the geographic and geopolitical and the balance-of-power questions of the region. The following five chapters discuss the political problems of the individual countries in the five subregions of the area: Australia and the Southeast Asian countries of the Indian Ocean; subcontinent India and its neighbors; the countries of the Persian Gulf; the Horn of Africa and Red Sea area; and the southwest, which includes South Africa and other states in the southern and eastern parts of Africa as well as the islands along their shores. Chapter 9 examines the political presence of the strategic triangle—the United States, the Soviet Union, and China—while Chapter 10 deals with the residual influence of former colonial powers in the region. Chapter 11 discusses the oil problem, navigation, and the law of the sea in their impact on the political issues of the region. And, finally, Chapter 12 adds some concluding observations with special emphasis on the global balance of power in the context of regional problems.

When discussing the plethora of conflicts, internal and external, of the regional countries and the impact on the region of exogenous forces, a certain selectivity as to topics had to be practiced. It was unavoidable that greater space had to be devoted to topics which appeared to this writer more important than others. Such a selection may not be approved by some readers. But if more attention had been given to specific geographic areas or problems, well-balanced treatment of significant issues, as attempted, would not have been possible.

I attempted to refrain from too many cross-references, which make reading rather cumbersome. However, the comparehensive character of the work, which demanded the examination of questions from widely different angles, rendered certain duplications inevitable. But I wished to abstain, for the sake of brevity, from citing a source for every item and piece of data; rather, I have added a selective bibliography at the end of each chapter.

Chapter 1

Historical Survey

*Let it be known to your Majesty that if you are strong in
ships the commerce of the Indies is yours; and if you are
not strong in ships, little will avail you any fortress
on land.*

Francisco de Almeida, first viceroy of the
Indies, to King Manoel I of Portugal, 1505

Introduction

The eminent historian of the Indian Ocean, Auguste Toussaint, called it "a
neglected ocean."[1] This may be true if we compare the number of publications
on this ocean with those treating the Atlantic and Pacific. On the other hand,
the Indian Ocean *has* a history, whereas no comprehensive history of the
Atlantic or the Pacific has yet been written. This may be a reflection of the
"closed" character of the Indian Ocean, the continuum of its historical development, and the interrelations and interactions between events in its various
corners, which provide a centrality that better permits a consistent narrative and
pertinent analysis of its multimilennial story.

Any historical presentation in a work on contemporary international politics
necessarily must be even more selective in what it treats than is the case with
historical publications. The historian's task is to describe and analyze what has
happened and why. If his orientation is historical, the student of contemporary

[1] Auguste Toussaint, *History of the Indian Ocean* (Chicago, 1966), p. 1.

1

politics uses the past to cast light upon the patterns of present-day developments.[2]

It is an illuminating endeavor in itself to divide the chronology of events into logical and consistent frames. K. M. Panikkar, the prominent Indian historian, differentiated thus between three separate eras or historical frames for us: the period before Vasco da Gama; next, the "Vasco da Gama epoch of Asian history," that is, the period between the arrival of the Portuguese admiral at Calicut and the end of World War II; and, finally, the contemporary period.[3]

Evidently, the "da Gama epoch" presented singularly important aspects, for during this era the control of the Indian Ocean and its riparian territories was held by nonregional maritime powers. However, the intensity of control along with its aims and purposes varied and ultimately changed according to the different actors and the times of their action. In time, the original emphasis on ideological (religious) motivations and on trade gave way to colonial acquisitions on a scale unprecedented in earlier centuries. Power and prestige considerations played a role which was uncommon in prior eras. Nonregional control did not end in 1945; it did end to a large degree when the British withdrew from the Indian subcontinent in 1947, but not completely even then for the British. Finally, the "da Gama" distinction does not take account of the by no means negligible presence and impact of the United States and the Soviet Union in the post-World War II period, although the nature of these influences has differed from those which European powers exercised during the previous four and a half centuries.

If we are to consider the nature and the methods by which influence and control were achieved, the use of maritime power in that oceanic region must first attract our attention. But in the past the Indian Ocean region was affected not only by the exercise of sea power; land power, foreign invasions led to major developments in the Indian subcontinent as well as in East and South Africa before and during the time when great maritime powers reached out into these waters.

Another past and present characteristic of the power relations between littoral nations of the area is their dependence on the balance of power existing outside the area. Historical developments in the Indian Ocean area during most of the time before the completion of the British conquest have been a function of events, or the power balance, in the Atlantic or European theater of confrontations.

In the pre-Gaman period the historical events of the area were largely divided between developments in the western and eastern parts of the ocean. After the arrival of the Portuguese, interrelations between different parts of the Indian Ocean have become more manifest. While major historical events took place in the northern section of the Indian Ocean basin, that is, in the Asian lands, the role of the African coast and, lately, of Australia is not negligible. The Euro-

[2]See Hans J. Morgenthau, "The Intellectual and Political Functions of a Theory of International Relations," in Horace V. Harrison, ed., *The Role of Theory in International Relations* (Princeton, N.J., 1964), pp. 104-105.

[3]See K. M. Panikkar, *Asia and Western Dominance. A Survey of the Vasco da Gama Epoch of Asian History, 1498-1945* (London, 1959).

peans arrived from around the southern tip of Africa. Before that the principal history of the Indian Ocean region unfolded in the area north and east of the Persian Gulf, across India, further east into the Malay Peninsula and through what is now Indonesia. The area around the Red Sea and the band of territory on the eastern coastland of Africa about halfway to the Cape of Good Hope constituted another stage of historical developments.

The early reports on navigation and travel in the Indian Ocean provide fascinating reading. We read of Egyptian expeditions in the period around 1500 B.C. which reached the Land of Punt (most likely Somaliland), of Phoenician shippers who brought from Ophir "gold and silver, ivory, and apes, and peacocks."[4] Traders and colonists from pre-Islamic Arabia, from India and Malaya, and also from China, sailed along the northern coast of the Indian Ocean exchanging goods and spreading their civilizations into distant lands. These maritime exchanges were favored by monsoon winds (the secrets of which must have been known to these Asian sailors from times immemorial), favorable climate, and the absence of dangerous currents. Probably even before the Mediterranean became an avenue for the seafarers of many nations, the sea routes from the Persian Gulf and the Red Sea toward India and beyond as well as along the northern part of East Africa were frequented by the sailing boats of Arabs, Persians, Indians, Malays, and possibly also Chinese. The first European—according to historical evidence—who traveled in the Indian Ocean was a Greek by the name of Scylax; commissioned by Darius I, the Persian king, he led an expedition from the Persian Gulf around Arabia to Egypt.[5]

From our point of view, these were curiosities which did not affect the power relations of the region. The ancient Persian Empire which reached to the Indus River never had ambition for sea power in the Indian Ocean. But it was no doubt the land power that held overwhelming control in the northwest corner of that region. With the overthrow of this empire and the arrival of Alexander the Great's Macedonians, the first organized European force penetrated into the area. After Alexander reached the Indus Valley, he was able to accomplish his retreat only by transporting part of his army by sea under the expert leadership of his admiral Nearchos.

Two successor states of the Alexandrine Empire had access and influence over this northwestern part of the Indian Ocean: the Seleucids, who ruled from Syria to the confines of India, and the Ptolemaids, whose domain was Egypt with its Red Sea coast. The Romans inherited only the western part of the Seleucid Empire; the eastern half fell to the Parthians, who barred commercial access toward India. Egypt, however, became a Roman province in 31 B.C. and thereby the Graeco-Roman period, lasting for about 400 years, opened in the western half of the region. The first centuries of the Christian era were the years when fewer power influences but significant expansions of cultures made themselves felt over almost the entire basin of the Indian Ocean.

[4] I Kings 10:22.

[5] Toussaint, pp. 24-27.

Culture and Power before the Portuguese

Roman influences were never imperialistic in the Indian Ocean; they were commercial and, to some extent, cultural. It is even doubtful whether we are justified in speaking of Rome in this context. Those who traveled in the Red Sea and beyond were ethnic Greeks and Orientals, often the subjects of Rome. Typical among them was the anonymous author of the famous *Periplus of the Erythrean Sea,* a kind of mariners' directory, written by a Greek sea captain from Berenice on the Red Sea in the first century A.D. This mariner described his voyages to India, to the Persian Gulf, and down the African east coast, giving information and advice on his experiences.[6]

Until the late fourth century Graeco-Roman fleets sailed annually to India. Adulis, the present Massawa, served as the major entrepôt for this interoceanic trade. Along with trade went a civilizational impact, the remnants of which are still to be found all around the western basin of the Indian Ocean.

The second, even more important contacts were established between India and the Malay world. It is no exaggeration to call this cultural orbit "Greater India."[7] Indians, especially Tamils from south India, settled in Malaya and Indonesia and merged with the local population (these Indian colonies should not be confounded with the Indian settlements in the ninetenth century). Hindu and Buddhist influences have not disappeared in those countries, though they have become submerged in the autochthonous substratum. There is proof that Indian traders moved westward into the Red Sea and Persian Gulf areas.

After the fourth century A.D. Graeco-Roman shipping into the Red Sea and Indian Ocean diminished with the political and economic collapse of the Roman Empire. In Iran the Parthians were replaced by the native Sassanid dynasty. Under the Sassanids, Iran for the first time possessed a navy which controlled the sea routes from the Persian Gulf to the Arabian Sea and even to the Red Sea. In the sixth century Ethiopia (the Axumite Kingdom) confronted Iran in Arabia and the Red Sea; the former occupied for half a century the Arabian coast of that sea. For that period, expansionism obtained primacy over commercial objectives.

In the seventh century the rise of Islam brought about a complete reversal of power relations. Arab conquest made Egypt and Iran into integral parts of the Islamic world and the Red Sea an Islamic lake. These were conquests by land and not by sea. The Islamic wave reached the confines of India (also by land) in the eighth century. However, there was no Arab-Muslim political-military expansion across the Indian Ocean; rather, the golden age for Arab merchantmen flourished for 700 years. During that period important shifts occurred in the

[6] A good description is found in Roland Oliver and Gervase Matthew, eds., *History of East Africa,* Vol. I (Oxford, 1962), p. 94.

[7] The names of Indonesia or Indochina attest to the validity of this thesis. The expression "Greater India" is used, among others, by Toussaint, pp. 60-73.

power relations between the countries bordering the eastern half of the Indian Ocean basin; and in the later years of that era the Chinese made their most spectacular appearance in force.

Since the first century of the Christian era, several Southeast Asian states have emerged, some of them from time to time claiming overlordship over others. The Funan Empire, centered in what is now Cambodia, extended its power over the Malay Peninsula. In the fourth century Funan power was largely replaced by the kingdom of Shri Vijaya, which was centered in Sumatra. But by the eighth century Shri Vijaya was made dependent on the Sailendra Kingdom, which had earlier originated in Java. All of these, in particular Shri Vijaya, were maritime powers.

In south India several maritime kingdoms existed in the first century A.D.; among them the Chola Empire held a genuine thalassocracy in the Gulf of Bengal and eastward. In the eleventh century the Cholans attacked Shri Vijaya across the sea, and for a hundred years battles were fought for the control of the Malacca Strait.[8]

Islamic influence had not yet reached the eastern Indian Ocean at that time. Arab traders and colonists did penetrate into the coastland of East Africa, where they set up towns and intermingled with the local population. But as mentioned before, the Arab-Islamic advance was commercial and religious-cultural and not expansionist in the political-military sense. Aden, at the entrance of the Red Sea, was held by the sultan of Egypt from 1175 for half a century and then given up. By the thirteenth century Muslim settlements, established for trade purposes, became widespread along the Malabar coast of India. After 1300 Islamic influence spread out into the eastern Indian Ocean, reached Malay areas, and the Malacca Strait, and moved further beyond.

Muslim political domination entered India by the tenth century from Afghanistan and established itself in Delhi by the thirteenth century, advancing further south in the next.[9] This Islamic expansion did not, however, affect power relations on the sea, nor did it interfere with the shipping and trade pursued peacefully from one end of the ocean to the other. On the other hand, the entry of the Chinese into the Indian Ocean in the thirteenth century and later in the first half of the fifteenth was motivated by considerations of political influence and prestige, though again activities connected with these did not affect commercial navigation and trade.

Traditionally, China conceded primacy to land power, for China's main strategic consideration lay with Inner Asia. But during the Southern Sung dynasty (1127-1279) sea power and overseas trade were given greater prominence. Subsequently, the Mongol Yuan dynasty organized maritime invasions of Java (1292), and Chinese warships exacted tributes from states in southern

[8]See K. M. Panikkar, *India and the Indian Ocean* (London, 1951), pp. 33-35. The Chola Empire at times extended to Ceylon and the Maldive Islands.

[9]W. H. Moreland and Atul Chandra Chatterjee, *A Short History of India,* 4th ed. (New York, 1957), p. 143.

India, Sumatra, and Malaya. Between 1405 and 1433, during the Ming dynasty, seven expeditions under the command of Admiral Cheng Ho, a eunuch, were sent into the Indian Ocean—to Aden, Hormuz, and the Persian Gulf and even to the coast of Africa. These Ming fleets demanded and received tribute and acknowledgment of the Chinese emperor's overlordship. After the 1430s these maritime expeditions suddenly ended. The Mongol menace detracted interest from these oceanic incursions, and expansion across the seas was thereafter abandoned.[10]

At the end of the fifteenth century, when the Portuguese made their dramatic entry into the Indian Ocean, there existed a power vacuum; that is, no major navy plied these waters and no country sought to exercise maritime control in the region. It seems interesting, yet idle, to speculate upon what would have happened if the Chinese presence had clashed with the Portuguese endeavors to rule the ocean.

The wave of Islamic advance preceded the Portuguese arrival by less than a hundred years; in some places, Indonesia, for example, it succeeded Vasco da Gama's advent.[11] It would be futile to speculate whether the Islamic advance would have been prevented or stopped had the Portuguese reached the Indian Ocean earlier. But one should be reminded that the Spanish annexation of the Philippine Islands forestalled the spread of Islam except for the southern islands of the archipelago, where Madrid was "just too late."

Portuguese Monopolism in the Indies

In the fifteenth century Christianity was critically engaged in a seemingly endless war against Islam in southeastern Europe, in the Mediterranean, in Spain, and in North Africa. At the same time, Europe depended on the Muslim world for the supply of spices and certain luxury commodities. Venice and Genoa, with great difficulties, acted as middlemen in furnishing these much-coveted articles at enormous costs. And behind the world of Islam stood legendary India, the source of wealth and—as it was believed—of Islamic might. There was also a widespread belief that behind the Islamic peoples, in Asia or Africa, Prester John, a Christian ruler, battled the common foe.

It was then well known, although not openly admitted, that the Ptolemaic geography was erroneous, that the world was round, not flat, and that the Indian Ocean was not a land-locked sea. Therefore India could be reached by either moving westward (as Columbus attempted) or by circumnavigating Africa. Religious dedication and a yearning for glory, power, and wealth inspired the

[10]See John K. Fairbank, "China's Foreign Policy in Historical Perspective," *Foreign Affairs* 47 (April 1969), 449-463.

[11]In Malacca the acceptance of Islam is estimated to have occurred in 1414, in Java around 1500, in the Moluccas around 1475, and in the lesser Sunda Islands only by 1600. F. J. Moorhead, *A History of Malaya and Her Neighbors,* Vol. I (London, 1959), p. 103.

Portuguese royal house to discover the route to the Indies. Under the leadership of Prince Henry the Navigator (1394-1460), expedition after expedition was sent along the coast of Africa pushing deep into the Gulf of Guinea and the South Atlantic. It was a most systematic and secret undertaking.[12]

In 1487 King João II dispatched the expedition under Bartolomeu Dias which succeeded in rounding the southernmost tip of Africa and entering the Indian Ocean. That same year two secret agents, Pero de Covilham and Affonso de Payva, were sent to India and Ethiopia via Egypt and the Red Sea. Disguised as Muslim merchants, they reached Aden, where they parted. Payva left for Ethiopia and was never heard of again. Covilham sailed to India, visited several places on the Malabar coast, went to Hormuz, and traveled along the East African coast. Upon his return to Cairo, he forwarded a detailed report to his king. He was then ordered to go to Ethiopia where, being prevented from returning to Portugal, he spent the rest of his life.

In 1497 when King Manoel I, the successor to King João, commissioned Vasco da Gama to sail around the Cape and to India, the Portuguese knew exactly where they were going. Unlike Columbus, they were familiar with the problems of navigation in those waters, the monsoon pattern, and the Indian ports to which they were heading. Da Gama's ships reached Calicut in April 1498, the first to have made a direct trip between Europe and the Indies. He returned to Lisbon the following year.

In such a way Portugal, with consistency and financial sacrifice incommensurate with its limited resources, opened up the trade route to the treasures of the Indian Ocean. But much more was thereby achieved. The Portuguese turned the flanks of the Islamic world, diverted the traditional flow of spices and other articles which reached the Middle East from the Indian Ocean region and the Spice Islands, and deprived the Arab world of the revenue they had realized by forwarding these commodities to Europe. And the Ottoman Empire that by the early sixteenth century gradually extended into Egypt, Arabia, and Mesopotamia now faced the Christian foe on a new front: the Red Sea and the Arab Indian Ocean.

At the time of the Portuguese arrival maritime traffic was almost entirely in the hands of Arab-Muslim sailors and merchants, but no naval-political control was exercised by any power in the Indian Ocean. In order to secure the maximum exploitation of the wealth of these areas, Portugal wished to monopolize to its own advantage the entire maritime trade. To that effect Lisbon endeavored to place the Indian Ocean under its naval-military control.[13]

During the next ten years, following the first voyage of Vasco da Gama, the Portuguese government came to the conclusion that in order to exclude all competition in the spice trade and also "to spread the faith," it had to make full

---

[12]A good description may be found in Alan Villiers, *Monsoon Sea. Story of the Indian Ocean* (New York, 1952), pp. 117-152.

[13]When Vasco da Gama allegedly told his Arab pilot that the Portuguese had come to India "to share in trade and to spread their faith, but not to conquer," he was told, "You will find that you will have to conquer, whether you wish so or not." Villiers, p. 142.

use of its naval superiority, sweep the sea of the Arab vessels, and capture the trade and divert goods directly to Lisbon. However, there were divergent views on how to achieve this grandiose plan.

The first Portuguese viceroy of India, Francisco de Almeida, who arrived in 1505, defeated combined Arab and Indian fleets. He believed that Portuguese supremacy could be maintained without territorial acquisitions, only requiring the assistance of local allies. However, his concept was not endorsed by his successor, Affonso d'Albuquerque, who became the architect of Portuguese empire in the Indian Ocean. He aimed to capture the strategic approaches to the Indian Ocean, to seal off these entrances to foreign shipping, and to set up territorial bases around the shore of the ocean. The Cape route was made secure by occupying key points along the East African coast; Socotra and Aden were captured to control the entrance to the Red Sea. Hormuz was taken to dominate the Persian Gulf. Albuquerque set out to conquer the eastern bottleneck leading to the Spice Islands, namely Malacca. Military stations were established on the island of Ceylon. And to set up a central command post to rule this vast maritime empire, the Portuguese settled in Goa, which became the supreme headquarters of their naval domination and the seat of the viceroy.

The Almeida-Albuquerque controversy, which was decided in favor of the latter, under entirely different conditions and in a different technological age, may still have some contemporary implications. The question remains basically the same: May naval (and air) supremacy be secured without naval (and air) bases? We shall have to come back to this question more than once in different contexts in this work.

The degree to which Portugal succeeded in excluding all foreign competition remains moot. Although Arab and Indian captains needed licenses issued by the Portuguese against payment to carry goods, their monopoly was not airtight. This is only natural, for blockades and embargoes never are. Nor was it unusual that Arabs and Indians considered Portuguese activities as piratical; the French considered the British blockade around their coast during the Napoleonic Wars to be piracy; so did the Germans when they were placed under a blockade in World Wars I and II; unrestricted U-boat warfare was also given the same epithet. Nevertheless, for a hundred years Portugal was able to obtain valuable cargoes—pepper, ginger, cinnamon, mace, cloves, nutmeg—all highly priced products in Europe. Portuguese ships also brought precious stones, silk, porcelain, textiles, and perfumes to Lisbon. The Indian trade was a royal monopoly and ended at the mouth of the Tagus. Portugal had no ships available to take the goods further. This was done by Flemish and Dutch shippers, mostly from Antwerp, who distributed these articles to England, France, Germany, and other countries.

Portuguese control and trade monopoly were made possible by the naval-military superiority of their galleons and *navs* over Arab-Turkish and other vessels in the Indian Ocean. Although European waters were shared by ships of every flag, a papal bull issued by Pope Alexander VI in 1494 gave the seas of the Western Hemisphere to Spain and the waters around Africa and India to

Portugal. A year later Spain and Portugal signed the Treaty of Tordesillas, which shifted the dividing line somewhat to the west so that Brazil was recognized as belonging to the latter. The Portuguese thus claimed sovereignty over the Indian Ocean and justification in "confiscating the goods of all those who navigate these seas without our permission."[14]

Portuguese rule served three purposes which, however, in the Lusitanian mind were closely interrelated. It satisfied aspirations for the glory and greatness of the country (so well expressed in *The Lusiads* by Camões); it offered an opportunity to convert "heathen" to the Catholic faith; and it brought unprecedented wealth to a poor country. In view of the limited resources of Portugal, what happened was a remarkable achievement. It was also a fortunate coincidence that no major local power existed which could have challenged the Portuguese ascendancy. The Ottoman Empire's naval strength was deployed in the Mediterranean and engaged in a desultory struggle with the Christian powers; only relatively small forces were available to fight the Portuguese in the Red and Arab Seas. Even so they caused considerable trouble to the "Rulers of the Indian Ocean." Ethiopia, the putative realm of Prester John, was invaded in the middle of the sixteenth century by Turkish-led Islamic forces; the Christian empire had to be rescued by Portuguese contingents but at the price of Ethiopia's conversion to Roman Catholicism. But when the danger was over, allegiance to the Pope was denounced, and the Portuguese were expelled.

The Mogul Empire, gradually extending its domination over India since 1526, was almost exclusively a land power, with little interest in maritime traffic or trade. This clear division of land power and sea power prevented any major clash between Portugal, with its monopoly of navigation and trade, and the rulers of Delhi, who controlled much of the interior of India.

Portuguese imperial power in the Indian Ocean lasted for about one century. This was the real Vasco da Gama epoch—an attempt by one European power to maintain a national monopoly of power and trade. Even in the heydays of British imperial dominance in the Indian Ocean region in time of peace, the sea lanes were left open to the shipping of all flags.

Dutch, British, and French Rivalry

Portuguese power was reduced in the Indian Ocean area by the arrival of other European fleets and not by the opposition of littoral powers. In any case, Portugal would have been unable to maintain its monocratic control if in competition with other, often more powerful European nations. But the decline of Portuguese power in the early seventeenth century was mainly due to historical developments in the European theater.

In 1580 King Philip II of Spain inherited the throne of Portugal. Inevitably, Portugal thus became involved in the wars that Spain fought against England and

[14]Panikkar, *India and the Indian Ocean*, p. 40.

its own rebellious provinces in the Netherlands. The Dutch so far had acted as middlemen in the distribution of Portuguese goods transported from the Indies; now they were banned from the mouth of the Tagus. They, and subsequently the English, therefore, resolved to trade directly with the Indies.

The Dutch also had a Covilham to brief them concerning sailing and trade in the Indian Ocean. Jan Huyghen van Linschoten, who for years had been secretary of the Portuguese Archbishop of Goa, provided the necessary information; he even published a book by the name of *Itinerario*, a detailed guide on navigation and geography of the region.

The first Netherlands fleet of four ships sailed in 1595 under the command of Cornelius de Houtman, who had previously served under the Portuguese. Following Linschoten's advice, after reaching the Cape, he sailed directly to Java, thereby avoiding the Indian waters and the Strait of Malacca so closely watched by the Portuguese. The Dutch even later preferred one of two more direct routes to reach the Indonesian islands—the middle route, which brought them along the island of Mauritius (named after Maurice of Nassau), or the eastern route along the western coast of Australia—for both were less frequented by the Portuguese. The center of their activity became Java, where they founded Batavia, subsequently the capital of their East Indian empire.

Although fully supported by the States General of the Netherlands, the Dutch sailed and traded under the aegis of their East India Company. The endeavor was essentially commercial; they were not interested in converting the natives or, in the beginning, in creating a colonial empire. They fought the Portuguese as rivals in business and ousted them gradually from their strongholds, east of Malacca, then in Ceylon, India, and the East African coast. In 1641 they captured Malacca. Previously, in 1620, with the help of the English, a strong Persian army took Hormuz. However, the Dutch were not able to altogether eliminate the Portuguese because they were faced by two more formidable rivals, the English and the French.

In 1601 the English established their East India Company, which was to outshine in every respect the similar companies of the Dutch and the French. The same year six ships under Captain James Lancaster sailed to Sumatra, returning with a rich cargo two years later. But first the English activities in the East Indies were rather modest compared to those of the Dutch, with whom they occasionally cooperated but whom they more often had to fight just as vehemently as the Portuguese. One of the most important ventures of the English was the peaceful take-over of Bombay Island from the Portuguese, a more convenient trading post than Surat further north. Soon Bombay grew into a major commercial center and outlet for Indian goods.

The East Indian Company of France was created in 1604 but at first was deployed almost inconspicuously. Only after 1664 did it set up trading posts in India. In 1710 the French seized uninhabited Mauritius (the Dutch had abandoned the island) and named it Isle de France.

In 1641 Portugal separated from Spain and tried to pursue an independent foreign policy. But it was too late to rescue its Indian empire. In 1648 the

Portuguese lost Muscat to the Omani Arabs and some of their East African outposts. The Portuguese were now more and more relying on the English against the Dutch and thus managed to retain Goa and other stations on the Indian mainland.

Admiral G. A. Ballard called the period between 1600 and 1750 an "interregnum" because no single European nation was able to wield overwhelming authority in the Indian Ocean area.[15] During that period some powers, indigenous to the region, established limited control in certain maritime areas. Aurangzeb, the last of the outstanding Moguls, equipped a navy which successfully operated in the Bay of Bengal against the kingdom of Arakan. It was during his reign (1658-1707) that the Mogul Empire spread over the major part of India; after his death the decline and fragmentation of this Muslim empire began. In 1698 Seif-bin-Sultan, ruler of Oman-Muscat, captured Mombasa, Kilwa, and Pemba from the Portuguese. Subsequently, the Omanis placed Zanzibar under their control. In the nineteenth century Zanzibar became an independent sultanate under an Omani ruler. The Portuguese fought back but eventually were able to keep only the area south of Cape Delgado (Mozambique). The Moguls had no navy on the Malabar coast of India; the Maratha Confederacy, which was in a state of revolt against the Great Mogul, maintained a fleet which fought the forces of Delhi. Subsequently these forces engaged in a long struggle against the English East India Company and captured vessels of any flag until, in 1756, their power was destroyed by the British.

A series of wars between the English and the Dutch in the latter half of the seventeenth century provided the reason that persuaded London to support the remaining Portuguese possessions. The main Dutch strength remained concentrated in what is now Indonesia, but the coast of Ceylon and the Cape of Good Hope also continued to be controlled by the Netherlands.

By the early eighteenth century France was showing greater interest in the Indian Ocean region. In 1735 the French, under Commander Bertrand Francois Mahé de la Bourdonnais, the governor of Isle de France (Mauritius), converted Port Louis into a major naval base. Port Louis is about halfway between the Cape and India. The British at that time had no such base between the Atlantic and their stations on the Malabar and Coromandel coasts of India.

The wars waged between the French and the British during the eighteenth and early nineteenth centuries determined the outcome of the struggle which these two imperial powers fought for the control of India and the ocean surrounding it. While it is correct to say that these wars were really decided on the European battlefield and by the naval battles fought in the Atlantic, changes in the military or naval balance in and around India in some cases resolved the distribution of power in this area.

During the War of the Austrian Succession (1740-1748), Joseph François Dupleix, governor of Pondichéry, the French stronghold on the Coromandel coast, struggled to establish French supremacy in India. With the help of his Indian allies, he tried to oust the British from Madras, their headquarters on the

[15]*The Rulers of the Indian Ocean* (London, 1927).

east coast of India. He was opposed by his British counterpart, Robert Clive. Dupleix failed, and the ensuing peace left the Franco-British balance essentially unchanged.

In 1756 the Seven Years' War began. Actually, in the interval between these two conflicts, wars by proxy were fought between the Indian allies of France and Britain. But now the struggle concentrated in the northeast where the Nawab of Bengal, an ally of the French, seized Calcutta, the British trade center. Clive defeated the Nawab at Plassey (1757), and Bengal became the first large territorial unit of the English East India Company. As in the previous war, the French were handicapped by a relative lack of naval power. Now Admiral Howe's victory at Quiberon gained naval control for the British in the Atlantic, and French forces in India were virtually cut off from their homeland. By the Treaty of Paris (1763) Britain annexed Canada and French influence in India was also largely eliminated.

Britain Conquers India

During the fifteen years of peace following the Treaty of Paris, the English East India Company further consolidated its control over large territories in India. In 1778 the peace was interrupted by hostilities between Britain and France, in which the following year Spain and the Netherlands joined France. Once more British and French fleets entered the Indian Ocean. Pierre André de Suffren, the French rear admiral, fought Sir Edward Hughes, the British vice admiral, in the Bay of Bengal and around Ceylon. Trincomalee, the naval base on Ceylon (which still belonged to the Dutch) was taken by the British but retaken by Suffren. On land Pondichéry was captured by the British.

The peace treaty of 1783, concluded again in Paris, more or less restored the status quo, leaving however an edge in favor of London. In the Atlantic theater Britain fared less well, for the independence of the thirteen American colonies had to be recognized.

It should be remembered that from 1783 until World War II no major naval encounter between capital ships took place in the Indian Ocean, and no concentration of large naval units occurred except during the Russo-Japanese War. In 1905 the Russian Baltic fleet passed the ocean on its ill-fated journey to the Far East.[16]

During the French Revolutionary and Napoleonic Wars, the British further extended their possessions on the Indian subcontinent and over other territories of the region. The Cape Province was captured and annexed in 1806, and Dutch settlements in Ceylon were seized in 1796. The Indonesian archipelago was restored to the Dutch after the Treaty of Amiens (1802) but retaken again after the renewed outbreak of the war.

[16]See Richard Alexander Hough, *The Fleet That Had to Die* (London, 1958).

The French naval strongholds in the middle of the Indian Ocean, the Mascarene Islands, were the bases from which the French directed a commercial war against enemy shipping. The French corsairs did considerable damage even during the Napoleonic Wars. In 1810-11 the Mascarenes, the principal island being Isle de France (Mauritius), were captured by the British. The Seychelles were taken earlier (1794).

In India, Tippoo Sahib, ruler of Mysore, followed in the footsteps of his father, who was an ally of the French, by invading Travancore, a British-protected state. He was defeated in 1799 and south India was incorporated into the possession of the British East India Company or turned into vassal states of the British. In north central India the company's power was advanced to the border of the Punjab, and Delhi was taken in 1804. The British Crown, represented by the company's governor general, claimed paramountcy on behalf of the Mogul, who was by then a mere puppet in the hands of the British.

France did not cease to consider India as the mainstay of British wealth and influence. Several times attempts were made to weaken or destroy that power: Bonaparte's Egyptian campaign was ultimately aimed at India; in 1800 the First Consul enlisted the help of Tsar Paul for a land invasion of British Asia; and in 1807 Emperor Napoleon negotiated with Persia for transit of a French army. But another even more urgent preoccupation, the Peninsular War, prevented an attempt to carry out this chimerical project. The French also flirted with Seyyid Said, the ruler of Muscat-Oman, and concluded a treaty with him in 1807. However, as soon as the tide turned against Napoleon, the sultan became eager to cooperate with the British.

Under the treaties of Paris which ended the Napoleonic Wars (1814 and 1815), Britain kept the Cape Province, Mauritius, and Ceylon. The Indonesian islands were returned to the Netherlands and the island of Bourbon (subsequestly, Réunion) to France. Trade posts in India (Pondichéry, Chandernagor, and others) were also restored to the French but prohibited from being fortified or maintaining a garrison. Thus the British took into their possession all the strategic key points of the Indian Ocean, removed French rivals from India, and were well on the way to place under their control the Indian subcontinent with its island annexes.

Pax Britannica over the Indian Ocean

Although it seems highly frivolous to pretend that the British Empire was built by absentmindedness, it appears still correct to maintain that the extension of British power over huge, populous India, as well as most of the countries around the Indian Ocean, was not the result of a preconceived plan. This, of course, was not true of the establishment of Portuguese mastery in that area. The English East India Company was the arm of British power which was instrumental in extending domination for its nation. It operated, fought, and ruled to secure markets, to trade, and to make money. Neither its founders nor subsequent leaders thought of establishing a gigantic territorial empire under the direction of the company with all the worries and risks involved in such an undertaking. The Portuguese, the Dutch, and the French were fought because they were rivals in the commerce to be conducted in the areas in question, a commerce which relied on the exploitation and the intimidation of the local population and its rulers. As the Portuguese discovered, to trade under such circumstances one has to control and in order to control one must have territorial supremacy. But, as we have seen, it was essentially the series of conflicts with the rival French, employing allies in India, which induced the British to use similar methods. And when the allies of the French were defeated or proved unreliable, the company, with the approval of its home government, resorted to the annexation of land which it had to govern. As is often true in world affairs, this procedure proved contagious; conquests were made for reasons of expedience or security or simply because a weak adversary was faced.

There is certainly much validity in the proposition recently submitted that the external domination of Indian Ocean countries was mainly the result of great power rivalries, conflicts between regional powers, and European interference in the affairs of the latter.[17]

The conquest of the still independent countries of India continued after 1815. The Maratha states gave up resistance in 1819, the Punjab was annexed between 1840 and 1850, followed by the North-West Frontier Province. Baluchistan was subjected to British control in 1875.

In 1815 Britain occupied the kingdom of Kandy in the heart of Ceylon, which neither the Portuguese nor the Dutch ever controlled. The rounding up of the areas east of India also continued. In 1824 Singapore was founded by Sir Stamford Raffles at the eastern entrance of the Strait of Malacca, on an island ceded to the British by the sultan of Johore. Malacca itself was exchanged by the Dutch for certain British settlements on Sumatra. Singapore soon outdistanced Malacca as the major entrepôt and harbor of the strait as well as of the areas to the east and west. By the end of the nineteenth century the sultans of the Malay Peninsula accepted British protection; in 1909 Siam ceded to Britain four other Malay states until then under its vassalage. The British conducted three wars against Burma between 1824 and 1885, which resulted in the annexation of the country, which was then placed under the administration of the government of India.

In 1857 a mutiny broke out against British rule in India which was swiftly suppressed; it led to the final elimination of the shadow ruler, the last of the Moguls. The outdated rule of the East India Company was ended in the same year, and direct control by the government in London was established. In 1877 Queen Victoria assumed the title of Empress of India.

[17]Report dated May 3, 1974, of the experts to the Ad Hoc Committee on the Indian Ocean pursuant to the United Nations General Assembly Resolution 3080 (XXVIII) of Dec. 6, 1973 ("Zone of Peace").

London also extended its rule in the western half of the Indian Ocean. In 1839 it secured the town of Aden with the adjoining island of Socotra at the entrance of the Bab el Mandeb Strait. Aden and the Red Sea grew immensely in strategic importance when the Suez Canal was opened in 1869. In 1882 Britain occupied Egypt and its Suez Canal zone, thus placing itself in control of the route to India. Nor was the Cape route neglected: In 1843 Natal was annexed to prevent the Boer republics, which lay north of the Cape Province, from obtaining an outlet to the ocean. And the South African War (1899-1902) led to the annexation of the Orange Free State and Transvaal, and ultimately the unification of South Africa under British rule. Along the northern east Coast of Africa, Zanzibar was made a British protectorate in 1890, and the British East Africa Company-administered territory (Kenya) was taken over by the London government in 1895.

In the southeast of the Indian Ocean region, Australia, including its west coast, became an undisputed British territory in the early nineteenth century. Formal occupation of what is now Western Australia took place in the 1820s to forestall the French from establishing a foothold.

Accordingly, British sovereignty extended over most of the countries surrounding the Indian Ocean. France, with British consent, turned the big island of Madagascar into a protectorate in 1885 and ten years later converted it into a colony. The Comoro Islands also came under French control. In 1888 France occupied the town of Djibouti, a key point on the southern entrance to the Red Sea. In the scramble for African colonies, Germany managed to obtain a large chunk on the east coast, later known as Tanganyika. The Portuguese continued to hold Mozambique between the German colony and South Africa.

On the Arabian coast of the Red Sea, the Hedjaz was under Ottoman control until 1916, and Yemen remained a vassal state of the Ottoman sultan. South of Egypt, what was to be known as the Anglo-Egyptian Sudan was brought under British control in 1898. In 1889, a year after France had taken Djibouti and after the British had settled opposite Aden in their Somaliland Protectorate, Italy, the latest comer in the race for African colonies, occupied Eritrea. On the other side of the Horn of Africa, the Italians established themselves in what was called Italian Somaliland. Thus the ancient empire of Ethiopia was placed in a pincer between the two Italian colonies to the north and south. But Italian endeavors to conquer this ancient land failed after the fatal Battle of Aduwa in 1895.

On the eastern shores of the Indian Ocean, Siam (Thailand) was the only country in the area which managed to retain its independence. Until World War II, the Netherlands remained the undisputed sovereign of their East Indian empire, from Sumatra to the Moluccas.

Britain had no further need for major naval forces in the Indian Ocean. It controlled most of the coastal lands and was in possession of practically all the strategically important strongpoints. Only the French could have been potential opponents in the western sections of the ocean, holding such key positions as Djibouti and Diego Suarez, the naval base at the northern tip of Madagascar.

But France was no longer a rival on the sea; after 1871, smarting under its defeat by Germany, it sought compensation in territorial acquisitions in Africa and Indochina. Although there were crises in the Anglo-French relationship, the French posed no challenge to British control in the Indian Ocean region. And after the conclusion of the *entente cordiale* in 1904, France became more a cooperative friend than a rival. The Netherlands, and even more so the Portuguese, relied on British protection for their colonies. But from the end of the Napoleonic Wars there was no potential foe that could have jeopardized the naval supremacy of Britain. The growing high-seas fleet of the Kaiser was still unable to reach out in strength into the vast blue of the Indian Ocean. Ships and warships were now fueled by coal; coaling stations were a necessity for any far-flung naval presence or operation. Only the British were in possession of bunkering facilities in every corner of the ocean. And bunkering on the high seas in time of war was a most hazardous undertaking.

For some time, around the middle of the nineteenth century, only light units of the British Navy were needed to carry out humanitarian actions: it remained its task to extirpate slave trade in the African waters. Not only Arab ships were engaged in this traffic, but also French, Portuguese, and vessels of other nationalities. Piracy was a menace to shipping for a long time in the Malay waters and the Persian Gulf. The Pirate Coast in the Persian Gulf, later known as the Trucial States or Trucial Oman, was pacified by the British in the 1820s. The sheiks or emirs pledged to keep the truce, that is, to place themselves under the protection of London.

The British imperial sway over India and the Indian Ocean region was unique. No European power, in fact no country ever in history, dominated such a huge overseas empire, one which was not territorially contiguous with the homeland. The vast tracts of Central Asia and Siberia under Russian sovereignty were territorial extensions of European Russia itself. But British India and its dependencies had become a self-sufficient imperial domain of the mother country. In the eyes of British statesmen and strategists, the security and protection of this realm were only slightly secondary to the safety of the homeland.

Although Great Britain carefully watched any danger which would have threatened the naval gateways leading to India, its main concern during most of the nineteenth and early twentieth centuries was the potential threat from land which would weaken or destroy its Indian Empire. The dreaded opponent was Imperial Russia. The mountain wall of the Hindu Kush, the Pamirs, Karakoram, and the Himalayas seems to have been considered insufficient to protect India, the "most precious jewel" of the English Crown. For many decades the defenders of India endeavored to push the first line of defense of this country further north and west. Several attempts were made to convert Afghanistan into a British protectorate; British protective measures were extended into Persia; an incursion was even made into Tibet to secure that country's dependence on Britain. In 1907, when a détente was reached with Russia, the southern section of Persia was declared a zone of British influence with the consent of St. Petersburg.

After 1907 the greatest danger to the Indian Empire was considered to come from Germany. The Berlin-to-Baghdad railway was sensed to be a menace to the British position in the Persian Gulf. It should be remembered here that Kuwait, at the far end of the gulf, had placed itself in 1899 under a British protectorate to escape Turkish domination.

Japan was acknowledged as a Far East great power after its defeat of Russia in 1904-05. Even before then, however, since the end of the nineteenth century, Japan had cooperated with the British, and in 1902 Japan signed a naval agreement with London which assured Britain that in the event of a war with Germany no danger would threaten its Indian Empire from the east. The fact that an Asian power was called upon to strengthen the balance in that part of the world was a significant foreboding of the events to come.

World War I and World War II

When World War I broke out, the British, in addition to thinking of the defense of India, had another reason for securing their control over the Persian Gulf. Since 1904 the British Navy had gradually turned toward oil as the fuel for its ships. The British Admiralty was the principal shareholder of the Anglo-Persian Oil Company. To safeguard the flow of oil from its main source, the Persian oil fields, units of the British-Indian Army occupied the mouth of the Shatt-el-Arab, including the town of Basra. During that long war, Mesopotamia and parts of Persia, along with German East Africa, were rather peripheral scenes of fighting. In the East African campaign against the Germans, contingents from South Africa participated at the side of forces from Kenya and the Belgian Congo. In 1910 the Union of South Africa was established as a self-governing dominion where Afrikaners (Boers) shared power with the English.

On sea no major action took place in the Indian Ocean. Commercial ships were raided by the three German cruisers which belonged to Berlin's Far Eastern fleet. The British had few warships in the Indian Ocean (the German cruiser *Emden* was able to shell Madras with impunity), and it took the British some time to destroy the privateering German vessels. It should be noted that Australian troopships sailing to Suez were escorted by Japanese destroyers. Because of the distance involved, no German submarine entered the Indian Ocean in World War I.

India proved to be an important source of manpower and also a logistic base for the British. For a hundred years Britain had tried to make India self-sufficient or nearly self-sufficient, both militarily and financially. Previously, the Indian Ocean possessions of the Portuguese, the Dutch, and the French, while producers of valuable commodities, were often a drain on the metallic monetary resources of the mother countries. There was little these countries could usefully export to their colonies. In the mid-nineteenth century, the British exported opium to China in exchange for Chinese tea and porcelain—opium which was grown in India. But with the industrial revolution in England, it was possible to transform India, with its teeming millions, into an area which imported industrial articles in return for the raw material it produced. During World War I India advanced on the road of industrialization, which reduced its dependence on British goods. Japanese competition was also sorely felt throughout the Indian Ocean region by Japanese underbidding of the more expensive British and other European articles.

But British territorial expansion still continued after the end of this war. Not only had German East Africa (now Tanganyika) become a British mandated territory, but the elimination of Ottoman control from all Arab lands led to the creation of the British mandated territories of Iraq (Mesopotamia), Transjordan, and Palestine. After the hostilities ended, no other territorial changes took place except that, in compensation for having been given no German lands in Africa, Britain ceded Jubaland (between Italian Somaliland and Kenya) to Italy, and the king of the Nejd annexed the Hedjaz, the country assuming the name Saudi Arabia.

After the war important internal developments occurred, particularly in India. The Wilsonian principle of national self-determination did not fail to impress the Asians. The claim for Indian independence was openly raised, and the status of the Indian Empire, as a colony of Britain, became less secure. Although India was nominally given "dominion status," it was no self-governing dominion; unlike Australia and South Africa in the interwar period, it did not grow into a genuine independent state.

But outwardly the British preponderance remained unchanged. It reached its zenith while internally weak and even hollow and evidently was as overextended as Aurangzeb's Indian Empire was at the end of his reign. Sooner or later the British hegemony in the Indian Ocean region would have declined. World War II, however, hastened this inevitable development.

A prelude to the war was played by Italy in East Africa. Mussolini attempted to accomplish what Italy had failed to achieve at the end of the nineteenth century: to conquer Ethiopia. In 1935 his armies invaded that country, and in the following year Ethiopia fell to the Italians. League of Nations sanctions proved ineffective; Britain, at the risk of war, could have prevented Ethiopia's conquest by closing the Suez Canal to Italian shipping. But weak in the air and intent on keeping the peace even at the sacrifice of Ethiopia, London shied away from any drastic steps. Thus an Italian empire, a very ephemeral empire indeed, was formed by the merger of Ethiopia, Eritrea, and Italian Somaliland.

World War II reached the Indian Ocean region in the summer of 1940; France had fallen and Mussolini's Italy cast its lot with Germany. Hostilities began along the Eritrean-Sudanese border and with the invasion of British Somaliland by the Italians. However, South African forces and British-Indian units soon invaded the Italian empire from the north as well as from the south. The Italian troops, cut off from their homeland, were swiftly defeated, and by the end of 1941 warfare ended in East Africa.

However, other actions soon threatened the security of the Indian Ocean region: the German-Italian advance in North Africa posed a real threat to the

Suez Canal, and less troublesome but potentially weakening pro-German movements surfaced in Iraq and Iran. The North African danger was eliminated only in 1943; but Iraq and Iran were made secure earlier. British forces seized key positions in Iraq, and after the invasion of the Soviet Union by Germany, British and Soviet forces moved into Iran from the north and from the south, deposed the pro-German Reza Shah, and established a line of supply across Iran to the Soviet Union. The most critical situation for all countries around the Indian Ocean was created when Japan entered the war against the United States, Britain, and the Netherlands.

On December 8, 1941, one day after the attack on Pearl Harbor, Japanese troops landed at a number of points on the Gulf of Siam and handed an ultimatum to the Thai government demanding passage to Malaya and Burma. By the end of December, the Philippines were considered lost. The Netherlands, Australia, and the United States were now faced with the problem of defending the "Malay barrier," the string of islands from the Malay Peninsula to New Guinea. Only by preventing the capture of this "barrier" could the Japanese be forestalled from entering the Indian Ocean.

The two British capital ships, the *Prince of Wales* and the *Repulse,* were sunk on December 10. Singapore, lacking defenses on the land side, was captured by the Japanese on February 15. Vice Admiral Nagumo, of Pearl Harbor fame, now moved with his carrier force into the Indian Ocean, mainly to prevent reinforcements from reaching the Dutch East Indies. The Japanese victory in the Battle of the Java Sea (February 27) sealed the fate of Java and the rest of the Netherlands possessions.

Nagumo's fleet now began raiding Indian Ocean shipping. The British Far Eastern naval forces had lacked protective air cover since the sinking of their carrier *Hermes.* Commanded by Admiral Sir James Somerville, the British forces withdrew first to the Maldives and then to Mombasa on the East African coast. The Indian Ocean was open and practically defenseless; air strikes hit Colombo and Trincomalee.[18]

Japan's failure to carry on its naval advance and to land troops on Ceylon, thereby cutting off communications with India, has puzzled historians.[19] The real reason for this reluctance was Japanese fear of overextension. Japan's war plan, agreed to by its Supreme War Council on September 6, 1941, did not envisage the conquest of India, but only those of the Philippines, Malaya with Singapore, Burma, and the Dutch East Indies. A defense perimeter was to be set up from the Burmese-Indian border along the Malay barrier and thence across the western Pacific to the Kurile Islands. This already huge area (which earlier was declared to be the "East Asian Co-Prosperity Sphere") was then to be defended against attempts at recovery.[20] In any case, advances in the South Pacific to cut off Australia were given priority by the Japanese strategy; and

[18]See Samuel Eliot Morison, *The Two Ocean War* (Boston, 1963), pp. 86-101.

[19]Toussaint, pp. 238-239; Villiers, p. 229.

[20]Morison, p. 34.

their defeat in the Battle of the Coral Sea forestalled any further ambitious naval offensives in the Indian Ocean, a war theater now deemed secondary by Tokyo. The Japanese did, however, occupy the Andaman and Nicobar Islands, which covered the entrance to the Malacca Strait.

Madagascar was under the control of the Vichy government. To prevent the use of Diego Suarez by German or Japanese submarines, South African and East African British forces captured this naval base in the summer of 1942.

As soon as the Japanese advance stopped, the Indian Ocean area became of second- or third-rate concern to the Western Allies as well. A stoppage in the badly needed food imports to India resulted in the death by starvation of about 1.5 million of its inhabitants.[21] After May 1943, German submarines moved into the Indian Ocean around the Cape, into waters where shipping was not yet assembled in convoys, and wrought havoc among Allied ships. The Germans even used the Japanese-occupied Penang Harbor as a submarine base. Japanese submarines also carried out raids, collaborating here with the Germans. In February 1944 a German submarine supply ship was sunk near Mauritius.[22]

In the spring of 1945 Allied forces in India and Ceylon prepared for the reconquest of Burma, Malaya, and the Dutch colonies. These military operations were partially successful before the Japanese surrender in August 1945.

The Japanese aggression in the Indian Ocean area temporarily ended Western domination in the eastern part of the region and threatened this domination in all other parts. With their sea and air superiority, the Japanese might have been able to take Ceylon, but it is still questionable whether they would have been able to conquer India. Sea and air power alone cannot secure control of land areas. The loss of these two elements of power might, but would not necessarily, jeopardize domination of the land. Ultimately, however, control of the land can only be permanently assured by land forces.

The fact that Western dominance had been eliminated in some areas and jeopardized in others largely contributed to the campaigns for independence which took place all around the periphery of the Indian Ocean. To enter into a discussion of these movements would be beyond the task of this work. We shall restrict ourselves to the mention of major events.

In 1947 the countries of the Indian subcontinent—India, Pakistan, Ceylon, and Burma—were given independence by Britain. The irony is that India, which had for the first time in history been united by the British, had to be partitioned because of the irreconcilable antagonism between Muslims and Hindus. This event not only sowed the seeds of an irredentist urge but resulted in a political monstrosity, the divided Pakistan.

Indonesia managed to obtain recognition of its independence by the Netherlands in 1949, though not without struggle and violence. Malaya, as the

[21] Maxwell Philip Schoenfeld, *The War Ministry of Winston Churchill* (Ames, Iowa, 1972), pp. 180-181.

[22] Morison, p. 314.

Federation of Malaya, was granted independence in 1957. The British possessions of North Borneo, Sarawak, and Sabah joined the federation, which thus became Malaysia. Singapore, however, withdrew from the federation in 1965 and established itself as an independent state.

On the east coast of Africa, Tanganyika in 1961 (and land-locked Uganda in 1962) obtained independence, as did Kenya in 1963. Also distant from the oceanic shore, Zambia (the former Northern Rhodesia) became independent in the same year. In 1964 Zanzibar joined Tanganyika to form the United Republic of Tanzania. Malawi (the former Nyasaland) became independent in the same year.

In 1949 the United Nations placed Italian Somaliland under the trusteeship of Italy. This trusteeship ended in 1960. Later that year, the British agreed to the union of their Somaliland Protectorate with what used to be Italian Somaliland, and the new state assumed the title of the Somali Democratic Republic.

In the Red Sea area, the Sudan achieved independence in 1956. Both countries at the head of the Gulf of Aqaba achieved independence—Jordan (originally called Transjordan) in 1946 and Israel in 1948. Saudi Arabia, which occupies most of the Arabian Peninsula, has been recognized as a fully independent state since 1925. Aden and its hinterland, the Aden Protectorate, were abandoned by the British in 1967 and formed the People's Democratic Republic of Yemen (South Yemen).

Along the Persian Gulf, British-protected Kuwait became fully independent in 1961; Muscat and Oman (since 1970 the Sultanate of Oman) have been recognized by Britain as fully independent in the post-World War II period. Since the announcement of withdrawal "from east of Suez" in 1967 by London, the formerly British-protected Gulf States have declared their independence: Bahrain and Qatar became fully independent in 1971; the seven Trucial States formed the United Arab Emirates that same year. Iraq had been formally independent since 1932.

Most of the major islands or groups of islands in the Indian Ocean have also become independent states. Madagascar (now the Malagasy Republic) was given full independence by France in 1960. The Maldive archipelago was confirmed as fully independent in 1965, and Mauritius in 1968. Three of the four Comoro Islands (French) became independent in late 1975 and the Seychelles (British) in 1976.

All these new countries are members of the United Nations. The former British territories, with slight exceptions, are members of the Commonwealth.

Relatively few territories of the region remain under European colonial rule. Mozambique, the Portuguese possession, achieved independence in 1975. In continental Africa only the French Territory of the Afars and Issas remains under European rule; in Asia no territory does. Those islands which are unlikely ever to obtain independence are miniscule specks of territory, such as those of the British Indian Ocean Territory.

The region, then, is presently fragmented to an extent which somewhat recalls the period when Europeans first entered the Indian Ocean. Relations between the regional nations permutate and move in a bewildering combination of enmities and rapprochements. These littoral powers maintain contacts with the superpowers and other nonarea great powers which reflect every shade of the spectrum.

While sovereignties and sovereign units have changed, while new ones arose or have arisen, and while some old ones have disappeared or became completely transformed, the geographic infrastructure has not. This is still the Indian Ocean basin of yore. But technological devices of transportation and communication have brought once distant countries and peoples of this basin closer together. If we are entitled to consider the region as a geopolitical or geostrategic entity, we are certainly more justified in doing so now than hundreds of years ago, although the political picture certainly has become more fragmented, mosaicized, and even kaleidoscopic in contrast.

Selected Bibliography

Auber, Jacques. *Histoire de l'Océan Indien.* Tananarive: Société Lilloise d'Imprimerie de Tananarive, 1955.

Ballard, (Admiral) G. A. *The Rulers of the Indian Ocean.* London: Duckworth, 1927.

Coupland, Sir Reginald. *East Africa and Its Invaders. From the Earliest Times to the Death of Seyyid Said in 1956.* London: Oxford University Press, 1956.

Duffy, James. *Portugal in Africa.* Cambridge, Mass.: Harvard University Press, 1962.

Fairbank, John K. "China's Foreign Policy in Historical Perspective." *Foreign Affairs* 47 (April 1969), 449-463.

Graham, Gerald S. *Great Britain in the Indian Ocean. A Study of Maritime Enterprise, 1810-1850.* London: Oxford University Press, 1967.

Harlow, Vincent T. *The Founding of the Second British Empire, 1763-1793.* 2 vols. London: Longmans, 1952 and 1964.

Harlow, Vincent T., Chilver, E. M., and Smith, Alison, eds. *History of East Africa.* 2 vols. Oxford: Clarendon Press, 1963 and 1965.

Hough, Richard Alexander. *The Fleet That Had to Die.* London: Hamish Hamilton, 1958.

Ludowyck, E. F. C. *The Story of Ceylon.* London: Faber & Faber, 1962.

Mahan, Alfred T. *The Problem of Asia and Its Effect on International Politics.* Boston: Little, Brown, 1900.

Moorhead, F. J. *A History of Malaya and Her Neighbors.* Vol. I. London: Longmans, 1959. Vol. II. Kuala Lumpur: Longmans of Malaya, 1963.

Moreland, W. H., and Chatterjee, Atul Chandra. *A Short History of India.* 4th ed. New York: David McKay Co., 1967.

Morison, Samuel Eliot. *The Two Ocean War.* Boston: Little, Brown, 1963.

Oliver, Roland, and Matthew, Gervase, eds. *History of East Africa.* Vol. I. Oxford: Clarendon Press, 1962. Vol. II. London: Oxford University Press, 1968.

Panikkar, K. M. *India and the Indian Ocean. An Essay on the Influence of Sea Power on Indian History.* London: George Allen & Unwin, 1951.

Panikkar, K. M. *Asia and Western Dominance. A Survey of the Vasco da Gama Epoch of Asian History.* London: George Allen & Unwin, 1959.

Schoenfeld, Maxwell Philip. *The War Ministry of Winston Churchill.* Ames: Iowa State University Press, 1972.

Toussaint, Auguste. *History of the Indian Ocean.* English ed. Chicago: University of Chicago Press, 1966.

Van Leur, J. C. *Indonesian Trade and Society.* The Hague: W. Van Hoeve Ltd., 1955.

Villiers, Alan. *Monsoon Seas. Story of the Indian Ocean.* New York: McGraw-Hill, 1952.

Chapter 2

Geography and Geopolitics

*For as Geography without History seemeth a carcasse
without motion; so History without Geography,
wandereth as a Vagrant without a certaine habitation.*

John Smith, *General History
of the Somers Islands* [Bermudas] , 1623

*It is easier to describe the position of the lands of the
Empire in relation to the oceans than to the continents. . . .*

C. B. Fawcett, *A Political
Geography of the British Empire,* 1933

The Geographic Setting

The Indian Ocean is an enormous gulf surrounded by the continents of Africa,
Asia, and Australia. Only below the latitudes 35 to 45 south is it open toward
the Atlantic and the Pacific. While the boundaries of the Indian Ocean are well
defined to the north, the determination of its southern confines depends on
whether one accepts or rejects the concept of a separate Antarctic Ocean. If the
separate existence of an Antarctic Ocean is disregarded, the Indian Ocean
reaches out to the Antarctic continent.

But in more usual practice the Indian Ocean is only that gigantic bay north of
the imaginary line between the Cape of Good Hope and Cape Leeuwin, the
southwestern tip of Australia. While open in the south, it is closed toward the
north. This distinguishes the Indian Ocean from the other two oceans, the

Atlantic and the Pacific, which stretch from the North Pole to Antarctica, a circumstance that in many respects determined the particular character of the ocean named after India.

Another peculiarity of the Indian Ocean involves the northern portion—historically and geostrategically the most important. This portion of the ocean is accessible from the west and from the east only through narrow straits. In the west, these narrows lead to two culs-de-sac, the Persian Gulf and the Red Sea. The latter lost its sacklike character in 1869 when the Suez Canal was completed and the Red Sea connected with the Mediterranean Sea.

The Persian Gulf and the Red Sea are gulfs of the Indian Ocean and, therefore, belong to this oceanic system. On the eastern side, the Indian Ocean is separated from the Pacific by the Indonesian island chain (and the narrow passages between the islands) and by the Australian continent. However, whether the Timor and Arafura Seas (between the Indonesian islands and Australia) belong to the Indian Ocean, or rather to the Pacific system, is a matter of more or less arbitrary choice.

In the north, the Indian Ocean is bordered by the Asian landmass; the Indian subcontinent, like a huge tongue, lashes out into its waters and divides its northernmost portion between what is known as the Arabian Sea and the Bay of Bengal.[1]

The Indian Ocean is the smallest among the three main oceans of the world. Even if measured by its largest dimensions (including the Southern Sea, that is, the ocean approximately between parallel 45 south and the Antarctica), it extends over only 30 million square miles, while the Pacific covers 60 million and the Atlantic (without the Arctic Ocean) 34 million square miles. In its more usual narrower meaning, the Indian Ocean covers only 16 million square miles. Even so, it is too large to connect culturally, economically, and politically all the countries washed by its waters as, for instance, the Mediterranean Sea did in the past and still does. Even the "countercoast" impact—the mutual impulses and sense of reciprocal dependence—which developed on both sides of the North Atlantic is much less in evidence here. Still, some very strong mutual impacts operated in the northernmost sector of the Indian Ocean, from Arabia to what is now Indonesia, across the Indian subcontinent, and in the reverse direction.

The question of how justified we are in considering the region around the Indian Ocean as a unit, from the political and strategic viewpoint, will be discussed later. Here we just wish to point out that this ocean is a gigantic water basin which separates, but at the same time loosely unites, the various lands which girdle its waters.

---

[1] The choice of geographic names is often fortuitous. Why the Arabian Sea is a "sea" and the equally large Gulf of Bengal is a "gulf," or why the Persian Gulf is a "gulf" and the Red Sea is a "sea," is a matter of historic tradition rather than a rational choice of names.

From times immemorial the northern section of the Indian Ocean has been a much-frequented waterway, second only to the Mediterranean in the period before the discovery of the Americas, and after that momentous event a close third behind the North Atlantic sea route. Both coastal and high-seas navigation were much favored in those waters by the climatic conditions prompted by the "closed" character of the ocean.

As life and civilization in Europe were aided by the warmth brought to them by the Gulf Stream, so monsoon winds and currents served to foster the growth of vegetation, the flow of navigation, and cultural exchanges in the northern section of the Indian Ocean region. The peculiar phenomenon of the monsoon,[2] alternating according to the seasons of the year, made deep-sea navigation, in the time of sailing ships, a relatively simple "sailing with the wind" operation.

North of the Equator, the winter monsoon winds blow from the northeast, and the summer monsoon winds from the southwest; this made possible a regular shuttle movement of sailing vessels between the Arabian and East African coast, on the one hand, and the Indian and Indonesian coast, on the other. The winter monsoon is dry and conveys coolness, whereas the summer monsoon draws abundant moisture and heat, thus providing for the necessities of agriculture.

Along the Equator, a regular flow of trade winds, alternating between the easterly and westerly directions, also furnished a dependable source for ship movements. Further south, in the "roaring forties" (along parallel 40 south), ships were able to move quickly from the Cape to the Australian west coast and then north to the Spice Islands.

Winds and currents affected shipping and also the migration of some peoples. The coming of Malay-Indonesian ethnic groups to Madagascar, on the east coast of Africa, probably is due to these phenomena. Atmospheric and hydrographic manifestations even today have a bearing on navigation and continue to have political-strategic significance, as, for instance, in the case of the Agulhas Current near the Cape.

Geography provides the "infrastructure" for historical and political as well as cultural and economic developments. The Indian Ocean is no exception in this respect. A comprehensive maritime survey around the periphery of this ocean does not solely explain the historical or political developments in the region. Movements of people and of ideas, impacts of the nations on each other, clashes, and conquests have taken place and are still taking place on land and often without reference to the power relations upon the ocean itself. No monopoly should, therefore, be conceded to the oceanic outlook. However, if only for the purpose of organizing and delimiting the subject matter to be scrutinized, the Indian Ocean may be deemed to be central to the investigations pursued in this study. Such a methodological approach seems also to be amply substantiated by the experiences of both geography and history.

[2]The original meaning of "monsoon" in Arabic (*mawsim)* is "season." From this the Portuguese made *moncao,* the Dutch *monssoon,* and, eventually, the English "monsoon."

Divisions of the Indian Ocean Region

The division of the material for a study is an artificial but still indispensable tool for systematization and better understanding. For the purposes of research, the division of the Indian Ocean region into several subregions is also quite artificial but necessary. The same applies to the ocean itself, which in the course of history was often quite arbitrarily divided into component parts. These divisions resulted from the successive penetrations of the Indian Ocean by travelers from the west—from areas we now call the Middle East and subsequently from Europe.

The Red Sea and the ocean beyond the Strait of Bab el Mandeb (the Arabian Sea) were known to ancient Greeks and Romans as the Erythrean Sea (that is, the "Red Sea"). At times the Erythrean Sea north of Bab el Mandeb was also known as *Sinus Arabicus* (Arab Gulf). The maritime area east of the Erythrean Sea was named *Mare Prasodum* (Green Sea) or even more appropriately *Mare Obscurum* (Dark, or Mysterious, Sea).[3]

In the Middle Ages the Islamic world gave its own divisions and names to the areas frequented by its sailors and merchants.[4] The presently used expressions for the ocean and its constituent portions originated from the period when Europeans, beginning with the Portuguese, entered these waters in strength.

The Portuguese, and after them the Dutch, English, and French, were aiming to reach the shores and riches of fabulous India. It was only natural for them to name the sea after the land they were all striving to reach. Inlets and deep sinuosities of the ocean, as well as those parts of it separated by strings of islands, were given separate names, often quite arbitrarily. In addition to the two large inlets of the Indian Ocean in the northwest, the Persian Gulf and the Red Sea, the Gulf of Oman and the Gulf of Aden covered large maritime areas in front of the Hormuz and Bab el Mandeb Straits. The Arabian Sea and the Gulf of Bengal have already been mentioned. The Andaman and Nicobar Islands divide the Gulf of Bengal from what is known as the Andaman Sea, lying before the funnel-like Malacca Straits. The Timor and Arafura Seas are also extensions of the Indian Ocean; the latter ends in the Torres Strait, which divides it from the Coral Sea, definitely a portion of the Pacific Ocean system.

For the purposes of our investigation, the division of the land areas around the water is more important than the divisions of the ocean itself. While using the maritime conspectus, our main concern should be directed toward the land and its people.

[3] Auguste Toussaint, *History of the Indian Ocean* (Chicago, 1966), pp. 6-11.

[4] Muslim travelers divided the western Indian Ocean region as between *Sind* (probably the Persian Gulf area and the northern shore of the Arabian Sea), *Hind* (India), and *Zinj* or *Zang* (East Africa). The name of Zanzibar (originally Zanjebar) derives from *Zanj*.

In a study by the Australian Department of Foreign Affairs,[5] the following divisions of the Indian Ocean area were suggested: (1) East Africa and the ocean region east of it; (2) the northwest from Somalia around to Iran, including the Red Sea, the Gulf of Aden, and the Persian Gulf; (3) the Asian subcontinent and the sea southward; and (4) Southeast Asia and Australia.

An Indian scholar divided the region into four "pivotal areas": (1) South Africa, (2) Southwest Asia, (3) India and Pakistan, and (4) Southeast Asia and Australia.[6] These two schemes are basically similar except that the Australian version is more precise and comprehensive.

In view of the great importance of the western approaches to the Indian Ocean, the Red Sea and the Persian Gulf, the joint discussion of both these areas seems impractical and the separation of the areas around the Horn of Africa and the Red Sea area from those around the Persian Gulf appears more appropriate. For these reasons, the present study will discuss the problems of the Indian Ocean region in the context of five, instead of four, subregions: (1) the southwest, which includes southern and East Africa and the islands east of the African coast; (2) the Horn of Africa and the Red Sea countries; (3) the Persian Gulf countries; (4) the subcontinent of India and its neighbors; and (5) the southeast, including Australia.

The disadvantage of this division is that it divides the Indian Ocean countries of the Middle East. However, the Middle East is a vague and somewhat artificial geographic concept; and while some of the problems are similar, quite evidently the questions relating to the Persian Gulf area and those of the Red Sea-Horn of Africa area are dissimilar. The subsequent discussion of these two subregions is likely to prove this point.

These divisions of the region around the periphery of the Indian Ocean should not be viewed as watertight compartments; on the contrary, trends, policies, and interests between neighboring subregions frequently overlap. International relations are too complex to be confined to certain perdetermined areas without allowing for their impact on neighboring or even more distant nations. The geographic fact of being located along or near the shores of one ocean increases the interrelationships that manifest themselves in tangible and intangible ways. The geographic vicinity creates stronger impulses between the nations thus involved; but in certain situations the impulses affect even more distant, but geopolitically still close, communities. And the ultimate truth has been poignantly expressed by the leader of an Indian Ocean nation:

The importance of a universal, intercontinental understanding and association is in no way diminished by the assertion that geography continues to

[5]"The Indian Ocean," background paper, Canberra, Aug. 14, 1973, p. 4. (Mimeographed.)

[6]R. C. Sharma, "The Indian Ocean and Its Community. A Geographical Appraisal," in *Indian Ocean Power Rivalry,* ed. T. T. Poulose (New Delhi, 1974), p. 209.

remain the most important single factor in the formulation of a country's foreign policy.[7]

The Geopolitical Setting

Historic developments occur within the space on our globe and within the flow of time. Actions are carried out by men, but the potentiality of such actions depends only partly on the will of individuals or collectivities. Plans and their realization are restricted by various factors, geography[8] being one of them. Geography may serve not only as a restraint to human endeavors; it may also be an inducement or motivation.

Geopolitics describes and analyzes the influence of the geographic factor on politics in general or on the politics of certain regions or nations. While the Napoleonic dictum according to which "geography determines a nation's history" is clearly exaggerated, the constants of geography have a bearing, in some cases a determining bearing, on the variables of both national and international politics. In other words, "the political significance of any area bears a well-defined relation to its climate, landforms and natural resources."[9] And we may add to this the nonphysical factors of human geography: ethnicity and social, cultural, and economic conditions.

It is hardly possible to give even an approximation of the weight of the geographic factor on political developments. While rejecting determinism, it should be recognized that in certain situations it was geography which prescribed what was possible and what impossible. Geography even may determine what may be inevitable. The history of the Indian Ocean region provides classic examples to this effect.

The land barrier between the eastern Mediterranean and the two protrusions of the Indian Ocean (the Red Sea and the Persian Gulf) prevented massive maritime penetration of European influence—political, military, and cultural—into the Indian Ocean area. Overland penetration (Alexander the Great's) was ephemeral and scanty.[10]

The regular monsoon winds allowed for a movement of men, goods, and ideas across the northern segment of the Indian Ocean. Before the arrival of Europeans from around the Cape of Good Hope, there resulted an intercourse between peoples of these shores not unlike that which took place along the Mediterranean.

[7]Zulfikar Ali Bhutto, *The Myth of Independence* (London, 1969), p. 28.

[8]We understand under "geography" both physical geography and political geography, which includes demographic, ethnic, social, and cultural elements.

[9]Derwent Whittlesey, *The Earth and the State* (New York, 1944), p. 585.

[10]See G. A. Ballard, *The Rulers of the Indian Ocean* (London, 1927), p. 7.

The contemporary economic, political, and strategic significance of the Persian Gulf has immeasurably increased due to the exploitation and quantity of its oil. .

The fact that Muslims in India were concentrated in the two extreme corners of the subcontinent led to the creation of two Pakistans, East and West; and their ethnic, linguistic, and social differences, in turn, resulted in the partition of this country.

Movements of peoples along the coastal areas of the Indian Ocean and across its waters have had momentous impacts on its history. The impulses—military or naval conquests, political or diplomatic pressures, religious and cultural influences—have proceeded overland or from the sea. Before the arrival of the Europeans, invasions on land were predominant but by no means exclusive. Since the advent of Vasco da Gama the history and political development of the region, in general, have mostly been determined by impulses which emanated from Europe and reached the region from the sea. The sea power versus land power dilemma may thus be analyzed in the context of events which shaped the fate of the area in question.

The particular geographic configuration of this ocean—its shape resembling a gigantic gulf, the narrow entrances leading to it, as well as other characteristics—may give rise to fruitful geopolitical scrutiny.

But, primarily, another question has to be answered: Are we justified in discussing the Indian Ocean region as one unit, as a single geopolitical or geostrategic division? Is one entitled to envisage, for scholarly or practical purposes, the area synoptically, as one whose component parts bear significant relations to one another? This is a question both of correct and systematic presentation and of sound and pragmatic political thinking.

Is the Indian Ocean Region a Geopolitical Unit?

Geographers operate with the concept of a "geographic region," although they more often disagree than agree as to the characteristics or requirements for an area to be considered as such.[11] The French expression *compage*,[12] also used by English-speaking geographers, to whom it means "framework" or "structure," is even more to the point. The *compage* is an area interrelated by natural and societal features relevant for a specific consideration or study. Characteristics of a geographic region overlap into other, neighboring regions; therefore there exists no "total" region, that is, one which has features not shared with other regions. Geographic regions may differ in size; they may even extend to a large sphere of continental dimensions. From the point of view of the student of a region, what matters is that in addition to similar features its differing character-

[11]Saul B. Cohen, *Geography and Politics in a World Divided* (New York, 1963), p. 61.

[12]*Compage* is derived from the Latin (con)*pangere,* (to place together).

istics should be amenable to assimilation. Ultimately, we should keep in mind Richard Hartshorne's advice: "Any regional division is not a true picture of reality, but it is an arbitrary device of the student . . . depending on what elements appear to him as most significant."[13] It should furthermore be remembered that " 'region' is a term of art, not science, and regions in world politics emerge only because policy-makers find within a given territorial area a number of interrelated problems that are discreet."[14]

Little attention has so far been paid to the consideration of whether the Indian Ocean area should be regarded as an independent geopolitical region. Among geopolitical scholars, Saul B. Cohen not only recognized the character of this area but even anticipated its eventual emergence as a "third geostrategic region." In his vocabulary a "geostrategic region" possesses certain "globe influencing" characteristics; the two such regions—according to this view—are at present the Western world and the "Eurasian Continental World," that is, the Sino-Soviet sphere.[15]

Objections against the acceptance of an Indian Ocean geopolitical region have been sporadic, and few arguments have been offered. For instance, a report of the Joint Committee on Foreign Affairs of the Australian Parliament, while on the one hand submitting an elaborate presentation on the "Indian Ocean Region," on the other hand refused to recognize it as a "unit" because "it consists of countries which have a great diversity of race, politics, strengths and opportunities."[16]

Nobody could deny that the region around the Indian Ocean is beset by diversities of all kinds. If judged solely on the basis of ethnicity, culture, and religion, one would be compelled to refuse unity to this area. Still, it should be remembered that the region is not clearly divided on ethnocultural and religious grounds. There are massive such centers, Islamic, Hindu, Buddhist, and also Christian, but they are by no means exclusive; from these centers, waves of influences have branched out creating new centers as well as ethnic and religious diasporas of many shades.

Islam, one of the chief religions and cultures of the region, is predominant in the northwest: in Arabia, in northeast Africa (except for the Christian enclave of Ethiopia), and in Iran and Pakistan. It has branched out in a latitudinal direction into Malaysia and Indonesia, creating another massive center. Bangladesh, the former eastern portion of Pakistan, is also Islamic, and there are millions of

[13]Richard Hartshorne, *The Nature of Geography* (Lancaster, Pa., 1969), p. 285.

[14]W. Wilcox, "The Indian Ocean and the Great Powers in the 1970's," in *Collected Papers of the Study Conference on the Indian Ocean in International Politics* (Southampton [England], 1973), pp. 25-26.

[15]Cohen, pp. 63-65 and 280-281. It should be remembered that this work was published in 1963 when the real nature of the Sino-Soviet conflict could not have been recognized.

[16]Joint Committee on Foreign Affairs, *Report on the Indian Ocean Region* (Canberra, Dec. 7, 1971), paras. 13 and 89.

Muslims scattered in all parts of India and also in many other parts of the region. Ethnically, Muslims are divided mainly between Arabs, Iranians, Pakistanis (themselves divided), Bengalese, Malays, and Indonesians, although the religious-cultural bonds between these groups are by no means negligible.

Hinduism, whose adherents outnumber Muslims in the region, is ethnically more homogeneous. India is predominantly Hindu, but followers of Hinduism also are to be found in Bali (ethnically Indonesian); the Indian diaspora has brought Hinduism into every corner of the region, to Malaysia, Singapore, East and South Africa, Mauritius and the Seychelles and other places.

Buddhism, the third major religious-cultural group of the region, is to be found in Ceylon, Burma, and Thailand. Chinese minorities (a majority in Singapore) in Malaysia, Indonesia, and other corners of the region are also mostly Buddhists. The Himalayan lands north of India and Pakistan are also inhabited by Buddhists.

Christians of all denominations are the inhabitants of Australia (overwhelmingly of British descent) and of southern Africa (both the white minorities and Bantus and coloreds); Christian majorities are to be found in the southern half of East Africa and in Madagascar; Ethiopia has already been mentioned.

Indeed, ethnic-religious differences divide the population of the Indian Ocean region. However, most of the sea is simultaneously tied together by followers of the same faith, culture, and often also language. There is division, but amidst the division there is unity.

In the social-economic sphere differences between the peoples in various parts of the region are striking. Except for Australia and South Africa, which are industrialized countries, and Singapore, a commercial emporium with a relatively high living standard, all nations are in the "developing" stage. But there are wide differences even between these countries; Iran, for instance, is on the threshold of the "take-off stage" of development. The oil bonanza which descended on some countries of the Persian Gulf has created another dimension: we can now distinguish between those which "have oil" and those which "have not." The picture is therefore far from being uniform; it is highly divergent. Really, if one desired to judge the region according to developmental and social-economic standards, a disparate image would emerge.

Jacques Auber has projected concepts not of one but of two Indian Ocean regions: one which he called the "World of Cancer," north of the Equator on both sides of the Tropic of Cancer; the other the "World of Capricorn," south of the Equator parallel with the Tropic of Capricorn.[17] The first "World" is the home of the three major civilizations, of Islam, Hinduism, and Buddhism. The second is less inhabited and mostly by immigrant populations who came from various parts of the world. Evidently, this division ignored the cultural and religious cross-currents which prevail throughout the areas. The emphasis on white South Africans and Australians hardly takes account of Africans and islanders south of the Equator.

[17]Jacques Auber, *Histoire de l'Océan Indien* (Tananarive, 1955), pp. 4 and 431.

The ethnic-religious-cultural chessboard of the Indian Ocean region provides a rather confusing but not entirely negative presentation concerning unity or disunity. It seems clear that the decisive answer to our question must be sought elsewhere, in the physical-geographic and political-strategic realms.

Physical Geographic Unity?

It may be interesting to recall that according to one school of geologists the Indian Ocean basin originated in the Paleozoic era from the division of the hypothetical landmass Gondwana which had earlier been separated from the landmass Laurasia in the Northern Hemisphere. Gondwana in the Southern Hemisphere split into what are now South America, Africa, and Australia. What was to become the Indian subcontinent parted from Africa, drifted northward and collided with the Eurasian landmass, an impact which uplifted the Tibetan Plateau and erected the Himalayas. We are also told that the fracture known as the Great Rift Valley will eventually result in the breaking off of East Africa from this continent (Madagascar is a broken-off part of Africa) and that Australia is moving north and will eventually squeeze together the Indonesian islands.[18] All this has nothing to do with geopolitics but demonstrates the geological unity of the Indian Ocean basin.

While submitting his concept of two Indian Ocean regions, Jacques Auber also pointed out the physical unity and symmetry of the Indian Ocean area when comparing it with the shapeless vastness of the Pacific and the corridorlike form of the Atlantic.[19] Starting with the African continent, he demonstrated that South Africa faces the Indian Ocean rather than the Atlantic because a desert stretches along its western borders. The Great Rift Valley divides East Africa from the rest of the continent along the great lakes. The Ethiopian highlands emerge between the desert and the Red Sea area. The corridor from the Cape to the Sudan is thus formed by desert, jungle, and the Rift Valley.

The Indian Ocean region is markedly separated from the rest of mainland Asia by the Arabian Desert and the mountain wall which stretches from Anatolia to Thailand: the Ararat, the Elburz Mountains, Hindu Kush, the Pamirs, Karakoram, the Himalayas, the mountains of northern Burma. These long and massive chains, which include the highest peaks of the world, form the northern land frontier of the South Asian rimland.[20]

The Burmese-Thai border mountains, the Malay Peninsula, and the chain of Indonesian islands provide a natural barrier dividing the Indian Ocean basin from the South China Sea, a subsidiary sea of the Pacific Ocean system. Though

[18]See Alfred Wegener, *The Origin of Continents and Oceans* (New York, 1966), pp. 62-64; Alexander L. Du Toit, *Our Wandering Continents* (Edinburgh, 1937), pp. 226-228.

[19]Auber, pp. 2-4.

[20]See D. H. Cole, *Imperial Military Geography* (London, 1950), pp. 150-151.

Australia's face is turned to the Pacific rather than to the Indian Ocean it is also an Indian Ocean littoral state, as it slowly began to realize—the southeast pillar of the huge arc, 4,500 miles distant from the southwest pillar, namely South Africa. Western Australia, the principal state on the Indian Ocean, has now become Australia's "expanding western frontier."[21]

K. M. Panikkar also emphasized the geographic unity of the Indian Ocean region. Its geographic structure is such as being "walled off on three sides by land, with the southern side of Asia forming a roof over it." But the vital mark—according to him—which differentiates the region from the two other oceans "is not the two sides but the subcontinent of India which juts out far into the sea for a thousand miles to its tapering end at Cape Comorin." He concludes that, despite the vastness of its surface and oceanic character, the Indian Ocean has "some of the features of a landlocked sea."[22]

Thomson submits that "geography has created three Asias, one of the land and two of the ocean." Continental Asia is the huge landmass from Manchuria to the Urals; the oceanic Asias are those of the Indian Ocean and of the Pacific.[23]

While the Indian Ocean region is a geographic unit, it is not a cohesive economic region. Economic interdependence between the countries concerned is minimal; only 10 percent of their foreign trade is regional, the rest being directed to areas outside the region. Patterns of export-import relations between former colonial and metropolitan countries have largely survived. However, there exists local interdependence between certain subregions: thus Mozambique, Rhodesia, Botswana, Lesotho, and Swaziland are dependent on the Republic of South Africa; Malaysia and to some extent Indonesia are still dependent on Singapore as an entrepôt station; Bangladesh is an economic "basket case" that has to rely on India.

The Indian Ocean is considerably smaller than the Pacific or Atlantic; but distances between its key points are still respectable. The distance between the Cape of Good Hope and Cape Leeuwin, the line closing the arc of the Indian Ocean, is 4,500 miles. The distance from England's Land's End to New York, across the Atlantic, is somewhat shorter, but that between San Francisco to Singapore, across the Pacific, is 8,800 miles. From Aden to the Strait of Malacca (the northern width of the Indian Ocean) the distance is 3,500 miles. From Aden to Colombo it is 2,100 miles (same as the length of the Mediterranean Sea).

The more compact configuration of the Indian Ocean is best expressed by its latitudinal and longitudinal extent as compared with the Pacific and Atlantic. The southern width of the Indian Ocean extends over 80 longitudinal degrees, the northern width over 55 degrees. The longitudinal reach of the Pacific, from the Bering Strait to Antarctica, is over 130 degrees, the latitudinal span 170

[21] George G. Thomson, *Problems of Strategy in the Pacific and Indian Oceans* (New York, 1970), p. 34.

[22] Panikkar, *India and the Indian Ocean* (London, 1951), pp. 18-19.

[23] Thomson, pp. 14-15.

degrees. The longitudinal extent of the Atlantic from the Greenland Sea to Antarctica is also 130 degrees, while the latitudinal span of both the North and the South Atlantic is roughly 70 degrees.

The narrow gateways leading to the Indian Ocean north of the Tropic of Capricorn have been mentioned earlier. They are referred here as evidence of the "closed" character of that ocean. One may, of course, object that the Atlantic is also served by such narrow passages: the Gibraltar Strait, the English Channel, the Norwegian Sea between Scotland and Iceland, and the Denmark Strait between Iceland and Greenland. Evidently, except for the Strait of Gibraltar, these are not strategic bottlenecks as are those which lead into the Indian Ocean. It is true that on the western coastline of the Americas only the artificial waterway of the Panama Canal allows entrance. The other navigable entry from the Pacific into the Atlantic (if we ignore the difficult Strait of Magellan) is around the stormy Cape Horn, which is 20 degrees nearer to the South Pole than the Cape of Good Hope. Despite some analogies the entrances to the Atlantic (except for Gibraltar) have not been historically "sluiceways," have not played such roles as those of the Indian Ocean, where Portuguese, Dutch, French, and British vied for their control.

The geopolitical significance of the specific physical features of the Indian Ocean can only be fully appreciated when viewed from the perspective of historical precedents.

Historical Legacy

History creates political structures within set geographic limits. Even after these political entities crumble or disappear, the legacy of their erstwhile existence continues to impinge on the human environment. Many centuries after its collapse, the Roman Empire continued to make its heritage felt over large parts of Europe. The impact of former British or French mastery in Asia and Africa has not been fully expunged by the end of colonial rule. A quasi-invisible bond still survives between these Asian-African lands and the former metropolitan countries.

Before the arrival of the Portuguese, the Indian Ocean area was a picture of fragmentation. The exception was the cultural-religious link which connected the Islamic west with the Malay-Indonesian east. But the Islamic advance shattered Greater India, the link between the Indian subcontinent and Hinduized Malaya and Indonesia. However, the Islamic arm stretched out across the ocean merely created a religious-cultural identity with no political-military content.

In contrast, the Portuguese invasion was purely military and political, though the intent was also religious. Lisbon conceived the Indian Ocean area as a unit that could be subjected to naval control. The unique geography of the region was highly helpful: the choke-points, west and east, once occupied, barred entry and exit. As described earlier, this embargo was far from foolproof, but it still served its purpose: for a century naval superiority worked and major control of the sea remained established. Navigation and commerce by local shippers were markedly reduced, and Portuguese bottoms carried spices and other coveted articles to Europe.

It is, therefore, no exaggeration to assert that, despite its shortcomings, Portugal was able to establish a thalassocracy, a naval empire within the Indian Ocean basin, lasting for about a hundred years. It created a unity based on power, primarily naval power, but territorial control was also held in certain areas, harbors, and key positions. It was a naval-political unit helped by geographic factors. There were hardly cultural-social ties with the population of the Indian Ocean region; Christianization succeeded only to a limited degree among Hindus and practically not at all among Muslims.

Portuguese monocracy was challenged and destroyed by the Dutch and the English. The interregnum that followed was characterized by the struggle between the Dutch, English, and French for the succession to Portugal's trade monopoly. Eventually, the struggle developed into a prolonged duel between Britain and France. This rivalry turned into a scramble not only for trade but also for land; the Indian subcontinent and most of the coastland of the ocean fell to the British. As the Cole's book on British military geography could, as late as 1950, proudly state, "The lands round the Indian Ocean are chiefly British."[24]

During the heyday of British imperial power, as George G. Thomson expressed it, British policy was "bifocal." This policy wished to protect, on the one hand, the British homeland and, on the other, "the Indian core of its world power." India also was distinguished from other British overseas possessions by its being headed by a viceroy.[25] After the Napoleonic Wars no European or other power was able to challenge or intent upon challenging the overwhelming British position in the area; if there was any threat, it had to come from the land side, from Russia, and this was a remote peril to which London often overreacted.

British policy in the region was based on three fundamental conceptions: (1) that no other great power should be able to establish on the Indian Ocean bases and ports "having secure land and air communications with its own main base"; (2) the control by British sea and air power of the naval gateways into the Indian Ocean; and (3) the maintenance in India, "the geographical keystone of the whole region," of a strategic reserve for the defense of India herself and other parts of the Indian Ocean.[26]

During nearly one century and a half, Britain succeeded in turning the Indian Ocean into a virtual British lake. Unlike the Portuguese control, which consisted of occupation of scattered points along the coast, British sovereignty extended over most of the land surrounding the ocean. The region thus had a unification

[24]Cole, p. 149.

[25]Thomson, p. 35.

[26]Cole, pp. 149-150.

much more perfect and durable than that of Lisbon. Nobody would have denied the "oneness" of the region as a geopolitical or strategic entity.[27]

Both during the Portuguese century and under the British domination, India was the natural fulcrum and accepted center of British Asia. Its geographic location—a huge peninsula protruding deep into the sea, dividing the northern segment of the ocean—confirmed that paramount position. This was implicitly recognized by the fact that the ocean itself was called "Indian"; it has recently been suggested that it should more appropriately called the "Afro-Asian" ocean.[28]

In the post-World War II period the Indian Ocean region has again become politically fragmented. Is this another interregnum? Hardly so; it seems rather unlikely that any power—superpower or littoral power—would be able or willing to establish a hegemony or near hegemony over the region as a whole. In other words, an Indian Ocean empire, like that of the British, is now past history. Whether the alleged vacuum in terms of naval power will be filled in by a nonregional thalassocratic power depends on many contingencies. Both within and outside the region, there are fears that superpower rivalry might draw the area into a series of conflagrations, as the Anglo-French rivalry caused in India and in the waters leading to it. Hence the movement for a denuclearization or neutralization of the region.[29] The history of past control of the ocean and the region as a whole is vividly felt by foreign policy elites and influences policy making.

The legacy of history, however, has not only a negative effect, namely the tendency to prevent or preempt any recurrence of nonregional control. It is also positive in the realization that many or most of the Indian Ocean littoral countries, if not all of them, have something in common despite their state of fragmentation. Thus past political-military domination, the shadow of the unifying force of *Pax Britannica,* still lingers in the air and exercises some integrative influence.[30] After all, it was a Ceylonese memorandum which coined the expression "Indian Ocean Community."[31]

When policy makers, regional or nonregional, in their policy considerations and strategists in their planning are ready to deal with the Indian Ocean region in its entirety and not only with its constituent parts, then scholars are entitled to proceed in a similar manner. The weight of contemporary political-strategic reflections and contingency schemes, which take into account geography and

[27] See T. B. Millar, *The Indian and Pacific Oceans. Some Strategic Considerations* (London, 1969), p. 3.

[28] Dieter Braun, "The Indian Ocean in Afro-Asian Perspective," in *The Indian Ocean in International Politics* (Southampton, 1973), p. 179.

[29] See below, pp. 59-63.

[30] See G. C. Bolton, *Britain's Legacy Overseas* (New York, 1973), pp. 168-170.

[31] Memorandum presented by Ceylonese Prime Minister Mrs. Sh. Bandaranaike to the Singapore Conference of Commonwealth Heads, January 1971.

historical precedents, should become respected by all who face with some measure of scepticism the reality of a geopolitical unit in and around that ocean.

Geostrategic Considerations

Prominent students of geopolitics of the early 20th century were keen to distinguish between the Eurasian heartland and the oceanic South and East Asia. They foresaw a confrontation between Eurasian land power and maritime powers lining up along the Asian rimland. However, their conclusions greatly differed: some believed that the land power possessed a basic advantage over sea power; others predicted that ultimately sea power would prevail over land power.

Admiral Alfred T. Mahan, writing around the turn of the century, viewed the Asian world as a zone of conflict between British sea power and Russian land power.[32] Nicholas Spykman, writing at the time of World War II, rallied to Mahan's view except that he believed that threatening German land power, trying to place under its control the Eurasian plain land, would be defeated by a combination of Anglo-Saxon and Soviet forces.[33]

Halford J. Mackinder was the principal proponent of the heartland concept. This concept was finally expressed in his often quoted axiom which predicted a command of the heartland over the "Monsoon coastland" of Asia and ultimately over the world.[34] The leading German geopolitist, Karl Haushofer, envisaged German-Russian cooperation establishing an overwhelming land power capable of defeating British maritime power.[35] At the time of the Hitler-Stalin cooperation it might have appeared that his forecast was correct. Similarly, after World War II Sino-Soviet alliance seemed to justify Mackinder's prophesies. However, these combinations of Asian land power proved short-lived. And the control of Asian rimland by offshore maritime powers has come to an end in the post-World War II period. And with the falling apart of the Soviet Union and China, Eurasian land power became split; decolonization resulted in a fragmentation of the South Asian rimland and of the entire Indian Ocean region. Former considerations of the advantages or disadvantages of sea power over land power and vice versa have not entirely lost their validity; they have, however, become complicated by the advent of air power and nuclear power.[36] Furthermore, the Soviet Union has ceased to be a land power only; in the Indian Ocean and other parts

[32] Alfred T. Mahan, *The Problem of Asia and Its Effects upon International Policies* (Boston, 1900).

[33] Nicholas Spykman, *The Geography of the Peace* (New York, 1944).

[34] Halford J. Mackinder, *Democratic Ideals and Realities* (New York, 1942).

[35] Karl Haushofer, *Weltmeere und Weltmächte* (Berlin, 1937).

[36] See Gerald S. Graham, *The Politics of Naval Supremacy. Studies in British Maritime Ascendancy* (Cambridge [England], 1965), p. 124.

of the high seas Soviet naval power is a factor which makes its weight felt in the strategic balance.

The fragmentation of the area affects the strategic thinking both of non-regional powers and of the littoral states. It is no longer possible for any planner to focus on part of the region. Individual littoral powers have a primary interest in their more immediate neighborhood. But they cannot, for various reasons, remain unconcerned in regard to developments in a wider circle that would include the Indian Ocean basin or most of its parts. The superpowers, as well as Britain, France, or China, may be interested in special areas of the region more than in others. They must think in terms of priorities as to the strategic value of individual countries or places. At the same time, however, they must maintain a comprehensive outlook while laying down their contingency planning.

For the superpowers in their strategic thinking, the indivisibility of the ocean must be a fundamental principle. Neither the United States nor the Soviet Union is, in contrast to the situation in the Atlantic and Pacific, an Indian Ocean power from the territorial point of view. They are interested not just in some or all countries of the region, but primarily in the ocean, which is a potentially offensive field for the Americans and a defensive one for the U.S.S.R. Nuclear missiles launched from submarines in these waters may reach targets in the industrial heartland of the Soviet Union, while no American land targets are vulnerable by submarines from these waters. In the nuclear equation the superpowers are thus bound to deal with the waters of this ocean as a single theater of potential action.[37]

The Persian Gulf area, where 62 percent of the world's known oil reserves are located, has acquired immense global strategic interest. The entire seascape is involved in the quest for fuel oil. Most of this oil is being shipped across the Indian Ocean—into the Red Sea toward Suez, or around the Cape of Good Hope to Europe or the Americas, or through the grand oceanic trunk road to the Strait of Malacca toward Japan—but also some is being shipped to points on the Indian Ocean itself, to India, Australia, and Singapore. And this ocean is also the thoroughfare for the transportation of other vital commodities (tin, rubber, foodstuffs, minerals, etc.) and so its geostrategic significance cannot be denied.

Nor can individual riparian powers escape in their security interests from a conspectus of the entire region. India's conflict (or future conflicts) with Pakistan, for instance, involved the superpowers and China; it also involved other littoral states such as Iran, Sri Lanka, and the Arab countries through their feeling of solidarity with their coreligionaries. Even Malaysia and Indonesia may thus be, at least implicitly, involved.

[37]P. Lyon believes that the Indian Ocean is either too big or too small to be considered a "single strategic theatre." Too small for the superpowers because they are free to concentrate their navies on any ocean including the Indian; too big for conflicts between littoral powers which cannot "be construed as trans-oceanic (i.e., all ocean) issues." "The Indian Ocean as a Strategic Area," in *The Indian Ocean in International Politics* (Southampton, 1973), p. 14.

A violent confrontation between South Africa and Rhodesia, on the one hand, and black Africa, on the other, may envelop not only the immediate northern neighbors of the countries claiming white supremacy but also other members of the Organization of African Unity, including the island states of Madagascar and Mauritius. The superpowers and China might, in a quasi-chain reaction, also be involved. Reactions of sorts might be created as far as Australia, Indonesia, and India.

The former colonial countries around the Indian Ocean are not signatories of any *one* military or political pact, but their common or opposing strategic interests arise from the fact of their geographic environment and from the geopolitical reality in which they live. The North Atlantic Treaty Organization includes countries which are far from forming a geopolitical unit. Their solidarity stems from the realization of a common danger and has been corroborated by treaty commitments. Similarly, Soviet-led East Europe is not a geopolitical entity, but the ties with and dependence on the Soviet Union have turned it into a geostrategic unit. On the other hand, the Indian Ocean region is a geopolitical entity by nature, an entity which is attracting strategic interest from many sides from both littoral and non-Indian Ocean nations. The synoptic concern of the strategic significance of the area is also reinforced by memories of the past.

It should also be remembered that individual countries are in the position of controlling the vital choke-points leading to or from the Indian Ocean. A possible interference with vital traffic through these gateways could not be regarded as a local problem; it would develop into a question of regional or even global significance. Should any of the naval powers (we must primarily think of the superpowers in this respect) try to place impediments to maritime transportation *anywhere* in the Indian Ocean, at the exit-entry points (such as the Cape) or elsewhere, all the area would immediately be involved. Nations of the two other oceans, geographically more decentralized, would not react in a similar manner. But if something like the Cuban missile crisis should arise, for instance, in the neighborhood of the Hormuz Strait or the Cape, an embargo on oil or other material commodities would set many countries aflame.

That leaders of many littoral countries recognize the geostrategic unity of the region may be evident from such movements as the drive to establish a "Zone of Peace" in the area.[38] It seems also pertinent to quote a Soviet periodical which makes reference to the Indian-Pakistani war of December 1971: "Statements by politicians and press commentaries devoted to these events have clearly high-

[38]It seems hardly appropriate to believe that "the Indian Ocean is now only really a meaningful political entity to the Superpowers, and then only because they have mutually come to regard it as important to offset the presence of the other, or use it as a means to supporting allies in the area." J. Simpson, "The Indian Ocean Area. Zone of Disengagement or Balance of Power," in *The Indian Ocean in International Politics* (Southampton, 1973), p. 208.

lighted one thought: the Indian Ocean and the countries around it are now regarded as a gradually independent geopolitical entity."[39]

Since this quote can be considered as at least a semi-official pronouncement of Moscow, such an approach should induce (if such an inducement is needed) all other powers which have an interest in the region to adopt a similar comprehensive view in their strategic considerations.

Policy makers, when concerned with questions relating to the Indian Ocean region, or students dealing with the same problems, may devote their attentions to more localized conflicts which fail to have oceanic significance; but it may appear useful or even indispensable to review these questions in the context of overall Indian Ocean power relations.

From the strategic point of view of the superpowers, the Indian Ocean is to be regarded as a single theater of operations. Considerations concerning the global strategic balance require a comprehensive assessment of the power balances of the region. The local balance of power which exists between countries around the ocean may or may not be connected with the balance the chief naval powers wish to maintain. The interests which the superpowers may have in these local balances vary according to their policy goals. Their perceptions of the significance of an issue and the images they may have concerning the intentions of others may differ or may coincide. There is, however, an admitted or discreet interconnection in this web of intersecting relations and rivaling interests. Of course, this is so in many parts of the world. But it is submitted that for geographic, historic, and strategic reasons these interrelations are here generally more solid, more forcible, and more conscious than in most other parts of the world. It is for the reason that it is not only permissible but even demanding that the balance-of-power system of the region be submitted to a synoptic scrutiny.

Selected Bibliography

Auber, Jacques. *Histoire de l'Océan Indien.* Tananarive: Société Lilloise d'Imprimerie de Tananarive, 1955.

Australian Department of Foreign Affairs. "The Indian Ocean." Background paper. Canberra, Aug. 14, 1973. (Mimeographed.)

Ballard, (Admiral) G. A. *The Rulers of the Indian Ocean.* London: Duckworth, 1927.

Bhutto, Zulfikar Ali. *The Myth of Independence.* London: Oxford University Press, 1969.

Bolton, G. C. *Britain's Legacy Overseas.* New York: Oxford University Press, 1973.

[39] V. F. Davidov and V. A. Kremenyuk, "Strategiya SShA v Zone Indiyskovo Okeana" (United States Strategy in the Indian Ocean), *USA: Economics, Politics, Ideology* (Moscow) No. 5 (May 1973), 6.

Braun, Dieter. "The Indian Ocean in Afro-Asian Perspective." In *Collected Papers of the Study Conference on the Indian Ocean in International Politics.* Southhampton (England): University of Southhampton, 1973. (Mimeographed.)

Cohen, Saul B. *Geography and Politics in a World Divided.* New York: Random House, 1963.

Cole, D. H. *Imperial Military Geography.* 10th ed. London: Sifton Praed & Co., 1950.

Curzon, Lord (Curzon) of Kedleston. *Frontiers* (Romanes Lectures). Oxford: Clarendon Press, 1908.

Du Toit, Alexander L. *Our Wandering Continents.* Edinburgh: Oliver & Boyd, 1937.

Fawcett, C. B. *A Political Geography of the British Empire.* Boston: Ginn, 1933.

George, H. B. *The Relations of Geography and History.* 5th ed. Oxford: Clarendon Press, 1924.

Graham, Gerald S. *The Politics of Naval Supremacy. Studies in British Maritime Ascendancy.* Cambridge (England): University Press, 1965.

Hartshorne, Richard. *The Nature of Geography.* Lancaster, Pa.: Association of American Geographers, 1969.

Haushofer, Karl. *Weltmeere und Weltmächte.* Berlin: Zeitgeschichte Verlag, 1937.

Jeffries, William W., ed. *Geography and National Power.* 3d ed. Annapolis, Md.: U.S. Naval Institute, 1962.

Lyon, P. "The Indian Ocean as a Strategic Area." In *Collected Papers of the Study Conference on the Indian Ocean in International Politics.* Southhampton (England): University of Southampton, 1973. (Mimeographed.)

Mackinder, Halford J. *Democratic Ideals and Realities.* New York: Henry Holt, 1942.

Mahan, Alfred T. *The Problem of Asia and Its Effects upon International Politics.* Boston: Little, Brown, 1900.

Millar, T. B. *The Indian and Pacific Oceans. Some Strategic Considerations.* London: International Institute for Strategic Studies (Adelphi Papers No. 57), 1969.

Panikkar, K. M. *India and the Indian Ocean. An Essay on the Influence of Sea Power on Indian History.* London: George Allen & Unwin, 1951.

Sharma, R. C. "The Indian Ocean and Its Community. A Geographical Appraisal." In *Indian Ocean Power Rivalry.* Edited by T. T. Poulose. New Delhi: Young Asia Publications, 1974.

Simpson, J. "The Indian Ocean Area. Zone of Disengagement or Balance of Power." In *Collected Papers of the Study Conference on the Indian Ocean in*

International Politics. Southampton (England): University of Southampton, 1973. (Mimeographed.)

Spate, O. H. K., and Learmonth, A. T. A. *India and Pakistan. A General and Regional Geography.* 3d ed. London: Methuen & Co., 1967.

Spykman, Nicholas. *The Geography of the Peace.* New York: Harcourt, Brace & Co., 1944.

Thomson, George G. *Problems of Strategy in the Pacific and Indian Oceans.* New York: National Strategy Information Center, 1970.

Whittlesey, Derwent. *The Earth and the State.* New York: Henry Holt, 1944.

Wilcox, W. "The Indian Ocean and the Great Powers in the 1970's." In *Collected Papers of the Study Conference on the Indian Ocean in International Politics.* Southampton (England): University of Southampton, 1973. (Mimeographed.)

Chapter 3

Balance of Power in the Indian Ocean

Thou art weighed in the balances and art found wanting.

Book of Daniel

Most of the countries around the periphery of the Indian Ocean and in its hinterland gained independence in the period following World War II. The exceptions included Australia and South Africa. As British dominions holding dominion status, they had enjoyed independence since the Statute of Westminster of 1931. Iran, Ethiopia, and Thailand were also independent, although they were temporarily under British-Soviet or Japanese occupation during the war; this also had been the case earlier for Ethiopia, Italian from 1936 to 1942. Though officially a sovereign state, Egypt had been under British military occupation during the war, and the crucial Suez Canal area was only evacuated by the British in 1955. Only Saudi Arabia, Afghanistan, and Yemen have not been subjected to colonial status or foreign military occupation during the interwar period or thereafter.

Out of the present thirty-seven independent countries of the region, only nine were independent in 1945; but even among these nine, many lacked the elements of genuine sovereignty. Those which had gained independence since 1945 differed in size, population, political experience, and administrative skills; since 1947-48, when India, Pakistan, Ceylon, and Burma achieved sovereignty, the other twenty-four countries have gradually followed on the path of independence. At the time of this writing, the process of emancipation has not ended: the Seychelles and Comoro Islands appeared now on the list.

With notable exceptions, the Indian Ocean region is one of considerable instability. This instability is due partly to internal and partly to external causes. Generalization is, of course, misleading because of differences in homogeneity within these states and their respective magnitude in terms of size and population. The status of these countries also differ depending on the subregional structure or international environment in which they happened to be placed. These questions will be dealt with in the context of these subregions and also in regard to individual states in the following chapters. However, it is no exaggeration to submit that most of the countries of the region exist in a state of tension and conflict, the degree of intensity varying greatly. In some cases the tension or conflict is latent or potential; in others it is manifest and chronic. In both cases sudden exacerbation cannot be excluded. The relative stability which still prevails and prevents wars, disorders, or chaos is due to a complex of local balances between the regional units supported by nonregional powers (great powers and superpowers) and, ultimately, by the global balance of forces reaching out into the Indian Ocean area.

While scholars disagree on the role, significance, and nature of the balance-of-power concept and some even deny its reality in international politics, international practice, consciously or unconsciously applied, confirms its overall function and usefulness. It serves to maintain a modicum of stability or prevention of chaotic conditions on the international scene.[1]

Referring to the conflicting interpretations of the balance of power in scholarly writings, one author has pointed out that the trouble with the balance-of-power concept is not that it has no meaning, but that it has too many meanings.[2] Not only with writers on international politics but also among policy makers, the term is used with different connotations.

When policy makers speak of the balance of power, either explicitly or implicitly, they generally refer to the actual balance of forces or to the territorial status quo as it exists, which they do not wish to see upset or tilted in favor of another power. Occasionally, when the term "balance of power" is mentioned by an expansionist leader, it is a "better" balance which he has in mind. Sometimes it is assumed by spokesmen of governments that there is an equilibrium, an equal distribution of forces, between two or more powers or between two groups of powers which is implied by the use of this expression. In any case, the concept of the balance of power should mean a certain ratio of elements of power. If this be so, the countries of the Indian Ocean region have not departed from the European model when they seek security and stability by manipulating their relations with other area powers under the mantle of a desired distribution of forces. Despite their highly cherished membership in the United Nations,

[1] See Paul Seabury, ed., *Balance of Power* (San Francisco, 1965); and Inis L. Claude, Jr., *Power and International Relations* (New York, 1962).

[2] Claude, p. 13.

these states prefer to rely on the safeguards offered by the possibilities of having friends and protectors and by supporting others with due regard to their own national interest.

Power Balance and Power Vacuum

As was to be expected, the decolonization process and ensuing decompression resulted in rivalries and clashes between the many new sovereignties. A multi-state system was thereby created; the heirs to the British, Dutch, and French empires sought self-identity, jockeyed for status, and struggled in quest of legitimacy and permanence. History has witnessed other similar processes whenever empires have dissolved. This happened when the Ottoman Empire gradually disintegrated and the countries on the Balkan Peninsula became engulfed in rivalries and conflicts and sought support from various great powers. When, after the dissolution of the Austro-Hungarian monarchy, Central Europe was "Balkanized," strife and conflict in the area prevailed. But, despite the national minorities they encompassed, these states were nation-states. In contrast, most of the new states around the Indian Ocean were would-be nation-states and had to start with the arduous task of nation building *after* their creation as independent states.

The British withdrawal from east of Suez did not begin when it was first officially announced in the late 1960s. It began in 1947, when London gave up the paramount jewel of its territorial possessions—the Indian subcontinent. This is often overlooked, for the alleged "power vacuum" often is said to have originated with the retreat from east of Suez announced in 1968.

As was made clear before, British supremacy in the region relied on control over most of the riparian countries of the Indian Ocean. After the Napoleonic Wars, Britain refrained from maintaining a battle fleet in these waters—one with battleships or battle cruisers and escorted by the appropriate number of cruisers and destroyers. There was no foreign navy to challenge British supremacy; if so, London could have assigned reinforcements to the area. Thus, while British naval superiority in these waters was only potential, it could have been made actual both before and after World War I. A number of light cruisers and destroyers were deemed sufficient to protect the shipping and naval bases of the area. After the end of World War II, Britain again withdrew most of its naval forces. However, the real retreat from the region was not a naval retreat; it was the abandonment of the land around the periphery of the Indian Ocean.

The withdrawal from east of Suez, announced in 1968 and implemented in the early 1970s, again was not an essentially naval operation. It meant the relinquishment of control in the Persian Gulf and the partial pull-out of forces from Singapore (Aden had already been given up in 1967).[3]

[3]British ministerial communiqué issued on the completion of the Five Power defense talks in London, April 1971.

Some credit the British decision to give up most of the remaining territories under its control and to pull out land forces and naval units (though not all of them) with having created a "vacuum" or "power vacuum" in the Indian Ocean, a void which according to some views will have to be filled by some other naval power. But according to other opinions, the vacuum need not be filled. Finally, it is also held by others that there is no vacuum to be or not be replenished.[4]

Those who claim that the power vacuum must be filled base their view on the nature of the balance-of-power operation. They concur with its expansionist interpretation—that "political and social power are by nature expansionist."[5] Some of these opinions present this development as inevitable, a law of nature as prescribed by the Latin adage, *Natura abhorret vacuo* (Nature abhors the void); that is, air will penetrate into space devoid of air.

If we are to consider a vacuum as a situation in international politics which is causative of certain unwanted consequences, we should differentiate between a vacuum on land and a vacuum on the sea. This seems important because most of the writers and governmental spokesmen appear to have British withdrawal from the Indian Ocean in mind when expressing views on the alleged vacuum. One should also distinguish between a "military vacuum" and a "political vacuum" on land, though both situations are mostly intimately interlinked. One should also mention a territory with a "population vacuum," that is, an uninhabited area, a *terra nullius* which has no people and belongs to no state, such as the island of Mauritius before the arrival of the Dutch or before its subsequent occupation by the French. Of course, a territory may be inhabited but still not belong to any recognized state, such as parts of the American West or of tropical Africa before occupation and annexation by Americans or the European colonial powers.

A military vacuum may be created when a protecting military force is withdrawn, leaving the country defenseless and open to foreign invasion. History teaches us that when the Roman legions were withdrawn from Britain around 410 A.D., it became a vacuum and was threatened by Nordic barbarians; the inhabitants asked for help from the Anglo-Saxons, who came and settled in what then became England.

An area recognized as belonging to the sphere of interest of a state may turn into a political (and often also military) vacuum if the state declares itself disinterested. Thus, under the Hitler-Stalin Pact, Germany declared itself disinterested in the Baltic states and Finland in 1939. The Soviet Union duly moved into this vacuum, except that Finland proved by its resistance that it was not a

[4]See, for instance, George G. Thomson, *Problems of Strategy in the Pacific and Indian Oceans* (New York, 1970), pp. 15, 20-21, and 36; Howard Wriggins, "U.S. Interests in the Indian Ocean," in *The Indian Ocean. Its Political, Economic, and Military Importance,* ed. Alvin J. Cottrell and R. M. Burrell (New York, 1972), p. 362; and W. Wilcox, "The Indian Ocean and the Great Powers in the 1970's," in *Collected Papers of the Study Conference on the Indian Ocean in International Politics* (Southampton [England], 1973), p. 31.

[5]Max Beloff, *The Balance of Power* (London, 1967), p. 7.

military vacuum and so survived. After 1945 a defeated, prostrate, and demilitarized Germany was considered to be a political-military void, to be defended against a potential Soviet attack by the Western occupation forces. West Germany was rearmed to fill this vacuum.

However, it should be emphasized that the "filling process" to avoid these vacua has never been an inevitable operation prompted by quasi-natural causes. Whenever there was a military-political penetration into an area deemed to be a vacuum, it was a voluntary act, not a spontaneous development.

While there are different sorts of territorial vacua, it may be questioned whether the sea or an ocean may be considered to be a similar power vacuum. In times of peace, the high seas are open to the movements of naval vessels and interdiction of such movements is an act of war. The freedom of the seas is not an empty slogan of international lawyers; it is a reality. Only in time of war may belligerent shipping, that of both merchant and naval vessels, be excluded from parts of the high seas. Under certain circumstances, territorial waters, straits, or parts of the sea may be mined or otherwise blocked. Such operations may amount to the establishment of a quasi- (but not in every case fully effective) physical control over a part of the sea—but only as temporary wartime measures.

Accordingly, at least in peacetime, the high sea is and will remain a "naval vacuum," even if a powerful navy is in the position to potentially place it under its control. But, barring the case of war, any navy may ply unhindered the waters of the high sea even if its appearance in certain parts of the ocean may be unwelcome or considered a threat or an upset to the balance of power. Naval superiority globally or in certain parts of the ocean by one power cannot prevent movements of other naval forces anywhere in the seven seas, and naval superiority or even potential control of the seas does not mean that fleets of other powers are excluded from any corner of the oceans. Even in the heyday of British naval power, navies of all nations were free to enter the Indian Ocean. But they did so only sporadically (e.g., the passage of the Russian squadron in 1905, a force more powerful than the British had at station at that time), since there was no reason for them to enter.

Therefore, it does not seem wholly accurate to speak of the creation of a vacuum, in the maritime sense, by the British decision to withdraw east of Suez. The alleged military-political vacuum caused by London's relinquishment of its colonial possessions rests on the belief that the local successor states were unable to "fill the gap," and thereby to defend themselves against a potential nonregional aggressor. But those who mentioned the power vacuum in the Indian Ocean hardly meant the often precarious, weak, and unstable administrations left in the wake of colonial withdrawal—a more pertinent regional source of instabilities and conflicts. It appears, therefore, more appropriate to speak of the emergence of a new balance of power or an instable balance which followed the rule of European colonial powers in the region.

Soviet or American naval units could have moved into the Indian Ocean in force even before the British withdrawal was announced. There are various explanations as to why Soviet naval entry began in 1968 after the British announcement. This may have been a coincidence, and it was easy to apply the *post hoc ergo propter hoc* (after it and therefore because of it) fallacy to this event. But policy makers, just as scholars, are ready to hypothesize that Soviet political and military leaders may have assumed that this British announcement amounted to a declaration of disinterest; or they themselves may have believed in the "power vacuum" theory. As far as the British were concerned, they wished to reduce the quantum of their military and political responsibilities. In this respect, one really may think of a "vacuum of purpose."[6]

If it is true that "it is inherent in the nature of international politics for states to have a remorseless drive to expand into areas where little resistance will be encountered,"[7] the Indian Ocean region with its fragmentation and congenital instability, whether we call this phenomenon a power vacuum or not, must be attractive to the policy makers of dynamic and expansionist governments. The environment of shifting local power balances, so characteristic of the area, is particularly conducive to friendly or hostile interactions on the part of external powers.

Local Balances of Power

The relinquishment of colonial rule in the region proceeded gradually and intermittently. The change-over to the new order was at places accompanied by violence and bloodshed. This took place on a major scale on the Indian subcontinent, where India and Pakistan struggled to set the new borders and establish a balance, and also in Indonesia, where the Netherlands gave up control due to insurgent pressure.

The decolonization process began and continued in a period when the world became divided by the Cold War. The South and Southeast Asian members of the region formed a barrier between the ocean and Soviet-Chinese power. This circumstance introduced an element of insecurity. But their principal concern rested first with their internal instability and then with the uncertainty of their relations with other members of the regional power system. Many of the new states sought to maintain ties with the former colonial powers in some form or other. Some of these ties still exist now, twenty or more years since independence. India, however, a superpower among the others, chose a different course. New Delhi came to pursue a policy of nonalignment, a path followed subsequently by other countries of the region.[8]

[6]Thomson, p. 20.

[7]J. Simpson, "The Indian Ocean Area. Zone of Disengagement or Balance of Power," in *Collected Papers of the Study Conference on the Indian Ocean in International Politics* (Southampton [England], 1973), p. 205.

[8]Max Beloff wrote that by choosing nonalignment India "ignored the problem of balance of power and her own possible contribution to it." Beloff, p. 37.

India possessed almost half the population of the entire Indian Ocean region and believed itself the heir of the British Raj. New Delhi then had ambition to be the pivot rather than simply an element of any alliance system. With Communist China, it planned to form a duo which would attract Asian and African nations in the spirit of the Bandung Conference of Afro-Asian States of 1955. India's rift with China, highlighted by the invasion of its territory by Peking's forces, disabused Indian leadership of this illusion. Still clinging to ideological nonalignment, India sought to put cohesion into the heterogeneous group of neutralist countries. Still, after some hesitation, it felt compelled to lean toward the Soviet Union to find security in its confrontation with China and Pakistan. The Soviet orientation proved successful; with Soviet arms aid and diplomatic support, the artificial unity of Pakistan broke up and an independent Bangladesh emerged. Thus the balance of power on the subcontinent shifted in favor of India.

Pakistan's somewhat restrained support by China and India's support by the Soviet Union are correlated to the Sino-Soviet conflict. Thus extraregional powers participated in the balancing process of the area. After initial cooperation with Britain, Ceylon (now Sri Lanka) also has embarked on the road of neutralism. Under the shadow of an India whose protective might it fears, an insecure Ceylon is seeking a more secure balance by welcoming aid and political support from Moscow, from Peking, and also from Washington. Relying also, as weak countries often have to, on the United Nations, Ceylon originated the ambitious project of establishing a Zone of Peace in the Indian Ocean.

Indonesia, encouraged by its successful fight for independence, and later the acquisition of western New Guinea (West Irian), and led by the charismatic but hubristic leader Sukarno, attempted to establish its supremacy over the surrounding areas. "Confrontation," as it was called, was practiced against Malaysia, Singapore, and even the Nicobar Islands belonging to India were threatened. British forces were called to defend Malaysia and Singapore. Sukarno obtained substantial Soviet assistance but sought Chinese cooperation. The abortive Communist coup of 1965 led to the eclipse of Sukarno and also ended the aggressive expansionist period. Thereafter, Indonesia sought cooperation with other Southeast Asian countries—Malaysia, Singapore, Thailand, and the Philippines—and economic cooperation has been strengthened with the United States, Australia, and West European countries. Indonesia maintains cautious contacts with Moscow, though so far no contacts have been established with Peking. It now ambitions by peaceful means to exercise the leading role to which it feels to be entitled because of the magnitude of its population (more than twice that of the other Southeast Asian countries).

Malaysia and Singapore receive some protection as a result of a vague defense treaty with Britain, Australia, and New Zealand. Forces of these countries have been reduced and will be withdrawn entirely at some future date. Malaysia and Singapore, together with Indonesia on the maritime trunk road of the Malacca Strait, try to balance out their position between the United States, the Soviet Union, and China. Timidly they attempted or will attempt to set up diplomatic relations with Peking; the problem of the Chinese minority (in the case of Singapore, a majority) looms heavily over their domestic and foreign policy considerations.

West of India, Pakistan, amputated and frustrated, feels threatened not only by India and Afghanistan, but also by the Soviet Union, which stands behind these two hostile powers. To balance out this hostile environment, Pakistan attempts to lean on China, the United States, Iran, and the Muslim World in general.

After British withdrawal from the Middle Eastern corner of the Indian Ocean region, Iran undertook to become the hegemonial power in the Persian Gulf. While Tehran's relations with Moscow were "friendly," it was opposed by Iraq, an ally of the Soviet Union. Some of the Gulf States have accepted Iranian leadership, while Saudi Arabia, more concerned with its spiritual ascendancy in the Muslim World, remained passive. Oman, on the other side of the nodal Hormuz Strait, is supported by Iran in its fight against Soviet-supported guerrillas in the Dhofar. Iran is an ally of the United States and, through the Central Treaty Organization (CENTO), of Britain. Relying on its gigantic oil income, it has embarked on a major armament program. In this it is reluctantly followed by Saudi Arabia.

Ethiopia is the strategically best-located power around the Horn of Africa and on the entrance to the Red Sea. But beset by internal troubles, it is unable to play the role which otherwise might be incumbent on it. It feels isolated in a Muslim sea, surrounded by hostile countries except perhaps Kenya. Somalia, heavily armed by Moscow, and the two Yemens, on the other side of the Red Sea, are openly hostile; the other neighbors are potentially so. Eritrean guerrillas, supported by Muslim and Communist countries, threaten Ethiopia's territorial integrity in the north; Somali irredentism is the danger in the south. Ethiopia's most important outlet to the sea leads to the French Territory of the Afars and Issas, an area to be contested with Somalia in the case of a French withdrawal. In its isolation, Ethiopia seeks cooperation with the United States, with China, and with African states. It is a member of the Organization of African Unity, but its influence is limited, though the headquarters of the organization are in Addis Ababa. On the other hand, the Arab countries on both sides of the Red Sea, as well as Somalia, are members of the Arab League.

South of Ethiopia, the balance is set by the enmity between African states and the lands of white supremacy, South Africa and Rhodesia. These are confronted along the Indian Ocean and in its hinterland by Tanzania, Zambia, and to a lesser degree the Malagasy Republic. Mauritius stands somewhat apart. South Africa is constantly trying to weaken the front of African states lined up against it and has had some limited success with only Malawi.

Its opponents, however, are divided on issues other than white supremacy, as for instance, Soviet-Cuban intervention in Angola or the meaning of African socialism. They are also divided on the question of whether to seek support from the Soviet Union or from China, or from both or none of them. Tanzania has close ties with China. The Malagasy Republic, after having severed its close ties with France, feels rather isolated and attempts to steer a course of rigid nonalignment. In this part of the Indian Ocean region, as well as in the other sectors of the area, a great number of sensitive issues and latent conflicts of territorial and other natures keep the respective governments on the alert.

At the opposite ends of the oceanic semicircle, the two countries ruled by European descendants pursue diametrically opposing foreign policies. Australia, well protected by its alliance with the United States and traditional ties with the United Kingdom, seeks rapprochement with its Asian neighbors, and with the Third World in general. It maintains normal contacts with Moscow and Peking, and also with Japan. On the other hand, beleaguered South Africa remains isolated; confronted by the African black states, cold-shouldered by the United States and Western Europe, violently hostile to the Communist world, which supports the Africans, it is forced to rely on its own forces and resources and on the hope that ultimately it will not be abandoned by the West.

This short survey will be followed by more detailed analysis in the following chapters, which should serve to demonstrate that in the region under examination a cluster of local balances exists, that groups of states are interconnected by a chain of relationships, pressures, and counterpressures. The balances are also stabilized by the weight of extra-area power which has either a stabilizing or a destabilizing effect on the entire system.

Another important characteristic of this system is the prevalence of hegemonial or potentially hegemonial nations in the various corners of the region. Indonesia is seeking such a role in view of its numerical superiority. India feels predestined to extend its influence over the entire subcontinent and beyond, in imitation of the British Indian policy. Also acting under the imitative example of history, Iran wishes to control the Persian Gulf area and the Arabian Sea. Ethiopia is suspected and feared by its neighbors to aspire to such a historical role in its area.

The balance-of-power system which we discern in the region seems quite unique. There is no historical model which would even loosely resemble this type of structure. Very distantly, it may reflect the Central European and Balkan state system between the two world wars, which was characterized by a mosaic of local balances strengthened by alliance systems and relying on the support of extra-area powers or great powers. However, the number of state units was much lower, and the geographic configuration was more compact and continental. In our case we have to deal with units over thirty in number and with countries ranging from tiny size and population to the second most populous state of the world. There is also much greater economic, social, and cultural diversity here. Finally, the impact of nonregional powers, former colonial powers, and the superpowers is weightier here, constantly shifting, and volatile rather than constant; the internal instabilities allow or require interferences or even intrusions for the sake of stability or for the advantage of the protected state, the protector, or both.[9]

Role of Nonregional Powers

As described earlier, despite their massive withdrawal from the Indian Ocean region, the British still maintained a residual territorial base and some armed forces in the area. The French, powerful only in the western sector, have abandoned their military bases on the island of Madagascar and have given up most of the Comoro Islands. With Djibouti, they maintain a strategic position at the entrance to the Red Sea. The island of Réunion is another of their residual possessions. Direct political and military influence of the Netherlands has completely disappeared. Portugal lost earlier its remaining possessions in India and has given up Mozambique; it no longer holds half of the island of Timor at the border between the Indian and Pacific oceanic systems.

The United States and the Union of Soviet Socialist Republics are both newcomers to the region and without a territorial power base. After 500 years, China has made a limited comeback in the sense that it has established political influence in the area. Although Japan's influence is economic-commercial, it is most powerful in this respect.

Britain wished to avoid a precipitate pull-back which would leave behind disorder and chaos. Where it was possible and not incompatible with national pride, in fact, where it was asked to do so, it provided military assistance and administrative help, and even formal defense agreements were concluded. Thus until 1957 Trincomalee on the island of Ceylon was used by the British Navy and the Royal Air Force; the British Far East Command retained its headquarters in Malaysia and Singapore until its dissolution in 1971 and replacement by the Five Power Pact under which Britain, Australia, and New Zealand maintain token forces to train and support those of Malaysia and Singapore. Britain also participates in CENTO.

France concluded a defense agreement with the Malagasy Republic when the latter attained independence in 1960. Under this agreement France continued to use the Diego Suarez naval base and an air base near Tananarive, the capital. But in 1973 it had to withdraw its air force contingent and subsequently to give up the naval base as well.

The British pull-back from east of Suez reduced even more the physical presence of that country in the region. However, the British presence is felt in many respects because of historic ties which culturally, linguistically, and also

[9]Michael Brecher wrote in 1961, "The dominant feature of internal politics in Southern Asia is instability. The record is emphatic on this theme." "The Subordinate State System of Southern Asia," in *International Politics and Foreign Policy,* ed. James N. Rosenau (New York, 1969), p. 164.

economically attract local countries to the former ruler. In case of emergency, some countries may even appeal to the British for assistance, as occurred for instance when the British intervened to quell a military mutiny in January 1964 upon the request of the government of Tanzania.[10]

Whereas the British and French presences remain a subdued continuation of their former power positions, the United States involvement was the result of the dichotomous world situation after the end of World War II. The Indian Ocean was, however, first considered as an area where British responsibilities and capabilities were paramount. As in the Mediterranean, United States involvement was to be uncalled for until the British presence was deemed to be insufficient for maintaining the balance against potential Communist penetration. American support was soon required to step up Iranian resistance against the Soviet threat. In 1954 Washington was instrumental in establishing the South East Asian Treaty Organization (SEATO), together with the United Kingdom, France, Australia, New Zealand, the Philippines, Pakistan, and Thailand. In the Central Treaty Organization (CENTO), formed by Iran, Pakistan, Turkey, and the United Kingdom, the United States participated only in two key committees but provided financial and advisory support. With these collective security organizations, Washington has formally become committed to the defense of certain countries in the Indian Ocean region. States which were nonmembers of these oganizations have also benefited from United States economic and arms support, including uncommitted India.

The atmosphere of suspicion, quarrel, and conflict between the regional powers[11] necessarily draws the attention of the nonregional countries to these developments. Not only is the global balance of power directly or indirectly affected by many of these disputes. In addition, investments of nationals and the well-being of nationals of these outside powers have to be looked after. As mentioned earlier, the local balance-of-power constellations are mostly interconnected with the patronage exercised by the extra-area great powers and the superpowers.

Even before they made their presence felt, the Soviet Union and China were already represented by proxy, namely by the various Communist parties operating in the area, some of them pro-Moscow, others pro-Peking, and even some in between. In the 1960s the two Communist giant states gradually appeared

---

[10]This cooperation is based on the rather vague membership of the Commonwealth of Nations, whose head is the Queen or King of Great Britain. It is assumed that this membership implies some political and military commitments. Members of the Commonwealth in the Indian Ocean region are Australia, India, Kenya, Malawi, Malaysia, Mauritius, Singapore, Sri Lanka, Tanzania, Uganda, and Zambia. The three countries dependent on South Africa (which is no longer a member)—Botswana, Lesotho, and Swaziland—are also members.

[11]According to one source, from 1945 to 1972 there were fifty-nine military clashes, coups d'état, or revolts among the countries along the periphery of the Indian Ocean. T. N. Dupuy and Wendell Blanchard, *The Almanac of World Military Power* (New York, 1972), pp. 158-159, 191-192, 304, and 341.

directly on the scene. Diplomatic contacts were increased; leading statesmen exchanged visits; and economic and military assistance was extended. Finally, in 1968 the Soviet Navy began its regular visits and established its semipermanent presence in the Indian Ocean.

The possible reasons for the Soviet naval move are manifold and will be discussed later. Suffice it to say here that a state of rivalry between Moscow and Washington appears to have been extended to the Indian Ocean. The area, it is believed, thus became a field of competition between the superpowers. Although neither of them considers the region as an area of primary or vital interest, a competitive instinct compels them to show strength, show the flag, help friends or allies, and maintain local balances or possibly help to change the balance of power in favor of a friend. Thereby Moscow and Washington may increase their influence and prestige among friends and foes alike. In this competitive exercise, the roles of Britain and France are more restrained; the latter is geographically limited to the area around Madagascar and the entrance to the Red Sea. On the other hand, China is competing with the U.S.S.R. wherever it is possible; Peking condemns imperialism and "socialist imperialism," but its actions are directed primarily to oppose Moscow.

The original report of the three experts to the United Nations *Ad Hoc* Committee on the Indian Ocean implicitly reproached the superpowers as well as other nonregional great powers, claiming that their rivalries in the region would eventually result in a renewed subjugation to their control of one or more local nations.[12] The authors had the scenario of the eighteenth-century Anglo-French rivalry in mind, which, in fact, resulted in the subjugation of India and ultimately reduced the entire region to colonial status.

But it appears that this time the scenario may rather unfold the other way around. The twenty-five-year-old enmity between India and Pakistan was not foisted on these two countries by either of the superpowers. Sukarno's "confrontation" policy was Sukarno's own doing even if at times it had Moscow's or Peking's blessing. Similarly, the hostilities between Iran and Iraq were indigenous to the area. The national liberation movements in the Dhofar, in Eritrea, and elsewhere are not the direct result of superpower rivalry. Even if these and other irredentist movements or territorial claims are not approved by one or more extra-area powers, and even if they are not supported by weapons from outside the region, such tendencies or movements will still exist.

On the other hand, it is also true that the nonregional great powers and superpowers would exhibit interest in the affairs of the local powers even if the relations of the latter were not to such an extent beset by internal and international conflicts and strife. But in such a case there would be fewer opportunities for interference and no reason to support one party against the other in a dispute. By their mere presence and in their contacts with the locals, the external Powers will necessarily reflect their respective political inclinations, intentions, and desires. Even if they pay lip service to the policy of nonalign-

---

[12]For the report of the three experts, see below, pp. 61-62.

ment, insecure littoral powers will nevertheless seek, if not formal, then informal adjustment to the policies of the protector or would-be protector power. And hostile powers will each endeavor to find a protector or even more than one, aligning themselves often, but not exclusively, according to domestic policy lines. And more often the superpowers are ready to support governments whose ideological dedication they approve. Status quo powers are more often helped by the Western powers and expansionist ones by Moscow or Peking, but exceptions do occur.

In such a way, the nonregional powers, particularly the superpowers and China, impinge on the power balances of the regional states; and, vice versa, changes in the balances affect the local status or influence of extra-area powers and thus discreetly touch on the delicate global balance of power.

For instance, the Chinese invasion of India enhanced United States influence and prestige in the region because it discredited India's slanted nonalignment policy. On the other hand, India's victory over Pakistan and the birth of Bangladesh enhanced Soviet prestige and lowered that of the United States. The dethronement of Sukarno strengthened Britain, the United States, and their influence in that part of the world. Egypt's volte-face from a pro-Soviet to a pro-American policy brightened Washington's status in the Arab world, from Cairo to the Persian Gulf. The victory of FRELIMO (the Liberation Front of Mozambique) strengthened Soviet and Chinese influence in East Africa.

This is thus a situation of overlapping balances: the local balances are influenced by the policies of the nonregional powers, and these local power balances affect the status of the extra-area powers and also their mutual power relations.

Nonregional Powers and Their Bases

Portuguese power began with the establishment of naval-military bases at strategically important points. Subsequently the Dutch, British, and French, before embarking on large-scale territorial conquests, first secured fortified and garrisoned "trade posts" or "factories." The United States, the Soviet Union and China never had territorial possessions in the Indian Ocean region.

The superpowers' outreach into the Indian Ocean is from across the sea, and their navies are the tangible expression of their presence in the area. They are suspected of harboring plans to establish or having already established military bases in rivalry with each other and for the purpose of having their military strength felt vis-à-vis the local countries. Bases would certainly have a bearing on the balance of power, and therefore it seems appropriate to discuss their possible roles and significance.

Bases in the conventional meaning are fortified or garrisoned harbors, towns, or other demarcated areas having storage capabilities and facilities for the refueling and repairing of warships, as well as air bases having one or more airstrips, hangars for housing warplanes, and communication or monitoring equipment. Really valuable bases are those which are near manufacturing or ship-building sites capable of refitting vessels and planes and which provide the industrial backing to military installations. According to where a base is located, we may distinguish (1) bases located on the territory of a state which is in charge of the military base itself (fully sovereign bases); (2) bases established under a treaty, permanently or for a definite number of years, on the territory of another state with full jurisdictional rights within the demarcated area (limited sovereign base or leased territory); (3) separated harbor area (quayage) or airstrip to be used under agreement by a foreign power which exercises jurisdictional rights over its own personnel (the facilities may be used jointly with the naval or military forces of the host state).

Communication bases or stations have now almost surpassed in significance genuine military, naval, or air bases. These are establishments equipped with electronic devices to signal, monitor, or guide ships (naval and commercial), airplanes, and airborne missiles and satellites. Such round-the-world communication networks have become indispensable instruments of great power or superpower status.[13]

Britain maintained sovereign bases in territories under its sovereignty—in Aden, Singapore, and Trincomalee. These had to be given up either simultaneously with the abandonment of sovereignty over the respective territory (Aden) or after the expiration of right-of-user (Trincomalee), or have been transformed into the type of base described above under (3), as in the case of the Singapore base. At present Britain holds air or naval bases of type (2) in the Maldive Islands (Gan) and on Masirah Island (Oman).

The United States has no fully sovereign base in the Indian Ocean region or nearby. The extensive naval-air bases in the Philippines (Subic Bay) are leased from the Philippine government. The base rights enjoyed by Washington in Bahrein have the character of type (3). The base on British-owned Diego Garcia Island conforms to type (2) as listed above. American communication bases, which in some cases include an airstrip, are in Western Australia (North West Cape) and are of type (3).

All these bases on foreign territory have been approved by formal treaties or agreements (exchange of notes). If a formal agreement is considered as requisite for a base managed on the territory of a foreign state, then one may conclude that the Soviet Union does not operate any base in the Indian Ocean region. Still, it is held by many sources that there are Soviet bases in different places around the periphery of the ocean. It is not known whether the Soviet government has formal treaties or agreements with any of the Indian Ocean coastal countries whose harbors it uses for refueling, minor repairs, or recre-

[13] See Dieter Braun, *Internationale Interessenprofile in der Region "Indischer Ozean"* (Eggenberg, 1972), pp. 15.

ation for its crews. Evidently, without any binding agreement, relying just on informal arrangements, the use of these "bases" remains precarious. Admission can be denied by the territorial state unilaterally. In Egypt, Soviet forces were invited to leave with only a few days notice, and Soviet warships were barred from the use of Alexandria, Port Said, and Mersa Matruh as staging ports.

However, the informal character of the facilities which Moscow enjoys in a number of harbors permits it to deny having bases at all and encourages critics in the regional countries to practice a "double standard." Accordingly, these critics condemn the West for its military and naval presence, made tangible by the existence of genuine bases, while closing their eyes to the Soviet presence, which lacks sovereign or leased base facilities.

Bases on foreign territory are generally unpopular with the host population. A base should have the capability of defending itself in addition to that of fulfilling its main purpose, to house supply and repair shops. It should be near but not too close to potential enemy territory.[14]

Modern technology offers substitutes for naval and air bases: anchorages can be used for refueling, fleet trains may provide supplies to the naval units on the high seas, where minor repairs may be carried out; and aircraft carriers are substitutes for airstrips. Nevertheless, only major powers can afford to operate in distant waters, and bases in the neighborhood of the possible area of operation are still useful. For navies with extended capabilities, bases may be an advantage for their economy in operations rather than an absolute necessity.

Despite the advent of air power and nuclear power, naval capabilities are still useful, as has been lately discovered by Moscow. The uses of naval power, short of war, are manifold: The presence or appearance of naval forces may support foreign policy by impressing friends and foes; they can operate visibly or discreetly, according to their assignment. They can intervene in a friendly or unfriendly manner far away from their home territory. Their presence can serve to demonstrate a stance for or against a certain country or objective; still short of active belligerency, warships and carrier-borne warplanes may constitute a threat; finally, a pacific blockade, embargo, or landing of forces may be carried out by them. This is "gunboat diplomacy," and although it has a bad reputation, it still may be thought of as useful.[15]

The advantage of "gunboat diplomacy" lies in its flexibility and the fact that, except when there is resort to forceful measures, it can be implemented in a manner which does not violate international law. In time of peace naval units may freely move anywhere on the high seas and, with certain limitations, even

---

[14]T. B. Millar, *The Indian and Pacific Oceans. Some Strategic Considerations* (London, 1969), p. 2.

[15]See James Cable, *Gunboat Diplomacy. Political Application of Limited Naval Force* (London, 1971), especially pp. 115-116; and L. W. Martin, *The Sea in Modern Strategy* (London, 1967), especially p. 169.

into the territorial waters of other countries. On the other hand, land armies cannot enter foreign territory and thus cannot move into distant areas without committing overt aggression.

In most countries around the Indian Ocean gunboat diplomacy is naturally unwelcome, except when it is directed against an enemy. Most of the littoral states, for various individual reasons, would like to eliminate all non-regional navies from their adjacent waters. Perhaps with the exception of India, they would particularly like to remove both the American and the Soviet navies from their neighboring waters; but if both cannot be removed, they would prefer both of them to stay and thus to balance out each other. This is not openly admitted by the spokesmen of the interested countries; nevertheless, this is their *in pectore,* not disclosed policy. Therefore, almost all of the littoral countries, at least officially, support the motion for a Zone of Peace which is pending before the General Assembly of the United Nations.

Alternative to Power Balance? The Zone of Peace Move

The classical balance-of-power idea as practiced in eighteenth- and nineteenth-century Europe had not been endorsed by the United States, for Washington could afford to stand outside the Concert of Europe until World War I. The United States officially entered that war to secure the freedom of the sea and to make the world "safe for democracy." The real reason, however, was to prevent Germany from ruling over Europe. President Wilson believed that universally institutionalized collective security within the League of Nations could replace the discredited balance-of-power concept. The United States did not join the League, and in any case the major powers—League or no League—continued to think and act in terms of the balance-of-power concept; they would have been foolish not to do so in the face of aggressive Germany, Italy, and Japan. Having been long neglectful of the deteriorating military balance, the Grand Alliance, by a narrow margin, was able to resist the Axis aggression and finally defeat Germany and Japan. The United Nations took the place of the defunct League of Nations, now including both the United States and the Soviet Union. However, Washington now, at least implicitly, accepted the working of the power balance. Thus, among other less political but more successful activities, the United Nations served as a forum and instrumentality for the implementation of a peace policy rather than a supernational organ to secure peace by its own international police force.

For most of the new ex-colonial states the United Nations served as a platform where their voice could be heard; and some of them, reluctant to join sides in the Cold War, hoped to be protected for their security by reliance on the provisions of the UN Charter. Even so, these new countries, including those which professed nonalignment, soon learned that they would be well advised to seek security by practicing balance-of-power politics, either by equilibrating between their neighbors and nonregional powers or by entrusting their safety to one or more than one great power, even one of the superpowers.

Frustrated partly by the lack of cohesion of the nonaligned Third World, alarmed by the appearance of Soviet and American squadrons equipped with nuclear warheads (the British were an accustomed sight and so were the French in their area of interest), the alleged presence of United States ballistic missile submarines, and seeing plainly the interlocking regional and nonregional systems of power balances (which made great power intervention inevitable in the event of a major crisis), some of the nonaligned governments wished to promote a neutralization and denuclearization of the Indian Ocean region.

Understandably, the weak and most centrally located Indian Ocean country Sri Lanka (Ceylon) took the initiative first before a conference of the nonaligned states, and subsequently before the General Assembly of the United Nations. The Cairo Conference of the Nonaligned Nations in 1964 already had demanded an "atom-free zone" for the Indian Ocean. The Third Conference of Nonaligned Countries, held at Lusaka in September 1970, discussed for the first time a Zone of Peace in the Indian Ocean. At the meeting of Commonwealth heads of government in Singapore on January 21, 1971, Mrs. Sirimavo Bandaranaike, Prime Minister of Ceylon, raised the question of superpower rivalries:

> Until now . . . neither the United States of America nor the Soviet Union has had any bases on territories under their control in the Indian Ocean, for stockpiling of weapons or the conduct of dangerous operations in a moment of crisis. The substance of our position is that weapons attract weapons, and bases, whatever they may be called, will attract bases from the opposing parties. If either of the superpowers establishes a naval base in the Indian Ocean, it will only be a matter of time before the other follows suit. In this context, we feel that there is a world of difference between, for example, the British air base at Gan airfield in the Maldives, or the Indian or Pakistani military installations in their respective territories, and the base that Britain has recently agreed to place in Diego Garcia under the control of the United States of America.[16]

The impetus and supporting argument for the proposal concerning the Zone of Peace was largely drawn from historical precedent. The Indian Ocean should be freed from great power rivalries and tensions because "it was the intrusion of these power rivalries into the Indian Ocean that resulted in the loss of political freedom in Asia in the eighteenth century."[17]

The United Nations General Assembly at its twenty-sixth session in 1971 adopted a "Declaration on the Indian Ocean as a Zone of Peace"—sixty-one countries voting in favor, none against, and fifty-five member states ab-

[16]See Devendra Kaushik, *The Indian Ocean. Towards a Peace Zone* (Delhi, 1972), p. 191.

[17]*Ibid.*, p. 194.

staining.[18] The resolution called on the great powers to enter into consultations with the littoral states of the Indian Ocean with a view toward halting further escalation of their military presence and for eliminating all bases from the Indian Ocean; an invitation was extended to the littoral and hinterland states of the ocean, as well as to the permanent members of the United Nations Security Council, to promote international security through regional and other cooperation and to make arrangements for giving effect to an agreement on the Zone of Peace in the Indian Ocean.

At the twenty-seventh session of the United Nations General Assembly, a new "Declaration of the Indian Ocean as a Zone of Peace" was adopted—ninety-five nations voting in favor, none against, and thirty-two member states abstaining. This resolution established an Ad Hoc Committee on the Indian Ocean, consisting of fifteen members, "to study the implications of the proposal" and to report to the General Assembly at its next session. The Ad Hoc Committee consisted of the following states: Australia, China, India, Indonesia, Iran, Iraq, Japan, Madagascar, Malaysia, Mauritius, Pakistan, Sri Lanka, United Republic of Tanzania, South Yemen, and Zambia.[19]

The Ad Hoc Committee met several times during 1973 and listed the following questions for discussion: (1) the limits of the Peace Zone, (2) the definition of littoral and hinterland states, (3) the definition of a foreign military base, and (4) the cataloguing of the great powers' military presence in the area.

The General Assembly at its twenty-eighth session voted yet another resolution: the Ad Hoc Committee was requested to continue its work and the Secretary-General was asked to prepare a factual statement of the Great Powers' military presence in all its aspects in the Indian Ocean. The resolution was carried with ninety-five votes in favor, none against, and with thirty-five members abstaining. As earlier, the United States, the Soviet Union, Britain, and France were among those which abstained.[20]

Pursuant to the above resolution, Secretary-General Dr. Kurt Waldheim appointed a three-member panel consisting of Dr. Frank Barnaby, director of the International Peace Research Institute in Stockholm; retired Iranian Admiral Shams Safavi; and K. Subrahamanyan, director of the Institute for Defense Studies and Analyses in New Delhi, to submit a report on the great power military presence in the Indian Ocean.

The report, submitted on May 10, 1974,[21] drew strong protests from all the four great powers whose activities had been described by the three experts, namely the United States, Britain, the Soviet Union, and China. A number of smaller powers also objected. Dr. Waldheim thereupon returned the report to its

[18] UN General Assembly Resolution 2832 (XXVI) of Dec. 16, 1971.

[19] UN General Assembly Resolution 2992 (XXVII) of December 15, 1972.

[20] UN General Assembly Resolution 3080 (XXVIII) of Dec. 19, 1973.

[21] Report of the Secretary-General pursuant to paras. 6 and 7 of General Assembly Resolution 3080 (XXVIII), No. A/AC.159/1, dated May 3, 1974.

authors and asked for a revised text. The second, much shorter report, revised with the help of William Epstein, the Canadian head of the United Nations Disarmament Division, was made public on July 15, 1974.[22]

At the twenty-ninth session of the United Nations General Assembly on December 9, 1974, another resolution on the "Implementation of the Declaration of the Indian Ocean as a Zone of Peace" was adopted by 103 votes in favor, none against, with 26 abstentions.[23] The resolution urged the littoral and hinterland states of the Indian Ocean as well as the permanent members of the Security Council and other major maritime users of the Indian Ocean "to give tangible support to the establishment and preservation of the Indian Ocean as a zone of peace." It also invited the great powers to refrain from increasing and strengthening their military presence in the region. The resolution requested all interested governments to enter into consultations with a view to convening a conference on the Indian Ocean.

The promoters of the Zone of Peace proposal were evidently convinced that the "instabilities, inherent in the Indian Ocean", lend themselves to great power interference and intervention and that the rivalries of these powers would be "interacting with local conflicts, and then escalating."[24] These adherents of the Zone of Peace wished to prevent their countries from being dragged into a possible conflict between the superpowers. They considered that a balance of naval power in the Indian Ocean area would not preclude the involvement of local countries. Regional conflicts would become synchronized with the existing rivalry between the superpowers. The United States and the Soviet Union, while siding with one regional power against another, would aggravate local conflicts. If one of the regional powers should emerge victorious from such a conflict, "the mutual balance between Great Powers could not be maintained over a period of time."[25] Evidently, the Indian-Pakistani war over Bangladesh was in the minds of the authors.

The various Zone of Peace proposals and the United Nations resolutions passed concerning this question, if analyzed specifically, present an amalgam of often contradictory desiderata. The plan to establish a nuclear-free zone in the Indian Ocean is mainly directed against the United States and the Soviet Union, which do or may deploy nuclear weapons in the area. But in view of India's reluctance and its explosion of a nuclear device in June 1974, it is unlikely that a general ban of nuclear proliferation in the Indian Ocean region could be

[22]Statement pursuant to paras. 6 and 7 of General Assembly Resolution 3080 (XXVIII), No. A/AC.159/1/Rev. 1, dated July 11, 1974. For the story of the two reports, see *New York Times,* May 25 and July 16, 1974.

[23]UN General Assembly Resolution 3259 (XXIX), adopted by the twenty-ninth session.

[24]As expressed by the report dated May 3, 1974.

[25]*Ibid.*

acceptable.[26] And it is equally unlikely that either Moscow or Washington would be willing to prohibit the entry or transit of their surface vessels or submarines with nuclear warheads into or across the Indian Ocean.

The proposal to eliminate, limit, or restrict expansion of the military presence of the nonregional great powers, including their naval or air bases, might become feasible provided these powers, principally the United States and the Soviet Union, would agree to such measures. However, it seems clear that such restrictions could only be implemented by the same powers or just the superpowers and only in relation to their global strategic balance.

The proposal to remove "rivalries" and "alliances" and "spheres of influence" from the area by the great powers is much too vague to be suitable for realistic considerations. Similarly, the quest for a renunciation of the use of force and for a peaceful settlement of disputes between the regional powers appears to be at present unlikely in view of the deep-seated conflicts existing between some of them. Other objectives envisaged by these proposals, such as the complete elimination of colonial domination of islands in the Indian Ocean or that of "racist regimes" (South Africa and Rhodesia) in the area, are questions in which other agencies and committees of the United Nations are already, and not too successfully, engaged.[27]

It appears that the questions raised by the Zone of Peace proposals, insofar as they are realistic, can only be resolved by the great powers themselves, in particular through an understanding between Washington and Moscow. Those problems which relate to the conflicts or latent conflicts between the regional powers can hardly be settled or smoothed out by sweeping resolutions in the General Assembly of the United Nations. They have to be analyzed on their individual merits and be resolved, if resolved they can be, according to the traditional methods of diplomacy.

Selected Bibliography

Baldwin, Hanson W. *Strategy for Tomorrow.* New York: Harper & Row, 1970.

Beloff, Max. *The Balance of Power.* London: George Allen & Unwin, 1967.

Braun, Dieter. *Internationale Interessenprofile in der Region "Indischer Ozean."* Eggenberg: Stiftung Wissenschaft und Politik, 1972.

[26]The Shah of Iran proposed the establishment of a "nuclear free zone" (and also of a Common Market) in the Indian Ocean area. The former proposal seems to have been directed against the Indian progress in the field of nuclear development. See *New York Times,* Oct. 9 and Nov. 2, 1974.

[27]See Hedley Bull, "The Indian Ocean as a 'Zone of Peace,'" in *Indian Ocean Power Rivalry,* ed. T. T. Poulose (New Delhi, 1974), pp. 177-189.

Brecher, Michael. "The Subordinate State System of Southern Asia," In *International Politics and Foreign Policy*, pp. 153-166. Edited by James N. Rosenau. New York: The Free Press, 1969.

Bull, Hedley. "The Indian Ocean as a 'Zone of Peace.' " In *Indian Ocean Power Rivalry*, pp. 177-189. New Delhi: Young India Publications, 1974.

Cable, James. *Gunboat Diplomacy. Political Application of Limited Naval Force.* London: Chatto & Windus, 1971.

Claude, Inis L., Jr. *Power and International Relations.* New York: Random House, 1962.

Dupuy, T. N., and Blanchard Wendell. *The Almanac of World Military Power.* New York: R. R. Bowker Co., 1972.

Gretton, Sir Peter. *Maritime Strategy: A Study of British Defence Problems.* London: Cassell & Co., 1965.

Kaushik, Devendra. *The Indian Ocean. Towards a Peace Zone.* Delhi: Vikas Publications, 1972.

Martin, L. W. *The Sea in Modern Strategy.* London: Chatto & Windus, 1967.

Millar, T. B. *The Indian and Pacific Oceans. Some Strategic Considerations.* London: International Institute for Strategic Studies (Adelphi Papers No. 57), 1969.

Seabury, Paul, ed. *Balance of Power.* San Francisco: Chandler Publishing Co., 1965.

Simpson, J. "The Indian Ocean Area. Zone of Disengagement or Balance of Power." In *Collected Papers of the Study Conference on the Indian Ocean in International Politics,* pp. 195-209. Southampton (England): University of Southampton, 1973. (Mimeographed.)

Thomson, George G. *Problems of Strategy in the Pacific and Indian Oceans.* New York: National Strategy Information Center, 1970.

United Nations. Report of the Secretary-General pursuant to the General Assembly Resolution 3080 (XXVIII) on the Indian Ocean as a Zone of Peace, transmitting statement by three experts on the great powers' military presence in the Indian Ocean, dated May 3, 1974.

United Nations. Statement of the Secretary-General pursuant to the General Assembly Resolution 3080 (XXVIII) on the Indian Ocean as a Zone of Peace, transmitting the revised report by three experts on the great powers' military presence in the Indian Ocean, dated July 11, 1974.

Wilcox, W. "The Indian Ocean and the Great Powers in the 1970's." In *Collected Papers of the Study Conference on the Indian Ocean in International Politics,* pp. 21-54. Southampton (England): University of Southampton, 1973. (Mimeographed.)

Wriggins, Howard. "U.S. Interests in the Indian Ocean." In *The Indian Ocean. Its Political, Economic, and Military Importance,* pp. 357-377. Edited by Alvin J. Cottrell and R. M. Burrell. New York: Praeger, 1972.

Chapter 4

The Southeast

It is your own interest that is at stake when your next neighbor's wall is ablaze.

Horace, *Epistles*

If there were no elephant in the jungle, the buffalo would be a great animal.

Oriental proverb

The countries of the Southeast Asian subregion divide the Indian Ocean from the Pacific Ocean system. Before the arrival of the Europeans, Hindu-Buddhist and Chinese cultural-political trends swept over that oceanic divide; the Islamic drive was the last to pass over the area, its spearhead reaching the Philippines. When European domination was established in the Indian Ocean, its sway did not stop at the Strait of Malacca, nor with the string of Indonesian islands; it advanced into the Pacific (the Philippines had already been conquered by the Spanish arriving not from the west but from the east, from across America) and reached the shores of Indochina and China, stopping just short of Japan. Only in the 1940s did a reverse trend start; the dramatic Japanese sweep placed Southeast Asia under Tokyo's temporary control, and Nippon's sword even threatened Australia, exposing this country for the first time to a danger coming from the north.

The Allied victory in World War II seemingly restored the balance, but it proved to be a shaky restoration. The Indian Ocean nations achieved independence, and while Japan ceased to be a military menace, the dormant giant China turned alive. And while former colonialists disappeared or became reduced in influence, new forces—those of the two superpowers—appeared on the scene.

In the post-World War II period the southeast corner of the Indian Ocean experienced two traumatic events. The first was an attempt by Indonesia to establish hegemony over the neighboring Malay countries with the help of the Communist powers. The abortive Communist coup of 1965 brought this scheme to an abrupt end. The second traumatic development was the massive American intervention in Vietnam. Australia and the rest of the southeast subregion were affected by both of these events.

Except for Indonesia, the countries of the area were partners to various mutual defense treaties, among themselves and with outside guarantors. In 1952 a tripartite defense treaty, known as ANZUS, was concluded between the United States, Australia, and New Zealand. The South East Asian Treaty Organization (SEATO) was established between Australia, France, New Zealand, Pakistan, the Philippines, Thailand, the United Kingdom, and the United States.[1] The original bilateral defense agreements between Great Britain and Malaya were replaced by a Five Power Pact in November 1971 which only provided for "consultation" in case of aggression or threat of aggression. In 1967 the Association of South East Asian Nations (ASEAN) was founded as a forum of exchange of ideas and economic-cultural cooperation. The members of this organization were Indonesia, Malaysia, the Philippines, Singapore, and Thailand. India showed interest but was politely refused admission. One of the outstanding actions of ASEAN was the "Kuala Lumpur Declaration" of November 27, 1971, seeking recognition for Southeast Asia as a "Zone of Peace, Freedom and Neutrality."

Since the convulsions of the Indonesia *konfrontasi*, (confrontation) and the Vietnam War, the Southeast of the Indian Ocean region has experienced no major upheaval. But divisions and latent conflicts between the countries under review continue to engender an atmosphere of instability. In this subdued imbroglio, Australia—wealthy, white, stable, and democratic—stands apart. From its birth until World War II, Australia sat under the protective umbrella of the British Empire; thereafter, it suddenly turned to the United States for protection. Again, in the last few years, Canberra has gone through a painful reconsideration of its international status and foreign policies.

Australia

In recent years Australian attitudes toward international politics have undergone changes, mainly due to the Labor Party's victory in the 1972 elections. The foreign policy shifts underlined Australia's new role in foreign

[1]On September 24, 1975, signatories of SEATO decided to "phase out" the long-dormant organization; *New York Times*, Sept. 25, 1975.

relations—which involved the break with guidance by the United States, which stemmed from continued diminishing links with the British mother country. Military commitments were to be reduced, while loyalty to AN-ZUS was to be maintained. However, a broad attempt at rapprochement with the Third World and close cooperation with neighboring Asian countries were to be undertaken. Gough Whitlam's Labor government opened diplomatic relations with Communist China in 1973, severed those with Taipei, and recognized East Germany. The Labor Prime Minister sharply condemned certain aspects of United States policies and, traveling to many countries abroad, engaged in a personal diplomacy which provoked criticism in Australia and elsewhere.

In late 1975 Gough Whitlam's party was defeated in the elections and the coalition of Liberal and National Country parties, under the premiership of Malcolm Fraser, formed a new government. While the new government will not reverse some of the initiatives taken by the Labor Party, such as the recognition of Communist China, the greater Australian self-reliance in international politics, and the increased involvement in regional affairs, it indicated a greater willingness to cooperate with the United States on defense matters. In contrast to Whitlam's attitude, Canberra now welcomed the strengthening of the American base on Diego Garcia island. There is no doubt, however, that in the future Australia will pursue a course which will be independent of the goals, aims, and methods endorsed by either the United States or Britain.

Australia's basic attitudes to questions relating to the Indian Ocean region may be described as follows:

1. Australia cannot sever fundamental military ties with the United States and cannot completely isolate itself from taking into account American vital security interests, which, indirectly, are also its security interests. Complete abandonment by Washington of any interest in the Indian Ocean region would affect Australia almost as much as if the United States should declare itself disinterested in the stability and security of the southwest Pacific. Australia is bound to realize, if it has not already, that it is an Indian Ocean riparian nation, and that it is no longer covered from that side by Britain as it used to be prior to World War I. Its freedom of option in foreign policy must necessarily be limited by these considerations.

Links with the United States, however, will not be submissive, but rather cooperative. That Australia requires Washington to be a partner and not a patron is only understandable. Washington maintains a number of military installations on Australian territory, the best-known being the low-frequency communication station at the North West Cape (near Learmonth on Exmouth Gulf).[2] In January 1974 agreement was reached between Canberra and Washington allowing Aus-

[2]Other installations are located at Pine Gap, near Alice Springs, Northern Territory, and at Nurrungar, near Woomera in South Australia. These stations monitor nuclear explosions and reconnaissance satellites, and may guide orbiting missiles.

tralian personnel to participate in the operation of the station.[3] Such an arrangement, which does not impede American performance, meets the requirements of Australian sensitivity.

While Australia does not wish to eliminate American activity in the Indian Ocean area, it would counsel restraint and caution. However, should the Soviet Union meaningfully increase its naval deployment in the ocean, Canberra would hardly object to an adequate American response.

2. When Soviet naval units first entered the Indian Ocean in strength in 1968, the Australian government did not consider this event as a reason for alarm, but only as a new element in the power relations of the region. As the Joint Committee on Foreign Affairs of the Australian Parliament expressed it:

> The recent Soviet strengthening of its economic and military presence in the Indian Ocean region is only one facet of a world-wide plan by the Soviet Union to extend its influence and shape its foreign policy as befitting that of a super power. This must be regarded as permanent and likely to increase. . . .
>
> The Soviet surface naval presence, because of its size, vulnerability and lack of full naval base facilities, cannot, at present, be considered an aggressive military force or a direct threat to Australia. It can generally be classed as a political and psychological tool, which increases uncertainty in the region.[4]

Australia maintains normal relations with the Soviet Union. These relations were strained during the peak years of the Cold War; Soviet endeavors to spread influence and doctrine to Southeast Asia created hostility; Indonesian aggression under Sukarno and also North Vietnamese–Vietcong activities in Indochina were blamed on Moscow. The American-Soviet détente persuaded Canberra to soften its views on Soviet expansive and subversive moves. Since 1973, under the Labor government, relations have improved even more, although the preference given by this government to the strengthening of contacts with China was coolly received by Moscow.

Canberra, therefore, was disinclined to regard the Soviet naval presence in the Indian Ocean as representing a direct threat to Australia's security or lines of communication. The possibility that Australia's vital foreign trade, which to a large extent has to cross the Indian Ocean, would be interfered with by Soviet naval units is considered as remote. But it is also recognized that Australia itself cannot do more than pay close attention to Soviet performances in its immediate and more remote vicinity.

3. Since the time when the first settlers came to Australia, its population, industry, and major cities have all been concentrated along the eastern coast.

---

[3]When United States forces throughout the world were ordered on a nuclear alert during the October 1973 Middle East crisis, Canberra claimed not to have been informed in time. The Australian protest led to the agreement mentioned in the text; *Sydney Morning Herald*, Jan. 11, 1974.

[4]*Report on the Indian Ocean Region*, Dec. 7, 1971, pp. 5-6.

Half of the population of that country lives in Sydney and Melbourne or in their suburbs. The capital territory is about halfway between these two metropolitan areas. No wonder that Australia's strategic concern was focused upon the eastern and northeastern shorelines. No particular attention was paid to the security of Western Australia, a state which covers half the country's territory, and the Indian Ocean coastline, which is even longer than that of the Pacific. Britannia, the ruler of the Indian Ocean until 1942, was trusted to thwart any threat from that direction.

Only more recently, when London officially declared its major withdrawal from the Indian Ocean, did Australia realize that it is also "an Indian Ocean power." Australia's naval and other military installations were mainly in the east. However, Western Australia's relative economic importance has greatly increased in the past ten years: 20 percent of Australia's exports consist of minerals mined in that part of the country. Half of all exports and imports have to pass the Indian Ocean. Australia has island possessions in the Indian Ocean: the Cocos (Keeling) Islands and Christmas Island.

In consideration of the lack of a major naval base on the Indian Ocean, the Australian Parliament voted credits for the construction of such a base (which is modestly called a "Naval Support Facility") at Garden Island, Cockburn Sound, in Western Australia south of Freemantle. However, in 1973 the Labor government decided to slow down the construction, which is scheduled to be completed in 1978. The Fraser government now declared its readiness to make this base available to units of the U.S. Navy, probably including nuclear-powered vessels.

Australia thus wishes to play a role in the Indian Ocean, even if a modest role. This role must be commensurate with the country's economic and military resources and should be limited to Australia's neighboring areas. In case of an armed conflagration, it is being realized that the country would be unable to secure its trade and indispensable trade routes. But its concern is focused principally on the Southeast Asian territories north of its national territory.

4. Britain is still looked upon as a mother country, but as a mother who can no longer care for her child; in addition, the offspring has now matured. Commonwealth ties, in a subtle, legally undefinable measure, still are felt to exist, though Britain, by joining the European Economic Community, ended the illusions which many cherished until then.

The Five Power Pact of 1971 is the only formal defense agreement which commits Australia to some limited collaboration with Britain for the defense of Malaysia and Singapore. Under this treaty Australia, Britain, and New Zealand contribute to the ANZUK Force from land, naval, and air services, some on permanent station and some on rotation.

The Five-Power Pact only obliged Australia to consult with the other signatories in the event of an attack or threat of an attack against Malaysia or Singapore, and to assist these countries with training and equipment in operational and technical matters. In 1973 the Labor government decided to withdraw the Australian battalion and battery from Singapore. However, the Mirage Squadron of the Royal Australian Air Force, stationed at Butterworth, near the mouth of the Malacca Strait, will remain until the Malaysians have acquired an adequate air defense capability of their own.[5]

Since World War II, Australian armed forces have been involved in fighting in a number of theaters: in Malaya against Communist guerrillas, in Korea, in Borneo against Indonesian infiltrators, and lastly in Vietnam. It is now believed that Australia will not have to face any military threat during the next ten to fifteen years. Therefore, Canberra did not wish to increase military spending, while strength in numbers of people in service was reduced and the acquisition of new equipment slowed down.

Nevertheless, Australia is conscious of its vital strategic interests in Southeast Asia. Therefore it seems certain that even the limited commitments under the Five Power Pact will not be treated lightly. Close defense cooperation is strongly favored, not only with Malaysia and Singapore but also with Australia's nearest neighbor, Indonesia.

5. In recent years Australia has deemphasized its relations with Europe (including the United Kingdom) and also those with the United States. While it does not consider itself as belonging to Asia, its solidarity and community of interest with Southeast Asia are prominently displayed. Good relations with its next-door neighbor, Indonesia, the former opponent in Sukarno's "confrontation policy," is given first priority.

"Regional cooperation will be one of the keynotes of Australia's foreign policy for the seventies" was an often quoted pronouncement made by Prime Minister Whitlam on January 27, 1973, soon after he formed his government.[6] Realizing that Australia has no chance (and perhaps no wish) to enter ASEAN, during his visit to Jakarta Gough Whitlam proposed a new organization of Asian states, which in addition to the ASEAN group would include China and Japan. Indonesia politely declined; nevertheless, the Australian government continued to support diplomatically the programs of ASEAN, to assist Indonesia economically, and generally to maintain a relationship of sincere cordiality.

Two potential causes of conflict have been eliminated in their relations. Indonesia was for a long time suspected by Canberra of harboring irredentist ideas about Papua-New Guinea, the eastern half of New Guinea which until 1975 was administered by Australia. It was suspected that Jakarta was just waiting for an opportunity to take over that half of New Guinea. The post-Sukarno government of Indonesia has, evidently, no such plans.

The other controversial question was the delimitation of the continental shelf between Australia and Indonesia in the Timor and Arafura Seas. Since drilling for oil is proceeding in those waters, which are generally shallow, important economic interests were clearly at stake. However, in 1973 Canberra and Jakarta agreed on a division of the shelf, in a way which was regarded as advantageous to

[5]*Ibid.*, pp. 8-9.

[6]*New York Times*, Mar. 7, 1973.

Australia. In the Timor Sea the edge of the shelf (the "trench") is close to the shore of the Indonesian island chain; the Australian sea bed was, by mutual agreement, extended almost to the "trench." In the Arafura Sea there was no such problem; here there is no "trench," and the underwater border was fixed approximately along the median line between the two countries.

In respect to Malaysia and Singapore, Canberra considers the security of these two countries to affect directly the security of Australia itself. Although the Malacca Strait is of secondary importance for Australian shipping, public opinion has not forgotten that Australia faced mortal danger when the Malay Peninsula and Singapore fell into Japanese hands.

6. When Whitlam took over the reins of government, many believed that, due to his earlier statements, he would embark on a course of neutralism. But faced with the responsibilities of power and realities of international politics, he vowed loyalty to ANZUS and support to ASEAN. "All other arrangements are transitory or belong to the past," he said.[7] But even thereafter he continued flirting with and admiring the neutralist stance; this became particularly apparent when he visited India in June 1973. There he made an effort to convince his hosts that "Australia is now an Asian nation" and not an "outpost of the West." In a joint communiqué issued at the end of his conversations with Prime Minister Indira Ghandi, the Australian Prime Minister endorsed the policy that the Indian Ocean "should be free from international tensions, great power rivalry and military escalation."[8]

7. Faithful to his course toward friendship with Afro-Asian nations, the Labor government repeatedly expressed its sympathies with the antiracist attitudes of the African states and condemned the policy of white supremacy practiced by South Africa and Rhodesia. There were even hints of a break in diplomatic relations with Pretoria. While not seeking rapprochement toward South Africa, the Fraser government deemphasized its sympathies vis-à-vis aggressive African states. .

Officially, the Whitlam government supported the Arab states in their demand that Israel should unconditionally withdraw its forces from the occupied territory. However, on this issue the Labor party was split, and some party leaders spoke out in favor of Israel. Finally, Australia did not sever its diplomatic relations with that country. The Fraser administration is taking a more pro-Israel line.

8. One of the first acts of the new Australian government in December 1972 was to support the United Nations General Assembly resolution of 1972 concerning the establishment of a Zone of Peace in the Indian Ocean. Australia was then elected to the membership of the Ad Hoc Committee of fifteen nations to study the implications of the proposal.

In 1973 Australia again voted for the Zone of Peace resolution and participated actively in the proceedings of the Ad Hoc Committee. It generally exerted

[7]*New York Times*, Mar. 11, 1973.

[8]*The Times* (London), June 7, 1973.

a moderating influence and attempted to render the scheme more realistic, while trying to give the impression that it was "going along."

9. As long as Indonesia was a threat to the stability of the area north of Australia, Communist China was dreaded as the "demon" creating trouble. Also the Australian contingent fighting Malayan guerrillas faced the "mercenaries" of Peking. But with the Labor government's move to take up diplomatic ties with Peking and drop recognition of Taipei, the image of Communist China has changed in the eyes of the public. Canberra does not fear that Chinese involvement in the politics of the Indian Ocean may constitute a threat.

10. Unlike the Sino-Australian suspicion, the relations of Australia with Japan are characterized by cordiality and pragmatism. Trade relations are flourishing—Japan is now the principal trading partner of Australia, having replaced Britain. Australia recognizes Japan's trade and navigational interests in the Indian Ocean; in the unlikely case that Japan should develop its naval capability, Australia would not be alarmed, despite historic memories.

11. As an astute commentator wrote, the replacement of Britain by America after 1941 was not a triumph of the United States over the United Kingdom in Australian affections, but "of geography over history." And the policy which demanded collaboration with neighboring countries reflected the same pragmatic idea. "Geography is now reasserting its predominance over Britain and the United States."[9] This was the real rationale for Australia's new "independent" foreign policy. And this policy began to recognize that the country was an Indian Ocean, at least to the same extent as a Pacific Ocean, power.

The amateurishness of some of the actions or pronouncements by Prime Minister Whitlam provoked criticism by more experienced politicians and academicians. However, the main features of his policy line will in all probability survive the administration of the Labor Party because it is based on genuine national interest and correct assessment of the balance-of-power situation. Hedley Bull, one of the most competent experts on Australia's foreign policy, listed seven options for his country's international status: continued reliance on the United States; nonalignment; military self-reliance; a balancing policy between America, Russia, and China; regional involvement; partnership with Japan; and strategic passivity. He rejected all these seven options, but advised his fellow countrymen to borrow from each of them.[10]

Australia cannot be an independent actor; it is too weak to be one (not even the superpowers can be entirely independent). It has to achieve its political objectives within the frame of the exigencies of the global and regional system in which it lives.

[9]T. B. Millar, *Foreign Policy. Some Australian Reflections* (Melbourne, 1972), p. 9.

[10]Hedley Bull, "Options for Australia," an unpublished address to the Australian Institute of Political Science, January 1973.

Indonesia

Indonesia is a state composed of many islands, and therefore its maritime interests are paramount. Sukarno attempted to create a powerful Indonesian Navy with Soviet help. Two cruisers, seven destroyers, ten submarines, and various other craft were delivered by Moscow, but most of them are no longer operational due to a lack of adequate maintenance and spare parts. Since the end of the Sukarno regime, Jakarta has no longer sought confrontation, but cooperation with its neighbors—in particular with Malaysia and the Philippines and also with Australia and Singapore.

Indonesia is officially a neutralist, nonaligned state (except for ASEAN, which is not considered incompatible with neutralism), but its neutralism is not infused with anti-Americanism. In fact, Jakarta's nonalignment is tinged with a leaning toward the West. Its foreign policy orientation, apart from the ties which she maintains with her neighbors, rests on friendship with the United States, with the countries of Western Europe, and with Japan.

1. The reconstruction of the ruined economy after Sukarno's fall was the main concern of the "New Course," initiated by General Suharto, the President of the republic. The country, inclined to be moderately xenophobic, is inward looking and self-seeking and puts an emphasis on nation building and promoting economic advancement. The bankruptcy which the New Course inherited has given way to more orderly management of the economy and finances. Foreign capital has been successfully attracted. Indonesia is an oil-exporting country, and the discovery of new offshore oil fields may make it a major fossil-fuel-producing nation. Living standards have somewhat improved, but the gaps between the tiny minority of the wealthy (among them many Chinese) and the poverty-stricken rural masses of the population are still openly visible.

2. Relations with the United States are excellent. American companies, including oil companies, cooperate with the government, assist technically, and market products while leaving ownership of oil wells and plants, to a large degree to the government. There is no resentment because of Vietnam; there is a widespread belief that American action in Southeast Asia helped to counteract the Communist threat to which Indonesia almost fell victim in 1965.

With West European nations relations are more complex. The former colonial country, the Netherlands, has managed a strange (economic) comeback; the Dutch are naturally most knowledgeable about Indonesia and are able to provide excellent advice and effective assistance. West Germany is doing excellent business and is well received. With Britain, the military confrontation has been quickly forgotten and contacts have greatly improved.

Relations with the third leg of Indonesia's foreign policy tripod, namely Japan, are possibly the most important in terms of volume and in economic assistance. Japan is making huge investments in Indonesia, but not without creating friction. Japanese negotiators are harsh and undiplomatic and use Chinese[11] clerks and assistants.

[11] Indonesian Chinese, officially known as "nonindigenous Indonesians." Private companies

3. Among its members Indonesia is probably the most fervent promoter of ASEAN's goals. It is mainly Jakarta that wishes to introduce politics into the counsels of this organization. ASEAN, so far, has no permanent headquarters; it is the ambition of Indonesia that Jakarta be chosen for this purpose. It is strongly opposed to the extension of ASEAN by admitting India and other more distant Asian countries. India is mistrusted mainly because of its close contacts with the Soviet Union.

4. The memory of the 1965 Communist coup looms over relations with major and minor Communist powers. It is to be remembered that possibly 300,000 Communists or Communist sympathizers were slaughtered in the wake of their own bloody attempt to seize power. The Soviet Union retaliated by stopping shipments of spare parts for warships and military equipment already delivered and insisted on the payment of the debt incurred. Only in 1970 could an agreement be signed which rescheduled debts totaling $750 million payable over a period of thirty years.

Jakarta does not appear to be overly worried by the Soviet naval presence, at least not by the present extent of deployment. The Indonesians nevertheless foresee a future possibility that a more massive Soviet involvement in the waters of the Indian Ocean might provoke a similar response by Washington. They would like both the Soviet and American naval presence removed or restricted.

In this vein, President Suharto deplored the American plan for a continued build-up in Diego Garcia, saying, "The move is clearly against our wish and will not be favorable to peace in this region." And Foreign Minister Adam Malik added that the move could be detrimental to making the Indian Ocean a Zone of Peace.[12] In private conversations, however, Indonesian leaders express the wish that the United States should not leave the field entirely to the Soviets.

5. Since 1966 diplomatic relations with China have remained "frozen." Ties were not officially severed, but diplomatic and consular staffs have been mutually withdrawn. Foreign Minister Malik would like to resume official contacts with Peking, but military leaders and the security police are apprehensive of an active Chinese mission in Jakarta. They also view the 3 million ethnic Chinese as a potential danger. If Jakarta is to resume diplomatic relations with Peking it is likely to be last among the Southeast Asian countries to do so.

6. Indonesia's relations with Malaysia are very good, but there are frictions between them. Although both have extended their territorial waters to twelve miles and thus claim control over the navigational artery of the Malacca Strait, the delimitation of their maritime boundary is strongly disputed. Furthermore, Indonesia's interpretation of the "archipelago concept"

---

must be owned 50 percent or over by indigenous Indonesians; companies owned more than 25 percent by nonindigenous Indonesians receive no government credit.

[12] *Sunday News* (Jakarta), Feb. 10, 1974.

would place under its own jurisdiction waters which divide Western from Eastern Malaysia.

In Borneo, along the Malaysian-Indonesian border, the military of both countries cooperate in fighting local Communist guerrillas. Indonesia's relations with Singapore have greatly improved in the last years, but not as much as those with Malaysia. Two factors contribute to this reluctance: first, the memory of the executions of Indonesian soldiers who had infiltrated into Singapore during the confrontation period; second, the fact that Singapore is basically a Chinese city.

7. Although the grandiose schemes and jingoist aggressiveness of the Sukarno period have been given up, Indonesia is imbued with a nationalist spirit which is conscious of the numerical preponderance of the country among its neighbors, of the mythos of a successful fight for independence against the Dutch, and the ethnic brotherhood of the Malay races. MAPHILINDO, the federation of Malay nations (it stands for Malaysia, Philippines, and Indonesia) as proclaimed under Sukarno, is a matter of the past; still Jakarta does not cease to cast eyes to east and west, from Melanesians to Malagasies, to unite under its leadership all the Malay races. This "indoctrination" is pursued discreetly and cautiously so as not to offend its neighbors and to avoid comparisons with the Sukarno model, an object of derision in its time. Thus Indonesia very cautiously moved to implement the unification of Portuguese Timor with its portion of the island (see Chapter 10 below). Present leaders are aware that "great maritime power" pretension is hardly matched by economic or military capabilities.

However, the maritime tradition of Indonesia is invoked on every possible occasion. Therefore, the evident lack of naval power is sorely felt. The relatively few naval vessels in operation have to be employed to patrol the 13,500 islands stretching out for 3,000 miles from east to west. It is interesting to note that the Indonesian maritime outlook was more to the north and northeast than toward the south or southwest, toward the vastnesses of the Indian Ocean. While Java is overpopulated, the southern coast of the island is almost empty and there is no noteworthy harbor along that shore.[13]

Jakarta is also intent upon developing ASEAN according to its own philosophy. No dangerous rival should be permitted admission; neither India nor Australia would be welcome, while Sri Lanka, Burma, or Cambodia would be. Hence the rather frigid attitude toward India, which can also be explained by Indonesia's Islamic sympathies with Pakistan and the fact that India is being more and more regarded as an ally of Moscow.

Jakarta likes to speak of the "unity and integrity" of Southeast Asia but denies seeking a "dominant role." In the Indonesian view, this regional unity and integrity should enable the nations concerned to resist pressures from the great

[13]Tjilatjap is now being developed and also Mataram on Lombok Island to attract Japanese supertankers which use the Lombok Strait instead of the shallow Malacca and Singapore Straits.

powers. Thus ASEAN is considered to be more realistic than the obscure concept of a Zone of Peace in the Indian Ocean.

Indonesia genuinely advocates peace and cooperation among its much smaller neighbors; it does this, however, with the *arrière pensée* that peace and security may be attainable in the future for these countries only if they rally around the 132 million, in two decades to become 150 million, Indonesians. The local balance of power—in Indonesia's view—can only be maintained if it can occupy the weight in this balance.

Malaysia

Only Western Malaysia, formerly Malaya, is a country abutting on the Indian Ocean. The states of East Malaysia, Sarawak, and Sabah, which joined the original Federation of Malay in 1963, are located on the island of Borneo 400 miles east of the Malay Peninsula across the South China Sea. Malaysia is a multinational country: the Malays, who hold the reins of power, comprise only 44 percent of the population; the Chinese, predominant in trade, business, and finance, form 36 percent of the population; Indians (Hindus, Muslims and Buddhists) make up 10 percent. The remaining 10 percent are non-Malay autochtonous inhabitants of Sarawak and Sabah.

Malays are mainly rural, whereas the Chinese are mostly urban dwellers. The ethnic schism between these two communities creates the greatest internal problem for Malaysia. Serious racial riots broke out in 1969 in Kuala Lumpur, the capital city, and calm was restored only with the help of the proclamation of a state of emergency, which ended in 1971.

The Sino-Malay problem has hung over the Malaysian Federation since its beginnings. The union with Sarawak and Sabah was welcomed because it increased the number of Malays, while Singapore was evicted from the federation to reduce the number of Chinese. Incidentally, the merger with the two North Borneo states gave rise to Sukarno's confrontation campaign. Another problem for the country was the large-scale Communist revolt (with Chinese in the majority among the insurgents), which had to be suppressed in a long guerrilla war in which British and Australian forces participated. By 1960 the Communists were defeated, but they managed to maintain themselves in small numbers along the Malaysian-Thai border. Another much smaller Communist insurgency is being fought in the border area between Sarawak and Indonesian Borneo (Kalimantan).

1. The announcement of British withdrawal from east of Suez, that is, from the Indian Ocean region, proved to be a watershed in Malaysia's foreign policy. Until then little thought was given to the broad questions of foreign relations; the leaders were happy to live under the protective roof of the United Kingdom. It was then that they began to be seriously concerned with their international future. Soon the realization came that the Five Power Pact which had replaced previous British commitments was no longer an effective guarantee, only an

obligation "to consult." The stationing of British, Australian, and New Zealand forces was optional, and soon these forces were reduced to a skeleton or token size.

Malaysia, thereafter, envisaged its future as a nonaligned country, a status somewhat inconsistent with its still existing military ties. The ASEAN organization, of which Malaysia was a founding member, offered an appropriate frame to advertise to the world, together with its other members, the uncommitted course which Malaysia wished to pursue. Malaysia was instrumental in the drafting and acceptance of the Kuala Lumpur Declaration of 1971, which demanded the neutralization of Southeast Asia.

2. Kuala Lumpur entertains a pious hope that neutralization will be guaranteed or at least acknowledged by the superpowers and other great powers. No such action has so far been forthcoming from any side.

Whenever there has been an opportunity, Malaysia also has promoted the Ceylonese proposal for a Zone of Peace in the Indian Ocean. This motion—in Malaysian eyes—appears to be complementary to the ASEAN declaration for a neutralized Southeast Asia. In fact, it is much more interested in the latter concept than in the former, for the former is a much more grandiose, even visionary plan, while down-to-earth Malaysia is concerned with its immediate vicinity.

The Foreign Minister in Kuala Lumpur politely expressed misgivings about the United States-British project to expand further the communication facilities on Diego Garcia. Five days later, on February 11, 1974, the *Yang di-Pertuan Agong* (Paramount Ruler or Head of State), while receiving the credentials of the new American ambassador, stated:

> Our efforts are directed not only towards building a progressive and economically viable nation but also towards the creation of a peaceful South East Asia.
>
> We are also mindful of President Nixon's efforts to continue his foreign policy through the setting up of a new structure of peace that can free future generations of the scourge of war.[14]

These pronouncements are characteristic of the cautious, almost apologetic approach directed toward the superpowers to persuade them to leave Malaysia and its neighbors in peace and unaffected by possible rivalries among themselves. Criticism of the Diego Garcia installation is prompted mainly by the fear that "this will later encourage the Soviets to send more naval warships to the Indian Ocean."[15]

3. Behind these official utterances, the real desire of Malaysian leaders remains directed toward noninvolvement. But views differ on how to achieve this objective: Malaysians would agree that the best solution for them would be

[14]*Straits Times* (Kuala Lumpur), Feb. 13, 1974.

[15]*Utusan Malaysia,* Feb. 8, 1974.

if both superpowers and other powers exogenous to their area would pull out as the British did. But just to have the Russians around in their waters, possibly in rivalry with the Chinese, who can infiltrate on land, would create hazards they do not wish to incur. Thus the equilibrating American presence is desirable as long as both superpowers are ready to accept neutralization of the area.

Malaysians are thankful to the United States that this country supported their independence from the very beginning of their statehood and also the union with the Borneo states. This contrasted sharply with the Soviet attitudes. When the Federation of Malaya was to be joined by Sarawak and Sabah, Moscow denounced the move as a "neocolonialist trick" and thus cooperated with Sukarno in the destruction of the federation.[16] However, after the Sukarno adventure failed, the Soviet Union initiated trade talks with Kuala Lumpur in 1966, and then in 1967 full diplomatic relations were established. The Soviet Union is the major purchaser of Malaysian rubber.

Kuala Lumpur is thus prepared to synthesize, at least in the abstract, conventional systems which are antithetical or at least difficult to combine: neutralism for Southeast Asia, Zone of Peace for the Indian Ocean, collective security arrangements for Asia, and the Five Power Defense Pact. But Malaysians are certainly not so unrealistic as not to see the incompatibilities. They may think in terms of Malayan family attitudes: try to be friendly with all your neighbors and acquaintances, for then none of them will harm you because each of them will fear the hostile reaction, not only from you but also from all the others you have befriended.

4. The only relationship where the above "friends with all" principle is hard to apply is that with Communist China. This is both an external and an internal political question. There are over 4 million Chinese in Malaysia out of a population of nearly 12 million. Prior to World War II, China regarded Chinese everywhere as its nationals under the doctrine of *jus sanguinis,* the right of citizenship by blood. Once a Chinese, always a Chinese. Such an attitude would have rendered the position of overseas Chinese in the postwar period impossible. Thus loyalty to their countries of adoption is no longer objected to by Peking.

The overwhelming majority of Chinese in Malaysia, Singapore, Indonesia, and Thailand are thus citizens of these states. In Malaysia there are, however, about 200,000 "stateless" Chinese—immigrants who are not Malaysian citizens, perhaps because they failed to obtain naturalization papers or perhaps because they (or their parents) entered illegally. But Malaysian citizens or not, many Chinese are inclined to believe that in some way or other China will champion their cause.

Nor is the support given by China to the Communist guerrillas forgotten. And China for years denounced Malaysia as a product of British and American imperialism; Malaysia was always referred to as "Malaya," indicating a refusal to recognize the union with the Borneo territories.

[16] See Guy J. Pauker, *The Soviet Union and Southeast Asia* (Santa Monica, Calif., 1973).

In spite of these difficulties and potential dangers, Malaysia was the first among the ASEAN countries to begin slow and cautious negotiations with Peking for a resumption of diplomatic relations. The final touch to this endeavor was laid down by Malaysian Prime Minister Tun Abdul Razak when he was received in Peking as a guest of the Chinese government on May 29, 1974. The two countries agreed to establish embassies in their respective capitals. The Chinese press on this occasion emphasized that the social system of each country can be determined only by the people of that country itself and that no interference by external forces is permissible. This was interpreted as a commitment by China not to take up the case of Malaysian Chinese.[17]

Malaysia has thus become the first ASEAN country to enter into diplomatic relations with Peking. In Kuala Lumpur it is believed that Chinese willingness to open up these contacts conforms to the latest pattern of Chinese foreign policy, that is, to drop support of national liberation movements where useful ties can be established with recognized governments. Peking may believe that this is a better strategy to counter Soviet influence in many parts of the world.

Simultaneously with its acceptance of an embassy by the People's Republic of China, Malaysia withdrew its mission from Taipei and closed the consulate general of the Republic of China in Kuala Lumpur.

5. The two closest neighbors of Malaysia, partners in ASEAN, Singapore and Indonesia, require special mention.

Singapore was forced out of the Federation of Malaysia in August 1965. The friction that preceded this move has not entirely disappeared in the past ten years. This is partly inevitable when a body politic is being amputated, but in this case it is partly due to the heterogeneity of the two entities concerned. Suffice it to mention here the essentially Chinese ethnic character of Singapore (Chinese are a minority in Malaysia, in Singapore Malays are the major minority), the commerical advantages which Singapore derives from being the nearby monopolistic commercial and transportation outlet for Western Malaysia, the jealousies created by Singapore's greater financial and commercial skills, and many other points in which Malaysia is still dependent on Singapore.

In the past ten years, despite the economic and cultural collaboration stipulated since 1971 by the ASEAN convention, Kuala Lumpur has gradually severed all administrative, financial, and organizational ties with Singapore. In order to depend less on Singapore's role as the traditional entrepôt (warehouse and transshipment point) for Malaysian export and import goods, the Malaysian government was keen to develop the harbor of Klam (Port Swettenham) near Kuala Lumpur as an outlet for tin and rubber, and Johore Harbor (on the northern shore of Johore Strait opposite Singapore Island) for the exportation of palm olive.

Although Malaysia managed to make impressive advances in economic development and may soon cease to be a "developing country," the per capita income of Singapore is $2,217, compared to the $392 of Malaysia.

[17] *New York Times,* May 30 and June 1, 1974.

Frictions are less acute with Indonesia than with Singapore. Still, despite the Malayan brotherhood and ASEAN collaboration, suspicions prevail. In the background looms the disproportion of Indonesia's size and population numbers, 132 million as against the 11.8 million of Malaysia. Although the vicious hostility of Sukarno's time has been eliminated, many of the grievances tacitly survived. Indonesia's hidden claim to be the big brother in the partnership is resented and some of Jakarta's actions, considered high-handed, are objected to. Furthermore, there are differences in the political ethos between the two countries: Malaysia was raised in the British political tradition, whereas Indonesia was under Dutch administration. Although Malay is spoken on both sides of the Malacca Strait, they do not always "speak" the same "language."

Besides its gigantic proportions, Indonesia has another advantage over Malaysia. Despite being a country divided by many islands, it succeeded largely to overcome insular divisions and established a measure of homogeneity. Even a common Malay tongue was created, which now serves as the official language and as the *lingua franca* for all the people. The 3 million Chinese, the only minority (except for the Papuans in Irian), count for less than 4 percent of the population. In contrast, the Malays in Malaysia are a minority if all other nationalities are counted together. And the Chinese community controls possibly more than 90 percent of private trade, industry, and finance. Malays are Muslims; assimilation with Chinese is thus out of question.

Malaysia is a divided country, not only ethnically but also territorially; it consists of two parts, east and west, divided by the sea. The disintegration of Pakistan must not have escaped the attention of those who are thinking of the future of the state.

All these debilities of Malaysia contrast with the soundness of its developing economy. Indonesia is ethnically strong, but its economy needs many years to develop fully and to prosper. Amidst these two countries lies Singapore, a political dwarf but an economic giant.

Singapore

Chinese form 74 percent of Singapore's population; 14 percent are Malays and 8 percent are Indians (Hindu and Muslim). As a remnant of Singapore's former membership in the Malaysian Federation, Malay is the "national language," while Chinese, English, and Tamil are official languages. The administration, however, uses English as its language, and this language is used in business and among professionals and is taught in schools.

In this cosmopolitan atmosphere with a Chinese majority overshadowing political, cultural, and economic activities, it is difficult to imagine how a national ethos could be developed. In contrast to Malaysia, racial harmony exists in the city-state and tolerant attitudes prevail. Chinese themselves are divided between the traditionalists (Confucian) and the English-educated, mostly of the younger generation. However, Singapore's exclusion from the Federation helped to develop a Singaporean national consciousness. Most of the Chinese now consider themselves Singaporeans rather than members of the Chinese people living in diaspora.

1. Singapore's foundation and continued existence in the past 150 years are basically due to its geographic location at the gateway between the Indian and Pacific Oceans. Navigation alone would not have created its present prosperity; ships passing through the Singapore Strait do not contribute to its wealth. The loading and unloading, refueling, and repairing of ships and the collection and distribution of goods provided work and wealth to its inhabitants. The strategic location of the city made it a center of military and naval activity.

When Singapore was deprived of its Malaysian hinterland in 1965, many doubted its continued viability. Abandonment of the naval base by the British and the withdrawal of forces all added to the economic plight of the population. But under the energetic and purposeful leadership of Prime Minister Lee Kuan Yew industrial projects were initiated. Today Singapore lives on manufacturing as well as on entrepôt activity and shipbuilding trade.

2. For many observers the political future looks less promising for Singapore than the economic future. But even the economy of the city-state is extremely vulnerable. It still depends on trade and entrepôt activity, since industrial development has its limits. Singapore is most sensitive to outside pressures because of its geographic location; repercussions of global or local conflicts and international economic crises could hit the country hard.

Singapore is dependent on its immediate neighbors, Malaysia and Indonesia. They could squeeze and ruin it if they wanted to do that, although they would also be hurt. Depression in Singapore, revolutionary upheaval in the city, or a Communist take-over would spill over into the neighboring areas and cause disaster. Thus Malaysia and Indonesia feel bound to cooperate with Singapore, although often they do so only reluctantly. Malaysia is eager to sever the remaining community ties and so to assert its economic-administrative independence.

Between Indonesia and Malaysia, Singapore is regarded as the "odd man." It is essentially Chinese, not Malay, in character; it is an exclusively urban, profit-oriented community. Its neighbors consider Singapore an artificial state (it was created by the excluding act of Malaysia) and are hardly inclined to accept it as a nation. Singapore's agility, flexibility, and high living standards are also resented. The cooperation with Singapore is for its neighboring nations a "utility," not a "love match." They have to live with the city-state whether they enjoy the partnership or not.

3. Perhaps even more than in the case of Indonesia and Malaysia, the nightmare of potential Chinese encroachment disquiets the leaders of the Singapore Republic. Prime Minister Lee, a shrewd and pragmatic politician, is particularly aware of his country's exposed position. Officially a socialist, he is ardently anti-Communist, but manages to disguise this attitude because he practices

skillful opportunism. He is far from enthusiastic about seeing Soviet warships passing the waters of Singapore but openly he would say, "Why should they not sail where they can freely sail?"

Indonesia, conscious of its size and potentials, may stay aloof from developments in the Indian Ocean region; Malaysia pursues an unobtrusive and quiet balancing policy; and the frail status of Singapore forces Lee to curry favor in every direction. He is ready to display a humiliating posture to appease potential opponents or to eliminate such dangers.

The dangers surrounding Singapore are both economic and political. Lee's foremost preoccupation is to promote employment. Large-scale unemployment would cause unrest among the urban masses and undermine his government and the country.[18] As long as matters proceed successfully, Lee and his People's Action Party are popular despite some of the high-handed police measures which are practiced. But Lee and his assistants feel that they live in a permanent state of emergency. Singapore's tiny army, navy, and air force, under instruction by British, Australian, and (strangely) Israeli advisers, will hardly ever be able to offer more than token resistance should the republic be attacked. Chinese direct aggression—probably just an obsession at this time—is less feared than interference which could endanger the delicate task of nation building.

4. Singapore has, at the time of this writing, refrained from approaching Peking for the purpose of establishing diplomatic relations, although Premier Lee visited Peking. He endeavors to maintain friendly relations with all the great powers and both superpowers. This is not always easy. With Britain (and Australia and New Zealand) the traditional ties are upheld. Rumors that Singapore would be ready to invite the United States Seventh Fleet into the more or less abandoned Sembawang naval base were promptly denied by the government.

On the other hand, Lee allowed the refueling and repair of Soviet naval craft in Singapore. It meant the earning of money, and he knew that Washington would not resort to reprisals because of such an attitude. When Singapore was threatened by Arab oil-producing countries with an oil boycott unless it would refrain from supplying oil to the American Seventh Fleet, the government quickly complied. Lee was anxious to explain the situation to Washington and found it understanding.[19] It is quite clear that Singapore is desperately anxious to continue with this tightrope performance to balance out pressures and possible dangerous situations.

5. Singapore holds the key to the shortest route from the Indian Ocean to the South China Sea and beyond that to Japan and parts of the Pacific. This navigation line is indeed a lifeline for Singapore, depending economically on the maintenance of unhindered navigation. The city is thus vitally interested in questions relating to the use of the Malacca Strait and, more generally, in the

[18]Singapore, the fourth harbor in the world in terms of tonnage handled, is also a center of oil refining and distribution of oil products. This monopolistic position was threatened when Indonesia began constructing an oil port on one of the islands opposite Singapore.

[19]*New York Times,* Nov. 15, 1973.

freedom of the sea. Therefore, it refused to endorse the declaration of November 18, 1971, in which Indonesia and Malaysia denied the "international" character of the Malacca Strait, wishing to place the strait under their sovereign control. Singapore just took notice of the bipartite declaration and continued to stick to the traditional three-mile territorial limit. Nor did it endorse the archipelago concept promoted by Indonesia, the application of which would impede navigation toward the South China Sea and within islands of the Indonesian archipelago.

6. Singapore, naturally, supported the Zone of Peace proposal in the councils of the United Nations; it assiduously supported the proceedings of ASEAN and its Kuala Lumpur Declaration. Lee prides himself on heading a nonaligned government but tries to put strength into the Five Power Pact with Britain, Australia, New Zealand, and Malaysia. The Commonwealth has no more faithful supporter than Singapore; though it is now a republic, it recognizes the Queen of Great Britain as the head of the Commonwealth.

Singapore has successfully weathered the storms of British withdrawal, exclusion from Malaysia, the economic crisis, and—previously—the Indonesian "confrontation." Its future, however, is closely bound up with the political developments in its immediate vicinity, and, being along the artery of world trade and navigation on which it is fully dependent, its fate hinges on the international balance of power, both global and local. Singapore is too weak to be a balancer of sorts, and its weight in political-military terms is hardly noticeable. It has two important assets: its strategically nodal position and efficient commercial facilities. How these assets will be utilized will depend on the circumstances of potential conflicts.

The Malacca and Singapore Straits

The Malacca and Singapore Straits are among the most frequented routes of international shipping (about 37,000 vessels of all sizes a year). They are the principal maritime gateways between the Indian Ocean and the Pacific.

The Strait of Malacca[20] is funnel-shaped, with its wider end toward the west; it extends between the Malay Peninsula and the Indonesian island of Sumatra. The entire Malacca Strait area is 500 to 600 miles long but only its eastern section, where the Strait narrows down to a width of fifty miles or less, creates navigational problems. The passage is obstructed just below Port Klang (Malaysia) about midway between the two ends of the strait by a group of islets. Further south, the One Fathom Bank endangers navigation because on both of its sides the channel is not wider than four miles. Southeast of the town of Malacca, the depth varies between thirteen and twenty-six fathoms, except for the Long Bank in the middle of the fairway, where the depth is only three

---

[20] At some points the Malacca Strait is divided by islands, and therefore it is customary to speak of "straits" rather than "strait." There are "straits" within the "Strait"; K. E. Shaw and G. G. Thomson, *The Straits of Malacca* (Singapore, 1973), pp. 5-11.

fathoms. After widening to forty miles, the strait again narrows sharply between the Indonesian island of Groot Karimun and the island of Pulau Kukub off the Malaysian coast. Here the width is less than eight miles. From this point eastward, the strait is known as the Singapore strait.

The Singapore strait is bordered to the south by a cluster of islands (the Indonesian Riouw Archipelago). Another string of smaller islands is scattered along Singapore Island. Facing Singapore Harbor, the strait narrows to the extent that the navigable channel is no wider than four miles. This is the area where the Japanese 237,700-ton supertanker *Showa Maru* ran aground on January 6, 1975, spilling thousands of tons of oil. At the eastern entrance of the Singapore Strait stands Horsburgh Light in the middle of the fairway, a landmark which ships moving from and to the South China Sea must pass.

Singapore Island (on which lies the Republic of Singapore) is separated from the Malaysian mainland by the narrow Johore Strait but is connected with the Malaysian side by a one-third-mile long causeway carrying both road and railroad.

The Malacca and Singapore Straits produce considerable navigation problems because the tides of the Indian Ocean are constantly silting up their channels and also because they are relatively shallow and unsuitable for oversize loaded tankers. Therefore, Japanese tankers above a certain tonnage have to avoid them and use alternative routes when moving from the Indian Ocean to the Pacific. The Sunda Strait between Sumatra and Java is one of these alternatives. However, at its narrowest section, this strait is confined to a width of less than two miles and is strewn with rocks and shoals which render navigation somewhat difficult.

Another alternative route which substitutes for the Malacca Strait is the Lombok Strait between the islands of Bali and Lombok. It is only twenty-five miles long, and its width ranges between fifteen and twenty miles. The island of Penda lies at its southern entrance, but channels on both sides of the island may be safely used by larger vessels. Yet another passage for larger vessels would be the Ombai Strait between the Alor Islands and the island of Timor, and its continuation the Wetar Strait between the island of that name and Timor. These are fairly wide and deep channels, but there is no harbor of any significance in the area. Further east, the Arafura Sea and the Torres Strait are both shallow and scattered with rocks, shoals, and sandbanks.

Except for the large supertankers, the Malacca Strait will continue to serve the international navigation of most ships. Dredging and otherwise rendering the strait less hazardous may prove helpful. The alternative of an artificial canal across the Kra Peninsula appears less realistic at present. But if such a project would appear feasible, Thailand would directly become involved in the navigational problems of the Indian Ocean region.

Thailand

Thailand has a 324-mile-long coastline on the Andaman Sea, that is, in the Indian Ocean system; but an almost three times longer shoreline on the Gulf of

Siam, that is, on the South China Sea and thereby in the Pacific Ocean region. Thailand is thus only marginally an Indian Ocean country; its main maritime interest is concentrated elsewhere. Still, it is a member of ASEAN and in certain features is like the Southeast Asian countries of the Indian Ocean region.

Unlike Indonesia, Malaysia, and Singapore, Thailand has never been a European colony. Thais are neither Malays nor Chinese, though their language is distantly related to Chinese. Their population of 40 million includes about 3 million ethnic Chinese who, unlike those in Malaysia, have mostly become integrated into Thai society. There are about 800,000 Malays in the areas of Thailand bordering Malaysia.

During the Vietnam War, the United States set up, with Thai consent, a number of air bases from which planes attacked targets in Vietnam and Cambodia. Thailand sent a contingent to South Vietnam that participated in the fighting. In such a way, Thailand became a close ally, a military comrade-in-arms, of the United States. However, with the end of American intervention in Vietnam and Cambodia and with the acceptance of the so-called Nixon Doctrine as United States policy in Asia, Bangkok-Washington relations were bound to undergo basic changes.

Thailand cannot claim to be nonaligned and had, so far, expressed no wish to be regarded as such. It abstained from voting for the resolution to establish a Zone of Peace in the Indian Ocean before the United Nations General Assembly. On the other hand, it, together with other ASEAN members, endorsed the Kuala Lumpur Declaration for the neutralization of Southeast Asia.

Thailand is intent upon disengaging from the American embrace. It has discovered, as allies often do, that United States assistance does not serve its national interests now or in all contingencies. Particularly, the air bases of the Americans have served the military and political interests of the United States and have become a political millstone in the conduct of Thai foreign policy.

Bangkok, like Malaysia, has to deal with an insurgency problem, which is even more serious because of proximity of the area to Laos, Vietnam, and even China. In July 1975 Thailand and the People's Republic of China resumed diplomatic relations. Bangkok also undertook to establish normal contacts with Hanoi and Phnom Penh and to break away from exclusive American dependence. In the past, Thailand has successfully played a diplomatic tightrope act between menacing great powers; it hopes to perform a similar operation in its present predicament.

In the nineteenth and early twentieth centuries, Bangkok most successfully practiced a balancing-off policy vis-à-vis European powers—in particular Britain and France, which held colonies east and west of Thai territory. Thailand even managed to extricate itself diplomatically from the wartime accusation against it of having been an ally of Japan. It appears to be the desire of the Thai leadership to return to this time-honored policy of strictly national self-interest. Fear of Communist aggression may, however, deter Thailand from pursuing such a course. However, close identification with one superpower would still be risky, especially when this superpower is unlikely to come to the rescue of Thailand as it tried to do in case of Vietnam. Bangkok will, nevertheless, try to solve this awkward dilemma and lean closely on its ASEAN colleagues to avoid creating an "alliance vacuum" that might be exploited by hostile forces.

The mainstream of shipping from the Indian Ocean to the Pacific avoids Thai ports; there is no significant harbor along the Andaman Sea coast, and Bangkok and other ports are deep in the Gulf of Siam outside the main shipping routes. Thus Thailand is not directly affected by navigational or legal questions which worry other countries of Southeast Asia.

Thailand is, however, concerned with a plan to cut a canal across the isthmus of Kra, on the Thai side of the border with Malaysia, which would not only shorten the route between the two oceans but would be deep enough to allow passage for Japanese and other supertankers which cannot use the Malacca Strait because of its shallowness. In such a way, one of the entrances to the Indian Ocean, a counterpart to the Suez Canal, would fall under Thai jurisdiction and would render Thailand directly dependent on developments in the Indian Ocean region.

Selected Bibliography

Agung, Ide Anak Gde. *Twenty Years of Indonesian Foreign Policy, 1945-1965.* The Hague: Mouton, 1969.

Australian Department of Defence. *Defence Report 1973.* Canberra: Australian Government Publishing Service,1973.

Australian Federal Parliament, Joint Committee on Foreign Affairs. *Report on the Indian Ocean Region.* Canberra: Australian Government Publishing Service, 1972.

Backhouse, Sally. *Singapore.* Newton Abbot, Devon: David & Charles Ltd., 1972.

Bell, Cora. "The Indian Ocean. An Australian Evaluation." In *The Indian Ocean: Its Political, Economic and Military Importance,* Edited by Alvin J. Cottrell and R. M. Burrell. New York: Praeger, 1972.

Bellamy, Ian, and Richardson, James L. *Australian Defence Procurement.* Canberra: Australian National University Press, 1970.

Bull, Hedley. "Options for Australia." Paper presented at Australian Institute of Political Science, Canberra, January 1973.

Chawla, Sudershan, et al., eds. *Southeast Asia under the New Balance of Power.* New York: Praeger, 1974.

Kahin, George M., ed. *Government and Politics of Southeast Asia.* 2d ed. Ithaca, N.Y.: Cornell University Press, 1967.

Kakkar, A. N. "Singapore and the Indian Ocean." In *Indian Ocean Rivalry.* Edited by T. T. Poulose. New Delhi: Young Asia Publications, 1974.

Kennedy, R. H. *A Brief Geographical and Hydrographical Study of Straits Which Constitute Routes for International Traffic.* United Nations Document A/Conf. 13/6, 1957.

Millar, T. B. *Foreign Policy. Some Australian Reflections.* Melbourne: Georgian House, 1972.

Palmier, Leslie. *Indonesia.* New York: Walker & Co., 1965.

Pauker, Guy J. *The Soviet Union and Southeast Asia.* Santa Monica, Calif.: Rand Corporation, 1973.

Richardson, James L. *Australia and the Non-Proliferation Treaty.* Canberra: Australian National University Press, 1968.

Roesnadi, C. Sutome. "ASEAN and the Great Powers." *Indonesian Quarterly* 1 (July 1973), 15-25.

Saksena, K. P. "The United Nations and the Indian Ocean." Paper presented at the Seminar on the Indian Ocean, Nehru University, New Delhi, Feb. 18-19, 1974.

Shaw, K. E., and Thomson, G. G. *The Straits of Malacca.* Singapore: University Education Press, 1973.

Singh, Vishal. "Indonesia and the Indian Ocean." In *Indian Ocean Power Rivalry.* Edited by T. T. Poulose. New Delhi: Young Asia Publications, 1974.

Vandenbosch, Amry, and Belle, May. *Australia Faces Southeast Asia. The Emergence of Foreign Policy.* Lexington: University of Kentucky Press, 1967.

Wilson, Dick. *The Future Role of Singapore.* London: Oxford University Press (for the Royal Institute of International Affairs), 1972.

Wilson, Dick. *The Neutralization of Southeast Asia.* New York: Praeger, 1974.

Chapter 5

Subcontinent India and Its Neighbors

> *Ill fares the land to hast'ning ills a prey*
> *Where wealth accumulates and men decay.*
> *But how much more unfortunate are those,*
> *Where wealth declines and population grows!*
>
> Hilaire Belloc

Under the British Raj, India radiated power in every direction, north and south, east and west. The Himalayan states (Nepal, Bhutan, and Sikkim), Ceylon, the Maldives, Burma, and Baluchistan were all dependencies of the British Empire, ruled either from Delhi or directly from London. Only Afghanistan, in the northwest, succeeded in maintaining its independence, and that was due to its balancing policy, Russia stretching out along its northern border.

More than half of the population of the Indian Ocean region lives on the subcontinent. Its long tongue extends far south; the island chain of the Maldives even crosses the Equator. It is the Indian Ocean subregion *par excellence*, located in the center between the Middle East and Southeast Asia.

In 1947, when independence was achieved, British India and the Indian native states became divided between India proper and Pakistan. This split was the consequence of irreconcilable Hindu-Muslim incompatibilities and the price of independence. To achieve this, Punjab and Bengal—the most populous provinces of India—had to be partitioned, and northern India came between the pincers of East and West Pakistan. As it happened, the deep-seated enmity which erupted four times into violent hostilities between Pakistan and India was kept alive by the problem of Kashmir—a territory claimed by both countries and divided between them, a division which gave the major part of the province to India. The unnatural union between East and West Pakistan came to an end in 1971; with Indian armed help, East Pakistan became independent under the name of Bangladesh. With this transformation, the regional balance of power, which already favored the more populous India, definitely tilted in its favor.

In Southeast Asia Indonesia is the population giant among its immediate neighbors, but Australia is a sturdy, modern industrial power. On the subcontinent, India is the uncontested supergiant; amputated Pakistan and newly formed Bangladesh are medium-sized powers in comparison. Thus India is not the first among equals; it is the second biggest country of the world, and its population is well over 600 million. These dimensions, together with India's coincident political ambitions, determine the role that this country is to play in the power relations of the subregion under examination.

India

The partition of the Indian subcontinent, accepted most reluctantly by India, was considered by Nehru and leaders of the Congress Party as a temporary expedient. They were convinced that Pakistan would not last.[1] On the other hand, Pakistani leaders doubted whether the unity of India could be maintained. Kashmir became the bone of contention; here the principle of self-determination (the Kashmiri Muslim majority would probably have sided with Pakistan) was thrown overboard for the sake of pan-Indian nationalism, which opposed the concept of "two nations" under which Pakistan had been created. The Kashmir case convinced the Pakistanis that they had to continue their struggle for the existence of their Islamic state. Thus the two ideologies, the concept of a nation based on Islam and India's concept of a "secular" state, inevitably collided.

As mentioned earlier, India rejected the instrument of balance of power and wrapped itself in the cloak of nonalignment. Relying on its immense dimensions, confident in its moral superiority, overestimating the role of the United Nations, it endeavored to provide an example, if not to the world at large, then at least to the countries of Asia and Africa. No doubt its intention was to apply the moral forces in the international scene with the help of which Gandhi's India had achieved independence. The forces of international politics differ, however, from those which may be successfully employed in the theater of domestic politics.

India failed to apply in its foreign policies the abstract principles which it preached to the world. Self-determination was never applied in Kashmir; the Portuguese possessions in India were acquired by the use of force; nonalignment was interpreted in an arbitrary manner so as to suit India's national interests.

[1] Neville Maxwell, "Jawaharlal Nehru. Of Pride and Principle," *Foreign Affairs* 52 (April 1974), 637.

In Nehru's vision the natural ally of India was to be China. India was the first non-Communist government that gave recognition to the Peking regime. At the Bandung Conference of Afro-Asian States in 1955, India and Communist China appeared to collaborate in brotherly love. Whether this desire to align with China was compatible with neutralism was never asked or questioned.

The honeymoon with China came to an abrupt end. When Peking extended its authority over Tibet in the late 1950s, Nehru, closely following Britain's Himalayan policy, attempted to take up advanced positions in the rather undefined border areas of northeast and northwest India. The ensuing rout of the Indian armies and Chinese penetration into Indian territory toppled the neutralist stance of Nehru's foreign policy and forced India to seek military assistance from the United States, from Britain, and eventually from the Soviet Union.

There is a dual personality in India's external outlook: there is a resort to *Realpolitik* and the use of force when its national interest is at stake, but noninvolvement in internal affairs, nonviolence, and pacifism are preached when other nations are advised or directed what to do.

With a hostile China along its long northern border and a hostile Pakistan on both its flanks, India has been faced with the realities of an international world. Unsurprisingly then, New Delhi has obeyed the rules of balance-of-power politics. Washington and London were allies of Pakistan and supplied it with arms. On the other hand, as the Sino-Soviet conflict grew in intensity, Moscow came to be regarded as the natural ally of India. Did not the ancient Hindu statecraft of Kautilya advise its disciples to seek alliance, not with neighbors, the natural enemies, but with neighbors of neighbors, the natural allies?

1. With the help of Soviet military supplies and diplomatic backing, in 1971 India was able to break the Pakistani ring around it; with the creation of Bangladesh, its strategic position improved and a grateful client state came to border it on the east. Having proved its usefulness, the Soviet relationship, as formulated by the Treaty of Peace, Friendship, and Cooperation of August 9, 1971, remains the keystone of India's foreign policy. The controlling provision of this Indo-Soviet treaty is included in Article 9, which reads as follows:

> Each of the High Contracting Parties undertakes to refrain from giving any assistance to any third party taking part in an armed conflict with the other party. In case any of the parties is attacked or threatened with attack the High Contracting Parties will immediately begin mutual consultations with a view to eliminating this threat and taking appropriate effective measures to ensure peace and security for their countries.

The treaty calls only for "consultations" between the two governments in case of aggression or threat of aggression against one of them. But there are many mutual defense treaties providing only for "consultation" which are considered defensive alliances. The question in the case of India is really whether this country may still be considered nonaligned. That the leaders of India had some scruples in this regard is demonstrated by paragraph 1, Article 4, of the treaty, in which the Soviet Union promises to respect India's policy of nonalignment. While there is no present intention to relax the quasi-alliance with Moscow, India is anxious not to be completely enmeshed in this relationship and to retain largely its freedom of action.

It appears that New Delhi was able to resist certain Soviet pressures. So far the Asian Security Plan, urged on several occasions by Brezhnev, has not met Indian approval. Since it is clearly directed against China, its conclusion would put an end to Indian attempts to come to terms with Peking.

The Soviet Union is shouldering the main burden of supporting India's development effort and increase in weaponry. Some Indian leaders fear the *de facto* dependence on the Soviet Union more than formal commitments. They would prefer a more even-handed policy which in a way would balance out the Soviet Union with the United States. On the other hand, the obsessive alarm over China and China's contact with Pakistan make the present reliance on Russia acceptable in the eyes of many. The 150 years of British rule—it is stated—created the image of India as a "Western" nation whereas it is both geographically and ethnically Asian. After all—it is rationalized—the U.S.S.R. is partly an Asian country too, if not racially at least geopolitically. Khrushchev's statement "If you shout over your hill we can hear you!" is quoted. Since India is in Asia and is Asian, a counterpoise against China should rightly be sought with Moscow. But there are also voices warning that Nehru once burned his fingers with China and that his daughter, Prime Minister Gandhi, may also be disabused of an excessive leaning on Moscow.[2]

2. The border dispute with China which sparked the violent clash in 1962 still remains unsettled. India would now be ready to settle it on less demanding terms than it insisted upon before the 1962 crisis. New Delhi would also like to establish normal relations with its northern neighbor. The Indo-Soviet Treaty of 1971, the troubled relations between India and Pakistan, and the status of Bangladesh were used by Peking to delay productive negotiations. And the Chinese have elephantine memories; they like to refer to British penetration into Tibet and the drawing of the McMahon Line (which Nehru claimed as the valid borderline) as acts of imperialism. It is ironic that in the eyes of the Chinese the Indians have replaced the British "imperialists."

China continues to worry India. The humiliating experience of 1962 is not forgotten, and border incidents keep the issue alive. During the 1971 Bangladesh crisis, the Chinese exerted pressures along the demarcation line, capturing Indian border guards. Bhutan and Sikkim are also harassed; loudspeakers diffuse anti-Indian propaganda. There are recriminations on both sides: Indians are accused of supporting Khamba fighters in Tibet; New Delhi suspects Peking of arming Naga guerrillas in India. However, the Indian government trusts that Soviet military pressures along the northern border of China will keep Peking at bay.

[2]See *Times of India,* Mar. 6, 1974.

3. Despite the agreement on the return of Pakistani prisoners of war and the recognition of Bangladesh by Islamabad, relations with Pakistan remain acrimonious. However, diplomatic relations are to be restored and movement across the border between the two countries allowed. It is India in this case which is dragging its feet; New Delhi has stated that in the past diplomatic relations did not prevent wars between the two countries.

The splitting up of East and West Pakistan has strengthened the strategic posture of India vis-à-vis Pakistan. But contrary to what is generally believed in Pakistan, India is by no means intent upon promoting that country's further dismemberment. It would rather correspond to India's political aims if Pakistan could be converted into a friendly cooperating state (the expression "client state" is being avoided).

All this is, however, just a pious hope. The bogey of an aggressive Pakistan, preparing for another battle, is very much in mind. India is also resentful that Pakistan is trying to find security and assistance by turning toward China, Iran, and the Arab states, while continuing to seek arms from the United States. As a well-informed commentator put it:

> New Delhi can go on deploring, as it has done in the past, Pakistan's lack of interest in promoting and preserving the *autonomy of the subcontinent* and its determination to bring in *external powers* to undermine this country's [India's] natural status. But it is a futile exercise because it is just not conceivable that Islamabad will in the foreseeable future revise its attitude sufficiently to warrant the hope of insulating the peninsula from developments around it.[3]

4. While it is thus deplored that Pakistan seeks allies from among powers outside the subcontinent, India, in addition to the Soviet Union, is attempting to establish cordial relations with countries on Pakistan's western flank and thus to isolate the arch-enemy. India's ties with Afghanistan are close, not only in a political sense but also in a military one.

With Iran the contacts are more complex. During the Bangladesh crisis, relations between India and Iran reached an unprecedented low. Tehran's open support for Pakistan, including military shipments, was deeply resented in New Delhi. Since 1972 successful attempts have been made to improve the situation. In February 1974 an economic agreement of a comprehensive nature reflected a certain cordiality between the two countries. This agreement sought to alleviate India's predicament following the increase in the price of oil. Iran, however, insisted upon referring to the agreement as merely economic, to calm Pakistan's apprehensions. India's earlier fears that the large-scale purchase of modern arms by Iran may be directed against it may have been somewhat dispelled.

For many years India supported the Arab countries, in the United Nations and outside the world organization, in their endeavors to resist Israel. India is, so to speak, surrounded by Islamic countries, and some critics of Nehru would have

[3]Girilal Jain in *Times of India,* Feb. 28, 1974 (italics added).

considered ties with Israel more natural. However, Nehru was keen to prove to the world that India is a "secular" state and, therefore, does not necessarily take sides against the coreligionaries of Pakistan.

5. The United States has been a strong supporter of India's independence. When independence was achieved, mainly in the economic field that Washington could and did contribute to the strengthening of New Delhi's position. Political contacts were less amicable. The policy of nonalignment was incompatible with the Dullesian "pactomania" which sought to create alliances against international communism. Pakistan's inclusion in this alliance system (CENTO and SEATO) and accompanying arms deliveries by the United States became the source of chronic bitterness against Washington.

More recently, the hostility culminated during the war of 1971, when New Delhi accused Washington not only of supporting Pakistan with weaponry but also of threatening India with a naval squadron led by the nuclear carrier *Enterprise,* which sailed into the Bay of Bengal.[4] Since then, relations have again improved except for the cloud caused by the joint American-British announcement to enlarge the naval-air communication facility on the island of Diego Garcia. While the Indian nationalist press reacted violently, the government of Indira Gandhi quietly protested without taking the case before the United Nations.[5]

India evidently wished to maintain friendly relations with Washington, which, in view of the United States-Soviet détente, is far from being incompatible with close cooperation with Moscow. In view of India's economic troubles, American economic help would be welcome. But relations with Washington hinge, as they have over the past twenty years, on the intensity of contacts the United States maintains with Pakistan. It is hinted at by New Delhi that the introduction of arms by Washington "into the subcontinent" (meaning Pakistan) will cause tension.[6] The same approach evidently was not made to Moscow when it supplied arms to India.

[4]There were several reasons for the dispatch of the naval units: (1) a fear that after disposing of East Pakistan the Indian Army would invade West Pakistan; (2) to induce Moscow to prevent this second round of military operations; (3) President Nixon was due to go to Peking, and China was to be assured that the United States would do everything in its power to forestall a complete collapse of Pakistan; and (4) to demonstrate American strength in order to bolster negotiations in Vietnam and give a warning to Arab countries preparing an assault against Israel. This "gunboat diplomacy" was not intended to save Bangladesh for Pakistan (which was already lost), but was aimed "beyond the Bay of Bengal," and there it worked. See C. L. Sulzberger in *New York Times,* Apr. 21, 1972.

[5]United States Ambassador to India Daniel P. Moynihan in a talk with journalists described the Diego Garcia extension as a normal and sensible move. Referring to the fact that Diego Garcia is more than 1,100 miles distant from India, he jestingly remarked, "Why call this ocean the Indian Ocean? One may call it the Madagascar Sea." In the Indian Parliament, Foreign Minister Sardar Swaran Singh said in response to questions, "Who is he to change the name based on the geographical situation? It is no gift of the United States or the Ambassador." *New York Times,* Mar. 7, 1974.

[6]*New York Times,* Aug. 11, 1974.

6. With reference to the controversy about Diego Garcia, Sir Alec Douglas-Home, the British Foreign Secretary, remarked that India is applying double standards in voicing concern at the Anglo-American plans to expand military facilities on the island while being silent as the Russians build up their naval power in the Indian Ocean. "When *we* do something there is a squeal!" The Indian reply to this "peevish" remark was simply "Insofar as there is no Russian base in the Indian Ocean, what can we protest about?"[7]

This rather good-natured exchange of recriminations is characteristic of the relations between India and its former ruler, now a partner in the Commonwealth. Britain maintains a low-profile presence vis-à-vis India; personal contacts between Indian and British leaders are generally free and easy; Indians feel more at home in Britain than in other English-speaking countries, and cultural exchanges are frequent. Britain's influence on Indian affairs, political and economic, is difficult to circumscribe but still more than negligible.

7. Present-day India is not only the heir of the British Indian Empire; it is the heir of the ancient Hindu empires, the Maurya and Gupta kingdoms, Asoka's empire, and also that of the Moguls (the Muslim rulers who built their empire on Hindu civilization). The world outlook of a multinational empire of 600 million is traditionally imperial and hegemonial. It is induced to look upon itself as a world center, the sun, surrounded by planets which receive the light from their sun. The image India has of itself is not the image it presents to the external world.

Pakistan and now Bangladesh are considered as secessionist fragments of the eternal Indian body politic which eventually will return to the bosom of Mother India. Other surrounding nations, disproportionately small in comparison with India, are regarded as cultural vassals of the Hindu civilization and, therefore, politically subordinate.

Even if these historical-philosophical ideas are not applied in practice, they influence political thinking. Hence the instinctive Indian desire for "subcontinental unity" and condemnation of Pakistan when Islamabad seeks assistance and alliances from outside the subcontinent.

The emphasis that India is, in contrast to Pakistan, a "secular" state is a political program: in the Indian view nations of the subcontinent, in the widest sense, could and should join India. The hegemonial perception of India's role in what it considers its part of the world (a kind of Indian Monroe Doctrine) extends to all neighboring lands that belonged to the British Empire: the Himalayan states, Ceylon, Burma, the Maldives, and even more so Pakistan and Bangladesh.

It was perhaps this self-centered world outlook, the "superior don" complex, which prevented India, and in a way still impedes it, from fully practicing the politics of balance of power. Nor were attempts made to establish a regional organization system, like ASEAN, in South Asia. Not only the rift with Pakistan but also the suspicions created by India's gigantic size prevented the small

[7] *Times of India*, Feb. 20, 1974.

neighbors which were not already client states from entering into the orbit of the giant.

While India, in comparison with the nations surrounding it, is huge and mighty, its effective power potentials are by no measure proportionate to its size. It is beset by a myriad of internal problems, centrifugal tendencies, strife between ethnic and linguistic groups, and a chronically calamitous economy. It needs economic assistance; Soviet economic help is insufficient, and so it is in need of United States support. Still, its supernation sensitivity and disdain prevent it from asking. At the same time, it has embarked on a large-scale armaments drive to increase the strength of its army, navy, and air force. On May 18, 1974, India exploded a nuclear device, thus entering the ranks of nuclear powers. This was to assert its great power status and was a response to Peking's atomic capabilities. Whether India's nuclear capabilities will further tilt the balance of power in the Indian subcontinent in its favor depends on whether it will be willing to spend major portions of its resources on this venture.[8]

But Indians maintain that an increase of their military power remains a vital necessity even with the reduction of Pakistan to its western portion. Islamabad is able to concentrate forces along the Indian border faster than India can because the latter's forces are dispersed all over a large country. It is also alleged that India has to maintain twelve divisions along the Chinese border, which cannot be replaced quickly or exchanged since they are stationed at an average height of 12,000 feet—an altitude which requires acclimatization. Overall, India would be able to mass eighteen divisions against Pakistan's sixteen.[9]

The Indian Navy—it is maintained—has to be strengthened because of India's long coastline and because of the moves of foreign fleets in the Indian Ocean. The Nicobar and Andaman Islands are 500 to 700 miles distant from the mainland and, at the nearest point, only seventy miles from Indonesia. It is still remembered that Sukarno's "confrontation" threatened these islands.

Evidently, after the frustrating results of Nehru's pacifism, India wished to rely on strength rather than neighborly goodwill, international treaties, or the United Nations. In this endeavor it is supported by the Soviet Union.

Pakistan

The concept of Pakistan dates back to the Lahore Resolution passed by the twenty-seventh session of the All-India Muslim League in March 1940, which demanded that in the northwestern and eastern zones of India where Muslims

---

[8]"India's nuclear explosion did not change the balance of power on the Asian subcontinent since India's resources will be relatively limited . . . ," remarked Secretary of State Henry Kissinger. *New York Times,* June 7, 1974.

[9]In Pakistan these data are denied. It is stated that there are not twelve Indian divisions on the frontier facing China; the bulk of the Indian Army is said to be concentrated close to the Pakistani border.

are numerically in a majority "independent states" be constituted. Later this resolution was amplified to mean that these Muslim homelands should enjoy complete independence with full control over defense, foreign affairs, currency, customs, etc., and not to be constituted under a government of an all-Indian character. During the negotiations on independence in 1946-47, Nehru wished to establish a kind of paramountcy for India which Mohammed Ali Jinnah refused to accept. This claim, however, did not disappear from the Indian subconscious and was invoked at the time of the Bangladesh crisis, when India laid claim to be the guardian of peace and security on the subcontinent.

Secular hatred between the Hindu and Muslim communities was inherited by Pakistan and India and raised to the boiling point by the dispute over Kashmir. Pakistan accused India of high-handedness in this matter as well as in acts of force against Hyderabad and Goa. Nehru's moral approach to international affairs and teacherlike demeanor became an object of ridicule and contempt in Pakistan.

Under such circumstances Pakistan threw itself with joy into the arms of the United States when economic and military aid were offered to it in 1954 and when it was invited to participate in CENTO and SEATO. Illusions about the nature of this alliance—which was an alliance against possible aggression by the Soviet Union or China—led it to believe that, armed to the teeth, it also could accomplish its supreme dream, the march to Delhi.

Frustration followed frustration. In 1962 the United States and Britain rushed arms to India when the latter was invaded by the forces of Peking. It is still believed in Pakistan that this was a lost and possibly last opportunity for it to reconquer Kashmir. At that time it was Washington which advised it not to move. Its determined orientation toward China began after the 1962 incident. But in 1965, when war broke out between India and Pakistan, neither the United States nor China provided assistance. The events of 1971, the loss of the eastern region, and the abandonment by all its allies proved to be traumatic for Pakistan. A search for genuine friends and allies to redress the upset balance of power has plagued Pakistan ever since.

1. The average Pakistani is convinced that India plans to destroy Pakistan or to weaken it in order to dominate it. It seems that the destruction or annexation of Pakistan can hardly be the political-military aim of New Delhi. A partition of that country into its component units would create a high measure of instability on India's northwest borders, which would be detrimental to India itself. Annexation, even if that were feasible (as it is not) would increase the Muslim population of India (already over 60 million) with another compact 60 million, a hardly desirable objective. It is a more reasonable assumption that India would like to transmogrify Pakistan into a pliable, friendly satellite, if such a marvel could be achieved. As things are, Pakistan is likely to remain a sullen, hostile, and suspicious neighbor even if, at least temporarily, it may have given up designs of reconquering the Indian portion of Kashmir.

Islamabad is definitely on the defensive: obsessed by the specter of encirclement by India, the Soviet Union, and Afghanistan, it is desperately trying to counterbalance this threat and the increased strength of India. Islamabad is unable to match India's military spending (which is considered to be ten times that of Pakistan) and to obtain military assistance comparable to that which India received from Moscow. Not only is India now far superior on land and in the air, but the losses suffered by the Pakistani Navy in the 1971 war and the gradual increase in India's naval strength turned Pakistan into an inferior maritime power as well. The "alliance" between Moscow and New Delhi is viewed as a deadly threat to the existence of the Islamic nation on the subcontinent.

2. In the official and unofficial opinion that prevails in Pakistan, there exists a Soviet design to weaken and eventually to break up Pakistan, a design in which India and Afghanistan cooperate. Pakistanis have been watching Moscow's policy in Soviet Central Asia; there the Muslim-Turkic nations have been split into often artificially created linguistic groups (Uzbek, Kazak, Kirgiz, Turkman, Tadjik, and others) so as to dominate them easier. Should Moscow obtain control over the area, the same policy could be applied to Pakistan with its diverse linguistic groups—the Punjabi, Sindi, Baluchi, and Pushtun. The text of the secret draft protocol presented in Berlin in November 1940 to Molotov by Ribbentrop, in which Moscow claimed that its territorial aspirations centered south of its national territory "in the direction of the Indian Ocean," is well remembered. Pakistan suspects that the Soviets plan a two-thronged advance—one via Iraq to the Persian Gulf and the other via Afghanistan and Pakistan to reach out to the Indian Ocean. No outright military action is envisaged, but penetration is possible with the help of "allied" governments, with subversion as the principal weapon. As far as Pakistan is concerned, such subversion is being practiced in the North-West Frontier Province and in Baluchistan.

It is alleged in Islamabad that, with the treaty of 1971, Moscow has given almost a blank check to New Delhi. Article 9 of the treaty contains a stronger guarantee for India than the promise of assistance provided in the NATO Convention. Whereas the latter speaks of assistance in case of "aggression," the Soviet-Indian treaty mentions "attack" against one of the signatories. And "attack" may be provoked, as when India supported the "rebels" in East Pakistan and forced Pakistan to react.

Whether the dread of the Soviet threat is exaggerated or even an obsession, as some observers submit, seems almost of secondary importance as long as such views prevail. The belief in the danger that threatens Pakistan is a political factor which impinges on the actions and reactions of the governments concerned and on the balance of forces they are seeking to establish.

3. Afghanistan is often believed to be simply a cat's-paw of the Soviets. There is no doubt that the Afghan Army is being supplied and trained not only by Moscow but also by the Indians. Kabul intermittently raises the issue of Pushtunistan, that is, the territory inhabited by Pushtu-speaking tribes (Pathans) which were divided between British India and Afghanistan in 1893 by the Durand Line. Islamabad could, of course, easily handle the Afghan "danger" if there were not the impression that "behind every Afghan there stands a Russian."

After the ouster of King Mohammad Zaher in July 1973 and the setting up of a more nationalist regime under General Mohammad Daud Khan, the dispute flared up again. Pakistani Prime Minister Bhutto reacted skillfully and refrained from violent recriminations when he said:

> We have nothing but most fraternal sentiments toward Afghanistan. While there is no question of our compromising our sovereignty and territorial integrity, we will spare no effort in establishing cordial relations with Afghanistan.[10]

Nor did Pakistan interfere with transit shipments from Afghanistan to India, or to Karachi, which is the main maritime outlet of that land-locked country.

4. Shortly after Britain recognized the People's Republic of China, Pakistan followed, in 1950. Relations became close only following the short Sino-Indian hostilities in 1962, when both governments became conscious of their common interest in opposing India. Pakistan, unlike India, concluded a boundary agreement in March 1963 with Peking in which it gave up excessive claims to inhospitable areas in the Karakoram Range of the Himalayas. Economic and cultural agreements followed, and regular civil air communications were established between the two countries. China extended economic and military assistance to Pakistan.

Neither in 1965 nor in 1971 did China join in the military struggle between Pakistan and India. The support which was given to Islamabad remained restricted to the diplomatic field except for border harassments, which did not influence the military operations of India. Frustrated but helpless, Pakistan continued to nurture its Chinese relations.

5. It is realized in Islamabad that China cannot compete with the help which Moscow may afford to extend to India. It is still hoped that perhaps in twenty or thirty years China might be ready to stand up against the Soviet Union and then the Chinese orientation would become invaluable. But until that time the Soviet pressure on China neutralizes the impact which the latter power may exert in the Indian subcontinent.

The Sino-Pakistani ties rest on the mutuality of interest against India and the Soviet Union. The lack of any ideological community between Islamabad and Peking hurts the harmony of cooperation. There is a constant link of consultation between the two governments, in which, however, Pakistan is more the seeker than the receiver. It is even suspected that the conversations which often take place between mutually visiting leaders and diplomats remain barren while extremely cordial in nature.

During the 1971 hostilities, Washington placed an embargo upon the shipment of military supplies to both India and Pakistan. Upon protests of Pakistan, in February 1975 the embargo was finally lifted from both Pakistan and India. This move provoked in turn sharp protests by New Delhi. Still, for the Pakistani

[10]*New York Times*, Aug. 4, 1973.

leadership it appeared incomprehensible and unfair that Pakistan was handled at the same level as a much more powerful and unfriendly India. Bhutto claimed that the United States had an obligation to resume the shipment of arms to Pakistan. "The Soviet Union," he said, "gives India $2 billion to $3 billion in arms. Pakistan is an ally of the United States. Why should India get upset if Pakistan received arms from the United States?" Islamabad continued to feel that there was a "conspiracy" against Pakistan; India and Afghanistan are arming themselves; and the explosion of a nuclear device by India on May 18, 1974, are all intended to force Pakistan to submit. But Bhutto declared, "We would rather see our whole country a wasteland than to put up our hands."

What displeases India, pleases Pakistan. Although the Pakistani leaders express dislike about the buildup on Diego Garcia, discreetly they encourage Americans to carry on. If the Russians are moving with their warships in the Indian Ocean, so should the Americans to avoid an imbalance of forces. To redress the imbalance of power which perilously affects them, they feverishly seek allies in the Muslim world.

6. For years Pakistan has been an only lukewarm member of CENTO, the alliance with Britain, Turkey, and Iran. After the Bangladesh debacle, Islamabad discovered the advantages of closer ties with these countries. Both Turkey and Iran had given some modest logistic help during that crisis. Due to the vicinity of Iran, this country's friendship is of particular value to Pakistan.

Iran's massive armament program is viewed in Pakistan not only with satisfaction but also with envy. Tehran will soon be amply equipped with the most modern weaponry money can buy, while Pakistan's armaments are still on a World War II level.

In Islamabad, Iran is considered a "genuine" friend. However, the question being raised is, how genuine? Can Iran be trusted to commit its armed forces in support of Pakistan?

But Iran must fear a possible dismemberment of Pakistan. The community of interest between these two powers is genuine. They share the Baluchi problem; these tribesmen live on both sides of the border, well over 1 million in Pakistani Baluchistan, and a smaller number in Iran. The unrest among the Baluchi in Pakistan (whether they really want independence and union with their kinsmen in Iran is less certain) may spread over the border.

It is, however, resented in Islamabad that Tehran has lately much improved its relations with India. Evidently, Iran has a much greater possibility of diplomatic maneuvering than Pakistan: while the latter needs Iran, Tehran may equilibrate between Pakistan and India.

7. Pakistan's earlier unconditional reliance on its alliance with Britain and the United States has not earned for it the friendship of its Arab coreligionaries. In the Suez conflict of 1956, Pakistan sided with Britain and France, an attitude which is still not forgotten among Arab nationalists. Since the early 1960s, however, Islamabad has begun to woo Arab friendship. Pakistani technicians and military personnel work for some Arab countries, particularly in Saudi Arabia

and in the Persian Gulf sheikdoms. The bulk of Pakistanis, unlike the Iranians, are Sunni Muslims similar to most Arabs. There are no intrinsic conflicts of interest between Pakistan and the Arab world, which again differentiates them from their Iranian neighbors.

In the wake of the Bangladesh disaster, the "community interest" between Islamic peoples became a political program for the Bhutto government. This political line culminated in the Islamic Summit Conference held in Lahore in March 1974. It was attended by many top leaders of the Islamic world, conservatives and revolutionaries alike (the Shah of Iran abstained from attending). The summit conference was held first to demonstrate Muslim solidarity with despondent Pakistan; second, it provided an excellent opportunity for the recognition of Bangladesh, so far opposed by the military.

This successful performance, however, was not and could not be followed by further similarly impressive expressions of the "togetherness" of the Islamic community. Bhutto's personal ambition—to become a recognized leader in the Third World or at least in its Islamic sector—bogged down, partly due to the difficulties of Pakistan's external questions, partly because of the quagmire of his country's domestic problems.

8. Possibly the greatest weakness of Pakistan is to be found, not in the perils menacing it from the outside, but in its lack of internal cohesion and consequent lack of identity. The present four provinces—Punjab, Sind, North-West Frontier Province, and Baluchistan—are *disjecta membra* in their historic-ethnic and linguistic nature. The country is divided by the Indus River, traditionally India's northwest border. Despite their Islamic faith, Punjab and even Sind continue to set their eyes toward Delhi and perceive a cultural unity with India though they may hate the Hindus. On the other hand, the North-West Frontier Province and Baluchistan, west of the Indus River, feel a cultural affinity with their western neighbors Afghanistan and Iran, where their ethnic brothers, the Pathans and Iranian Baluchis, live.[11]

Pakistan has no real center. Karachi served as the capital until it was transferred far north, first to Rawalpindi and then to a newly built center.

---

[11] Pakistan's geopolitical duality was thus explained by its Prime Minister: "Pakistan's destiny is inevitably intertwined with that of the subcontinent. Nevertheless, her geopolitical position is not circumscribed by the subcontinent. There is a 371-mile-long border between Chinese Sinkiang and Pakistan-controlled Kashmir with its ancient silk route, and only Afghanistan's Wakhan corridor, varying in width from seven to thirty-one miles, divided the Soviet Union and Pakistan along 188 miles. Situated at the head of the Arabian Sea, Pakistan flanks the entrance to the oil-rich Persian Gulf and is therefore of strategic importance to many countries of the Middle East. Pakistan is also strategically placed in relation to the sea-lanes between Europe and the Indian Ocean, once they regain their former importance with the reopening of the Suez Canal. Moreover, Pakistan provides an overland passage from Europe to the Indian Ocean, an area on which international attention is being increasingly centered. Throughout history the part of the subcontinent now comprising Pakistan has been of vital importance as a gateway for trade and the passage of peoples." Zulfikar Ali Bhutto, "Pakistan Builds Anew," *Foreign Affairs* 51 (April 1973), 553.

Islamabad, in northwest Punjab. The country is still in search of its identity. As the example of Bangladesh has shown, Islamic faith is insufficient to engender a genuinely cohesive national sentiment. Centrifugal factors, ethnicity, language, historical tradition, and, last but not least, geographic location prevail over religious community.

The example of Bangladesh should be a warning. Internal disorder and local uprisings would be invitations for India and Pakistan's other neighbors to intervene. And they would not hesitate to exploit such weakness. Only in this respect can the status of Pakistan be considered potentially unstable.

The best-organized force is still the military, and as long as Bhutto is able to cooperate with the army leaders, he can be considered safe. But at the same time, he must be careful in his balancing act between the foes and often unreliable friends of his country.

Bangladesh

The division between India and Pakistan was based on the two-nation theory, namely, that on the Indian subcontinent there is a Hindu and a Muslim nation. Because the Muslim-majority areas existed in the northwest and in the east, the original Lahore Resolution of March 1940 spoke of independent Muslim "states" and not one "state." It was only subsequently that the establishment of one Muslim state, consisting of the western and eastern regions, was agreed upon. With the secession of East Pakistan, the original idea of two Muslim states materialized.

Bangladesh is the eastern half of the province of Bengal (plus the Sylhet District of Assam) as it existed under the British administration. Its population exceeded that of (West) Pakistan; still the national capital was located in the west, and East Pakistan was ruled from Islamabad. The inability to reconcile the demand for autonomy with the centralistic tendencies prevailing in Islamabad led to the secessionist movement, its cruel suppression by the military, and ultimately the intervention by India.

The overwhelming majority of the people of Bangladesh are Bengalese and speak the same language as the Hindu majority in Indian Bengal. So far, no movement exists which would call for a union of Bangladesh with India or unification of *all* the Bengal nation ("Bangladesh" means "Bengal Nation"). Bangladesh was admitted to the United Nations in 1974. Thus its existence as a member of the international family has been secured. However, doubts as to its genuine independence and continued viability have frequently been raised. When Bangladesh was born, Secretary of State Kissinger aptly called it "an international basket case." Its economic problems are now worse than before, and there seems to be no hope that it could physically survive without foreign assistance, which must include food and the means to find occupation for its fast-growing population, whose average density already is 1,400 persons per square mile.

India, the country which "liberated" and surrounds Bangladesh (except for a 120-mile border with Burma), remained the main source of relief and economic assistance to its "ward." On March 20, 1972, a Treaty of Friendship, Cooperation, and Peace was signed in Dacca between the two countries which in many respects reminds one of the treaty of 1971 between the Soviet Union and India. One was probably justified to consider India as the protector of Bangladesh's independence and the protected state as a kind of semi-satellite of New Delhi. In view of the geographic location of Bangladesh, which appeared to exclude a useful balance-of-power policy, and its economic dependence on India, it no doubt offered a target for New Delhi's aspiration for paramountcy on the subcontinent.

Since August 1975, when the charismatic liberator-leader Sheik Mujib was killed in a military coup, a military junta (whose members have frequently massacred each other) has ruled Bangladesh, staging a number of further bloody coups. While corruption and inefficiency figured as the official reasons for the revolts, there is reason to believe that dependence on India, objections against socialism and secularism as advocated by Sheik Mujib, and a demand for Islamic solidarity have added to the discontent so widespread in this flood- and drought-ravaged country. The events in Bangladesh reflect the instability which pervades subcontinent India.

Sri Lanka

Geographically, the island of Ceylon hangs at the southernmost tip of India—a country of 14 million overshadowed by one of 600 million. Despite the massive cultural impact of India which has descended on Ceylon in the course of history, the political development of the island was largely independent of India. Even during the British rule, the governor general of Ceylon depended directly on London and not on the viceroy of India, in contrast to the situation in Burma and other dependencies of India.

Ceylon (the name of Sri Lanka was officially assumed later, but in the Sinhalese text of the Constitution it was always Sri Lanka) attained full independence on February 4, 1948. Since 1970 the Sri Lanka Freedom Party, in coalition with the pro-Moscow Communist Party, has ruled the country under the Prime Ministership of Mrs. Sirimavo Bandaranaike. The Sri Lanka Freedom Party, according to its program, wishes to serve Buddhism, nationalism, and "democratic socialism." It is supported by the majority of the Sinhalese ethnic element (about 70 percent of the total population). The Tamil minority (about 22 percent) is represented by two opposition parties.

The Tamils are Hindus, whereas the Sinhalese are Buddhists. Only the "Ceylon Tamils," whose ancestors have lived on the island for many generations, are citizens of Sri Lanka. Other Tamils (the "Indian Tamils"), whose families had come to Ceylon only in the second half of the last century or later, are stateless. But even the Ceylon Tamils consider themselves to be treated as second-class citizens and are striving to have their language accepted as one of the official languages.

However, the greatest danger to the stability of Sri Lanka was faced in April 1971, when an unexpected revolution was exploded by a group calling itself the People's Liberation Front. This group consisted of Sinhalese youths who had been indoctrinated with Maoist-type ideology. It took a major effort on the part of the government to defeat the uprising.

Sri Lanka is weak economically and militarily. The fourfold rise of the price of oil has further upset the balance of its foreign trade. It professes to pursue a nonaligned foreign policy but is realistic enough to realize that without skillful adjustment of its relations with the exterior world, it would stand isolated and abandoned.

1. The balancing operations which Sri Lanka executes in its contacts with India are ambivalent and complex. Their actual differences are less significant than the general aura of reserve or suspicion, which is often acerbated.[12] The dispute over the Indian Tamils was settled by two agreements which provided for the grant of citizenship to part of these Tamils while the other were to be repatriated. However, the Tamil view is that neither of these agreements was fully implemented.

To all appearances, Indian-Sri Lanka relations are excellent but lack warmth. During the 1971 uprising, India concentrated forces across the Palk Strait and Indian warships patrolled the waters around Ceylon. The Indian assumption (which later proved incorrect) was that China stood behind the revolt. For India, it would have been intolerable to have a Chinese satellite at its southern doorstep. Should an extreme movement gain power in Sri Lanka, India would be ready to invade the island, for which, it is believed, plans have been prepared by the Indian Army Staff.

During the Bangladesh crisis and entry of Indian forces into what used to be East Pakistan, Sri Lanka became openly suspicious. When India prohibited overflights of Pakistani aircraft, a shuttle service between Karachi and Dacca was maintained with stopovers and refueling on Bandaranaike Airfield near Colombo.

Pakistan's loss of power was perceived in Colombo as an opportunity for India to bolster its ambition for paramountcy in the subcontinent and its neighborhood. In Sinhalese circles there exists some apprehension of "Indian imperialism"; they wish to prevent a satellite relationship from developing between the small and big neighbor.

2. Because of its exposed oceanic location, Sri Lanka is highly sensitive to naval movements in the waters around its shore. For this reason, the Soviet naval presence (just as an American naval presence) is highly unwelcome. On the

[12]Thus the question of the uninhabited Kachchaitivu Island in the Palk Strait (which is a place of pilgrimage from both Ceylon and India) could be easily solved except for the opposition by Madras against a cession to Sri Lanka. *New York Times,* June 20, 1974.

whole, Sri Lanka is reluctant to follow Soviet initiatives and accept Soviet advice. The ruling party does not need the participation of the Pro-Moscow Communists in the cabinet; still, it is more convenient to have critics within the government than to face them as outside opposition.

To balance out possible pressures from the Soviet side and also because China appears more remote, good relations with that country are being given much prominence in Colombo.

3. Since 1971, when it was realized that Peking was innocent of the uprising in that year, China has risen as the number one great power with which the best contacts have been sought. The Chinese have reacted cautiously. They were pleased to have obtained a diplomatic *pied-à-terre* wherefrom they can counteract Moscow and watch the other side of India. The measure of intimacy between Sri Lanka and China is hard to assess, but relations are mutually cordial.

4. Britain has maintained a subdued but still important role in the affairs of Sri Lanka. On May 22, 1972, the country pronounced itself a "Socialist Republic," but remained a member of the Commonwealth.

5. Relations between Sri Lanka and the United States have improved during the last half-dozen years. The economic assistance provided by Washington has remained moderate but constant. But there is no intention on the part of the United States to further intensify cordial relations, as possibly Colombo would be prepared to do: no expectations in the political or economic field should be raised—expectations which cannot be fulfilled.

Even the Diego Garcia matter did not cause a crisis in the ties between Washington and Colombo. Sri Lanka has been the initiator and main protagonist (next to India) of the Zone of Peace proposal for the Indian Ocean; yet when the plan for an extension of the facilities on Diego Garcia was announced, beyond expressing disappointment and misgivings, Colombo refrained from international action. Although Ceylonese leaders would never openly admit it, a United States interest in the Indian Ocean is welcome as long as it is directed to counterbalance Soviet activity.

6. Sri Lanka is rather focused on its internal problems. Its only major international initiative is the Zone of Peace proposal before the United Nations. It first referred to the dangers of great power rivalry and adduced the historic example of the competition which led to the British domination of most of the littoral of the Indian Ocean. Colombo believes it already has scored a victory by having drawn attention to the potential dangers in the Indian Ocean region and by having been able to enlist the support of the majority of members of the United Nations, including China.

The significance which Sri Lanka attributes to the Zone of Peace project is naturally prompted by its geographic location as an island particularly exposed to maritime rivalries. In its insular position it is unable to lean for support on any neighboring country in order to balance out potential pressures from India or those which may threaten it from seaside. While being a geographic appendix of India, it does not wish to become a political or economic appendix of that gigantic country. Its historic individuality and separate nationhood explain its reluctance to become submerged in the arms of Mother India.

The Maldives

The Maldive Islands have been a British protectorate since 1887. Britain handled foreign relations, defense, and security matters for the sultanate, but otherwise it remained internally self-governing. The protectorate ended in 1965 when the Maldives became fully independent; but Britain retained the right to maintain military facilities until 1986 on Gan Island, the principal island of Addu Atoll, the southernmost atoll of the long island chain running from north to south. In 1968 the sultanate was abolished and the Maldives became a republic.

The Republic of the Maldives is a member of the United Nations and is ready to enter into diplomatic relations with any country which so desires. But it maintains only one resident ambassador in Colombo (and some secondary representation in New York to the United Nations). Ambassadors accredited to the Maldives mostly reside in Colombo (as is the case with those of the United States and the Soviet Union); the British high commissioner in Sri Lanka is also his country's representative to the Maldives.

The government of the Maldives wished to keep aloof from international entanglements and to remain nonaligned. In fact, it is a passive onlooker at international developments. Thus it has failed formally to oppose Soviet or American naval activity, although it supports the concept of the Zone of Peace in the Indian Ocean. The determination to minimize involvement in outside conflicts led the Maldives, a strongly Muslim country, to avoid taking sides in the Arab-Israeli conflict. The Maldives declined an invitation to attend the Islamic Summit Conference at Lahore in March 1974. India and Pakistan, neighbors across the waters, somehow compete for the friendship of the island republic.

The Republic of the Maldives has no defense forces. Britain is no longer bound to defend it in case of aggression. Whether the British air base on Gan will be available after 1986 seems uncertain.

The Maldive state is slowly emerging from its "Arabian Nights" existence. For more than a century it was living under the protective shield of the British Navy, and now it is trying to find its place in the international community. The Maldives believe that their best protection is to remain outside international politics so that international politics will not involve them. They are no danger to anybody. Still, they have one asset: their strategic real estate value in the Indian Ocean for those who wish to control it. Had the Japanese entered the Indian Ocean to conquer in 1942, the Maldives would have been an ideal place to invade and fortify. Whether the calculation to rely on their peacefulness and harmlessness is justified will depend on the future political developments in the Indian Ocean region.

The Himalayan States: Nepal, Bhutan, and Sikkim

These states are remote from the Indian Ocean and are located at the southern slopes of the Himalayas, facing China and Tibet in the north and India in the south. But this geographic location confers significance to their position in relation to the power balances in the Indian Ocean region. Their territorial immunity from Chinese control is vital for the security of India.

Nepal. The high barrier of the Himalaya range divides Nepal from Tibet; the flat land along the Indian border is the continuation of the Gangetic plain; in between is a hilly country where most of the people live and where Kathmandu, the capital city, is situated. This strategic constellation determined that Nepal is more open to India than to Tibet and China. Indian cultural influences have been overwhelming; the main religion is Hindu.

For centuries isolation was the device by which Nepal managed to maintain its independence and national identity. The leaders of the country intuitively practiced power-balance politics, equilibrating between British India and China. As long as Tibet was independent or semi-independent, India was regarded as the greater danger. China was distant and separated by Tibet, and the almost inaccessible range of the Himalayas. Indian political influence was felt to be preponderant, even too much for the Nepalese. Thus when China conquered Tibet in 1951, little alarm was felt in Kathmandu. The country, it was believed, had gained a wider freedom of maneuver.

Since 1951 Nepal's foreign policy has been officially guided by the principle of nonalignment. In 1955 diplomatic relations with China were established, and Kathmandu could pride itself on being a "link" between the two gigantic powers. However, when relations between New Delhi and Peking turned tense, especially after the clash in 1962, this idea of a link was tacitly dropped. Thereafter, the guiding motto was "Equal friendship toward both India and China."

Nepal is the home of the reputable fighters the Ghurkas (both Britain and India may by treaty recruit Ghurka units there), but Nepal's army would hardly be able to resist a military invasion. The short-lived 1962 war between China and India was an eyeopener insofar as it proved that the Himalayas are not impassable for a modern army. Despite Nepal's reluctance to submit to New Delhi's hegemony, it still has confidential staff agreements with India which may be in fact plans for defense against China.

Diplomatically, Nepal is most skillfully managing its politics of balance, "tacking with the winds," obtaining economic help from China but trading mostly with India, from which economic assistance also is forthcoming.

Nepal is one of the strategic barricades along India's northern border against China. Its loss to the northern giant would fundamentally alter India's interests, and therefore New Delhi will support Nepal's endeavors to maintain its independence, though always watching developments with a cautious eye. A partition of the country would result in India's annexation of the southern plainland of

Nepal and the seizure of the high ranges and mountain passes of the Himalayas by China. Militarily this would be tantamount to the potential descent of China's armed forces into the Gangetic plains of India. Accordingly, Nepal's defense must be India's defense as well.

Bhutan. Isolation from the outside world has characterized Bhutan's position for centuries. It was as late as 1910 that Bhutan signed an agreement with Britain under which the country's foreign relations were to be "guided" by the advice of the viceroy of India, representing the Crown. When India became independent, a new treaty was agreed upon in 1949; New Delhi continued to guide Bhutan in its foreign relations. With the consent of India, Bhutan applied for membership in the United Nations and was admitted in 1971. Except for the Indian representative, there are no other diplomatic missions in Thimphu, Bhutan's capital.

Bhutan's international status is somewhat anomalous. She is an independent state, but dependent on India's "advice" in foreign relations and without other direct external contacts except a Permanent Mission to the United Nations. Her small army is being trained by the Indian military, and strategic routes are being built by India. China has published maps claiming part of Bhutan's territory. The High Himalayas extend along the northern borders of the country; if for no other reason, the strategic terrain compels India to remain a guardian of Bhutan's national existence.

Sikkim. While the kingdom of Bhutan possesses quasi-independence, Sikkim was a protectorate of India. Lying between Nepal and Bhutan, Sikkim shared the geopolitical characteristics of its two neighbors: the strategic passes across the main Himalayan range also separate it from Tibet.

New Delhi always managed Sikkim's international relations and maintained military forces (at times two divisions) in the country, and Indian advisers and top political officers directed its administration.

In April 1975 Sikkim's ruler, who tried to bring his country into the United Nations, was deposed by the Indian-influenced legislature, and his country was incorporated into the Indian Union. China protested and refused to recognize the annexation of Sikkim by India.

Burma

Burma is the borderland between Southeast Asia and the Indian subcontinent. While its long coastline faces the Bay of Bengal and the Andaman Sea, high mountains divide it from China and India, and wild jungles from Thailand.

The Union of Burma was formed and granted independence by the British in early 1948; it declined to join the Commonwealth. It embarked on a foreign policy of nonalignment and neutrality, attempting to exclude all foreign influences. However, it felt compelled to accept foreign economic assistance from both Communist and non-Communist sources. Membership in the United Nations was highly valued. Otherwise, Burma displayed a passive, almost autistic attitude, ignoring alliances or balance-of-power concepts. In view of its 1,200-mile-long border with China, its attention (which almost amounts to a fixation) is directed toward Peking.

Burma's main security problems are internal, not external, although some of the internal problems are rooted abroad. Only 70 percent of the population is Burmese; the rest belong to different ethnic groups (Karens, Shans, Chins, Kachins, and others). The Union of Burma is a federated state; in addition to Burma proper, there are four constituent states (Kachin, Shan, Kawthule, and Kayah). Some of the ethnic minorities live in a state of chronic insurgency. They are led by members of the outlawed Communist parties (White Flags and Red Flags). The White Flag organization is pro-Chinese and controls large sections of east and northeast Burma. It provides a good example of the tribal insubordination fostered by ideological motivation and supplied from abroad.

Since the beginnings of its independence, Burma has attempted to placate its big northern neighbor and to establish cordial relations. A historic border problem was settled and a Treaty of Friendship and Mutual Non-Aggression was concluded with Peking in 1960. Since 1972 the Communist-led insurgency has gained territorially and has been in slow advance. In order not to disturb normal diplomatic relations, Rangoon refrained from accusing Peking of supporting the rebels. The official Chinese position holds that it is the Chinese Communist Party which helps the insurgents, not the Chinese government, an argument which convinces few Burmese. Peking considers Burma to be a suitable area where it can compete with potential Soviet influences.

Thus Burma, willy-nilly, will eventually be dragged into the arena of Sino-Soviet rivalries. Whether it can maintain "neutrality" or will be compelled to seek protection through alliances and enter into the balance-of-power game will depend not only on developments on the subcontinent but also on the resistance the Burmese state may demonstrate vis-à-vis the centrifugal tendencies within. Burma's lack of political stability offers an invitation for intervention by outside powers.

Afghanistan

Like Burma, Afghanistan lies along the border region of the Indian subcontinent. While the former borders the Indian Ocean and divides India from China, Afghanistan is land-locked but forms a bridge between the subcontinent, on the one hand, and Soviet Central Asia, on the other. The Muslim invasions which descended on India from the eleventh century originated in what is now Afghanistan. When the Mogul Empire disintegrated in the eighteenth century, the Afghan Kingdom emerged by consolidating diverse principalities and tribes into one country.

Between 1880 and 1919 the foreign affairs of Afghanistan were conducted by London, and only after World War I did Afghanistan become an independent country. During the time of the British influence, the border between India and Afghanistan became delimited by the so-called Durand Line, the present frontier between Pakistan and Afghanistan.

After the formation of Pakistan in 1947, the Afghan government attempted to raise the border issue and claimed the North-west Frontier Province (and occasionally Baluchistan too). Since Pushtun-speaking people (also called Pathans) live on both sides of the border, Afghan nationalists raised a demand for the establishment of Pushtunistan, a country which has not existed in the past.

Since 1919 Afghanistan has successfully balanced its foreign relations between the Soviet Union and British India. After World War II, the United States provided economic and military assistance to Kabul, and subsequently there was almost a competition between Moscow and Washington to assist this backward country. However, after 1955 Soviet help increased, American aid decreased, and Moscow's influence came to overshadow that of other countries.

In July 1973 Afghanistan declared itself a republic under the leadership of General Mohammad Daud. He is known as an ardent nationalist and promoter of Pushtunistan. As Prime Minister from 1955 to 1962, his anti-Pakistani policy led to a rupture of diplomatic relations between Pakistan and Afghanistan.

Whether the coup d'état to oust the king was masterminded in Moscow (as Peking suggested) or not, the new Afghan head of state seems to enjoy strong Soviet support. With this change, the Soviet Union has certainly further strengthened its power potentials in the direction of the Indian Ocean.

Since 1954 the Afghan Army has been trained and supplied almost exclusively by Moscow. Several treaties of an economic nature have been concluded between Kabul and Moscow, as well as agreements for military assistance.

The expulsion of King Mohammad Zaher has created an unfavorable impression in Iran. The relations between Iran and Afghanistan, officially normal and even friendly, have occasionally suffered because of Afghanistan's leanings toward Moscow and to sporadic frictions along the Iranian border. Indeed, any aggressive action by Afghanistan with Soviet support would be a potential cause for a global crisis.

Selected Bibliography

Beloff, Max. *The Balance of Power.* London: George Allen & Unwin, 1967.

Bhutto, Zulfikar Ali. *The Myth of Independence.* London: Oxford University Press, 1969.

Bhutto, Zulfikar Ali. "Pakistan Builds Anew." *Foreign Affairs* 51 (April 1973), 541-554.

Brown, W. Norman. *The United States, India, Pakistan, and Bangladesh*. Cambridge, Mass.: Harvard University Press, 1972.

Burke, S. M. *Pakistan's Foreign Policy. An Historical Analysis*. London: Oxford University Press, 1973.

Chaoudhury, G. W. *India, Pakistan, Bangladesh, and the Major Powers*. New York: The Free Press, 1975.

Feldman, Herbert. *Revolution in Pakistan. A Study of the Martial Law Administration*. London: Oxford University Press, 1967.

Feldman, Herbert. *From Crisis to Crisis. Pakistan 1962-1969*. London: Oxford University Press, 1972.

Gopal, Madan. *India as a World Power*. New Delhi: Sagar Publications, 1974.

Hartmann, Horst. "The Indian Subcontinent with Bangla Desh." *Aussenpolitik* (English ed.) 25 (1974), 450-457.

Kaushik, Devendra. *The Indian Ocean. Towards a Peace Zone*. Delhi: Vikas Publications, 1972.

Kaushik, Devendra. *Soviet Relations with India and Pakistan*. New York: Barnes & Noble, 1972.

Maxwell, Neville. "Jawaharlal Nehru: Of Pride and Principle." *Foreign Affairs* 52 (April 1974), 633-634.

Menon, K. P. S. *The Indo-Soviet Treaty. Setting and Sequel*. Delhi: Vikas Publications, 1972.

Rao, Gondker Narayana. *The India-China Border*. Bombay: Asia Publishing House, 1968.

Rose, Leo E. *Nepal. Strategy for Survival*. Berkeley: University of California Press, 1971.

Rubinoff, Arthur G. *India's Use of Force in Goa*. Bombay: Popular Prakashan, 1971.

Siriwardene, Justin. "Sri Lanka and the Indian Ocean." In *Indian Ocean Power Rivalry*, pp. 88-95. Edited by T. T. Poulose. New Delhi: Young Asia Publications, 1974.

Spellman, John W. *Political Theory of Ancient India*. Oxford: Clarendon Press, 1964.

Syed, Anwar H. "Pakistan's Security Problem: A Bill of Constraints." *Orbis* 16 (Winter 1973), 952-974.

Syed, Anwar H. *China and Pakistan. Diplomacy of an Entente Cordiale*. Amherst: University of Massachusetts Press, 1974.

Chapter 6

Countries of the Persian Gulf

> *Certainty, surely, is beyond human grasp. But however that may be, the usual thing is that profit comes to those who are willing to act, not to the overcautious and hesitant. Just think how the power of Persia has grown: if my predecessors had felt as you do . . . you would not have seen our country in its present glory.*
>
> King Xerxes to Artabanus, 480 B.C.,
> in Herodotus

The Persian Gulf is a bay of the Indian Ocean. This geographic verity is to be remembered when discussing the political or strategic issues of the countries located around this very nearly "closed sea." The gulf was never a politically-strategically self-contained area; it was a place of constant outward or inward movements, coming from the valley of the Euphrates or entering from the Indian Ocean through the Strait of Hormuz. Since times immemorial the gulf has been a trade route, an alternative to the Suez route, from the Mediterranean to the Indian Ocean and from that ocean toward the Mediterranean lands.

At the height of Persian power, under the Acheamenides, and later under the Sassanids, the gulf was not only ruled by Persia but witnessed the extension of the Great King's military sway far into the Indian Ocean. And between these two zeniths of Persian history, the Macedonians of Alexander the Great navigated the gulf on their way back from India. Albuquerque's decision to capture Hormuz and seal the traffic to and from the gulf in 1515 demonstrated the interconnection between the gulf and the Indian Ocean.

While Arabs and Persians moved from the gulf into the ocean, the British arrived from the ocean to protect and extend their domination over the subcontinent; Russian and later German designs to reach the gulf and advance from there toward India motivated Britain to place this area under its control.

The economic-strategic significance of the gulf rose sky-high when it became the world's principal source of petroleum. In two world wars the protection and exploitation of this oil wealth, indispensable for warfare on land, sea, and air, has been a paramount task of the British Army and Navy. This petroleum is no less significant to both the industrial and agricultural economies of the world's countries.

About 60 percent of the world's oil reserves lie under the waters and around the Persian Gulf. More than a quarter of the world's used oil originates in and around the gulf, and most of it is being shipped out into the Indian Ocean and to destinations in Europe, Japan, and the United States, as well as to other countries. About 90 percent of Japan's oil arrives across the ocean from the gulf. The same is true for 50 percent of Europe's oil. It is calculated that by 1980, 35 percent of the oil needed in the United States will have to come from the gulf unless other sources of energy are tapped. American oil companies have earned $1.5 billion yearly from their investments in and around the gulf.

The British withdrawal from the gulf area, which formally ended on December 1, 1971, fundamentally changed the power balance in that part of the world. A second, equally radical transformation was the result of the fourfold increase in oil prices in 1973, which increased by that same measure the financial potential of the oil-producing countries in that area. While the second development in a way confronted the Persian Gulf countries with the oil-importing world, the first increased tensions among the area powers and permitted Iran to strive for a hegemonial role.

The confrontation in the Persian Gulf region derives from a divergent ethno-religious substratum, now supplemented by power rivalries, along with territorial and other conflicts. The primary divergence stems from the ancient hostility between the Aryan (Persians) and Semitic (Arab) ethnic groups, on the one hand, and the Shiite and Sunni sects of Islam, on the other.[1] This schism remains deeply buried in the ethnic subconscious, but becomes blurred when other, more urgent and more vital interests interpose and require different alignments.

Conservative and revolutionary forces are well represented among the littoral powers of the Persian Gulf, and the latter receive support from the Soviet side (and occasionally from the Chinese). The conservative governments are more sympathetic toward the United States or Great Britain. The Arab-Israeli conflict impinges strongly on the relations with Western powers, particularly those with the United States. Atheistic communism deters conservative and strongly Muslim

[1]Arabs demand that the gulf be named the "Arab Gulf," a demand which is indicative of the deep-seated antagonism prevailing on both sides of these waters. The oil-rich Iranian province of Khuzistan (ceded in 1847 by the Ottoman Empire to Persia) is called "Arabistan" by the Arabs.

governments from collaboration with Moscow, but anti-Israeli sentiment makes them cautious vis-à-vis Washington. Iran refused to boycott Israel and thus provoked enmities on the part of Arabs.

These cross-currents of sympathies and antipathies between the regional powers and concurrent attitudes toward the outside powers produce a highly volatile and dynamic field of forces, replete with potential dangers and violent reactions. The area is traditionally prone to sudden upheavals, military or civilian coups d'état and assassinations of heads of state or government.

The British withdrawal, as might be expected, had a destabilizing influence and created a vacuum of power. Iran's dramatic endeavor to establish its own dominating influence may, if successful, constitute a surrogate to the British Raj.

Iran

There are three medium powers on the periphery of the Persian Gulf: Iran, Iraq, and Saudi Arabia. Among these three, Iran is by far the most powerful. Its oil production is somewhat lower than that of Saudi Arabia, but its population of 32 million is far larger than the 8 million of Saudi Arabia and 10 million of Iraq. Under a determined leadership, with modernization and industrialization on the way, Iran's power potential, together with its geopolitical location and historical tradition, appears predestined to secure for it a paramount position in the gulf area.

The tremendously improved financial situation of the country has instilled great self-confidence. Iran's monarch, Mohammad Riza Shah, predicted that his land will become one of the five great powers in the world by 1985, equal in status to France, and "the Japan of West Asia."[2] The Shah, while not repudiating existing alliances and friends, wished to rely primarily on the economic and military strength of his own country. The predictions in these two fields of development may eventually prove to be overoptimistic but have to be accepted as the targets which the policy makers hope to attain.

To achieve this ambitious goal, Iran has embarked on a crash industrialization and massive armament program. The avowed purpose of Iran's armament effort is to assure passage through the Hormuz Strait and within the gulf. This is Iran's "jugular vein," a matter of "life and death." Because Iran's oil is not only produced in the gulf area and exported across the Hormuz Strait but also beyond that strait, its interest extends beyond the exit to the Indian Ocean out into the ocean itself. Iran therefore remains highly concerned with the events of that ocean. The construction of a major military-naval complex at Chah Bahar, some 250 miles east of the Hormuz Strait and about fifty miles west of the Pakistani border, demonstrates that interest. How far Tehran may be able to extend its security perimeter into the ocean depends on capabilities of naval and air power.

[2]From the Shah's interview with the correspondent of the German periodical *Der Spiegel*, Jan. 5, 1974.

Iran's dramatic initiatives and the ambition to raise itself into the rank of a major power and to claim interest in areas distant from its national territory have been prompted and supported by three important developments: (1) the British withdrawal from the gulf, (2) evolutions in the field of international politics (American-Soviet détente, Pakistan's dismemberment), and (3) the bonanza resulting from the fourfold rise of the price of oil.

1. British military and political withdrawal from the gulf was carefully prepared in agreement with Iran. The termination of Britain's defense treaties with the Trucial Sheikdoms and with Bahrein, Qatar, and Kuwait and the recall of British forces from the gulf area upset the existing balance of power. With the Iranian decision to assume responsibility for the security of navigation within the gulf and, especially, through its gateway to the Indian Ocean, Tehran emerged as the dominant power in that subregion. To demonstrate its role and to obtain physical control over the entrance to the Hormuz Strait, on the day when the British protectorate over the Trucial States ended, that is, on November 30, 1971, Iranian troops occupied the strategic islands of Abu Musa, Greater Tunb, and Lesser Tunb.[3]

London, Washington, and Tehran were collaborating to fill the vacuum caused by the British pull-out and to replace it by the principal custodianship of Iran. The many-billion-dollar defense program of Iran is being supported by the United States, Britain, and other members of the Western alliance system, such as France and West Germany. Together with the acquisition of a full range of modern weaponry, Iran developed its airfields and port facilities—within the Gulf (Khurramshahr on the Shatt el-Arab, the island of Kharg and Bushire) and east and west of the Hormuz Strait (Bender Abbas, Jask, and Chah Bahar).

In addition to the arms deliveries, Washington has sent service and training personnel of the army, air force, and navy to assist the Iranians in the use of the modern weaponry. Nearly 11,000 Iranian officers and enlisted men have received military training in the United States.[4]

2. Iran is not a newcomer in the field of balance-of-power politics. In fact, it owes the preservation of its national existence to the balance which was maintained between its two powerful neighbors to the north and to the south. Since the end of the eighteenth century Russia has threatened to swallow up more and more of Iranian territory. In the south, the British, who operated in the gulf, came to oppose a Russian advance toward India. The balancing-out policy worked until Russia and Britain achieved collaboration, as in 1907 or during World War II. Considering the Soviet Union as the greater danger, in 1955 Iran aligned itself with the Western powers by signing the Baghdad Pact (later to become the CENTO alliance). But Soviet hostility toward Iran relaxed after 1962 and relations turned not only normal but also friendly. Despite the hegemonial aspirations and its massive military build-up, Iran was able to avoid direct confrontation with Moscow.

[3]*New York Times,* Nov. 7 and Dec. 3, 1971.

[4]*New York Times,* May 20 and July 22, 1973.

The Iranian arms program is, nevertheless, at variance with Soviet foreign policy goals and against the interests of countries and movements supported by Moscow. But, so far, Moscow has showed reluctance to oppose directly Iranian endeavors lest the antagonism of the past be repeated. Similarly, Tehran is happy to maintain the official "border of friendship" with the Soviets so as to have a freer hand in its activity in the gulf area.

3. Peking, which is challenging Soviet influence in Southeast Asia and on the Indian subcontinent, is also making its presence felt in the area of the Persian Gulf. Diplomatic relations between Tehran and Peking were established in 1971, and since then relations between the two governments have become friendly, almost intimate. In this respect, Iran was following Pakistan's example; to counterbalance possible Soviet pressures, closer contact with China served useful purposes. Creation of such a favorable atmosphere was also due to Peking's pragmatic thinking: it has given up all assistance to the insurgents in Oman, a thorn in the eyes of the Iranian government, and seemingly also the support of other "national liberation movements" in the Middle East.

China also expressed readiness to support Iran in its policies for the protection of navigation and security in and around the gulf.

4. Tehran considered the dismemberment of Pakistan to be a serious warning; it became genuinely alarmed about the future of this eastern neighbor. It advised moderation to Islamabad and, to the extent India was willing to listen, also to New Delhi. The Shah realized that he was not in a position to put pressure on Soviet-supported India except in the form of friendly persuasion.

The rise in the price of oil completely upset India's foreign trade; it had to obtain oil on credit lest most of its foreign exchange revenue be expended on the importation of oil. This may have been one of the factors which induced New Delhi, after an unprecedented low in Iranian-Indian relations at the time of the Bangladesh crisis, to mend fences with Tehran, although the massive Iranian arms program was looked upon with suspicious eyes.

In April 1974 Prime Minister Gandhi journeyed to Tehran. The communiqué issued at the end of the talks affirmed Iranian and Indian support for the Indian Ocean as a "Zone of Peace" without mentioning either the Soviet presence or Diego Garcia. India agreed that "safeguarding stability and peace in the Persian Gulf" was the exclusive duty of the Gulf States themselves (thus recognizing its own disinterestedness in this area). Iran pledged to provide India with oil on generous terms of credit.[5]

This rapprochement between Iran and India is to be considered as a phase in the balancing-out operations which both countries pursue to gain temporary advantages and to feel out each other. The Shah assured Pakistani Prime Minister Bhutto that normalization of his ties with India could only favorably affect those between Pakistan and India.

In the case of the Afghan danger, Iran would proceed not only in the interest of Pakistan but also in its own considered interest. Tehran would not be willing

[5]*New York Times,* May 6, 1974.

to tolerate the creation of a Pushtunistan which included Pakistani Baluchistan or an independent Baluchistan or the annexation of these areas by Afghanistan; such developments would jeopardize the future of the Iranian portion of Baluchistan. In the event of such a danger, even a "protective reaction," that is, an occupation of Pakistani Baluchistan by Iran, cannot be excluded.

In the Shah's eyes the CENTO alliance did not possess any tangible value. On the other hand, the economic offspring of CENTO, the Regional Cooperation for Development, the organization of which Iran, Pakistan, and Turkey are members, was held in much higher esteem. Under the aegis of this organization, communications between these three countries are improved and various economic projects undertaken. Pakistan was also able to obtain Iranian oil on favorable terms.

5. Among the neighbors of Iran, Iraq was for a long time considered the arch-enemy. The latent Arab-Persian animosity found open expression in the Iraqi-Iranian confrontation. There were concrete grievances galore: navigation on the Shatt al-Arab, dividing the two countries (where Iraq claimed control over the entire riverbed); Baghdad's opposition to Iranian prominence in the gulf; accusations according to which Iran is supporting the Kurdish spearatists in Iraq; and border incidents and hostile attitudes of the Iranian minority in Iraq.

During the Algiers summit conference of the Organization of Petroleum Exporting Countries (OPEC), on March 6, 1975, the Shah of Iran and Saddam Hussein, deputy chairman of the Revolutionary Command Council of Iraq, agreed to settle the differences between their two countries: to demarcate their borders, delimit the Shatt al-Arab frontier according to the median line of the navigational channel (the so-called *thalweg*), and end subversive activities along their boundaries. The latter promise implied the cessation of aid to the Kurds by Iran.

Iran has its Kurdish problem, but this creates no headaches comparable to those created by the Kurdish problem of Iran's Iraqi and Turkish neighbors. No attempts were made on the Iranian side of Kurdish-inhabited areas to disrupt the existing traditional tribal system. Whenever hard pressed, Kurds from Iraq used to move over the Iranian border, where they were well received by their conationals. Under the agreement reached between Iran and Iraq in Algiers, Tehran discontinued its assistance to the Kurdish rebellion, which thereafter collapsed.

6. Iran's relations with the Arab world are selective: it is hostile toward radical-socialist states, somewhat reserved toward moderately socialist Arab countries, and more cordial toward conservative and Western-oriented Arab regimes. On the whole, Iran's attitude is influenced by the notion of power balance, here and elsewhere.

Despite the pressures which Arab countries have exerted to isolate Israel, Iran has continued to maintain discreet but important links with that country. Jerusalem maintained an "economic office" in Tehran, as the Israeli Mission is officially called. Iran is the main source of foreign oil for Israel; the oil is sold by the Iranian National Petroleum Company to foreign concerns, which then resell it to Israel. At the same time, however, Tehran paid lip service to the Arab demand for an Israeli withdrawal behind the 1967 borders.

Iran objected to the Arab oil boycott imposed on Western, allegedly pro-Israeli countries in the fall of 1973, but did promote the increase in the price of oil.

In the political field, Iran is trying to be accepted by the Arab countries around the gulf as the leading power. Iran has submitted plans for a regional defense pact linking all the littoral states of the Persian Gulf. Iraq was not expected to rally to this proposal; but other Gulf States, including Saudi Arabia, have also been reluctant to accept the Iranian project. Only with Oman did Tehran succeed in establishing close ties and agreement on common defense. Iranian forces assist Oman in its fight against the Dhofari rebels.

7. Iran's impressive initiative in asserting its growing military and naval power in order to safeguard stability and security in the gulf so far has not been seriously challenged. Protests against the occupation of the islands at the entrance to the Strait of Hormuz has been uttered, but even Saudi Arabia abstained from overt opposition.

Whether Iran, in the long run, will be able to maintain its primacy among the states of the Persian Gulf and whether it will be able to build up an industrial infrastructure, as it proposes to do, for the support of a great power status remain to be seen. To overcome its internal deficiencies requires much more than the acquisition of modern weaponry and the accumulation of monetary reserves. For it to catch up with the per capita income of West European powers, simultaneously with the steady increase of its population within the next twenty or thirty years, seems somewhat unlikely. To bridge the gap between town and rural areas in terms of education, economic status, and national consciousness appears to be a task which would require the energy of more than one generation.

The presence of non-Persian-speaking minorities (some claim that the Persian-speaking element itself is in a minority) and the semiautonomous tribal groups contributes to the internal weakness of the Iranian state. While Persian culture (a symbiosis of many nationalities for centuries) and the strong leadership of the Shah are factors of cohesion, the question remains whether these factors may in the long run successfully counteract the centrifugal or debilitating forces stemming from the ethnic divergencies and the dependence on an ephemeral personal leadership.

It is clear that, while seeking to play a prominent role as a military power in the Persian Gulf region, Iran should not lose sight of its limitations. Only in union with other stabilizing forces will it be able to carry out the task of maintaining an equilibrium of forces and a stable situation.

Iraq

Iraq is rather remote from the main body of the Indian Ocean, and its coastline on the Persian Gulf (apart from the estuary shore of the Shatt al-Arab) is only ten miles. Nevertheless, its location at the head of the oil-rich gulf at the confluence of two historic rivers, the Tigris and the Euphrates, enhances its strategic and political significance. Being the only country among the littoral states of the Persian Gulf which maintains close ties with the Soviet Union makes it something of an exponent of Moscow's policies and further increases its importance. For Iraq's size and economic potentials, it is armed to the teeth. She is, therefore, a weighty factor in the balance of power in the gulf area and, tangentially, also in that in the Indian Ocean region at large.

On April 9, 1972, Iraq signed a Treaty of Friendship and Cooperation with the Soviet Union which is to last fifteen years—one which in many respects resembles the Indo-Soviet Treaty of 1971. Among the provisions of the treaty corresponding to Iraqi desiderata, Article 4 pledged the two countries to continue "their determined struggle against imperialism and Zionism and for the total elimination of colonialism." Article 9 announced that it was in the interest of two countries "to pursue cooperation in the field of strengthening each other's defense ability."[6]

An ominous clause which provides for the obligation "to consult" in case of an attack against one or both of the signatory governments, as contained in the treaty between Moscow and New Delhi, has not been repeated in the Soviet-Iraqi treaty. Therefore, for many observers (among them the Iranians), the provision concerning the strengthening of each other's defense capabilities sounded more threatening.

Iraq is separated from Soviet territory by Turkey in the northwest and Iran in the northeast. Turkey, having a community of interest with regard to Kurdish nationalist ambitions, displays a relatively friendly attitude toward Iraq; between Iraq and Iran head-on collisions have not been infrequent. But even in the case of Turkey, the transit of military supplies by land or by air from the Soviet Union to Iraq was hardly to be approved except under special circumstances. A more reliable way of access to Iraq is by sea. Here, however, geography is unfavorable to Iraq. Its main commercial port is Basra, seventy-three miles upstream on the Shatt al-Arab; the secondary is Fao, some ten miles from the gulf on the same river. Access by ocean-going vessels to these ports is difficult; an artificial channel, sufficiently deep only at the time of the spring rains which feed the river and at high tide, cannot be depended on permanently. All shipping is open to the sight of the Iranians from the eastern shore of the river.

In the last years, Iraq, again with Soviet assistance, has developed the port of Umm Qasr. But this harbor is located at the far end of Khor Abdullah, a funnel-shaped creek between the Kuwaiti islands of Bubiyan and Warba, in the south, and the Iraqi territory, in the north. The width of the channel leading to Umm Qasr is at places less than one mile. The border of Kuwait is also close to the harbor itself.

Since Kuwait attained independence in 1961, there have been several attempts on the part of Iraq to annex part of that country or even all of it.

[6]*New York Times,* Apr. 10, 1972.

Subsequently, Iraq laid a formal claim to the two islands, Bubiyan and Warba, in the Khor Abdullah channel leading to Umm Qasr. The Iraqi Foreign Minister, Murtadha Said Abdul-Baqi, asserted that the ownership of these two islands was essential for his country, that they were closer to Iraq than to Kuwait, and that sovereignty over them was open to question. It is not difficult to imagine that this probe was implemented to secure a safer passage for Soviet warships to Umm Qasr.

The weakest point of Iraq's internal situation lies in the northeast of the country, where the Kurdish minority maintained for many years a *de facto* autonomous state, defending its area in intermittent combat against the forces of Baghdad. Only when Iraq and Iran settled their differences in 1975 and Tehran discontinued its support to the Kurdish cause did the revolt collapse.

For Iran, any diversion of Iraqi military power can only be welcome. Even if Iraq is strongly supported and armed by Moscow and other Communist countries, so long as Baghdad remains isolated in the gulf area, the weight of the balance will rest with the more conservative forces—and Iran's leading position will not be seriously challenged.

Kuwait

Despite its small size and population, Kuwait is the third biggest oil producer in the Middle East, after Saudi Arabia and Iran. Extremely vulnerable to outside attacks, consisting of one city by the same name where half the population lives, and situated on the flat, dry desert, Kuwait is dependent on the goodwill of other countries as far as its security is concerned. When the British withdrew in 1971, Kuwait was forced to fend for itself. It embarked on a program of arms acquisition which is still in progress. But in other respects its foreign policy resembles that of other militarily exposed city-states such as Singapore, which have to make up for their lack of strength by a shrewd and cautious foreign policy and place the weight of their wealth in the balance.

Kuwait, however, must find safety in the community of Arab states; it relies upon the moral and physical pressure of this community in part to contain Iraq. For this reason, Kuwait acted as the champion for the Arab cause against Israel; it has been the "Santa Claus" to the Palestinian movements; together with Saudi Arabia, it compensated Egypt for the loss of Suez Canal revenues and gave assistance to Jordan. Thus Arab solidarity was enlisted to support the wealthy little brother in its hour of need should such an occasion arise.

Internally, Kuwait appears to be more stable than many other Arab Gulf States. Popular representation has replaced the absolute rule of the emir. But Kuwaiti citizenship is hard to obtain, and more than half of the population is foreign-born Arabs, many of them Palestinians. There are also a sizable number of Iranians. A high standard of living, the highest among Arab nations, free education, and extremely generous social welfare provisions will, for some time, satisfy the disfranchised part of the population. However, in the long run, discrimination between Kuwaiti citizens who wield voting power and noncitizens who do not may prove a source of debility.

Saudi Arabia

Next to Iran and Iraq, Saudi Arabia is the major power in the Persian Gulf area. Its population is smaller than that of Iraq, but its size is gigantic for such a population: three times the size of France. Saudi Arabia stretches from the gulf to the Red Sea; its gulf coastline extends 296 miles, while its Red Sea coast is 1,020 miles. Saudi Arabia is thus both a Persian Gulf and a Red Sea Power. The capital, Riyadh, is located in an east central position, but the commercial center is Jidda on the Red Sea. The holy cities of Islam, Mecca, and Medina, of which Saudi Arabia is the "guardian," lie near the Red Sea shore. On the other hand, Saudi Arabian oil is exploited near the Persian Gulf; its strategic air center is Dharan, and the principal oil port is at nearby Dammam.

Saudi Arabia's enormous extent—most of it being barren desert land—and sparse population are a source of weakness. Its vast oil wealth has helped it to pursue an active foreign policy using the "oil weapon," especially since prices were increased fourfold in 1973. Its mammoth foreign exchange surplus enabled it to initiate large-scale development plans and also to purchase arms from the West, mainly from the United States.

Unlike Kuwait, Saudi Arabia does not maintain diplomatic contacts with the Soviet Union or any Communist country. It is an ardent opponent of leftist Arab governments; it claims a spiritual leadership role in the Muslim world. Such attitudes limit its maneuverability and the flexibility of its foreign policy; a deep-seated, ideological anti-Israeli sentiment restrains its pro-American sympathies. While hostile to the East, it remains suspicious of the West.

The withdrawal of the British from the gulf persuaded the otherwise cautious Saudi leaders that they, like Iran and Kuwait, had to strengthen their military establishment. Iraq's venture against Kuwait and the "national liberation movements" supported by the Soviets and their agent state, South Yemen, were considered warnings that could not be ignored.

When the armament build-up reaches its initial goal and Saudi personnel have been trained by the British and American advisers in the use of sophisticated weaponry, Saudi Arabia will emerge, next to Iran and Iraq, as a military power which could effectively oppose pro-Soviet attempts to gain further footholds in the gulf area. So far, however, the Saudi armament effort has not been accompanied by any formal defense treaty. Saudi Arabia has no mutual defense arrangements with either Britain or the United States or with any of the Arab states or Gulf States. Save for Saudi Arabia's membership in the Arab League, Riyadh is and prefers to remain isolated as far as alliances or defense agreements are concerned. Its geographic location, except for its exposed oil shore in the Gulf, permitted a "splendid isolation," a status without formal commitments to other countries and with no commitments of others to her. It may be noted that

Saudi Arabia, a genuinely uncommitted state, never boasts of being uncommitted, while clearly committed countries, such as Iraq, loudly claim to be neutralist.

Domestically, the Saudi Arabian state presently appears solid and stable in its traditional archaic setting. With more than half of its population still nomads or seminomads, ruled by ancient customs and the Koranic law, and thus only a minority settled in villages or urban communities, full modernization and industrialization will take time.

So long as the paternalistic but autocratic rule of the monarch and royal family continues, any revolutionary change is excluded. With the increase in numbers of a Western-educated, intellectual segment, discontent may spread, but not enough to allow a Libyan-type revolution. On the other hand, as militarization proceeds, a professional officer corps may be one organized element that could become a danger to the largely antiquated system which appears inconsistent with the technological and computerized industrial society demanded by the bonanza of oil production and mammoth earnings. How Saudi Arabia's politics will eventually evolve and what its status will be after a change in the confrontations within the gulf area will very much depend on the way the transformation takes place; whether the change is evolutionary or revolutionary will greatly determine its place on one or the other side of the international political fence, and this will also determine where its weight in the local balance will fall.

Bahrain and Qatar

Bahrain consists of a group of islands in the gulf of the same name, between the peninsula of Qatar and the Arab mainland of Saudi Arabia. Bahrain and Qatar share a common history and have common interests; they are both oil producers and have lived under British overlordship before London terminated the respective protectorate treaties and granted full independence to the two states.

In the seventeenth century Bahrain itself was subjected to Iranian suzerainty, a claim which Iran relinquished only in 1970. Both Bahrain and Qatar refused to join a federation with the Trucial Sheikdoms, which joined together in late 1971 and early 1972 and called themselves the United Arab Emirates.

Bahrain and Qatar, both larger in terms of population than any of the members of the United Arab Emirates, refused to become "equals" in a union of states which accustomed to look down on. Politics in that area are governed by long-standing feuds and jealousies among the ruling families. A natural union between Bahrain and Qatar, neighbors across narrow waters, is thwarted by the memories of Qatar's former dependence on Bahrain and by an unsolved dispute over the island of Howar (or Young Camel), which both countries claim for themselves.

Since the ending of the British connection, neither Bahrain nor Qatar has entered into any alliance or defense treaty. However, both joined the Arab

League. Both states entertain friendly relations with the two prominent gulf powers, Iran and Saudi Arabia. But if there is collaboration it is only on an ad hoc basis. These governments, by tradition and instinct, still look toward Britain, although Britain no longer has a commitment to protect them.

Since the early 1960s Bahrain had been the home port for the United States Middle East Force, a symbolic rather than powerful naval unit, consisting of a converted seaplane tender (serving as flagship) and two destroyers which often make tours out into the Indian Ocean or along the coast of East Africa. The American squadron was a "guest" of the British-operated Jufair naval base; after the departure of the "landlord," Washington opened negotiations with the ruler of Bahrain for an agreement allowing more permanent use of the port. Before the negotiations could be completed, the October 1973 war broke out between the Arabs and the Israelis. As a gesture of solidarity with the Arab cause, Bahrain served notice to the United States to evacuate its base before October 20, 1974. Subsequently, the notice was rescinded, and the Americans continue to operate the base.

Both Bahrain and Qatar maintain diplomatic relations with the Soviet Union; however, they view Iraq's association with Moscow with utter suspicion.

Bahrain, in contrast to Qatar, runs a recently established constitutional regime with an elected assembly. More than 20 percent of the population are nonindigenous Arabs. These and the largely increasing class of the educated are the elements striving for more radical change. Qatar is less stable; in a 1972 bloodless coup the ruler, while on a hunting trip in Iran, was replaced by his cousin, who promised reforms. More than half of the population of Qatar consists of nonnative Arabs, among them Palestinians and Yemenites.

These two Gulf States practice a pro-Western and pro-Arab oriented non-aligned foreign policy, relying for their protection on the existing balance of power in the gulf area, which they hope and expect none of the major regional states will disturb. Against a potential aggression by leftist forces (Soviet- or Chinese-supported revolutionary movements), they depend on their conservative neighbors or, if necessary, on direct or indirect British or American assistance. But primarily they wish to confide in Arab solidarity due to their own military weakness and innocuousness.

United Arab Emirates

After prolonged negotiations, Oriental haggling, and intermittent crises, six of the seven Trucial States (Abu Dhabi, Dubai, Sharjah, Fujairah, Ajman, and Umm-al-Qaiwain) joined together on December 2, 1971, to form the federation of the United Arab Emirates. The seventh, Ras-al-Khaimah, first refused to join but subsequently, in February 1972, also adhered to the federation.

Under the federal Constitution the Supreme Council, consisting of the seven rulers, is the main governing body, and the presidency is to alternate among the heads of the member states. The ruler of Abu Dhabi, the richest of the emirates, was elected first President, and the emir of Dubai, the second richest, was named Vice President. Abu Dhabi and Dubai have veto power in the Supreme Council, a privilege also claimed by Ras-al-Khaimah. There is a forty-member legislature in which membership differs from four to eight, according to the population of the member states. It was agreed by the Supreme Council that the provisional seat of the federation will be in Abu Dhabi for the next five years, during which time a new capital will be built on the border between Abu Dhabi and Dubai. The first diplomatic act of the federation was to conclude a treaty of friendship with Britain, which, however, does not amount to an obligation of defense on Britain's part. Britain's primary task was to assist the United Arab Emirates in creating a military force using the former Trucial Oman Scouts, a British-maintained unit, as a nucleus.

The United Arab Emirates was almost immediately admitted to the United Nations and to the Arab League, as were Bahrain and Qatar. But the new federation entertains no treaty ties with either Saudi Arabia or Iran. Its members are beset with conflicts among themselves and with their respective neighboring states. Unless the central authority can assert itself (which would, in fact, mean Abu Dhabi-Dubai condominium over the rest of the states), the centrifugal and disruptive tendencies among its members will prevent any clear-cut foreign policy line.

The geopolitical location of the federation is rather unfavorable. It extends for over 400 miles along the Persian Gulf, from the bottom of the Qatar peninsula to the Musandam peninsula, which belongs to Oman. Its inland boundary toward Saudi Arabia and Oman is largely undefined. Except for Abu Dhabi and Dubai, the territory has no town of any importance and no harbor. It is a strip of desert with fishing villages on the coast and scattered oases inland. Abu Dhabi and Dubai are oil-rich and prosperous; Sharja lived off the presence of a former British military base and airfield; otherwise, there is poverty. The rulers of the smaller states obtained some income from oil companies for exploration rights, but uncertainties concerning the boundaries of the sea bed (where the search for oil is being conducted), as between one state and the other, often prevented the conclusion of such contracts. Whereas the continental shelf of the upper section of the gulf has been divided between Iran and Saudi Arabia, the southern section, between Iran and the emirates, is still undemarcated.

Iran's claim to the three islands off the Hormuz Strait has been mentioned earlier. Much of the opposition against the Iranian move is traceable to hopes by Sharja, Ajman, or Ras-al-Kharma that oil might be found around these islands. Furthermore, Ras-al-Khaimah has laid claim to the Musandam peninsula which is owned by Oman. Sharja and Ajman raised conflicting claims on the sea-bed area before their shores. The entire territory of the United Arab Emirates south of Musandam resembles a jigsaw puzzle rather than the frontiers of respectable states: enclaves around other enclaves and pieces of territory far away from the major body of the state are not uncommon. Most borders are undefined; they are in dispute between Sharja and Fujaira, Ajman and Oman, and Sharja and Oman, respectively.

Internal instability is also due to feuds between the ruling families and within the families themselves. Attempts at assassination are not infrequent. Nonindigenous Arabs and members of other ethnic groups (Iranians, Indians, Pakistanis, and many Palestinians) hold leading posts, particularly in those states where industry (oil) and commerce (in Dubai) are more developed. Arab nationalist movements (Baathist and Palestinian) entertain agents and have followers mostly among the nonnative Arabs. Arab nationalists have considered the rulers mere puppets in the hands of the oil companies and Western imperialists-colonialists. As long as Palestinians are busy against Israel and the Dhofari rebels against Oman, the former Trucial sheiks may be left undisturbed. But should these movements, supported by South Yemen and, indirectly, by Iraq and the Soviet Union, concentrate on the vulnerable emirates, an end to the present seemingly stable situation can be expected.

The asymmetry between the federation's member states, in terms of wealth, population, and influence, is likely to lead to secessionist attempts by the dissatisfied rulers. Unless the United Arab Emirates is able to strengthen its military potential so as to be in a position to defeat internal upheavals or separatist actions and limited aggressions or incursions by outside powers, the future of this federated entity appears to be fragile.

In view of this state of affairs, it seems rather understandable that the Shah undertook to provide for the defense of the gulf area. The rulers of the emirates are rather conservative and strictly anti-Communist; but many of their inhabitants are not. The reluctance to enter into any formal defense arrangement which would be a warning to potential troublemakers encouraged Iran's unilateral action. Unlike the emirates, or Bahrain and Qatar, the strategically important and endangered state of Oman has shown readiness to accept the helping hand offered by Tehran.

Oman

Following the expulsion of the Portuguese and successful resistance against the Ottomans and Persians, the Omani dynasty exercised control over the western coast of the Arabian sea. Omani domination was extended to the Makran coast of what is now Pakistan, and along the East African coast including the island of Zanzibar. In 1861 the Omani Empire was divided between the two sons of the last ruler; Zanzibar and the African dependencies were separated from Muscat and Oman, as the sultanate was called until 1970, when "Muscat" was dropped from its name.

Until the accession of the present Sultan Qabus in 1970 (his father Sultan Said bin Taimur was deposed in a bloodless coup and exiled to London), Oman was practically closed to outside influences and lived under medieval circumstances. Oil had been discovered in the early 1950s, but the income failed to be used for the increase of general well-being. The new sultan introduced many reforms and opened up the country to currents of modernization.

Since 1970 Oman has entered the international community, become a member of the United Nations and the Arab League, and set up diplomatic relations with many countries, including the United States. Sultan Qabus was especially intent upon securing close contacts with Saudi Arabia and Iran. However, due to the reserved and secretive nature of Saudi politics, the relations with Iran proved to be more felicitous and fruitful.

For over ten years the southern province of Oman, the province of Dhofar found itself in a state of chronic rebellion against the government of Muscat. Among the goals which the new administration set before itself was the liquidation of this insurgency, supported from across the border by the People's Republic of (South) Yemen.

The sultan's forces, led by British officers, were for years unable to dislodge the guerrillas of the Dhofari Liberation Front, many of them trained in the Soviet Union, China, and East Germany, and supplied by these countries and also by South Yemen and Iraq and other leftist powers.

However, by 1973 it became evident that the Dhofari insurgents were not only aiming at the "liberation" of Dhofar and of Oman but had set a much higher goal, namely, the overthrow of the traditionalist-conservative regimes of Arabia. The affected monarchies began considering how to help the hard-pressed Omani regime. But only Iran was ready to dispatch armed forces to assure the sultan's victory. Iran's motives were not only ideological: Tehran was vitally interested in preventing a pro-Communist take-over of the southern shore of the Strait of Hormuz.

The alliance between Iran and Oman is momentous; thus Tehran not only secured as well as possible the control over the vital strait route from and to the Persian Gulf but also stretched out its influence along the shores of the Indian Ocean. How highly the Shah must value this "special relationship" with Oman is proved by the agreement which the two countries have concluded concerning the delimitation of the waters within the Hormuz Strait.

The Strait of Hormuz

Except for the relatively small quantities of oil which are pumped through pipelines to Mediterranean ports, the bulk of crude or refined oil exported from the Persian Gulf area is shipped through the Strait of Hormuz on its way to Western Europe, Japan, the United States, and other parts of the world.[7] If only for this reason, the Hormuz Strait is one of the most important maritime thoroughfares of the world. Iran, jointly with Oman, its ally and client, secured strategic control over this indispensable oil "sluiceway."

While Kharg Island is Iran's principal naval base (connected by an oil pipeline

---

[7]In 1971 the number of loaded oil tankers passing through the Strait of Hormuz was 1,050, carrying 650 million tons of oil. Among them 578 were headed toward Europe, 280 toward Japan, and 40 toward the United States. See Henri Labrouse, *Le golfe et le canal* (Paris, 1973), pp. 152-155.

with the coast), some 400 miles eastward another Iranian harbor and naval base, Bender Abbas, is located at the bottom of a bay, behind the islands of Qishm and Hormuz.

Near the eastern extremity of Qishm Island lies another small island, Larak. The strategic Hormuz Strait extends between Larak Island (on the Iranian side) and Perforated Rock, a small islet off the Musandam peninsula (on the Omani side). The distance between Larak and Perforated Rock is twenty-six nautical miles. Within the strait are the Qoins, three islets seven to nine miles north of the Musandam peninsula. Sovereignty over these islets (also called the Salamah Wa Binatahan group) was claimed both by Iran and Oman; they are situated around the median line between these two countries. Iran has now recognized them as belonging to Oman.

Ships passing through the Hormuz Strait mostly use the channel which is widest, namely, that which extends north and east of the Qoins, where the depth varies between thirty-two and fifty fathoms. The strait thus is easier to navigate than, for instance, the Malacca and Singapore Straits.

From the southeastern end of the Hormuz Strait, the Iranian coastline runs generally east along the Gulf of Oman for about 200 miles, reaching a natural bay where the newly constructed military-naval base of Chah Bahar is located. Along the southern shore of the strait, the Sultanate of Oman, protected on the ground and from the air by Iran, is a dependable partner in its guardianship.

The greatest immediate peril which threatens or may threaten the security and stability of the Persian Gulf stems from the regime which has become the heir to the strategic corner of Aden, the gateway to the Red Sea. The government of the People's Republic of Yemen controls the northern shore of the strategic Bab el Mandeb Strait; on the opposite side of this strait, the lands of the Horn of Africa present another picture of instability and strife.

Selected Bibliography

Albaharnam, Husain M. *The Legal Status of the Arabian Gulf States. A Study of Their Treaty Relations and Their International Problems.* Dobbs Ferry, N.Y.: Oceana Publications, 1969.

Amirie, Abbas (ed.). *The Persian Gulf and Indian Ocean in International Politics.* Tehran: Institute for International Political and Economic Studies, 1975.

Braun, Dieter. *Neue Konstellationen zwischen dem Indischen Subkontinent und Westasien.* Eggenberg: Stiftung Wissenschaft und Politik, 1974.

Braun, Ursula. "Wachsende Polarisierung in der Region des Arabischen Golfs." *Europa-Archiv,* No. 17 (1973), 603-612.

Chandra, S. "Iran's Role in the Indian Ocean." In *Indian Ocean Power Rivalry,* pp. 103-116. Edited by T. T. Poulose. New Delhi: Young Asia Publications, 1974.

Chubin, Shahran, and Sepehr Zabih. *The Foreign Relations of Iran.* Berkeley: University of California Press, 1975.

Cottam, Richard. *Nationalism in Iran.* Pittsburgh: University of Pittsburgh Press, 1968.

Heravi, Mehdi. *Iranian-American Diplomacy.* Brooklyn, N.Y.: Theo. Gaus' Sons, 1969.

Holden, David. "The Persian Gulf. After the British Raj." *Foreign Affairs* 49 (July 1971), 721-735.

Hopwood, Derek, ed. *The Arabian Peninsula. Society and Politics.* Totowa, N.Y.: Rowman & Littlefield, 1972.

Labrousse, Henri. *Le golfe et le canal.* Paris: Presses Universitaires de France, 1973.

Landis, Lincoln. *Politics and Oil. Moscow in the Middle East.* New York: Dunellen Publishing Co., 1973.

McLane, Charles B. *Soviet Middle Eastern Relations.* New York: Columbia University Press, 1973.

Monroe, Elizabeth, ed. *The Changing Balance of Power in the Persian Gulf.* Report of an International Seminar at the Center for Mediterranean Studies. New York: American Universities Field Staff, 1972.

Nakhleh, Emile A. *Arab-American Relations in the Persian Gulf.* Washington, D.C.: American Enterprise Institute, 1975.

Ramazani, Rouhollah K. *The Persian Gulf. Iran's Role.* Charlottesville: University of Virginia Press, 1972.

Saleem Khan, M. A. "The Persian Gulf Security System." In *Indian Ocean Power Rivalry,* pp. 117-133. Edited by T. T. Poulose. New Delhi: Young Asia Publications, 1974.

Steinbach, Udo. "Saudi Arabia's New Role in the Middle East." *Aussenpolitik* (English ed.) 25 (February 1974), 201-212.

Chapter 7

The Horn of Africa and the Red Sea Countries

There is always something new from Africa.

Pliny, *Historia Naturalis*

When spider webs unite, they can tie up a lion.

Ethiopian proverb

For nations of the world engaged in commerce and navigation or interested in the strategic aspects of the Indian Ocean region, the incomparable value of the Horn of Africa rests with its geography and its geopolitical potentials. Here lies the entrance to the Red Sea, a sea which served as the main artery between the world of the Mediterranean and that of the Indian Ocean even before the narrow Suez isthmus was pierced by the Canal of the same name.

Since ancient times trade, people, and armies have moved along the maritime highway of the Red Sea and either out into the Indian Ocean toward India or south around the tip of the Horn. Other movements crossed the Red Sea in both directions: the ancestors of the Semitic Ethiopians crossed from Arabia to Africa here, and so did the preachers and warriors of Islam. At times it was the Ethiopian Empire which extended its way across the Red Sea. The Portuguese and the British entered from the ocean, while outposts of the Ottoman Empire occupied points on both sides of the Red Sea and even beyond. At the height of Egyptian military power in the middle of the nineteenth century, Cairo extended its influence in the valley of the Upper Nile, along the African coast of the Red Sea, and on the farther side of the Bab el Mandeb Strait.

The Ethiopian highlands rise like a massive fortress in the center of the Horn of Africa surrounded by barren coastal strips along the Red Sea and the Gulf of Aden in the northeast, the Nubian Desert in the north, the Valley of the Nile in the west, and semiarid grazing lands in the southeast. Not only is the landscape sharply divided geographically between deserts and highlands, and by the sea separating Asia and Africa, but the area also suffers from many kinds of other divisions—religious, ethnic, and ideological. The ancient Christian "island" of Ethiopia on its high plateau is surrounded by the turbulent waves of Islam. Among Muslims we find Somalis, Arabs, and Bantus, while pagan Negroid or Nilotic peoples inhabit the border areas of Ethiopia and the Sudan. In the southern Sudan Christian tribesmen oppose the ruling Afro-Arab Sudanese of the north.

The area is also divided ideologically: traditional conservative regimes alternate with revolutionary leftist governments, patriarchal rulers with military dictatorships. There are pro-Soviet and pro-Western administrations. The shock waves of the Arab-Israeli conflict have affected foreign policy orientations and established new dimensions in the complex net of interstate relationships. Soviet, American, and Chinese influences overlap in many parts of the subregion, while French control is maintained in one strategically crucial corner of the Red Sea-Indian Ocean route.

In geopolitically connected areas there often exists one power which feels entitled to claim paramountcy or a leadership role. This may be due to the fact that it stands above its neighbors with its central geographic location, the size of its territory or population, or its economic-military strength.

In the area in and around the Horn of Africa, Ethiopia seems to be favored to compete for such a position. Due to its past, its central geographic location and the leadership tradition of its elite, Ethiopia held such a position through most of its history until the advance of European colonial powers in the middle of the nineteenth century. At present it might still be destined to play a paramount role in the Horn of Africa if grave internal frailties, the hostile attitudes of neighboring powers, and the impact of great power and superpower rivalries did not stand in its path.

Ethiopia

Ethiopia's territory extends almost to 472,000 square miles—an area larger than France and West Germany together. Its estimated population is over 27 million, but probably not more than 35 percent are Christians, and only 30 percent belong to the ruling Amhara-Tigrean stock. The majority of the population consists of many other ethnic groups, the Galla being the most numerous. Most of the Galla are Muslims; Arabs, Somalis, and Danakils are also Muslims. Amhara ascendancy in the core provinces is secured by the military and administrative monopoly exercised since times immemorial. However, nearly half of Ethiopia's present territory was only acquired by Emperor Menelik II at the end of the nineteenth century; in these often backward areas, remote from the center of the country, Amhara influences have penetrated less than elsewhere and tribal regimes prevail. Eritrea, an Italian colony for fifty years, was united with Ethiopia after World War II.

Except for the period of the Italian conquest between 1936 and 1941 and subsequent British military administration, Ethiopia has been able to escape foreign colonial rule. Thus despite attempts at modernization the country has retained its essentially archaic-traditional structure. A revolutionary movement, led by the armed forces, has, since February 1974, managed to dismantle the power of the established government. In September 1974 the eighty-two-year-old Emperior Haile Selassie was deposed; the Ethiopian (Coptic) Christian Church also suffered a diminution of its erstwhile influence.

Whether under an imperial or military rule, Ethiopians perceive a sense of real isolation due to their historical experiences and the fact that they are Christians amidst a Muslim world. Emperior Haile Selassie enjoyed tremendous prestige among African and Asian countries. This stemmed from the 1936 Italian invasion, when this defeated but unyielding "Lion of Judah" warned the West before the Assembly of the League of Nations of the aggressive intentions of dictatorial powers, having thus acquired the stature of a martyr to colonialist invasion. In order to improve his country's image in Africa, the emperor set himself up as a protagonist of African cooperation. He was one of the founders of the Organization of African Unity (OAU). Nevertheless, Ethiopia is not regarded by black African states as genuinely African, nor by the Arab-Muslim powers as sharing their views of anti-imperialism, anti-Zionism, or anticolonialism.

Ethiopia faces a number of foreign policy problems which are linked with its immediate neighbors, the great powers, and its present internal instability.

1. Ethiopia's relations with Somalia are as bad as possible, although diplomatic ties are maintained. Somalia claims almost one-third of Ethiopia's territory on ethnic grounds. The contested border areas are inhabited by nomadic Somali tribesmen who wander with their herds to find suitable grazing land. Feuds between these tribes lead to raids (so-called *shiftas*). On the Somali side these are often described as actuated by Somali national feeling. However, Ethiopian and other observers point out that the Somali "irredentism" is prompted not so much by nationalism as by a concern for the water and other natural resources of the disputed area.

There is considerable anxiety in Ethiopia over Soviet arms deliveries to Somalia. The military balance between the two countries has shifted in favor of Somalia; Somali tanks, armored vehicles, and artillery now outnumber those of Ethiopia. Many of the Ethiopian armed forces are pinned down in the north to fight Eritrean rebels. While a direct attack on Ethiopia is not considered likely, a possible arms clash may arise in regard to Djibouti when the French abandon their colonial possession of the Territory of the Afars and Issas.

2. A railroad completed in 1915 connects Addis Ababa, the Ethiopian capital, with the harbor of Djibouti in the French Territory. This is the principal outlet of Ethiopia to the sea, although the country has two harbors of its own in

Eritrea: Massawa and Assab. The Ethiopians consider the free flow of goods and persons through Djibouti vital to their interests. As long as the French are in control of the territory the Ethiopian government will feel secure and content. However, when the Territory becomes independent, the situation is likely to become unstable and Somali intrusion a heightened possibility. Ethiopia has let it known that it would consider any such action as a *casus belli*. In that case, a full-fledged armed conflict with Somalia might ensue.

3. Freedom of passage through the Bab el Mandeb Strait is also considered vital for Ethiopia's commercial and safety interests. With Somalia's annexation of the French Territory both sides of the strait were to fall into potentially hostile hands, South Yemen being the other. The fact that during the Arab-Israeli war of October 1973 Israeli ships were deterred from passing the strait has added to the Ethiopian disquiet.

South Yemen is considered to be Soviet-dominated and to harbor subversive plans against Ethiopia; therefore, Addis Ababa maintains not diplomatic but only consular ties with Aden. On the other hand, full diplomatic relations are kept with the Yemen Arab Republic and, at least officially, these relations are considered good. The same is true in regard to contacts between Saudi Arabia and Ethiopia. Nevertheless, real harmony and sympathies are lacking. Arab countries admitted the obviously non-Arab (but Muslim) Somalia into the Arab League. And Ethiopia, like other oil-importing Third World countries, suffers from the increase in the price of oil.

4. Besides the Somali threat the other principal weakness of Ethiopia is the insurgency, supported from abroad, which exists in the northern province of Eritrea, bordering on the Sudan. The two insurgent organizations, the Eritrean Liberation Front and the Popular Liberation Front of Eritrea, now cooperate, though they have been fighting one another. They are supported by South Yemen, Syria, Libya, and the Palestinian liberation organizations. They are equipped mostly with Soviet arms.

The guerrillas control most of the open country, while the Ethiopian forces manage to maintain control in the principal towns and along the main highways. The insurgents are a mixed lot: they consist mostly of Eritrean Arabs (Muslims), but there are also Christian Eritreans among them. They demand complete independence for Eritrea, but many Christians would probably settle for autonomous Eritrea.

For years Ethiopia's relations with the Sudan were strained for two reasons: one was the leftist tendencies of the Sudanese regime; the other was the support it was giving to the Eritrean rebels. Addis Ababa retaliated by giving assistance to the chronic rebellion of Christian and pagan tribesmen in the southern provinces of the Sudan against the ruling Muslim majority. However, in 1972 Ethiopia and the Sudan concluded a border agreement and promised to refrain from helping insurgency on each other's territory.

5. For years Arabs accused Ethiopia of collusion with Israel. Tel Aviv provided technical, economic, and military assistance to Addis Ababa, including the dispatch of military advisers to the Ethiopian Army. During the Arab-Israeli

war of 1973, Ethiopia was hard pressed by Arab countries and, complying with a similar resolution passed by the Organization of African Unity, ostentatiously severed its diplomatic ties with Israel. It was admitted in Addis Ababa that this action required a painful decision for a country whose dynasty allegedly traced its origin from the union of King Solomon and the Queen of Sheba. In its isolation, Ethiopia is intent to demonstrate its solidarity with African countries, but only with modest success.

6. Since 1951 Washington has provided economic, technical, and military assistance to Ethiopia. In 1953 a mutual defense assistance agreement and an agreement providing for an American communication station (the Kagnew station) near Asmara were concluded. In view of the massive arms deliveries to Somalia by the Soviet Union, Addis Ababa began pressing Washington for increased supplies of arms. However, the United States refused to deliver what it considered to be "offensive weapons."

Washington has never concluded a treaty of alliance with Ethiopia; still, the readiness to supply and train Ethiopian armed forces was considered in Addis Ababa to be an implicit commitment to assist it in case of an aggression against its territory. Ethiopian leaders believe that the Christian West should help their country against non-Christian and Communist threats. It is sadly remembered that when Ethiopia was attacked by Italy in 1935, Western Europe remained a passive onlooker. Unlike Somalia vis-à-vis Moscow, Addis Ababa has no leverage to use against Washington. The latter has now decided to phase out the Kagnew communication station.

7. In order not to displease either the neutralist governments or the United States, Addis Ababa has refrained from expressing views on the American base at Diego Garcia in the Indian Ocean. But unhappiness about the Soviet naval presence in this ocean prevails, and for this reason Ethiopia is officially supporting the Zone of Peace plan in the United Nations.

Relations between Ethiopia and the Soviet Union are overshadowed by the military assistance Moscow is giving to the Somali Democratic Republic and, indirectly, to insurgents in Eritrea and possibly elsewhere. When Addis Ababa cautiously asked Moscow whether it would not supply certain types of arms to Ethiopia, the answer was "We would give weapons to friends only." It seems evident that the Soviet Union is not interested in the maintenance of the present balance of power in the Horn of Africa and would prefer a shift in favor of its protégés, which would increase its influence in the crucial area around the Red Sea and the Bab el Mandeb Strait. Since the reopening of the Suez Canal the strategic importance of this area has even increased in the eyes of Moscow.

Ethiopia maintains good relations with Peking, but the Chinese are more reserved in their dealings with Addis Ababa than in other parts of Africa.[1] In early 1974 Ethiopia renewed its request to Peking for arms (some Chinese aircraft had been delivered earlier) but so far without avail.

[1]In 1971 Ethiopia established diplomatic relations with the People's Republic of China and simultaneously severed its ties with the Republic of China on Taiwan.

It seems highly probable that the revolutionary unrest in Ethiopia has caught both Russians and Chinese by surprise. Previously, the prevailing view had been that no radical change was to be expected before the emperor's natural demise. The removal (and subsequent death) of the emperor and the advent of military rule are likely to at least temporarily weaken the hard-pressed Ethiopian state.

8. It is believed that, especially in the border areas where tribal regimes prevailed, the personal and feudal relations which existed between the tribal leaders and the emperor might be difficult to replace. This is particularly true in regard to the sensitive ties with the sultan of the Afara and the Ugaz of the Issas, both in the neighborhood of the French Territory of the Afars and Issas.

Ali Mirrah Hanferi, the paramount sultan of the Afars (who sought refuge in the French Territory when threatened by the military junta in Addis Ababa), owed allegiance to the emperor, his liege-lord, and while preserving his autonomous role, he strove to protect the foreign interests of Ethiopia. The position of the Ugaz, the tribal and religious head of the Issas, is similar to that of the sultan of the Afara, though his control over Issas is tenuous compared to that of the sultan over his subjects.

There is thus an acute danger, aggravated by the often incompetent handling of delicate issues by the military, that the multiethnic and multireligious Ethiopia may fall apart or at least offer easy possibilities for outside interventions. The Somali threat is particularly dangerous because it affects all the three weak spots of Ethiopia: it is Islamic (the majority of Ethiopia's population being Muslim), irredentist (aiming at the Somali-inhabited regions of the country), and revolutionary (exploiting the still conservative-archaic structure of the empire).

Somalia

The Somali Democratic Republic was founded in 1960 when former Italian Somaliland and British Somaliland were given independence and became united. Somali territory consists of a band of land averaging 200 miles in width along the Gulf of Aden and the Indian Ocean. On the inland side it surrounds Ethiopia's eastern provinces in an acute angle; on the sea side a sharp corner juts out into the ocean, forming the tip of the Horn of Africa. Ships entering from the Red Sea (and the Suez Canal) must pass its coast, and so must those sailing from the Persian Gulf toward the Cape.

Although much smaller in numbers than Ethiopia, Somalia comprises a wholly homogeneous ethnic and religious population of 3 million. Somalis speak a non-Arab Cushitic language, which is now written in the Roman alphabet.

After it achieved independence regional differences and divergent policy goals divided the country. A pro-Arab trend sought to give first priority to unification of Somali-inhabited territories, while a pro-African faction wished first to strengthen and modernize the nation. In 1969 the military intervened and a Supreme Revolutionary Council headed by Major General Mohamed Siad Barre took over the reins of government and initiated policies guided by "scientific socialism."

1. One-third of the Somali nation lives outside the borders of the Somali Republic: in Ethiopia, Kenya, and the French Territory of the Afars and Issas. The basic political goal of Somali leaders is the unification of all Somali-inhabited areas. This endeavor is symbolized by the Somali flag: a five-pointed white star in an azure blue field; the five points of the star represent Somali-peopled territories: former Italian Somaliland, British Somaliland, the French Territory, the Ogaden region of Ethiopia, and the northeastern districts of Kenya.

According to the Somali view it is not the uncertainty of the boundary lines separating Somalia from Ethiopia or Kenya or the difficulty of controlling tribesmen wandering across these lines which is the problem. Somalia wishes to change the frontiers, to acquire territory that in its view is inhabited by its Somali kinfolk. It is stressing these issues before African regional conferences, and was ready to create incidents, some of them violent, in order to attract attention to these questions.

In return, both Ethiopia and Kenya tried to enlist African and Arab support against Somalia's land claims. They concluded in 1963 (even before Kenya obtained independence) a defense agreement directed against Somali aggressiveness. When Addis Ababa suddenly decided to sever its ties with Israel, this action was aimed at supporting Ethiopia's diplomatic front against the claims for a "Greater Somalia." Such defense is made more difficult by the support Somalia is receiving from the Soviet Union.

2. Somalia has been obtaining Soviet military aid since 1964. After 1973 the military build-up was further intensified. In return, Somalia has allowed the Soviet Navy extended use of its port facilities. In Berbera, Soviet warships dock, refuel, and do repair work in a part of the port reserved exclusively to Soviet shipping. The Soviet Union also runs a communication station east of Berbera, at Alula, near Cape Guardafui, the easternmost tip of the Horn of Africa.[2] The Soviet Union and Somalia signed a Treaty of Friendship and Cooperation on July 11, 1974, when Soviet President Podgorny visited Mogadishu.

The Soviet establishment in Somalia reflects Soviet interest in the Horn and an appreciation of its great strategic value for Moscow. This provides a leverage to Mogadishu to press Moscow for the delivery of more and more modern weapons, an advantage which Addis Ababa does not possess vis-à-vis Washington. Moscow at times has appeared to be reluctant to comply with Somali requests, and in such cases Somali leaders have reminded the Soviets of the advantages to using their port facilities. As a result of these mutual pressures (or mutual "blackmail," as Ethiopian observers commented), the "collaboration" and arms deliveries both increased.

[2]It is believed that orbital correction of Soviet FOBS (fractional orbital bombardment system) missiles is to be carried out in the region around the Horn of Africa should such missiles be launched. The relative proximity of the U.S. Kagnew base near Asmara (now abandoned) and the Diego Garcia communication station (to be expanded) may also have been an incentive for Moscow to establish a similar facility in that area.

3. The French Territory is openly coveted by Mogadishu as one which should be included in Greater Somalia. Ethnically, the claim is supported by the presence in the territory of members of the Issa tribe, a people speaking a Somali dialect. Historically, Mogadishu refers to the fact that prior to 1967 the official name of the Territory has been *La Côte française des Somalis* (French Somali Coast). The Somali government rejected the "new absurd title" which the French "foisted on the unwilling people of the French Somali Coast."[3] It is impatiently waiting for the day when Paris will abandon its hold over the territory.

The Somali-Ethiopian confrontation endangers the delicate balance in the Horn of Africa more than the other conflicts or potential conflicts in the area. Soviet involvement on the side of Mogadishu lends an even more ominous element to this state of affairs. The future of Djibouti is closely allied with the possibility of a violent conflagration between the armed forces of historical Ethiopian preponderance and those of young Somali nationalism.

French Territory of Afars and Issas

The British had occupied Aden on the Arabian coast in 1839, and in 1884 they descended on the Somali coast of Africa opposite Aden; the acquisition of Djibouti was the French response to the British move on the African side of the Gulf of Aden.

The French concluded treaties with the Afar (Danakil) sultans on the northern side of the Gulf of Tadjoura and with Issa tribes on the southern side. Djibouti itself soon became a busy port and its commercial significance was greatly enhanced by the railroad from Addis Ababa constructed with French financial help.

Relations between the French colony and the regime of Emperor Menelik II were cordial from the very outset. Paris disapproved of Italian ambitions to expand in East Africa and to establish an Italian protectorate in Ethiopia. From Djibouti the emperor obtained the guns and ammunition which enabled him to defeat the Italian Army at Aduwa in 1896. When in the following year an agreement was reached concerning the construction of the Addis Ababa-Djibouti railroad, the French consul general of Addis Ababa wrote a letter to Emperor Menelik in which France recognized that Djibouti constituted "the natural outlet for Ethiopia."[4] Addis Ababa relied on this text when claiming the right of access to Djibouti and, in a broader interpretation, a right to succeed France in the territory should it decide to end its rule.

The 1972 population of the territory was estimated to be 125,000. It consists of Somalis (mostly from the Issa tribe) and Afars (also known as Danakils) as

[3]*Le Monde* (Paris), Sept. 24, 1971.

[4]In the original French, *le débouché naturel de l'Ethiopie.*

well as extraneous residents, mostly Arabs and French. Afars and Somalis are almost equal in numbers; there is a small edge in favor of the latter.

Although Afars and Issas (as well as members of other Somali tribes) are both Muslims and both speak Cushitic languages, their social and political outlooks are different. Issas are individualists and their tribal loyalties are loose, whereas the Afars strongly rally to their tribes and tribal leaders.

Another interesting feature of the ethnic composition of the territory is the fact that the majority of both the Afars and the Issas live outside its borders. Three hundred thousand Afars live in the adjoining area of Ethiopia, stretching from the territory to the harbor of Massawa in Eritrea. They belong to different tribes, the most important being that of Aussa. The Issas inhabit an area straddling the border of the territory, Somalia, and Ethiopia. Their tribal differentiations are less pronounced, and the tribal areas are not clearly delimited, unlike those of the Afars. On the other hand, like the Afars, they are inclined to ignore national frontiers in their wanderings.

The internal politics of the territory and to some extent its future international status are largely influenced by the rivalries of the two major ethnic groups. On the whole, the majority of Issas appear to demand independence (and possibly subsequent union with Somalia, so Mogadishu believes), while almost all the Afars wish to maintain some form of French protection, mainly because they dread both an Issa majority domination or incorporation into Somalia. Nor do they favor incorporation into Ethiopia.

Elections in the territory, as well as the referendum of 1967, are influenced by the nomadic character of about half of the inhabitants. Afars, disciplined voters following the advice of their leaders, vote according to uniform patterns. The sultan of the Afars, to please his liege-lord the emperor, invited his people to vote against independence or, in elections, to vote for Afar candidates. Afars living outside the territory may also have participated and influenced the outcome of the referendum and various elections.

In the Chamber of Deputies, the legislature of the territory, the Party for the Progress and Defense of the Interests of the Territory, supported by the Afars, holds a decisive majority, and the executive is composed mostly of Afars.

For years, the Organization of African Unity has urged the "decolonization" of the territory and departure of the French, a demand supported particularly by Somalia. At the same time, to prevent an outbreak of hostilities between Somalia and Ethiopia, the Organization has tended to bring about an agreement between these two countries concerning the future of the territory before pressing Paris to give up the area.

The French government, in accordance with its policy of accommodation to African demands, announced on January 1, 1975, that it was granting independence to the Territory of Afars and Issas. At the same time, it assured the inhabitants of the territory that it would safeguard the integrity and security of the area. Paris is to retain a military base in or around Djibouti in order to be able to control the western shore of the Bab el Mandeb Strait, the entrance of the Red Sea, where vital oil shipments pass on their way to the Mediterranean and further to France.

The Strait of Bab el Mandeb

Since the time of Albuquerque, who captured Aden for the Portuguese to block the Bab el Mandeb Strait, this was recognized as a highly important strategic thoroughfare. Britain and France were eager to secure a base near this narrow pass. There are in fact two straits here: one between *Ras* (Cape) Bab el Mandeb on the Arabian side and Perim Island, the other between the island and *Ras* (Cape) Si Ane on the African coast. Ras Bab el Mandeb lies in the disputed border area between South and North Yemen; Perim Island belongs to South Yemen; the African coast along the straits is part of the French Territory of Afars and Issas.

Between Perim Island and the Yemeni coast the strait is only about one and a half to three miles wide, while the channel between the island and the French Territory is nine and a quarter to twelve and a half miles wide. The fairway in the latter is about 100 fathoms deep, while the narrower strait has a varying depth of only five and a half to twelve fathoms. Deep-sea vessels mostly use the wider strait, which is only obstructed by the Jezirat Saba group of tiny islands near Ras Si Ane.

Aden lies about 100 miles east of Bab el Mandeb. In addition to Perim Island, South Yemen inherited from the British Aden Protectorate sovereignty over the island of Socotra off Cape Guardafui, the easternmost tip of the Horn of Africa, and its dependencies (the island of Abd al Kuri being the principal one).

All the powers which are interested in the use of the Suez Canal are, naturally, equally interested in free navigation through the Bab el Mandeb Strait. As mentioned earlier, Ethiopia is closely affected; and Israel is eager to keep open its access to the Indian Ocean via the Gulf of Aqaba, the Red Sea, and ultimately these straits.

While the blockade of the Bab el Mandeb Strait during the war of October 1973 between Israel and the Arab countries remained controversial as to its efficacy, the present occupation of Perim Island by Egyptian naval forces lends greater probability to the effective blocking of the straits in case of another outbreak of hostilities between Israel and Egypt.[5]

The area around the Bab el Mandeb has thus even increased as a neuralgic point not only of the region itself but for the world at large as well. The fact that this sea route could be controlled fully by the People's Republic of Southern Yemen, a close confederate of Moscow, greatly enhanced the geostrategic role of this waterway and also the dangers concomitant with such a controlling position.

[5] In October 1974 at the Rabat meeting of Arab heads of state, it was announced that Southern Yemen had leased Perim Island for 99 years to the Arab League for payment of $150 million, and that Egyptian forces had taken up positions on the island; *New York Times,* Oct. 30, 1974.

People's Republic of Southern Yemen

This former British colony (Aden Crown Colony) and protectorate (Eastern and Western Aden Protectorates) was given independence in 1967 when London became tired of the violence and terrorism practiced by the two nationalist movements, the Front for Liberation of Occupied South Yemen and the National Liberation Front. In 1969 an even more radical branch of the National Liberation Front took over and declared the country a "People's Republic." Since 1968 Southern Yemen has concluded arms agreements with the Soviet Union and also with China. While professing to be nonaligned, it maintains close relations with Communist countries and with radical Arab governments.

The strategic location of Southern Yemen, its main value in the eyes of Moscow, is clearly prominent: it commands the exit from the Red Sea to the Indian Ocean. Aden itself, although no longer the busy and wealthy commercial port and refueling station that it was under the British, is still a major deep-water harbor now frequented by Soviet merchant, fishing, and naval vessels, and Soviet advisers, civilian and military, abound in the town and countryside.

The Soviet-trained armed forces of Southern Yemen, with a population of 1.4 million, are probably more powerful than those of Northern Yemen, consisting mainly of tribal levies. However, since the end of the civil war, Saudi Arabia appears to be ready to prevent any "reunification" of the two Yemens under the red banner.

Yemen Arab Republic

Yemen obtained independence from Ottoman rule at the end of World War I. In 1962 the government of the king was overthrown by a military-republican coup; years of civil war followed, in which Egypt supported the republicans and Saudi Arabia the royalists. During the Arab-Israeli war of 1967 Egyptian forces were withdrawn and an agreement was reached between different factions and tribes accepting the republican regime. For the next years, similarly to the situation in Egypt, Soviet influence predominated in Sanaa. Two weeks after Egypt invited Soviet advisers to leave, in August 1962, North Yemen followed the example and asked Moscow to remove its advisers and experts. Thereafter it sought closer relations with more conservative Arab forces and the West, restoring diplomatic relations with Washington in 1972.

The forces of status quo and revolutionary forces thus confront each other on the Arabian side of the Red Sea, as they do on the African side. Shifting policies alternatively strengthen one of these fronts and then the other. On the African side, Sudan also has experienced similar transformations.

Sudan

The Democratic Republic of the Sudan, formerly under joint Anglo-Egyptian administration, achieved independence on January 1, 1956. Parliamentary and military regimes followed each other; in May 1969 the civilian government was overthrown by a military coup under a Revolutionary Command Council, headed by Major General Jafar Muhammad Nimeri, who later was made Prime Minister.

By 1971 it appeared as if the Sudan would sail deep into Soviet waters; economic grants and military deliveries arrived, and over 500 Soviet military advisers were attached to the army and air force. However, overzealous Communist leadership attempted a coup in July 1971; the Sudan thereafter changed its foreign policy course, carried out a rapprochement to Western Powers, including the United States (diplomatic relations had been broken off in 1967); peace also was restored in the three southern provinces, where non-Muslim insurgents were pursuing endemic warfare against the central government.

With the events of 1971, the threat of a pro-Soviet or directly Communist take-over in Northern Yemen and in the Sudan had been averted. In the same year, Egypt managed to escape from a firm Soviet grip that almost reduced it to the status of a satellite. Without these reactions in the three countries the balance in the Red Sea area, affecting the entire region of the Horn of Africa, would have been tilted in favor of revolutionary forces.

Egypt, Israel, Jordan, and Saudi Arabia

The Arab Republic of Egypt lies at the northern end of the Red Sea; the state of Israel and the Hashemite Kingdom of Jordan abut on the Gulf of Aqaba, at the northeastern extremity of the same sea. Both Egypt and Israel are littoral countries of the Mediterranean. Except for sixteen miles of coastline on the Gulf of Aqaba, Jordan is a land-locked country. On the other hand, the kingdom of Saudi Arabia is both a Persian Gulf and a Red Sea Power.

All these four governments are preoccupied with their mutual problems, with questions of war and peace, so that they have had little opportunity to express themselves on the general problems of the Indian Ocean region. But both Egypt and Israel are closely interested in navigation of the Suez Canal and along the Red Sea to and from the Indian Ocean. And the Arab-Israeli conflict, as seen from earlier reflections, extends its impact into wide areas of the Middle East and Africa, not only to Arab countries but to other Muslim nations and, more indirectly, to non-Muslim peoples as well. The shock waves of events within the Arab-Israeli context thus have significantly influenced power relations and the balance of power in the entire western Indian Ocean region, coincidently with the relative attitudes taken by the superpowers and other powers exogenous to the area.

Egypt closed the Suez Canal to Israeli shipping in 1948 by invoking Article X of the Convention of Constantinople of 1888, which provided for free passage to vessels of all nations across the canal. Article X permitted the temporary closure of the canal if necessary for the maintenance of public order.

With inability to use the canal, shipping from Eilat, the Israeli port on the Gulf of Aqaba, acquired prominent importance for that country. Israel obtains from the Middle East (Iran) most of its oil; it exchanges goods with countries of the Indian Ocean.

The Strait of Tiran can easily be controlled from the Sinai Peninsula. One of the officially announced reasons for the outbreak of the 1967 war was the closure of the strait by Cairo. To keep the entrance to the Gulf of Aqaba open remains one of the objectives of Israeli policy.

During neither the war of 1967 nor the hostilities in October 1973 did Egyptian naval forces or Israeli naval units in the Red Sea interfere with each other's shipping. The only recorded incident is the rather dubious "blockade" of the Strait of Bab el Mandeb in 1973. The rumors relating to this "blockade" may have served as a warning by Egypt that freedom of passage across the Tiran Strait does not secure for Israel access to Eilat, because its shipping might be closed at Bab el Mandeb to the Indian Ocean.

Jordan, closely cooperating with its powerful Arab neighbor Saudi Arabia, has never ceased to follow the general policies of the West and oppose Soviet influence in the region. The Soviets have had no leverage over Jordan in the past, nor do they at present.

Even more momentous than the expulsion of Soviet forces and advisers in 1971 was the unexpected volte-face of Egypt in late 1973 which restored diplomatic relations with the United States. Cairo's reliance on Washington to press Israel into concessions somewhat changed the power balance in the northern part of the Red Sea area and at least temporarily excluded direct interference by Moscow into matters pending between Egypt and Israel. In March 1976 Egypt denounced its treaty of friendship and mutual assistance with the Soviet Union, thus creating an even wider rift between the two countries.

Saudi Arabia's capital, Riyadh, as mentioned earlier, is located near the center of the country; its window to the outside world is Jidda, a harbor on the Red Sea. In the Red Sea, Saudi Arabia is strongly opposed to the revolutionary leftist policies and activities of Southern Yemen. Riyadh is, if not legally, politically and ideologically committed to defend Northern Yemen. For this purpose, it has, with American advice, developed a big army base at Khamis Mushait, near the Yemeni border. But the complicated power relations in that part of the world render its role rather ambivalent: Riyadh is anti-Soviet but at the same time anti-Israeli. It opposes Southern Yemen but would not object to a blockade of the Bab el Mandeb Strait in another Arab-Israeli outbreak. It is dependent on American arms deliveries but criticizes Washington for its assistance to Israel.

But be this as it may, Saudi Arabia is basically an important counterforce against revolutionary upheavals masterminded by Moscow or Peking and implemented by subversive movements or pro-Communist regimes in that area. While unhappy with a Christian Ethiopia that rules over millions of Muslims, Saudi Arabia would be rather hesitant to support the socialist-type Soviet-allied regime of Somalia. Neither would it acclaim a highly nationalist military government, in the place of Haile Selassie's traditional-conservative rule in Ethiopia.

Kenya

The Republic of Kenya is the geographic bridge between the Horn of Africa and East Africa. Although it cooperates with its southern and western neighbors—Tanzania and Uganda—some of its major foreign policy concerns are directed toward the eastern and northern adjacent countries—Somalia and Ethiopia. For this reason it seems justified to discuss these problems within the context of this chapter dealing with the Horn of Africa.

The center of Kenya's economic activity and also the center of population concentration is in its southern segment between Lake Victoria and the Indian Ocean; this area includes the city of Nairobi, the capital, and Mombasa, the principal harbor. The northern areas of Kenya are sparsely populated, and this is particularly true for the eastern portion of the Northern Frontier Province, where about a quarter-million Somalis live and which Somalia wishes to detach from Kenya.

The equilibrium of forces in the relationship between Kenya and Somalia largely rested on the defense treaty with Ethiopia. However, the treaty is regarded in Nairobi as a personal arrangement between two friends, President Jomo Kenyatta and Emperor Haile Selassie. Furthermore, the revolutionary events in Ethiopia and the removal of the trusted emperor have shattered the confidence in Ethiopian assistance. Nairobi is also apprehensive lest Ethiopia, overwhelmed by internal struggles and external aggression, disintegrate or become so weakened that it would be unable to offer any help. This danger appears to be compounded by Uganda's unprecedented increase of arms. A strong army may be an inducement, especially for a person of General Amin's mentality, for aggression against a weaker neighbor.

Kenyan armed forces, unlike those of many African states, were kept on the "colonial level." This level approximately equaled that of the two other members of the East African Community—Tanzania and Uganda. During the past two years Uganda under the irascible President Idi Amin began receiving Soviet arms shipments, which considerably raised the firepower and mobility of his armed forces. Under the impact of these developments, Kenya also embarked on a modest rearmament program, supported mainly by Britain.

Kenya does not feel threatened by her southern neighbor, Tanzania, although their relationship is now far from being as intimate as in 1963 when Tanzanian President Julius K. Nyerere offered to unite with Kenya and Uganda in an East African confederation.

Kenya's foreign policy relies on nonalignment; but it has no inhibitions against maintaining most friendly relations with the countries of the West. It wishes to promote self-determination to the peoples of southern Africa without involving itself in the support of guerrillas. It favors disarmament and therefore voted for the Zone of Peace in the Indian Ocean resolutions in the United Nations. It refrained, however, from placing the blame for naval activity on the shoulders of the United States and did not condemn the Pentagon's plans for the island of Diego Garcia. The changing power balance in the Horn of Africa may seriously affect its foreign policy outlook and force it to modify some of its restrained attitudes. The question of succession to the charismatic person of Jomo Kenyatta may also add to its worries in the international field.

The central question which looms over the political future of the area in and around the Horn of Africa concerns developments in Ethiopia. The possible collapse and fragmentation of this realm would have consequences analogous to the fall of other historic multinational empires. Having once disintegrated they proved irreplaceable, and their downfall created chaos not only within their own boundaries but in geographically interrelated territories as well.

A breakdown of the central power which holds the Ethiopian realm together would seriously upset the present balance of power in the subregion. One could assume that in such an eventuality the ethnically and religiously homogeneous Somali state would be able to achieve its goal: the creation of Greater Somalia by incorporating large chunks of Ethiopian territory. Somali expansionism would not stop at this point; it would receive further impetus. Kenya's north-eastern districts would be exposed to the danger of Somali invasion. French presence in the Territory of the Afars and Issas would become untenable under Somali nationalist and decolonizing pressures, no longer balanced out by Ethiopia's counterpressure. An independent Eritrea would be likely to become a victim of a fratricidal struggle between Christians and Muslims. In the western and southwestern provinces of Ethiopia, attempts would be made to establish a new and therefore unstable Galla independent state.

However, history does not always and promptly choose between alternatives. Empires, like the Ottoman can vegetate for a long time before collapsing, and sometimes being resurrected later in a rejuvenated form. The political conditions in the area under our investigation may remain in a state of flux for a long time. Ethiopia may continue to live in a state of uncertainty without collapsing, and the power balance in the Horn of Africa may remain essentially unchanged. But in any event, the geopolitical significance of that area deserves the keen attention of all the powers which have a stake in peace and order of that part of the world.

Selective Bibliography

Abir, Mordechai. *Sharm al-Sheikh—Bab al-Mandeb. The Strategic Balance and Israel's Southern Approaches.* Jerusalem: Hebrew University of Jerusalem, 1974.

Bell, J. Bowyer. *The Horn of Africa. Strategic Magnet of the Seventies.* New York: National Strategy Information Center, 1973.

Beshir, Mohamed Omer. *Southern Sudan. Background to Conflict.* London: Hurst, 1968.

Drysdale, John G. S. *The Somali Dispute.* New York: Praeger, 1964.

Gertzel, C. J., et al., eds. *Government and Politics in Kenya.* Nairobi: East African Publishing House, 1969.

Hess, Robert. *Ethiopia. The Modernization of Autocracy.* Ithaca, N.Y.: Cornell University Press, 1970.

Kennedy, R. H. *A Brief Geographical and Hydrographical Study of Straits Which Constitute Routes for Internationl Traffic.* United Nations Document A/Conf. 13/6, 1957.

Little, Tom. *South Arabia. Arena of Conflict.* London: Pall Mall, 1968.

Luttwak, Edward, and Horowitz, Dan. *The Israeli Army.* New York: Harper & Row, 1975.

Mitchell, C. "The Horn of Africa and the Indian Ocean." In *Collected Papers of the Study Conference on the Indian Ocean in International Politics,* pp. 153-178. Southampton (England): University of Southampton, 1973. (Mimeographed.)

Mosley, Leonard. *Haile Selassie. The Conquering Lion.* Englewood Cliffs, N.J.: Prentice-Hall, 1965.

Oberlé, Philippe. *Afars et Somalis. Le Dossier de Djibouti.* Paris: Presence Africaine, 1971.

Perham, Margery. *The Government of Ethiopia.* Evanston, Ill.: Northwestern University Press, 1969.

Thompson, Virginia, and Adloff, Richard. *Djibouti and the Horn of Africa.* Stanford, Calif.: Stanford University Press, 1968.

Touval, Saadia. *Somali Nationalism. International Politics and the Drive for Unity in the Horn of Africa.* Cambridge, Mass.: Harvard University Press, 1963.

Touval, Saadia. *The Boundary Politics of Independent Africa.* Cambridge, Mass.: Harvard University Press, 1972.

Wolde-Mariam, Mesfin. "Ethiopia and the Indian Ocean." In *The Indian Ocean. Its Political, Economic and Military Importance,* pp. 181-196. Edited by Alvin J. Cottrell and R. M. Burrell. New York: Praeger, 1972.

Chapter 8

The Southwest

Money is sharper than a sword.

Ashanti proverb

Even an ant may harm an elephant.

Zulu proverb

Africa divides the Indian Ocean from the Atlantic, as Australia and Southeast Asia separate the Indian Ocean basin from the Pacific oceanic system. Australia, a continent in itself, settled by European immigrants, faces north toward the Malay-Melanesian-Chinese world. However, the white settlers of southern Africa live next door and intermingled with the African-Bantu peoples of that continent.

White Australia is clearly divided from Asians, although these races continue to live peacefully next to each other's shores. In contrast, on the southwestern, African side of the Indian Ocean, a confrontation between black and white peoples is the most outstanding political-military factor impinging heavily on the power relations of that part of the Indian Ocean region.

The strain of this confrontation between the countries of white supremacy, on the one hand, and the black African nations, on the other, extends throughout the subregion discussed in the present chapter. It includes, first of all, the Republic of South Africa, the principal actor of the scene, and its willing or reluctant entourage: the former British High Commission territories, now the independent states of Botswana, Lesotho, and Swaziland; and the former mandated territory of South West Africa (designated as Namibia by the United Nations), which, however, extends along the Atlantic Ocean and therefore falls, rather outside the range of our scrutiny. The South African "buffer" toward the

144

north is Rhodesia (whose independent statehood has so far not been recognized by any country). In the same "buffer" status was Mozambique, a Portuguese overseas territory, until 1975, when it attained independence.

The black African countries north of the area of South African hegemony, now including Mozambique, are not unanimous in their opposition to the white-dominated states of southern Africa. Zambia and Tanzania are the staunch enemies of white minority governments, while Malawi is not. The subregion also includes islands east of the African continent: Madagascar (its political name is the Malagasy Republic), Mauritius, the Seychelles, and the Comoro Islands, mainly inhabited by people of Asian or mixed Asian-African origin.

In this confrontation the outside powers are positively involved. In one way or another the Soviet Union and China support the black African countries diplomatically and by military assistance in their policies help to topple the white regimes; they also support the various liberation movements and their guerrilla operations. The major battlefield for the diplomatic offensives is in United Nations bodies—the General Assembly, the Security Council, and various committees. It is here that the Afro-Asian bloc, supported by the Communist powers and most of the democratic governments of Europe and American, scored victory after victory—which, however, hardly changed the factual situation.

Since the keystone of white supremacy is South Africa and the tilting of the balance of power to the detriment of South Africa would affect the Western world, these powers are confronted with the dilemma of how far considerations of a humanitarian nature can or should influence their broader foreign policy goals, and their military-strategic safety. In other words, the geopolitical-strategic significance of the entire southern African theater and, more specifically, that of the South African Republic, have to be evaluated against demands of equity, morality, or even international legality—an agonizing dilemma for leaders of nations.

Republic of South Africa

The domestic politics of South Africa influence its international relations much more than is the case for most other countries. Accordingly, when discussing the present internal structure and political ethos, together with the ethnic composition of this republic, we are dealing with matters tightly interlinked with its international position.

The total population of the republic was estimated in 1974 to be 24,887,000; the number of whites was 4,160,000; of blacks (officially called Bantu), 17,712,000; of coloreds (of mixed, mainly black-and-white descent), 2,306,000; and of Asians (mostly Indians), 709,000.

Blacks, therefore, outnumber whites five to one. This ratio in favor of Bantus is constantly rising; in the last four years (prior to 1974) the black population rose by 11.3 percent; the white, by 8.5 percent.

However, neither the whites nor the Bantu people are homogeneous. The whites are divided by their mother tongues between the Afrikaans-speaking (a language developed by the Dutch settlers of South Africa) and English-speaking groups. Nearly 60 percent of the whites belong to the first (the Afrikaners) and about 37 percent to the second; the remainder are members of splinter ethnic groups (Afrikaans-English bilinguals, Germans, Italians, and others).

It is much emphasized in South Africa that the Bantu peoples themselves are divided in very distinct ethnic-linguistic groups, such as the Zulu, Xhosa, Tswana, Sotho, and other nations. Even the coloreds are not uniform: 88 percent speak Afrikaans and over 10 percent English. And the Indians provide a similarly heterogeneous religious-linguistic picture like that of the inhabitants of the Indian subcontinent.

It is evident that a policy of integration, as practiced in the United States, would result in reducing the whites to a vastly outnumbered minority group that would lose everything they now cherish: their European-derived culture, income level, and style of life. According to the patterns developed elsewhere in Africa, many if not most would be forced to emigrate for a variety of reasons, leaving behind a heritage accumulated in 300 years. A viable compromise between this gloomy, hopeless choice and the present system of "separate development" (known by its Afrikaans name *apartheid*) might be possible, but has not been officially advocated.[1]

After the victory of the National Party at the elections in 1948, the policy of *apartheid* was systematically and consistently introduced in all the four provinces of the Union of South Africa (as the country was called prior to 1961). In 1959 Prime Minister Verwoerd announced the program to create "Bantustans," native homelands for the Bantus, with the ultimate goal of granting them an independent status.

The policy of "separate development" was enforced with discriminatory legislation. Resistance was suppressed; the Sharpeville incident in March 1960 (in which many protesting blacks were killed or wounded) in particular drew international attention to and condemnation of the South African government.

The National Party is the political party of the Afrikaner (Boer) segment of the white population; it has obtained absolute majorities in all elections (only whites participating) since 1948. Although the ideal of a "South African nation," Afrikaans- and English-speaking together, has not been officially abandoned, the Afrikaans-speaking community acts and speaks as if it were identical with that nation. The *Weltanschauung* of the Afrikaners is the key to the understanding of their sociopolitical values and attitudes by the world at large.

1. The Afrikaners are descendants of the seventeenth-century Dutch settlers of the Cape Province and also of Huguenot, German, and additional Dutch

[1]The plan supported by the opposition United Party at the 1974 election only differed in nuances from the program of "independent homelands" endorsed by the ruling National Party. The bid for "one man, one vote," as advocated by the small Progressive Party, would eventually create a situation of a black majority in Parliament and disestablishment of white supremacy.

refugees (mostly for religious reasons) in the following century. Britain annexed the Cape Province as a result of the Napoleonic Wars, and British settlers have come since 1820. In 1836, to escape British rule, groups of Afrikaners moved northward, a migration known as the "Great Trek." These *Voortrekkers* (Pioneers) had to fight their way for nearly twenty years against the warlike Bantu tribes which since the late eighteenth century had been moving from north to south and at times established control over certain areas.

The *Voortrekker* spirit—with its religious implications (an analogy with the Israelites escaping from Egypt to find refuge in the Holy Land), its missionary zeal (to spread the Gospel and civilization among heathens), and its determination to fight or die—has remained an important feature of the Afrikaner mind.

The two Boer republics—Transvaal (officially, the South African Republic) and the Orange Free State—had to struggle against the British who were threatening their independence from the south (Cape Colony) and east (Natal). The discovery of diamonds and of gold deposits in Transvaal first proved to be of "doubtful blessing"; they attracted masses of *uitlanders* (foreigners), who were not given civil rights but still jeopardized the Afrikaners' control of their republics. These frictions led to the first and second Boer Wars, which ended in the annexation of the two republics by Britain in 1902.

Ever since that traumatic defeat, the Afrikaner nation has been intent upon having its "revenge" on the Britons. Whitehall's policy of reconciliation eventually led to the unification of the four South African provinces in 1910 with dominion status, and an opportunity to regain by peaceful means what had been lost on the battlefield. While paying lip service to the concept of an Anglo-Afrikaner nation, Afrikaners and their National Party consider themselves as the real upholders of South Africa's national existence.

For the average Afrikaners, the policy of discrimination toward nonwhites is a purely South African way of handling the "multinational" (not "multiracial") problems which resulted from their historical development. It is a move of "self-defense," of "nation saving." The Afrikaners' mentality is rather defensive and isolationist. They would defend themselves if attacked, as they did in the past, or "trek away" if they could. Their strategic outlook recalls historic analogies: behind their *laager*, the fortress of the circle of their ox-driven wagons, they fought the onslaught of the Zulus or other tribes. They realize that their country is isolated in the world. But they also know that, unlike the French of Algeria or the Britons in Kenya, they have nowhere to go should they lose their land. And they are not looking over their shoulders to see if there are boats to take them away as the Portuguese did. So they say they must stay and die rather than give up.

This "hedgehog" attitude created among Afrikaners an encirclement syndrome, a state of mind which is more understandable than with other "beleaguered" nations in the Indian Ocean region, such as the Pakistanis or Ethiopians. Providence—they say—provided them with a land of incomparable mineral wealth, a land that is coveted by others. These "others" are not primarily the African states, which Afrikaners do not recognize as a serious threat to themselves. The real, serious menace stems from the Communist great powers, the Soviet Union and China. Rightly or wrongly, the antigovernment activity of opposing *apartheid* is often construed as pro-Communist. In 1950 the "Suppression of Communism Act" was passed, which permits the dissolution of organizations and arrest of individuals who further the aims of "communism."

The problems of the Indian Ocean region, then, are seen in the light of a global dichotomy, of a conflict between pro- and anti-Communist forces. The intervention by Soviet-equipped Cuban forces in the civil war of Angola appeared to support the accuracy of this belief. Pretoria views the Soviet naval presence in these waters as serving the purposes of subversion and establishment of Communist influence. The Soviet presence and help, as well as Chinese assistance, impress the credulous and uneducates Africans, while their leaders, as Nyerere or Kaunda, are too often naive idealists who ignore the ultimate aims of Moscow or Peking.

2. In 1960 a referendum in South Africa supported the move to transform that country into a republic. When in the following year the Republic of South Africa requested to remain in the 'Commonwealth, other members wished to make compliance with this request dependent on a change of South Africa's racial policies. Thereupon, Pretoria withdrew the request and South Africa remained excluded from the Commonwealth.

As a member of the United Nations since 1946, South Africa has been the target of attacks because of its *apartheid* policy. African states proposed draft resolution after draft resolution in the General Assembly condemning Pretoria for its violation of human rights. While South Africa was frequently censured by the General Assembly, the Security Council declined to apply sanctions because its policies, while endangering peace, were not considered a "threat to the peace, breach of the peace, or act of aggression" (Article 39 of the United Nations Charter).

Another conflict arose between the United Nations and South Africa in regard to the former German colony of South West Africa, which had been assigned after World War I to South Africa as a "mandated territory" under the League of Nations. In 1946 South Africa wished to incorporate this territory, but the United Nations refused this request; in return, Pretoria declined to conclude a trusteeship agreement and, subsequently, refused to allow independence for the territory, renamed Namibia in the United Nations. In June 1971 the World Court ruled that the presence of South Africa in Namibia is illegal and it is under the obligation to withdraw from that country.

Namibia, or South West Africa, is located along the coast of the Atlantic. From its northeast corner a narrow panhandle juts out, the so-called Caprivi Strip (named after the German Chancellor Count Caprivi, under whose administration this strip was ceded to Germany in 1893 so that South West Africa should have an outlet to the Zambesi River), which embraces the Republic of Botswana from the north.

3. Threats of expulsion from the United Nations, a resort to military sanctions, and other harassments failed to prevail upon Prestoria to alter its policies.

It insisted that resolutions by the General Assembly and advisory opinions by the World Court were only recommendations. It is, of course, doubtful whether South Africa would have complied with any binding decision in matters which it considers vital for its national existence.

What South Africa demands is time; time to carry out its plans for the establishment of "homelands," to crown its concept of separate development Eight separate areas are being set aside, or already set aside, to become Bantu homelands. Transkei and KwaZulu (Zululand) are the most developed homelands and the former is to attain "independence" on October 26, 1976. When fully developed, the homelands—according to official planning—will be given independence and will apply for membership in the United Nations. Pretoria believes that such a request will embarrass the world organization (or the voicferously hostile Afro-Asian bloc) and place before it a dilemma: whether to admit these "independent" homelands to membership, an action that would vindicate South Africa, or to reject such demands, in which case African countries will have been refused admittance. Leaders of the National Party realize that the creation of "internationally independent" homelands will not make these countries economically independent, as Botswana, Lesotho, and Swaziland are economically dependent on South Africa.

4. South Africa maintains no diplomatic contacts with the countries of Africa except for Malawi, with no Communist state, and, apart from the countries of Western Europe and the United States, with only few other governments in Asia and in the Americas. Afrikaner introversion has tended to ignore the unfavorable image which South Africa presented to the world. Nevertheless, since 1967 passive attitudes have been replaced by diplomatic moves, known as the *uitwardse beweging* (outward movement or outward-looking policy), whereby Pretoria has attempted to establish ties with African states, often confidential contacts, and has used for this purpose the economic advantages which South Africa could offer. Only with Malawi could a complete breakthrough be achieved; otherwise, discreet or clandestine connections could be maintained with some governments and also a few personal visits exchanged, especially with francophone African leaders.

The "outward-looking" policy had little effect in the West. In those countries where, for economic or military-political reasons, the strategic and financial weight of South Africa is fully appreciated, their leaders were careful not to provoke the groundswell of opponents of the South African regime. This was particularly the case with questions of military supplies and strategic cooperation.

5. In the early 1960s South Africa began building up a powerful military establishment. Previously it felt secure under British protection, but because of its diplomatic isolation, it felt that neither Britain nor any outside power would support it. Afrikaners had always been "land-oriented"; it required a greater effort to develop the navy than the land and air forces. Still, the major geopolitical importance of South Africa rests with the Cape route, passing around its shores from the Indian Ocean to the Atlantic and more specifically, from the Persian Gulf to Europe and North America.

After the 1967 closure of the Suez Canal, shipping around the Cape of Good Hope rose by more than 50 percent. Even after the Suez Canal was reopened to traffic in 1975, many ships, especially supertankers of 200,000-ton displacements and above, continued to use the Cape route. In order to monitor ship movement around the Cape, the South African Government in 1973 completed the construction of a maritime operations and communications headquarters at Silvermine near Cape Town. Ships on the Cape route are electronically contacted and identified, whether they enter a South African harbor or not. If a vessel cannot be identified (Soviet ships, as a rule, refuse to give answers), all other ships in the vicinity are invited to provide data about the unknown vessel.

The arms embargo passed by the United Nations against South Africa did little to prevent that country from growing into a powerful military power. The South African Navy is well proportioned but still the weekest arm of the defense forces. The army is being trained to meet both an invading land force and guerrilla infiltration. South Africa maintains a powerful air force, and the country is dotted with good airfields, one of them in the strategic Caprivi Strip.

The strategic planning of Pretoria assumes that African countries, aided by one or more Communist powers, will attempt to seek a "military solution," as advocated by the Organization of African Unity, to "decolonize" South Africa. The military establishment should be prepared to meet such attempts, which are likely to resemble those practiced against Rhodesia, or practiced in the past against Mozambique and Angola. South Africa is confident that it will be able to handle any such emergency more successfully than other victims of such aggressions.

The South African military posture is defensive; no preventive actions are envisaged, particularly after the unsuccessful incursion into Angola in 1975. Even the dispatch of police forces to Rhodesia (now withdrawn) was done rather reluctantly. Afrikaners are not enthusiastic about Rhodesia's Unilateral Declaration of Independence (UDI); should Rhodesia crumble, an exodus of its white population to South Africa (tilting the Afrikaner majority) would be regarded with mixed feelings by many.

Thus while South Africa is preparing itself to stand alone in its fight against the surrounding hostile world, the lack of the accustomed backing by Britain is deplored by the English-speaking and Afrikaner South Africans alike. The abandonment by Britain of the Simonstown naval base south of Cape Town, strategically located to control navigation around the Cape, signified the end of a collaboration which survived until 1975. In that year London formally denounced the Simonstown Agreements, which provided that the facilities of this base would be available for the use of the British Navy and by navies of allies of the United Kingdom in any war in which Britain was involved. British officials asserted that the need for the Simonstown base was largely reduced with the reopening of the Suez Canal. The base will probably be available to Britain and its allies anyway, in times of emergency.[2]

[2]*New York Times,* June 17, 1975.

6. With its military and economic might, the Republic of South Africa appears to be able to maintain its white supremacy internally as well as to uphold its weight in the regional power balance of southern Africa. Still diplomatic isolation and lack of cooperation with the countries of the West, to which it feels it belongs, are a cause of disquiet. And many, especially the non-Afrikaans-speaking segment of the white population, feel that "they are dancing on a volcano."

Not only for South Africans is the status of their country embarrassing: for the countries of the West (especially those which in the past felt close to South Africa, such as Britain or the Netherlands) the "nonalliance" with this country appears anomalous and repugnant. Relations between the West and Pretoria are inhibited from following their rational course; they are disturbed by ideological considerations and the condemnation of racial discrimination, which do not permit the pursuit of requirements of national interest. While such a condemnatory attitude may be morally right, from the narrower foreign policy angle it is wrong. While it may please the overwhelming public sentiment in the United States, Britain, and other Western countries, while it prevents a break with many Afro-Asian governments (although not necessarily improving relations with them), as a foreign policy *per se* it is harmful. Ultimately it may—but not necessarily will—accrue to the benefit of Soviet or Chinese interests should an isolated South Africa crumble. What seems right from a moral, humanitarian point of view is prejudicial from a foreign policy point of view.

Because of this Sophoclean tragic situation, South Africa, an important geopolitical area in a global and regional sense, a factor in the balance of power in the Indian Ocean area, is left in limbo, not made use of, not enlisted in the group of states to which it would like to belong, and left isolated and exposed to the pressures of opposing forces.

Prophesies about the downfall of the South African minority rule have been rampant in the last twenty years. But embargoes and censure in the United Nations have so far proved to be abortive. There is hardly any likelihood that equality (one man, one vote) will be granted to the nonwhite population. The government of the Republic is more likely to proceed with its homelands experiment, the outcome of which cannot be foreseen.

Should, however, an international crisis occur which would require the use of South African real estate by the Western powers, or should, as a result of outside aggression, the national existence of South Africa as presently constituted be threatened, it is likely that the West will still throw overboard its prejudices against the domestic setup of that country and—as demanded by national interest[3]—come to the rescue of the "outcast."

---

[3]As Secretary of State Kissinger said in another context, "Where we believe the national interest is at stake we proceed even when we do not approve of a country's (domestic) policies." *New York Times,* July 25, 1974.

Botswana, Lesotho, and Swaziland

When the Union of South Africa was formed in 1910 and obtained "dominion status," Bechuanaland, Basutoland, and Swaziland remained British protectorates directly dependent on London. This state of affairs remained unchanged even when South Africa evolved into a completely sovereign country and even after it became a republic in 1961. Pretoria had wished, in vain, to have these protectorates placed under its control; it also opposed giving them independence. However, in 1963 the republic suddenly reversed its policy and welcomed the granting of independence to these three British High Commission territories, as was planned by the British government.

By abandoning any intention of incorporating these territories, Pretoria wished to appear consistent in its racial policy of "separate development." The three native states would also serve as models or "showpieces" for the Bantustans which the South African government desired to create on its own territory.

Furthermore, South Africa could afford to tolerate the existence of these independent black states because of their dependence on the South African economy and lack of any military power. This interdependence was mainly the consequence of the geographic location of these former British protectorates. Lesotho (Basutoland) is a complete enclave, surrounded by the territory of South Africa on four sides; likewise, Botswana (Bechuanaland) is encircled by South Africa and Rhodesia except that it claims a narrow piece of land on the Zambesi River opposite Zambesian territory, a claim contested by both South Africa and Rhodesia. Swaziland is surrounded on three sides by South Africa; in the east it is bordered by Mozambique.

The economic subjection of these population-wise mini-states rests primarily on their being included in the customs and monetary area of South Africa and the fact that large segments of their labor force work in South Africa and remit their earnings to keeping the economy of these otherwise poor countries going. This dependence, however, is not one-sided; all three tribal states possess some leverage on Pretoria, a fact which strengthens rather than weakens their interdependence.

Certain general usages have developed in the interrelation of these three countries with South Africa, certain understandings of a "live and let live" nature. Thus, while opposed to *apartheid,* these three are committed not to undermine the security of the republic, such as by allowing members of the guerrilla movements to operate on or even pass through their territories. At the same time, Pretoria does not require them to identify themselves with the policies of South Africa, and they try not to be identified with those. All the three countries are members of the Organization of African Unity, an organization which is dedicated to the destruction of the present white regime of South Africa. In return, this organization and the African countries with which the three maintain diplomatic relations have so far recognized the delicate situation of these three governments and refrained from demanding compliance with the "anti-white regimes" attitude.

Botswana, Lesotho, and Swaziland are members of the United Nations and of the Commonwealth, as well as other international organizations of which the Republic of South Africa is not a member or from which it has been expelled.

Perhaps the most peculiar situation prevails in the diplomatic field: there are no Botswana, Lesotho, or Swaziland ambassadors or diplomatic-consular missions of any kind in Pretoria; nor does South Africa maintain diplomatic representatives in Gaberones, Maseru, or Mbabane, although South African officials and advisors operate in the territories of these countries with their consent. The top-level exchanges between their governments and the government in Pretoria are mostly informal; they are referred to as a kind of "telephone diplomacy." South Africa has, for pragmatic reasons, laid aside formalities or prestige; it is satisfied as long as the system works. The differences in power relations and the physical dependence are so obvious that any insistence on "protocol" can be dispensed with. And the leaders of the three black ministates are able to pride themselves that they do not maintain "diplomatic relations" with a government censured because of its "white supremacist" policies.

For the South African Republic the three former British High Commission territories are convenient buffers against enemy infiltration and objects of display to demonstrate the feasibility of coexistence and collaboration between white South Africa and black nations on a basis of mutual satisfaction and legal equality. For the three ministates, South Africa presents the only alternative for economic viability and national existence.

Rhodesia

With the end of Portuguese colonial rule in Mozambique, Rhodesia, with the Republic of South Africa, remained one of the countries ruled by a white minority. However, the proportions between whites and blacks in Rhodesia were considerably more disadvantageous for the former than even in South Africa. In 1972 the population of Rhodesia numbered 5.6 million; among them 5.3 million were Africans and only 260,000 were Europeans (whites), the remainder being coloreds and Asians. Thus the ratio between Africans and Europeans was twenty-one to one. It has been pointed out that every one and a half years the African population increases by a number which is equal to that of the total European population of Rhodesia.

Rhodesia, previously known as Southern Rhodesia, was settled by British settlers under the charter given to the British South African Company by the British government in the last decade of the nineteenth century. From 1953 to 1963 Southern Rhodesia was a member of the Federation of Rhodesia and Nyasaland, formed together with Northern Rhodesia and Nyasaland, two British protectorates. However, after ten years the federation was dissolved because Northern Rhodesia and Nyasaland, which came to be led by their native African population, refused to be dominated by the influence of Southern Rhodesia's whites. Northern Rhodesia and Nyasaland thereafter became the independent states of Zambia and Malawi, in 1964.

It was now Southern Rhodesia's turn to achieve independence. Its 1961 Constitution already gave it complete autonomy except in the fields of foreign affairs and defense matters. It also provided for limited participation by the representatives of the black population in the parliamentary government of the country. London made compliance with the wishes of the black leadership for an extended participation in government the condition for granting full independence; the white leadership rejected these demands.

After two years of abortive negotiations, Rhodesia, under the Premiership of Ian Smith, declared itself independent on November 11, 1965 (the Unilateral Declaration of Independence). The act was considered unconstitutional by the British government and also by members of the United Nations; officially, the country is still regarded as a British possession. In 1969 the Rhodesian Parliament broke all ties with the Crown by declaring the country a republic. Prolonged and renewed talks between the Rhodesian and British representatives failed to result in a settlement.

The Security Council of the United Nations, first in 1966 and again in 1968, called upon the member states to refrain from trade with Rhodesia. These mandatory sanctions eventually extended to all articles (except medical and educational material) and were to apply both to importations to and exportations from Rhodesia. In compliance with these measures, the British Navy maintained a quasi-blockade along the Mozambican coast (the so-called Beira patrol). Proposals, however, to call on Britain to suppress the revolting colony with armed forces failed to be adopted by the Security Council. Both the Republic of South Africa and Portugal refused to carry out the sanctions, which fell short of being effective enough to change the policies of the Salisbury government.

No country maintained diplomatic relations with Rhodesia. After the declaration of the republic, all consular missions, including that of the United States, were withdrawn, except for those of South Africa and Portugal. After the April 1974 revolution, Portuguese consular contacts were also ended.

Although Rhodesia has so far refrained from introducing legislation of the strict *apartheid* type, as practiced in South Africa, more stringent measures have been passed to secure the rule of the European minority. The Land Tenure Act, for instance, divided the entire land area of the country between Europeans and Africans, reserving about half of the territory and the better farmlands to the former. Leaders of the black opposition movements have been imprisoned. Attempts by the liberation movements centered outside the country, the Zimbabwe African People's Union (ZAPU), the Zimbabwe African National Union (ZANU), and the Front for the Liberation of Zimbabwe (FROLIZI) to infiltrate guerrilla fighters into Rhodesia have so far had only limited success.[4]

[4]Zimbabwe is the name used by African countries to designate Rhodesia after the city (now in ruins) built between the ninth and thirteenth centuries near the town of Fort Victoria.

Rhodesia finds itself in a much more exposed position than South Africa vis-à-vis the inimical African forces. From the point of view of Pretoria, Rhodesia serves as a military *glacis,* a forward position for its own defense. However, with the establishment of a black government in Mozambique, this forward position has become dangerously exposed. Until this Rhodesia faced Zambia along an endangered border of about 500 miles on the easily controlled Zambesi River (including the more than 150-mile-long artificial lake created by the Kariba Dam). Infiltrators more easily managed to reach Rhodesian territory across the Tete Province of Mozambique. With the changed political situation in the former Portuguese possession, Rhodesia's entire northeastern and eastern border (over 650 miles), much of it mountainous, wooded, and rugged, has become a bridgehead for guerrilla infiltrators.

After the Soviet-Cuban intervention in Angola, the military position of Rhodesia further deteriorated in the spring of 1976. It now appeared evident that it might become the next victim in the program of the Organization of African Unity aimed at the destruction of white minority rule in southern Africa. The main concern of the Rhodesian government—and of South Africa—is the role which the modern well-equipped and well-trained Cuban forces would be playing in the implementation of this program. While Rhodesia felt strong enough to cope with African guerrillas, a massive onslaught by a Cuban expeditionary force, transported by Soviet vessels and Soviet aircraft to Mozambique, would be impossible to sustain.

Rhodesia maintains a permanent army of about 3,400, which may quickly be reinforced by a territorial force of 8,400. There are also reserve forces which number 25,000. The land army is highly mobile. It is supported by several squadrons of a fairly modern air force. The active police force is 6,400 strong and is trained for counterinsurgency activity. Less than one-third of the regular land forces and two-thirds of the police are blacks.

The Portuguese abandonment of Mozambique also affected Rhodesia's communications with the outside world. Before that development, Rhodesia's lifeline, transporting most of its vital imports and exports, was the railroad line from Salisbury to Beira, and to a lesser extent the line to Lourenço Marques (both Mozambican harbors on the Indian Ocean). In a way, the Rhodesian government foresaw the possible severance of these railroad lines; in 1972 the construction of a rail link with the South African network was begun, and it was completed in feverish haste by October 1974. It will prevent Rhodesia's complete deprivation of an outlet by rail for its heavy export articles, consisting of valuable minerals, chromite, nickel, copper, pig iron, asbestos, and all kinds of steel manufactured goods. Rhodesia is also completely dependent on oil and machinery imports from overseas.

Because of the changed situation in Mozambique, Rhodesia has become even more completely dependent on South Africa in order to survive economically. It is known that the South African Central Bank is providing credit to the government of Ian Smith. But apart from the economic menace, the most acute danger for Rhodesia consists in the assault that is being launched from the secure bases in Mozambique.

Mozambique

Prior to 1974 Mozambique was one of the three African overseas provinces of Portugal which were ruled from Lisbon. Portuguese settlements along the more than 1,600-mile-long coast of Mozambique date back to the time of Vasco da Gama, that is, to the years around 1500. But the interior of the country was colonized much later, and its present borders were only fixed in the nineteenth century. When Britain, France, and Belgium abandoned their colonies in Africa, Portugal consistently held onto its colonial possessions despite protests and condemnation in the United Nations and despite the insurgency movements, armed by Moscow and Peking and based in surrounding black African states. The bulk of the guerrillas were affiliated with the Mozambique Liberation Front (*Frente de Liberataço de Moçambique,* FRELIMO) and recognized by the Organization of African Unity. FRELIMO moved its guerrillas from their Tanzanian bases to the northern provinces of Mozambique, while others penetrated from Zambia into the Tete Province.

The war of attrition which started in 1964 came to an end in 1974, when, after the military coup in Lisbon in April of that year, the new democratic government showed readiness to recognize the independence of Mozambique. In September 1974 an agreement was reached between Lisbon and FRELIMO for the establishment of a provisional government, with the major participation of the guerrilla movement, and this was followed in June 1975 by the complete independence of that country. The President of the newly independent Mozambique, Samora M. Machel (also the leader of FRELIMO), promised to create a disciplined, austere socialist country which thus might become the first Communist nation in Africa. His model appears to be that of Mao Tse-tung's China rather than the Soviet version.

Landlocked Rhodesia's closest and natural outlet to the sea is through Mozambique; Beira has handled the bulk of Salisbury's foreign trade, while Lourenço Marques (now renamed Maputo) has offered another access to the Indian Ocean. However, in March 1976 Mozambique severed all rail and road connections with Rhodesia. It even declared a state of war between the two countries, and guerrilla operations were launched along Rhodesia's border. Whether Mozambique will invite Cuban forces to operate from its territory, still remains a matter for conjecture.

Strangely enough, no essential change has so far taken place in the complicated and interlocked relations between Mozambique and South Africa. The interdependence between the economies of Mozambique and South Africa has not only been commercial, for South Africa was the second largest trade partner of Mozambique after Portugal. About 100,000 Mozambicans were employed in South Africa's gold and coal mines.

Among schemes of mutual interest and interdependence, the Cabora Bassa hydroelectric project took a prominent place. Under this enterprise a South African-led consortium, with the participation of Portuguese, French, and West German firms, raised a dam in the Cabora Bassa gorge of the Zambesi River and built a hydroelectric complex with an initial capacity of 1,800 megawatts (the fourth largest of its kind in the world) to provide electric power to large parts of southern Africa. The dam's capacity can subsequently be raised to 4,000 megawatts. When in operation, it would transform the adjacent area of Mozambique into an industrial center unparalleled in Africa, except for the Republic of South Africa. The financial program of the project assumed that the major customer of electric power would be South Africa; cables leading to the Transvaal were laid down and the complex was to be ready in 1975. But construction was slowed down since Mozambique gained independence.

The different attitude displayed by Mozambique toward Rhodesia and South Africa, open hostility against the first, cooperation with the second, may just be tactics to last until the Rhodesian question is "settled." But it is possible that Mozambique will one day sever its ties of interdependence with South Africa irrespective of the outcome of the Rhodesian venture. National feeling and devotion to the pan-African cause and hatred against white discrimination could prevail over vital economic interests. In that case, economically South Africa would be the lesser loser. If the exit for its exports via Maputo (Lourenço Marques) should be cut, the shipments could be diverted to Durban and to Richards Bay, a port north of Durban, developed for the purpose of meeting such a contingency and to relieve the congestion in its other harbors. Workers from Mozambique could be, again with some effort, replaced by African workers from South Africa's own labor market or from the former British High Commission territories. While no other hydroelectric plant could substitute for Cabora Bassa, South Africa could find other, more expensive sources of energy. But Pretoria has no way to influence the policies of the new Mozambican government except to demonstrate to it the advantages of cooperation and the disadvantages of a break in relations.

The long Indian Ocean coastline of Mozambique is studded with a number of ports, located on deep bays which are most convenient for accommodating warships or fishing fleets. Maputo and Beira have extended quaysides. Others, like Quelimane, Porto Amelia, and Nacala, are ideal anchorages. The latter is being developed into a deep-water port, the terminus of a railroad from Malawi. The Mozambican government, especially if it receives aid from Moscow, may find itself in a situation somewhat similar to that of Somalia, South Yemen, or Iraq: the Soviet Union may require, in return, the use of one or more of the excellent anchorages or port facilities for its naval units or fishing vessels which frequently move north or south in these waters. Such naval facilities would greatly strengthen Soviet strategy in the southwestern section of the Indian

Ocean, where so far Moscow has enjoyed only very limited possiblilties for the refueling or repair of its vessels.

The independence of Mozambique has, no doubt, changed the power balance in Southern Africa. Depending on how far the new regime is willing to join the group of anti-Western African states, the Soviet naval presence may obtain further *points d'appui* in that part of the ocean. And depending on the determination of the government of Mozambique how to pursue the anti-white-supremacy campaign against South Africa, the military balance, so far much in favor of South Africa, will tilt in the latter's disfavor.

Zambia

The Republic of Zambia, formerly Northern Rhodesia, became independent in October 1964, after the dissolution of the Federation of Rhodesia and Nyasaland. Here the African majority managed to gain control in the Legislative Council, thus frustrating any attempts of the small white population to maintain its ascendancy. The number of Europeans was small, even compared with that in Southern Rhodesia (in 1969 only 43,000 in a total population of 4.4 million) and their self-government was never established as it was in Southern Rhodesia.

Zambia, although a member of the Commonwealth, adopted the republican form of government immediately upon attaining independence. The country is run under a strong presidential and one-party system with a unicameral parliament. Under the leadership of Kenneth Kaunda, Zambia embarked upon a foreign policy of nonalignment combined with the goal of ending white-supremacist rule in other parts of southern Africa. However, the economic and communication ties with her southern neighbors made the implementation of sanctions against Rhodesia a painful endeavor.

Zambia's relative prosperity is based on the exploitation of its copper deposits (it is the world's third biggest producer of copper after the United States and the Soviet Union). Since Zambia is a land-locked country, the exportation of copper (96 percent in value of its total exports) required cooperation with the neighboring countries. In the past a major portion of its exports and imports passed through Rhodesia, to or from the Mozambican port of Beira. The rest was routed over the Benguela railroad across Zaire to the Angolan port of Lobito, In retaliation for guerrilla infiltrations from Zambia, the Rhodesian government closed the border in 1973, thus forcing Zambia to find other routes for its foreign trade. And during the civil war in Angola the railroad to Lobito was also closed.

When the rail line to Dar es Salaam is opened, the most frequented route is likely to be the TanZam (Tanzania–Zambia) railway. This line stretches 1,163 miles from the Indian Ocean and reaches the Zambian rail net at the town of Kapiri Mposhi, 100 miles north of the Zambian capital city of Lusaka. This railway—also known as the *Uhuru* (Freedom) railway—was constructed jointly by China, Tanzania, and Zambia. (Peking provided a $400 million, interest-free loan.) However, Zambia will still have to rely on its outlet to Lobito because the TanZam railroad is single-track and because the port of Dar es Salaam will be unable to handle all the heavy copper shipments.

Zambia closely cooperates with Tanzania, not only in questions of transportation but also in its policies against Rhodesia and South Africa. But while Tanzania, mostly with Chinese assistance, is training and organizing guerrillas on its territory, Zambia, fearing retaliatory incursions into its land, only allows brief stationing and passage of guerrillas on and across its territory.

Despite Zambia's determined anti*apartheid* policy, trade relations with South Africa were not completely broken off. Among the unofficial and secret contacts which South Africa maintains with black African leaders, those with Zambia were made public in 1971. In 1975 Kenneth Kaunda openly met with South African Prime Minister John Vorster when they mediated between Rhodesian Prime Minister Ian Smith and his African opposition leaders. South African citizens still possess investments in Zambia, and the latter country was also deeply interested in the Cabora Bassa project and hoped to be included in the grid network to provide electric energy in large parts of southern Africa.

Although President Kaunda strongly opposed the policies of bridge building between Zambia's neighbor, Malawi, and South Africa, the economic and political benefits which the former Nyasaland enjoys from its relations with the economic giant of the south cannot totally escape the attention of an astute politician.

Malawi

The Republic of Malawi's territory is less than one-fourth that of Zambia, but its population exceeds that of the latter. Although consisting of many smaller tribes, Malawi showed greater cohesion and even developed more intensive national feeling than most of the ex-colonial states in Africa south of the Sahara.

Malawi's territorial location is less fortunate. Its territory stretches along the Great Rift Valley for a length of about 600 miles with an average width of 100 miles. It is land-locked and pressed between Zambia and Tanzania in the northwest and northeast, and surrounded by Mozambican territory in the southwest and southeast.

Malawi, under the former name of Nyasaland, formed part of the Central African Federation with the two Rhodesias; it also had urged a dissolution of the link with white-dominated Southern Rhodesia and achieved independence in July 1964. Since 1958 Malawi's charismatic leader has been Dr. Hastings Kamuzu Banda, who also heads the governing Malawi Congress Party.

Malawi does not possess the mineral wealth of Zambia, and therefore its per capita income was only $69 in 1972 (that of Zambia was $423). Its economic interdependence with Rhodesia and, in particular, South Africa is probably the main reason that Malawi refrained from joining the vehemently anti*apartheid* group of African states. Malawi might have had a choice (one which Lesotho,

Botswana, and Swaziland, because of their geographic location, did not possess); but it chose friendship and cooperation with the white-dominated countries of southern Africa. This attitude placed it in a position of confrontation with Zambia and Tanzania.

More than half of Malawi's labor force is employed abroad; two-thirds work in Rhodesia and one-third in South Africa. But more than half of workers' remittances arrive from South Africa, which is thus the more important labor market. Furthermore, South Africa provides economic aid to Malawi and is one of the most important trading partners for its exports.

Malawi's role as a bridge between whites and blacks—as Dr. Banda asserts—or as a traitor to the black cause—as Malawi is being depicted in the circles of the Organization of African Unity—has hardly affected the military balance of power in southern Africa. Malawi's British-trained army is rather insignificant, though, it could defend itself against Zambian or Tanzanian attacks. Its political significance is psychological: it is a black country, practically if not formally an ally of South Africa, which gives comfort to those South Africans who may be despondent because of their country's isolation. It is almost axiomatic in Pretoria that its isolation has to be broken, not in Europe or North America or the United Nations, but in Africa itself.

Tanzania

The United Republic of Tanzania consists of two territorial units: of Tanganyika (or mainland Tanzania) and the islands of Zanzibar and Pemba. Before World War I, mainland Tanzania was known as German East Africa, which, deprived of its two western areas Rwanda and Burundi, became the British-administered mandated territory of Tanganyika after the end of that war. On the other hand, Zanzibar and Pemba, ruled since the early eighteenth century by the Omani Arab dynasty of Sultan Seyyid Said, became British protectorates in 1890.

After World War II, Tanganyika became a United Nations trust territory, still administered by Britain. Having first received internal self-government in 1960, Tanganyika achieved full independence in December 1961 under the presidency of Julius Nyerere. Zanzibar obtained independence under the rule of its sultan in December 1963. One month later the sultan was ousted and a republican form of government adopted. In April 1964 Zanzibar-Pemba joined Tanganyika while retaining considerable autonomy. The union was renamed the United Republic of Tanzania in October 1964.

As its Constitution established, Tanzania is a one-party state: Nyerere is both President of the republic and leader of the TANU (Tanganyika African National Union). The President of Zanzibar is the First Vice President of Tanzania and Chairman of the Revolutionary Council, the legislature of the island, acting also on behalf of the Afro-Shirazi Party, the only permitted political organization. The party document adopted as law in 1967, the so-called Arusha Declaration, introduced a socialist economic program and an egalitarian social system with emphasis on rural development.

Tanzania is the prime promoter of the overthrow of the white-dominated regimes in southern Africa. Its intense hostility against South Africa, Rhodesia, and earlier against Portugal did not remain verbal; it allowed its territory to become the principal training base for guerrillas operating against Mozambique (before the Lisbon coup in 1974), Rhodesia, and South Africa. It is host to the "national liberation" organizations in charge of these guerrilla operations and others which wish to replace regimes in countries such as the Seychelles, Réunion, and Malawi.

Among African states, Tanzania was most outspoken in condemning both the United States and Britain for the establishment and extension of naval-air installations on the island of Diego Garcia. It is the most vocal protagonist among African states of the Zone of Peace project for the Indian Ocean, but—like the Indians—condemned the American presence in these waters while ignoring that of the Soviet Union.

While Zambia only permitted guerrillas to operate from its territory, Tanzania allowed the establishment of a network of training bases and camps under the direction of the Liberation Committee of the Organization of African Unity. Tanzania feels free to serve as host to these liberation movements because it is less apprehensive of retaliation than Zambia, which still maintains economic ties with South Africa.

Peking became the major power which provided economic and military assistance to Tanzania. The TanZam railway, to connect Dar es Salaam with the Zambian rail network, was planned by Chinese railway engineers of the People's Liberation Army. Its construction made possible with the help of Chinese labor, was begun in October 1970 and was partly completed in 1975.

Until 1965 the army and air force of Tanzania were trained and equipped by British instructors and with British weaponry. In January 1964 a revolt of two battalions of the Tanganyika Rifles could only be supressed with the help of British Royal Marine Commandos brought in by air upon the request of the Tanzanian government. Thereafter, the army was restructured, British influences eliminated (between 1965 and 1967 Tanzania broke diplomatic relations with Britain), and arms and training received from a variety of countries though predominantly from the Chinese. Tanzanian officers and military technicians are obtaining training in China.

Quite evidently, in Tanzania Peking has managed to obtain the upper hand over the Soviet influence. While Soviet ascendancy prevails in Somalia and in Southern Yemen (and possibly in Uganda), in Tanzania Peking has so far scored the major success. But it would be exaggerated to pretend that Tanzania has compromised its freedom of action. The collaboration with Peking remains voluntary and is conceived as beneficial for both parties.

Tanzania is internally more stable than most of the African countries south of the Sahara. Thus it can afford to engage in an agressive military policy toward Rhodesia and South Africa, neither of which is an immediate neighbor. The only potential nearby adversary is Uganda, with which border skirmishes are not infrequent.

The union with Zanzibar-Pamba has experienced less tensions since the assassination of Zanzibar's maverick leader, Sheikh Karume. But the island partners of the union are often out of step with the policies of mainland Tanzania, especially in matters of foreign assistance. Under the terms of the union, areas like foreign affairs, external trade, and defense are to be handled by the union government, an arrangement which is not fully respected by Zanzibar.

Tanzania, like other black African countries, is no major threat to the existing balance of power along the African coast of the Indian Ocean. The offensive against the white-dominated countries may continue (Mozambique counts as a major victory) and Tanzanian-trained and -based guerrillas may harass Rhodesia and even South Africa. But as long as these countries are determined to resist and as long as their black population remains largely passive, the guerrillas, though more than pinpricks, cannot overthrow the balance. The balance could nevertheless be tilted by massive military intervention from overseas.

Malagasy Republic

The fate of Madagascar was determined in 1890 when a Franco-British agreement recognized France's protectorate over the island in return for French recognition of British rule over Zanzibar. In 1895 French forces established France's effective domination, and in the following year Madagascar was declared a French colony and the last ruling member of the Merina Dynasty was exiled.

The population of Madagascar consists of many ethnic groups. From the point of view of present-day politics, the most important division is that between the Merina, the high-plateau people, descendants of Malay-Polynesian immigrants who arrived on the island in the first centuries of the Christian era, and the coastal people *(côtiers),* with their African and Arab admixtures of blood.

The Malagasy Republic (the political name) obtained independence in 1960 under the presidency of Philibert Tsiranana, a *côtier,* whose Social Democratic Party controlled the state until 1972, when Tsiranana was overthrown by the military and General Gabriel Ramanantsoa, a Merina, became the President. This internal change was accompanied by a drastic reshaping of the republic's foreign relations, including those with France.

When achieving independence in 1960, the Malagasy Republic accepted a mutual defense agreement with France which committed France to provide military aid and secured for Paris the rights to maintain land, air, and naval forces in Madagascar. The country continued to belong to the French monetary area and was given French economic aid.

From the outset, the government of President Ramanantsoa emphasized its pursuit of a policy of strict nonalignment, as opposed to the previous government's full commitment to the West and opposition to the East. Governmental spokesmen explained that the advantages of this policy had been minimal, whereas the disadvantages had been considerable. The Western orientation meant very little, if anything, from the economic or cultural point of view, and was clearly detrimental politically because it obscured the vision toward the East. The economy of Madagascar remained colonial under this regime, notwithstanding independence; French-controlled or other Western-controlled corporations carried out trade, exported, and imported but did not invest in the country and failed to help it to industrialize. French cultural assistance did little to educate the masses—only members of the elite were educated by it.

A change in foreign policy so governmental commentators explained, was also desirable because the Cold War had come to an end; both the capitalist and the socialist camps are now fragmented, and the lines of division between the two camps are blurred. China considers the Soviet Union to be a more dangerous enemy than even the United States. The Malagasy Republic does not wish to side either with Peking or with Moscow; it considers the Sino-Soviet conflict to be as futile as the Cold War was in its time. Diplomatic relations established with Moscow or Peking would not endanger the security of the country.

Malagasy nonalignment was intended to stress "even-handedness" in dealing with Communist and non-Communist countries. Foreign Minister Didier Ratsiraka, a former naval officer educated in France, expressed this in naval terminology as facing *tous azimuts* (every direction) or standing *sens muet* (halt). Strict interpretation of nonalignment led the Malagasy government of Ramanantsoa to ban the visits of all warships from Malagasy ports as of December 1973, including Japanese school ships and Iranian and even Kenyan naval vessels.

The Malagasy Republic was one of the sponsors of the Zone of Peace resolutions in the United Nations. When in February 1974 the plan for an extension of the Diego Garcia installation was announced in Washington, the Foreign Minister condemned this action. Balancing somewhat his statement, he expressed the wish that both superpowers and great powers (meaning Britain and France) would stop their rivalries in the Indian Ocean area.

The most consequential decision by the new government was to demand an end of the basic 1960 treaty with France, concluded at the time of the Declaration of Independence. By an agreement reached in June 1973 Madagascar left the franc monetary system.

The small French Air Force units stationed at Ivato and Antsirabe airports were withdrawn, as were all land forces (a Foreign Legion regiment was stationed at Diego Suarez). The important naval base at Diego Suarez, the bulwark of French naval power in the Indian Ocean, was liquidated in 1975. French teachers were withdrawn and other special ties with France ended.

While the Tsiranana government cared little for the black African states (although the republic joined the Organization of African Unity), the new Government of Madagascar endorsed a clearly pro-African policy. Earlier Tananarive stressed Malagasy's non-African, Asian descent; now the official line emphasizes that the Malagasy people are both African and Malay-Polynesians.

The Ramanantsoa government laid claim to fifty miles of territorial waters (previously it was six miles), plus 100 miles of an "economic zone" around

Madagascar, but has claimed no additional portions of the continental shelf (Madagascar's continental shelf abruptly deepens in almost every direction). With these claims Madagascar really expressed a wish to control the entire eastern half of the Mozambique Channel together with the small islands located in that channel.

The Malagasy authoritarian government is mild compared with other military leaderships in Africa. The Tsiranana government was less Merina-dominated than the present one, and *côtiers* complain that instead of Malagasization of business a great deal of "Merinization" is going on. While the army is mainly Merina-led, the gendarmerie and the special mobile police are *côtier* and there is much rivalry between these armed forces. Ethnic differences were at the root of the troubles which erupted in the first months of 1975.

When a coup was attempted against President Ramanantsoa, led by members of the special mobile police group, he handed over his powers to Colonel Ratsimandrava, the Minister of the Interior. On February 12, 1975, six days after he assumed power, the new President was killed and agents of the special police force were considered responsible. A new military junta under the leadership of General Andriamahazo has taken over the government. In June 1975 Foreign Minister Didier Ratsiraka was named head of the Revolutionary Council and elected President of the Malagasy Republic. These dramatic events reflected the deep-seated antagonism characteristic for the Merina-*côtier* feud.

In the balance-of-power equation of the southwestern corner of the Indian Ocean, the Malagasy Republic's position differs from that of the African states which oppose white-dominated South Africa. It is far from being aggressive; it only pays lip service to liberation movements and is indifferent to the success or unsuccess of guerrilla operations. However, as an island state, it feels exposed and vulnerable to conflicts which might erupt between naval powers. It fears the strength and resilience of South Africa; it envisages that a cornered South Africa might try to move into neighboring African territories to establish a protective belt around its land, a move which would ultimately involve the United States and the Soviet Union—a conflict into which Madagascar might be inexorably drawn.

The Seychelles, the Comoros, and Réunion

There are two groups of islands north of Madagascar and a single island east of it. All the three have French affiliations, cultural or political, and Réunion still belongs firmly to France at the time of this writing.

1. The Seychelles Islands, about a thousand miles east of the African mainland (Kenya), consist of about eighty-five islands, the principal one being Mahé Island with Victoria, the capital. The Seychelles were occupied by the British during the Napoleonic Wars and ceded by France to Britain in 1814. The inhabitants are mainly descendants of French settlers and their African slaves; the native tongue is Creole French, but the official language is English.

A Crown colony until 1970, the islands obtained self-government in that year. The governing party is the Seychelles Democratic Party, and the Chief Minister is its leader, James R. Mancham. The leader of the opposition is France Albert René, head of the Seychelles People's United Party.

Since the beginning of the parliamentary regime, the opposition demanded independence, while Chief Minister Mancham wished to maintain the islands' association with the United Kingdom. Because of the "meddling" by the Organization of African Unity, the Chief Minister, after the April 1974 elections, joined the bandwagon of the independence movement. On June 29, 1976, the islands became an independent republic, Mancham its first President, and Albert René the Prime Minister.

In 1963 the United States government was given permission to establish a space-tracking station on Mahé Island.

The Seychelles are too weak even to think of meaningful defense forces. Their security will rest on some defense agreement with Britain and otherwise on the power balance in the Indian Ocean.

2. The Comoro Islands have been under French sovereignty since 1886; previously, from the year 1841, only the island of Mayotte was under French protection since its inhabitants invited the French to protect them against Grand Comore, the largest of the island group (the two other islands are Anjouan and Moheli).

The inhabitants of these islands are not very unlike those of Zanzibar; they are partly of Bantu and partly of Arab origin, the former outnumbering the latter. Due to the ethnic and economic stratification, several political parties have been vying for control since the islands received internal autonomy.[5]

In 1972 the "whites" and "greens" formed a coalition cabinet, which pressed for independence in agreement with France. The Party of Mayotte Island desired continued French presence on the islands. While the population of Mayotte is mainly Christian, the other three islands owe allegiance to the conservative traditions of Islam, the religion of their settler forebears of the tenth century. They all speak a Swahili dialect, which creates a linguistic kinship between them and the coastal people of East Africa.

The islands declared their independence in 1975; it seems probable that Paris will continue to protect the inhabitants of Mayotte from the dangers which might threaten them from the other islanders.

The Comoro Islands lie across the northern entrance to the Mozambique Channel and therefore may possess considerable strategic significance in case of a conflict which would involve the use of sea lanes along the eastern coast of Africa.

[5]There is a "white" party (*Rassemblement démocratic du peuple comorien*), a "green" party *(Union democratique comorienne),* a *Mouvemént mahorais* (centered on Mayotte Island, which earlier was called Mahore), and also a *Parti socialiste des Comores,* which is suspected to be the arm of the Comoran Liberation Movement, whose headquarters is in Dar es Salaam. Except for the Socialists, the parties represent occupational, communal, and ethnic interests.

3. Since 1946 Réunion has been a French *département*, that is, a constituent part of metropolitan France which elects representatives to the French Parliament. The island belongs, together with Mauritius and others, to the Mascarene chain of islands and is located about midway between Madagascar and Mauritius.

The inhabitants of Réunion are descendants of French settlers, with an admixture of African blood. Because of their geographic location and contacts with Mauritius, they are inclined to compare their status with that of the latter, a comparison unfavorable both economically and politically. Réunion's even lower living standards are maintained only with the financial support of Paris; Michel Debré, Prime Minister under de Gaulle, served for years as the deputy of Réunion, and many of the benefits enjoyed by the islanders were due to his good offices. Reunion is governed under the centralized French administrative system and looks with envious eyes toward Mauritius, which has profited from its British-type self-government and present-day independence. The police in Réunion are not indigenous, but are officers sent out from France.

The political parties of France are represented in Réunion; next to the Gaullists, the Communist Party is particularly strong, especially among the agricultural laborers. In Réunion there is little evidence of a desire for independence, although there is an organization for the "liberation of Réunion" operating outside the island and the United Nations Committee for Decolonization lists Réunion as one of the territories on which it wishes "to impose independence."

With the loss of Diego Suarez, the headquarters of the French Indian Ocean Command has been transferred to St. Denis, the capital of Réunion. Although its harbor is much less suitable for stationing warships, in comparison to the French Territory of Afars and Issas (Djibouti), Réunion is "safe" in the sense that it will remain French. Because of France's evident interest in continuing its presence in the Indian Ocean, it is likely that Paris will be rather reluctant to abandon this, the "most French" of its overseas possessions in that part of the world.

Mauritius

The checkered history of this island began with the Dutch settlers, who named it after their Prince Maurice of Nassau. In 1715 the French took over the abandoned island and named it Île de France. For France, in its quest for the domination of the Indian Ocean, this island served as the chief naval base, especially during the Napoleonic Wars. The British captured it in 1810, and their possession was confirmed by the Treaty of Paris of 1814. The former name was reintroduced; henceforth the island was called Mauritius.

During the more than 150 years of British rule, the economy and population of the island underwent important changes. Sugar production became the mainstay of its economy. After the liberation of the African slaves, indentured laborers were brought from India to work in the sugar fields.

Nearly 69 percent of the population are of Indian origin, divided between a Hindu majority and a Muslim minority; 29 percent are of mixed European (mostly French) and African origin. There is a vocal group of Franco-Mauritians and a small but wealthy Chinese colony. Ethnic harmony is by no means perfect: Muslim Indians complain of the domination of "high-caste" Hindus. There is a "New Left" that opposes the rather conservative leadership; its members' orientation is either pro-French or pro-Communist. More conservative Indians wish to promote rapprochement to India.

After 1947 limited self-government was introduced, followed by more complete internal autonomy in 1961. Finally, in March 1968 the island became independent while not only remaining in the British Commonwealth but also continuing to recognize the British sovereign as its head of state, represented by a governor general.

The Mauritian Legislative Assembly is dominated by the Labor Party and its partner in the governmental coalition, the Mauritian Social and Democratic Party. The leader of the former is Sir Seewoosagur Ramgoolam, the Prime Minister since independence, a powerful political figure whose ultimate departure from the scene is likely to create a succession crisis. Until the end of 1973, the leader of the coalition partner, Gaétan Duval, was the Foreign Minister; he resigned because of his outspoken Western orientation. His motto was "We are first Mauritians, then Africans, and lastly friends of the West."[6]

Sir Seewoosagur prefers a more cautious, nonaligned foreign policy, less outspoken in its friendliness toward the West. The island is geographically isolated, a weak state which cannot and should not have ambition to play an outstanding role in international politics. Mauritius wants to be "left alone" in the rivalries between superpowers and great powers. Therefore it would, for instance, make no sense to express opinion for or against the Diego Garcia plan of the United States. The government takes a rather pragmatic view concerning the Zone of Peace plan for the Indian Ocean. The plan is considered unrealistic until the two superpowers are ready to end their rivalries in these waters. Privately, Mauritian leaders would even go so far as to say that Americans and British are correct to counteract Soviet activities in this ocean, and from this point of view Diego Garcia is well justified.

Mauritians sense their loneliness in the vast ocean. Unlike the Malgasy, they say they welcome foreigners and welcome ships of any nationality, which they feel offer a break in their monotony and insular situation.

It is the political principle of the Mauritian government not to give any special privileges to any foreign power, except for the naval communication station maintained by the British. It is strongly denied that the Mauritians have ever considered giving naval facilities to the Soviet Union. The August 6, 1969 Agreement on Mutual Assistance and Cooperation in the Field of Marine Fisheries is said to be completely nonpolitical. This agreement allows Soviet fishing vessels to be serviced in the port of Port Louis and in return promises the delivery of ships for Mauritius to develop its marine fishery in the Indian Ocean.

Mauritius is the most orderly and most prosperous among the other islands in its vicinity—Réunion, Madagascar, and the Seychelles. At one time, before

[6]*Jeune Afrique,* (Paris) Feb. 23, 1970.

independence, schemes were conceived about a "Federation of the Mascarene Islands" which would include Madagascar (which does not belong to this group), in addition to the real Mascarenes, Réunion, Mauritius and its dependencies. But nowadays, rather strained relations with the Malagasy Republic, a certain estrangement from Réunion, and slight frictions with the Seychelles have made any such plan inoperative.

Mauritius claims Tromelin Island (near the northeast tip of Madagascar), which is now controlled by Tananarive. The Agalega Islands, a dependency of Mauritius (but nearer in distance to the Seychelles) are feared to be willing to join the Seychelles when the latter achieve independence.

Shortly before Mauritius obtained independence, the islands of the Chagos Archipelago (which include Diego Garcia) became administratively separated from it by Britain and included in the BIOT (British Indian Ocean Territory), a move which has never been recognized by independent Mauritius.

Contacts with the United Kingdom, the former colonial power, continue to be intimate; although the British maintain a low-key posture on the island, their influence is still felt. The French, who had embarked on a cultural offensive in their former dependency, still predominantly francophone, find communications and contacts easy and fruitful. In the past, the Mauritans enjoyed Commonwealth preferences, vital for their sugar exports; with the British entry into the European Economic Community, they undertook to obtain a maximum of preferential treatment in the European continental market as well, and are in this respect dependent on France's goodwill.

Because of its oceanic location, Mauritius is highly interested in the development of the law of the sea. Its greatest concern is the recognition of a continental shelf far beyond the principles established by the convention of 1958 (the right to explore and exploit natural resources of the seabed and its subsoil outside the territorial waters to the depth of 200 meters). Mauritius claims the surrounding seabed reaching out to the outer edge of the geomorphic shell irrespective of the depth; and it seeks recognition of this claim by other powers. Mauritius hopes to find oil in the areas surrounding its coasts and those of its dependencies, a bonanza which would solve the economic problems of this overpopulated island.

Mauritius also adheres to the archipelago concept, but not in such an exaggerated form as, for instance, Indonesia. The Mauritian government would consider it unrealistic to extend its territorial waters to and around Rodrigues Island, its most important dependency, some 200 miles to the east. Other dependencies of Mauritius include the Agalega Islands (more than 400 miles north) and the Cargados and Carajos groups (about 200 miles northeast). The Mauritian government proposed a concept of "archipelagic waters," which would secure certain rights to its country in the surrounding portions of the sea but would not essentially interfere with free navigation.

Mauritius, because of its insular character and location in the Indian Ocean, realizes more intensively than the contenental countries adjacent to this ocean that its security and future depend on the relations and the balance between the oceanic great powers, in particular the Soviet Union and the United States. It is unable to influence peaceful developments between these giants but tries to avoid giving rise to conflicts between them. The motto of Mauritius, inscribed in its coat of arms, is *Stella Clavisque Maris Indici* (Star and Key of the Indian Ocean). Its people can only hope that rival powers will not endeavor to take possession of this starry and luscious island, one of the historic-strategic keys to the Indian Ocean.

Selected Bibliography

Adloff, Virginia, and Adloff, Richard. *Madagascar. Political and Economic Conditions.* Stanford, Calif.: Stanford University Press, 1965.

Austin, Dennis. *Britain and South Africa.* London: Oxford University Press, 1966.

Barber, James. *Rhodesia. The Road to Rebellion.* London: Oxford University Press, 1967.

Barber, James. *South Africa's Foreign Policy, 1945-1970.* London: Oxford University Press, 1973.

Benedict, Burton. *Mauritius. Problems of a Plural Society.* New York: Praeger, 1965.

Bierman, (Admiral) H. H. *The Republic of South Africa and the Southern Hemisphere.* Potchefstroom: University Centre for International Politics, 1973.

Bowman, Larry W. *Politics in Rhodesia. White Power in an African State.* Cambridge, Mass.: Harvard University Press, 1973.

Carter, Gwendolen M. *The Politics of Inequality. South Africa since 1948.* 3d ed. New York: Praeger, 1962.

Feit, Edward. *South Africa. The Dynamics of the African National Congress.* New York: Oxford University Press, 1962.

Feit, Edward. *African Opposition in South Africa. The Failure of Passive Resistance.* Stanford, Calif.: Hoover Institution Press, 1967.

Grundy, Kenneth W. *Confrontation and Accommodation in Southern Africa.* Berkeley: University of California Press, 1973.

Heseltine, Nigel. *Madagascar.* New York: Praeger, 1971.

Ostheimer, John, ed. *The Politics of the Western Indian Ocean Islands.* New York: Praeger, 1975.

Potholm, Christian P., and Dale, Richard, eds. *Southern Africa in Perspective.* New York: The Free Press, 1972.

Rotberg, Robert I. *The Rise of Nationalism in Central Africa.* Cambridge, Mass.: Harvard University Press, 1965.

Spence, J. E. *The Strategic Significance of Southern Africa.* London: Royal United Service Institute, 1970.

Stevens, Richard P. *Lesotho, Botswana and Swaziland. The Former High Commission Territories is Southern Africa.* New York: Praeger, 1967.

Tanzanian High Commission, New Delhi. "Tanzania and the Indian Ocean." In *Indian Ocean Rivalry.* Edited by T. T. Poulose. New Delhi: Young Asia Publications, 1974.

Tordoff, William. *Government and Politics in Tanzania.* Nairobi: East African Publishing House, 1967.

Vandenbosch, Amry. *South Africa and the World. The Foreign Policy of Apartheid.* Lexington: University of Kentucky Press, 1970.

Wilson, N., and Thompson, L., eds. *The Oxford History of South Africa.* New York: Oxford University Press, 1969.

Chapter 9

The Strategic Triangle: U.S.A., U.S.S.R., and China

> *Military positions, fortified posts, by land or by sea,*
> *however strong or admirably situated, do not confer*
> *control by themselves alone.*
>
> Alfred T. Mahan, *The Interest of America*
> *in Sea Power,* 1893

> *Distant waters cannot fight fires.*
>
> Chinese proverb

The preceding surveys have demonstrated the potential for conflict among the local nations in all five corners of the Indian Ocean region. This potential for confrontation, political or military, varies from subregion to subregion; it is less acute in the southeast, more so in the Indian subcontinent, threatening around the Persian Gulf, virulent in the Horn of Africa, and open and pervasive in southern Africa.

Beginning in the early sixteenth century, European naval powers established footholds, trading posts, and eventually immense colonial empires in the area. The Chinese visited the ocean before the arrival of Europeans but abruptly withdrew. The Japanese made a short-lived attempt to control at least the eastern portion of the region. The European powers, after World War II, gradually gave up all or most of their territories in the region, although Britain and France still maintain a modest but notable colonial-naval presence. On the

171

other hand, the United States and the Soviet Union, newcomers on the scene, have appeared with their naval forces and imposed their political-diplomatic and economic weight on the relations of the local powers. China, though without a naval presence, exercises pressures on the developments in the area.

The interrelations and interactions between great power presence (really, superpower presence is meant) and the possible or probable conflicts between regional powers have been thus described in a United Nations report:

> The vast majority of the littoral and hinterland States of the Indian Ocean are still developing socially, economically and politically. During this period of development there is, unfortunately, a considerable potential for local conflicts. But the involvement of the great Powers in a future local conflict would be neither in the real long-term interests of the great Powers nor in those of the littoral and hinterland States. Any attempt to derive advantage from this unstable situation by one great Power will inevitably lead to a countermove by the other great Power. Moreover, any attempt by one of the littoral or hinterland States to obtain undue support from one of the great Powers will probably in turn lead to some other littoral or hinterland State seeking countervailing support from the other great Power.[1]

This statement raises a number of questions which require answers and relates to the crucial problems inherent in the political status of the Indian Ocean region: (1) How far does the national interest of superpowers and other great powers demand their presence in the area? (2) Does their simultaneous presence necessarily lead to rivalry between them—a rivalry which is a potential source of danger to peace? (3) Would the superpower or other great power presence necessarily lead to interference in conflicts between local powers? Would such an interference be conducive to the stability or instability of the region?

These questions can only be answered empirically and in the context of the broader relations between the nonregional powers and the world's past experience of their general interests and foreign policy goals.

The United States, the Soviet Union, and China possess no territorial interests to protect in the area. Their worldwide interests partly collide and partly coincide, a situation which has rightly been considered "triangular." On the other hand, the naval-military and political presence of Britain, France, and up to 1974, Portugal was mainly due to their residual territorial interests in the area. The relatively modest power potentials of Britain and France also reduce their capacity to influence the relations of the local powers as well as the possibility of their interfering in local conflicts. Japan, an economic but not military superpower, has vital navigational and commercial interests in the Indian Ocean; its weight is thus felt in these matters.

---

[1] From the report of three experts, appointed by the Secretary-General of the United Nations, to the Ad Hoc Committee on the Indian Ocean, dated May 3, 1974 (A/AC.159/1).

American Presence

The Indian Ocean is the most remote major sea from the United States; its center is located on the antipode of the globe's Northern Hemisphere as seen from the center of the United States. It has been pointed out that Trincomalee, the historic naval strongpoint on the east coast of Ceylon, is 11,500 miles distant from New York in the easterly direction and also 11,500 miles distant from San Francisco in the westerly direction.[2] On American world maps the United States is placed in the center and the Indian Ocean is divided at both ends of the map, thus providing a distorted perspective of its expanse and shape.

American naval presence[3] in the region was prompted by the gradual erosion of British supremacy. The primary and most visible interest lay with oil investments in the Persian Gulf area. This interest was expressed by the establishment in 1948 of a modest Middle East Task Force (MIDEASTFOR), consisting of a small flagship—a converted seaplane tender—and two destroyers assigned on a rotational basis from the Atlantic Fleet, and based at the British naval station on Bahrain Island. On the Arabian mainland, with the consent of Saudi Arabia, the United States maintained a Military Airlift Command base at Dhahran Airfield.

During the 1950s, in addition to economic aid provided to many countries in the area, Washington sent military advisory and training missions to Ethiopia, Iran, and Saudi Arabia. Bilateral defense agreements were concluded with Iran in 1950 and with Pakistan in 1954, connected with the first's membership in the Baghdad Pact (later to become CENTO) and the second's participation in SEATO.

In 1968 the British government intimated its withdrawal from east of Suez, terminated its security arrangements with Kuwait, began to liquidate its ties with other Persian Gulf states, and gave independence to Mauritius (other British possessions in Southeast Asia and East Africa had already attained independent statehood). In view of the dangers and instabilities which prevailed in the Indian Ocean region, Washington also began considering its "longer-term strategic requirements" in the area.[4] In 1968 the U.S. Joint Chiefs of Staff recommended the setting up of a communication facility to be maintained jointly with the British on the island of Diego Garcia in the Chagos Archipelago. American requirements coincided with those of the British, who also wished to secure

[2]Howard Wriggins, "United States Interests in the Indian Ocean. An Introductory Essay," Appendix to United States, House of Representatives, *The Indian Ocean. Political and Strategic Future,* hearings before the Subcommittee on National Security Policy and Scientific Developments of the Committee on Foreign Affairs, U.S. House of Representatives, 92d Cong., 1st sess., July 20-28, 1971 (Washington, D.C., 1971), p. 206.

[3]The Indian Ocean, however, was not an unknown sea to American shippers; in the eighteenth century New Bedford whalers frequented Mauritius as a port of call, and in the nineteenth century clipper ships crossed the Indian Ocean on their way to China.

[4]Statement by Ronald I. Spiers of the U.S. Department of State, in *The Indian Ocean,* hearings, p. 164.

communications and transit rights across the Indian Ocean. By 1965 the administratively separated and sparsely populated groups of atolls, which until then had fallen under the administrations of Mauritius and the Seychelles, were formed into the British Indian Ocean Territory (BIOT). The Chagos Archipelago is one group belonging to BIOT.[5]

The geostrategic location of Diego Garcia is felicitous: it lies at the apex of an isosceles triangle, the base of which extends from Australia to South Africa. Airplanes placed on this island could protect tanker lanes from the Persian Gulf to the Cape and other shipping routes between the Arabian Sea and the Strait of Malacca. For these reasons, a plan of strengthening the capabilities of this station was submitted to the Congress of the United States: to deepen the harbor, to extend the runway to 12,000 feet so that it could handle reconnaissance aircraft and aerial tanker planes and be able to support a carrier task force operating in the Indian Ocean.

After 1942 the United States operated a communication station near Asmara in Ethiopia (Eritrea), known as Kagnew station. Subsequently, it developed into a relay and satellite-tracking facility which was also used for monitoring purposes. This station started to be phased out as a military facility in 1974 and ultimately will also be discontinued as a communication station for civilian use.

In 1967 the United States, in agreement with the Australian government, established a powerful very-low-frequency communication station at Learmonth, on Exmouth Gulf, south of North West Cape. The station is able to communicate with submerged submarines. In January 1974 Washington agreed to share the control of this facility with Canberra.

The United States also shared with Australia the satellite control and monitoring facility at Pine Gap (near Alice Springs in the Northern Territory of Australia) and also maintained a satellite control station at Nurrungar (near Woomera in South Australia). Yet another tracking facility exists on Mahé Island of the British-administered Seychelles group.

When London gave up its naval base at Jufair (in the harbor of Manama, the capital of Bahrain), the United States signed an agreement with the Bahraini government in December 1971 which enabled it to continue the existing facility as a homing port for MIDEASTFOR. In October 1973, under the pressures prompted by the Arab-Israeli hostilities, Bahrain denounced the agreement but subsequently consented to the continued use of the base.[6]

The units of MIDEASTFOR often participate with other units of the United States Navy and with allied naval ships in antisubmarine and other fleet exercises

---

[5]The right to use Diego Garcia (and possibly other islands of the BIOT) for U.S. defense purposes originally relied on an exchange of notes between the United Kingdom and the United States of Dec. 30, 1966 (U.K. Treaty Series No. 15/1967/Cmnd 3231, London, H.M. Stationery Office).

[6]*New York Times,* Oct. 4, 1974.

in the Indian Ocean.[7] Apart from these routine exercises and courtesy visits by American warships in Indian Ocean ports, some entries into the ocean have been occasioned by certain crisis situations. In December 1971, at the time of the Indian-Pakistani war, the aircraft carrier *Enterprise,* heading a task force which included the amphibious assault ship *Tripoli,* a battalion of 800 Marines, and other smaller units, entered the Bay of Bengal; it left the Indian Ocean in January 1972. In October 1973, at the time of the Arab-Israeli war, the aircraft carrier *Hancock,* escorted by four destroyers, was dispatched into the western section of the Indian Ocean; when the *Hancock* was withdrawn in December, it was replaced by the carrier *Oriskany.* In the spring of 1974, the aircraft carrier *Kitty Hawk* was for some time on station in the Indian Ocean.

Calculating the American naval presence in the Indian Ocean in "ship-days" (in number of days individual ships have spent in that sea), United States surface combat ships accumulated 872 ship-days in 1970, 858 in 1971, 990 in 1972, and 1,410 in 1973 (the year of the Arab-Israeli war).[8]

While there is no official information concerning the deployment of American nuclear ballistic missile-firing submarines (Polaris A3 and later Poseidon missile submarines), their presence has been assumed or accepted as real by many commentators.[9] This presence has also been listed as one or even the principal reason for the entry and stationing of units of the Soviet Navy in these waters.

Soviet Presence

While earlier American interest in the Indian Ocean region was only commercial, Tsarist interest was linked with Russian penetration into Central Asia and conflicts with Britain over influence in the Middle East and the border areas between India and Russian Asia, especially in Iran, Afghanistan, and Tibet. Russia's often invoked desire for "warm-water ports" was unlikely to be aimed toward the distant shores of the Indian Ocean, except the Persian Gulf, which, in

[7]In November 1974 warships of the United States (including the 60,000-ton carrier *Constellation*), Britain, Iran, Pakistan, and Turkey participated in the (so far) largest naval exercise in the Indian Ocean. The exercise bore the name "Midlink 74" and was conducted in the Arabian Sea. *New York Times,* Nov. 21, 1974.

[8]Report of three experts, dated July 5, 1974, to the Secretary-General of the United Nations, pursuant to the Declaration of the Indian Ocean as a Zone of Peace (A/AC.159/1/ Rev. 1).

[9]See, among others, Geoffrey Jukes, *The Indian Ocean in Soviet Naval Policy* (London, 1972), pp. 4-12; Oles M. Smolansky, "Soviet Entry into the Indian Ocean. An Analysis," in *The Indian Ocean,* ed. A. J. Cottrell and R. M. Burrell (New York, 1972), pp. 337-355; report of three experts, dated May 3, 1974, to the UN Secretary-General (A/AC.159/1), pp. 6-7 (omitted in the revised report).

case of a total collapse of the Ottoman Empire, might have been within the reach of a Russian advance.[10]

After the Bolshevik take-over, Lenin was interested in carrying revolution into colonial Asia, but the question of whether the revolutionary struggle for liberation from the colonial yoke was to be made a "one-stage" operation by introducing a Communist system directly or a "two-stage" operation by adopting first a national-bourgeois system could never be decided. Stalin came to believe that the leaders of the independence movements, such as Gandhi, simply were capitalist stooges. When the countries around the Indian Ocean gradually obtained their independence, Moscow continued to consider them as still dependent on their former colonial masters for some time. It was the task of Khrushchev to accept nonalignment as a foreign policy compatible with the aims of the socialist world.[11]

After 1954 Moscow became more closely interested in some countries around the Indian Ocean, particularly those of the Indian subcontinent and Indonesia. The "special tie" between the Soviet Union and India was first demonstrated when Khrushchev and Bulganin visited India in 1955. Soviet military and economic aid began to flow to this country and also to others in the region, often competing with the assistance the United States was abundantly providing. But Soviet relations with India and other regional states had their high and low points during the following years; as the Sino-Soviet rivalry grew in intensity, Chinese competition and attempts to establish diplomatic-political footholds rendered Moscow's status more difficult.

Whether the announcement by the British government of the decision to liquidate its positions in the area east of Suez prompted the Soviet move to send naval units into the Indian Ocean must remain moot. Whether the deployment or potential deployment of American Polaris-type submarines has been the principal motivation must equally remain doubtful.[12]

However, it may be assumed that the arrival of Soviet warships in the Indian Ocean was coincident with the stage of growth which the Soviet Navy reached in the mid-sixties. After Stalin's death (he had ordered the construction of large "cruisers" of the *Stalingrad* class), a much better balanced building program was adopted, first with an emphasis on smaller surface ships and submarines. By the

---

[10]During the German-Soviet negotiations in November 1940, the German draft of a secret protocol offered to recognize Soviet aspirations "south of the national territory of the Soviet Union in the direction of the Indian Ocean," and the Soviet counterdraft spoke of "the area south of Batum and Baku in the general direction of the Persian Gulf," which Moscow asked to be recognized as the center of its territorial aspirations in Asia. See Ferenc A. Váli, *The Turkish Straits and NATO* (Stanford, Calif., 1972), pp. 225 and 228.

[11]Geoffrey Jukes, *The Soviet Union in Asia* (Berkeley, Calif.: 1973), pp. 7-17.

[12]Geoffrey Jukes connects the dispatch of Soviet naval units into the Indian Ocean with the emergence of U.S. ballistic fleet submarines and, in particular, with the increases in range and payload of the successive versions of the Polaris missiles; *The Indian Ocean in Soviet Naval Policy*, p. 5. On the other hand, T. B. Millar notes the "coincidence" of the British announcement with the increased Soviet interest and involvement in the Indian Ocean; *Soviet Policies in the Indian Ocean Area,* Canberra Papers on Strategy and Defence, No. 7 (Canberra, 1970), p. 1.

late 1950s the strength of the Soviet Navy surpassed that of the United Kingdom; it became the second largest navy after that of the United States.

In the later 1950s and early 1960s the Soviet leaders smarted under the evident inferiority of their navy in comparison with that of the United States. The American landing in Lebanon in 1958 and the humiliation suffered in the Cuban missile crisis in 1962 brought home to them the shortcomings of their oceanic capabilities. While refraining from the construction of aircraft carriers (that would have slowed down the building of smaller craft), they concentrated on guided missile-carrying cruisers, frigates, and destroyers and on nuclear-powered missile submarines.[13] By the mid-1960s the Soviet Navy evidently possessed the strength to venture out in strength beyond the seas surrounding Soviet or Soviet-controlled areas: the Arctic waters and the eastern North Atlantic, the Baltic, the Black Sea, and the western Pacific. Since 1964 Moscow has maintained naval units in the Mediterranean in ever-increasing numbers, especially during the 1967 and 1973 Arab-Israeli hostilities.

The first ostentatious appearance of Soviet warships in the Indian Ocean occurred in the spring of 1968. Units of the Soviet Pacific Fleet, a *Sverdlov*-class cruiser and two guided-missile destroyers, visited India; the cruiser and one destroyer called on ports in Somalia, in the Persian Gulf, and Pakistan before returning to Vladivostok.

In the following years, the deployment of Soviet naval vessels was systematically continued; the average strength of the squadrons consisted of one cruiser and two destroyers with a number of supply ships. But at the time of the Bangladesh War (early 1972) their number increased to thirteen combat surface ships. In the spring of 1974 one cruiser, three destroyers, and two minesweepers sailed in the Indian Ocean. While the number of these warships has not grown considerably, the later arrivals mustered more modern types (such as the *Kynda*-class cruisers armed with eight Shaddock surface-to-surface missiles). In mid-1974 the Black Sea-based Soviet helicopter carrier *Leningrad* entered the Indian Ocean from around the Cape of Good Hope.

It should be remembered that long before the regular presence of Soviet warships in the Indian Ocean, these waters had been visited by large numbers of Soviet fishing vessels and some oceanographic craft. Soviet merchant ships crossed the ocean in considerable numbers; during the Vietnam War supply vessels sailed through the Suez Canal and, after the closure of the canal in 1967, around Africa to reach Hanoi.

The Soviet warships call on many ports of the region, and while they frequent certain countries, they prefer to omit others; but no direct political inferences necessarily need be drawn from the geographic distribution of these visits.[14]

[13]For details see Norman Polmar, *Soviet Naval Power. Challenge for the 1970's* (New York, 1972), pp. 27-43.

[14]The most frequent visits have been made to Somali ports (Berbera, Mogadishu, and Kismayu) but there have been visits also to Indian, Red Sea, and Persian Gulf harbors. For statistics of these visits, see Australian Federal Parliament, Joint Committee on Foreign Affairs, *Report on the Indian Ocean Region* (Canberra, 1972), Appendix L.

There is no evidence that the Soviet Union possesses an official (overt) treaty which secures any sovereign or leased naval or air base in the Indian Ocean area. From the auxiliary craft accompanying the Soviet warships, it may be inferred that these units rely to some considerable measure on floating support. But it also appears well substantiated that these warships enjoy extended shore-related support in some ports.

The question of whether the Soviet Union maintains "bases" in the Indian Ocean area has been raised on many occasions and answered in the affirmative or negative manner.[15] The ports which Soviet warships frequently entered, as Vishakapatnam (India), Hodeida (North Yemen), Aden (South Yemen), Berbera and Mogadishu (Somalia), Umm Qasr (Iraq), and Chittagong (Bangladesh), were often listed as "Soviet bases." Singapore and Mauritius, where Soviet ships occasionally called for minor repairs or bunkering, were also mentioned, although in these cases only facilities available were used. Naturally, much of the controversy depends on the definition of a "base" or "naval base."[16]

Even if the Soviet Union does not maintain any sovereign or treaty-secured naval or air base, it appears that Moscow was able to make solid arrangements with some friendly powers for the use of port facilities in certain harbors. It appears that the port where the most extensive facilities are offered is Berbera. In this Somali town a restricted port area is available to the Soviet Navy, with storehouses, barracks, a repair ship, and housing for Soviet military dependents.[17]

Another "Soviet base," a port with extended facilities, is Umm Qasr at the head of the Persian Gulf in Iraqi territory. This port was constructed with Soviet assistance, partly for commercial reasons (the Soviet-exploited Rumaila oil fields lie in the hinterland of Umm Qasr) and partly for the use of the Soviet Navy. However, the location of this "base" is such that it can be reached only through the narrow Khor Abdullah Channel, which is situated between Iraqi territory and the Kuwaiti islands of Bubayan and Warba. It is much too exposed and vulnerable for access by larger Soviet naval vessels unless Iraq manages to annex the two Kuwaiti islands.

There is no hard evidence that in other ports listed as "bases" the Soviet warships enjoy particular privileges (restricted quayage, storage facilities, buildings for housing of crews, etc.) not available for other visiting warships. If

[15]For instance, President Ford, in his press conference on Aug. 28, 1974, mentioned that the "Soviet Union already has three major naval operating bases in the Indian Ocean." Subsequently, these three bases were identified as being in Aden (South Yemen), Berbera (Somalia), and Umm Qasr (Iraq). The Soviet News Agency (TASS) promptly denied the existence of any Soviet bases in the Indian Ocean. *New York Times,* Aug. 29 and Sept. 1, 1974.

[16]See Chapt. 3, pp. 56-59.

[17]See UN report of three experts (revised), dated July 11, 1974, p. 7. On June 10, 1975, Secretary of Defense James R. Schlesinger, showed aerial reconnaissance photographs to the Senate Armed Services Committee to prove that the Soviet Union established a missile storage facility, a naval communication site, and other defense constructions at Berbera; *New York Times,* June 11, 1975.

they can obtain certain special advantages, these are due to the particular activity which Soviet technicians perform in the area: Vishakapatnam, the Indian naval base, is the receiving port for naval vessels delivered by the Soviet Union, and therefore Soviet training crews are often present; in Chittagong Harbor Soviet dredges cleared some wrecked hulks, remainders of the Bangladesh War, and lingered in the area for over one year. The report according to which Socotra Island has been turned into a Soviet air base has proved incorrect.[18] But there are fleet anchorages near Socotra and around the Chagos Archipelago which are used by Soviet warships, as well as permanent mooring buoys laid by Soviet vessels off the Seychelles Islands and Mauritius.[19]

If we measure the Soviet naval presence according to ship-days spent in the Indian Ocean, we find that their numbers are considerably higher than those the Americans. In 1970 the ship-days numbered 1,670; in 1971, 1,480; in 1972, 2,387; and in 1973, 2,487. In these years the average ship-days spent in that ocean numbered 2,006 for the warships of the Soviet Union, and only 1,032 for those of the United States—that is, about half as many for the Americans as for the Soviets. Other standards of measurement (size of ships, armaments, or port visits) would lead to a similar showing, namely, that the Soviet naval presence largely outstripped that of the United States. This raises the question of the meaning and nature of the superpowers' presence in the Indian Ocean—of what circumstances may explain or justify their entry into these waters. In other words, it appears necessary to analyze their political-military aims and objectives in the region.

Soviet Interest

The Soviet move into the Indian Ocean is evidently a multipurpose operation which cannot be separated from the broader political objectives of the Soviet state. The navy's arrival was preceded by gestures and actions directed toward that region which cannot be described here in detail. There were several landmarks of these political moves: the support for India at the time of the Sino-Indian border war in 1962; the Soviet memorandum of December 7, 1964, proposing a "nuclear-free zone" in the Indian Ocean area; Soviet mediation between Pakistan and India to end the war of 1965; the proposal by Brezhnev in 1969 (repeated several times since) for the conclusion of an Asian collective security pact (interpreted as directed against China); the Soviet-Indian Treaty of Peace, Friendship, and Cooperation of 1971, and the ensuing assistance by Moscow in the Bangladesh crisis.

In the context of Moscow's evident interest in the region, it appears almost natural that the successive "out-of-area" deployments of the growing Soviet

---

[18]The South Yemen government invited a correspondent of *The Times* (London) to visit the island; he reported having seen no special activities or suitable port facilities. *The Times,* Jan. 9, 1971.

[19]UN report by the three experts (revised), July 11, 1974, p. 8.

Navy should reach the Indian Ocean. Still, taking this naval entry separately, there has been much speculation as to the objectives of such a move, whereby purely military objectives may be distinguished—artificially, of course—from more political goals.

1. Among the military objectives, much prominence has been given to the Soviet strategic concern to detect and oppose in the waters of the Indian Ocean nuclear strike forces of the United States (submarines equipped with Polaris or Poseidon missiles, attack carriers) which, from positions in the northwestern points of the ocean, could reach targets in Soviet Central Asia and the Urals.[20] It should, however, be remembered that Washington never admitted such a deployment and that Moscow has never directly accused the former of posing such a threat.[21]

2. Another reason for the Soviet naval presence may be the geographic necessity to maintain the communication line between the European and the East Asian parts of the Soviet Union. The Soviet Navy is divided into four fleet areas: the Arctic, the Baltic, the Black Sea, and the Pacific areas. Assured connection between the three European fleets and the Pacific Fleet can only be maintained through the Indian Ocean.[22] Larger Soviet warships are not constructed in the Vladivostok shipyards; they have to be sent to the Far East. It is only natural that Moscow wishes to familiarize its crews with the sea and its harbors where many of its warships have to pass to reach their permanent or temporary stations in the Far East.

3. Another reason for Soviet naval presence in the Indian Ocean—a reason often adduced by major naval powers—is the protection of Soviet merchant-shipping and fishing fleets.[23] The Soviet merchant marine witnessed a sensational increase in the last twenty-five years: from 2 million gross tons in 1948 to over 16 million in 1973. Soviet merchant ships in the Indian Ocean are nu-

[20]Jukes, *The Indian Ocean in Soviet Naval Policy*, pp. 5-12; Smolansky, pp. 338-346.

[21]See James M. McConnell, *The Soviet Navy in the Indian Ocean* (Arlington, Va., 1971), pp. 1-2.

[22]"In the first place, the Soviet Navy uses the waters of the ocean's international zone, which is open to the ships of any country in accordance with international law. These sea communications are very important to the Soviet Union since they represent the only non-freezing sea-route linking Soviet ports in the Black and Azov seas with Soviet ports in the Far East. Soviet naval ships in the Indian Ocean have no permanent bases there; for purposes of refuelling, taking on fresh water and foodstuffs, they use the ports of the Indian Ocean states in accordance with the standards of international law. Moreover, most important of all, unlike the naval ships of the United States and other imperialist countries, they do not engage in shows of force and blackmail with respect to the states of the region." V. Kudryavtsev, "The Indian Ocean in the Plans of Imperialism," *International Affairs* (Moscow), November 1974, p. 117.

[23]During the Cuban missile crisis in 1962, Moscow felt unable to protect its merchant vessels en route to Cuba with surface warships (only submarines were in the neighborhood).

merous but not as numerous as ships of many other nations in the area.[24] Soviet trawlers visit many parts of the Indian Ocean but in lesser numbers than in the Atlantic or Pacific.

4. Soviet warships in the Indian Ocean have been suspected of being there in potential readiness to interdict—in the eventuality of an armed conflict—enemy shipping, especially that transporting oil from the Persian Gulf to Europe, the United States, or Japan. The narrows through which such shipping has to pass, such as the Hormuz and Bab el Mandeb Straits, or the maritime corner around the Cape of Good Hope, have been mentioned as "choke-points" for such operations.[25] Such an interference in the freedom of navigation would be a cause of—perhaps even global—hostilities and unlikely unless as part of a general military confrontation. Even so, for lack of air support, the Soviet Indian Ocean naval forces are hardly able to implement such a blockade so distant from their bases of strength. Should oil shipments or other trade with Europe, Japan, or the United States be intercepted, this could be effected by Soviet naval and air forces in more convenient places than those mentioned above—for instance, in the Mediterranean for shipping passing the Suez Canal or in the northwest Atlantic.

5. Should the Soviet squadron in the Indian Ocean participate in some action, it is more likely that such a move would be carried out in support of a "national liberation movement" or in support of one of the friendly littoral powers in order to protect it against foreign aggression. This is a possibility which cannot be totally excluded, but it might take place only when essential Soviet interests were at stake and only when Moscow could be certain that no American counteraction was to be expected. Probably, any such initiative will remain a "naval demonstration" only, a part of "gunboat diplomacy," which belongs rather to the area of political use of the navy than to the strictly military activity of the fleet.

The following possibilities seem to exist for the nonmilitary use of the Soviet Navy in the Indian Ocean:

1. The Soviet Union is seeking more recognition as a global power; it wishes to obtain at least "parity" with the United States in fields beyond the nuclear arms race. Having attained the capability of maintaining warships outside its coastal waters and adjoining seas, Moscow wishes to have its presence felt in the

---

[24]The traditional shipping nation of the Indian Ocean is Britain; 625 of its vessels of all categories sailed this ocean in 1971, whereas the Soviet flag was flown from only 121. Japanese, Greek, Norwegian, Indian, Liberian, Panamanian, and West German ships were there in higher numbers than Soviet. See Henri Labrousse, *Le golfe et le canal* (Paris, 1973), pp. 149-151.

[25]Such fears have been expressed by the British government and members of the European Community. See Anders C. Sjaastad, "The Indian Ocean and the Soviet Navy," *Norsk Militaert Tidskrift* (Oslo), October 1971 (as translated in *Congressional Record*, Mar. 30, 1972, p. E3145).

seven seas. In this respect, the Indian Ocean could not remain an exception; on the contrary, in terms of political importance, it may surpass the western Atlantic or the eastern Pacific.

To "show the flag" has been a time-honored device to increase influence and prestige; the Kaiser's Germany, trying to compete with the British global naval power, resorted to the same political stratagem before World War I. To demonstrate its naval strength in a manner consistent with international law and established practices, the Soviet Union undertook to advertise its superpower status by a naval presence in waters which, prior to the mid-sixties, did not see Soviet naval vessels. This "flag showing" is one objective, and certainly not the least important, of the entry of Soviet warships into the Indian Ocean.

2. Connected with the above purpose but still to be distinguished are the "goodwill" visits performed by the Soviet naval units since 1968 to Indian Ocean ports. In no other sea (except the Mediterranean) have Soviet port calls been so frequent since then as on the littoral of the Indian Ocean. They are "an important instrument of Soviet policy."[26] They can be made—as an expression of diplomatic courtesy—not only to uncommitted countries but also to allies of the Western powers without impinging on their political status. They may be interpreted as a symbolic gesture to provide help if needed or as a warning against provoking the wrath of Moscow. Goodwill visits thus provide tangible evidence of Soviet interest and help Soviet diplomacy on its endeavors vis-á-vis the host country. For countries which in one or another respect wish to rely on Soviet assistance—political, military, or economic—the visits of Soviet warships are considered to be a guarantee of the determination of Moscow to abide by its commitments.

3. Some writers have suspected the Soviet of aiming to replace Britain as the "dominant external power" in all or certain parts of the Indian Ocean.[27] However, such an objective seems hardly in the mind of Moscow's policy makers. As pointed out earlier, British power depended on the territorial sovereignty which London possessed in many countries around the Indian Ocean, including primarily its sovereignty over the area of the Indian subcontinent. Any influence which Moscow might have ambition to exercise cannot rest on such an exclusive and absolute a prerogative as the United Kingdom held—and still holds, in a diminutive measure—over some islands of the Indian Ocean.

4. Among the many reasons and motivations for the Soviet interest and presence in the Indian Ocean, the containment of China appears highly plausible. Some countries of the region, especially India, dread China. The Soviet naval presence serves as a political sedative to assure these countries of Moscow's

[26]McConnell, p. 9.

[27]Millar, p. 20; G. W. Wheeler, "The Indian Ocean Area. Soviet Aims and Interests," in *Collected Papers of the Study Conference on the Indian Ocean in International Politics* (Southampton [England], 1973), p. 71.

countervailing strength.[28] On the other hand, in many other countries of the region Moscow resents their flirtations with Peking. There is an often overt rivalry for influence between these two "Asian" powers, a rivalry in which the fact that Russians are considered Europeans proves to be an obstacle for easy and friendly rapport. Although Chinese economic and military aid is small compared to that which Moscow can and does provide, Chinese negotiators, advisers, or trainers are often preferred to those of the Soviet Union. But China is unable to muster a naval presence in the Indian Ocean; it cannot match the demonstrative effect of Soviet warships in the harbors of the region.

Most of the above-listed Soviet objectives for maintaining a naval presence in the Indian Ocean are a correct assessment of individual considerations. But it is to be suggested that, aside and above these military and political reasons, a broader stategic motivation is the main determinant.

Soviet descent—political, diplomatic, and also naval—into the Indian Ocean region is basically motivated by geopolitical considerations which, not unlike the imperial German approach to *Weltpolitik,* dominates Soviet strategic thinking.

By way of analogy, the British approach to the European continent of the eighteenth and nineteenth centuries may be remembered. Britain confronted the European continent and, alternatively, had to fight the great powers which sought predominance—Spain, France, Russia, and Germany. At the beginning of the eighteenth century, Britain established its naval presence and bases in the Mediterranean (Gibraltar, Malta, and, for half a century, Minorca are good examples) so that it could better face any of these opponents. It is important to note that this took place long before the construction of the Suez Canal which opened up the route to India via the Mediterranean.

Viewing it from England, the Mediterranean was Europe's backyard. Strategically, it was the "soft underbelly" of Europe long before Churchill coined this expression in relation to the Axis powers. By dominating the Mediterranean and being able to threaten its coastal countries, Britain outflanked Europe and was able to put pressure (diplomatic and military) from behind its potential enemies on the continent—an elementary strategic move.

This micro-European strategy is now being duplicated on a macro-Asian scale—by the Soviet Union—and is being applied to the Indian Ocean. The U.S.S.R. controls more than one-third of Asia and faces the rest of this giant continent along its southern border. It is an instinctive, if not preconceived, strategy to use the Indian Ocean area to outflank any potential Asian opponent by confronting the "soft underbelly" of Asia simultaneously from the north and from the south. The Soviet Union claims to be a "Mediterranean Power"; by the

---

[28]This is to be distinguished from the direct military assistance which Moscow could provide for an Asian country endangered by China. In India it is expected that the Soviet Union will, in case of a Chinese threat, place pressure on that country along the Sino-Soviet border rather than by its naval power in the Indian Ocean.

same token it could also claim to be an Indian Ocean power, "directly interested in insuring the security of its southern borders."[29]

Although the Soviet Union is separated from the countries of South Asia by gigantic mountain chains, the distances—as the crow flies—from Soviet territory to the Indian Ocean are relatively short: from the northern shore of the Arabian Sea, 750 miles, and from the northwest tip of the Persian Gulf, only 550 miles to the Soviet border. The broad strategic requirements of Moscow to have a naval force in the Indian Ocean, together with more specific political-military objectives, such as to undercut Chinese penetration and to oppose, if needed, American missile threats, may provide ample explanation for the Soviet presence. It may also be assumed that only political considerations, the distances involved, the limited number of vessels available for this purpose, and the geographic impediments to reach the area have so far prevented Moscow from maintaining an even larger force in those waters.

American Interest

A modest American naval presence preceded the Soviet appearance in the Indian Ocean. The Soviet presence was, however, no response to United States presence; nor can the Diego Garcia base or periodic naval visits in strength by American warships be considered to be a direct riposte to Soviet activities in the area. Naturally, political developments around the periphery of this ocean influenced Washington's short- and long-range decision making in regard to the region, but the Soviet presence, in itself, was hardly the trigger which induced this policy. For the United States the Indian Ocean region, generally speaking, is not one of the areas closely associated with its vital interests. As expressed by a spokesman of the Department of State, "The Indian Ocean area, unlike Europe and Asia, is one which has been only on the margins of United States attention. Never considered of great importance to the central balance of power, it has been on the edges of great power rivalry."[30]

Nevertheless, the elements which stimulated limited American interest in the region are as complex as those which stimulated the Soviets. They may be thus described:

[29] In an evidently Kremlin-inspired article, *Pravda* wrote on Nov. 27, 1968, "Soviet ships entered the [Mediterranean] sea on the strength of the U.S.S.R.'s sovereign right to make free use of the open sea. . . . As a Black Sea, and in this sense, a Mediterranean Power, it is closely connected with all problems involving the interests of the peoples of this area of Europe, Africa, and Asia. It is directly interested in insuring the security of its southern borders." (As reported by the *New York Times*, Nov. 28, 1968.)

[30] Statement by Ronald I. Spiers, Director of the Bureau of Politico-Military Affairs, Department of State, before the House of Representatives Subcommittee on National Security Policy and Scientific Developments of the Committee on Foreign Affairs; see United States, House of Representatives, *The Indian Ocean*, hearings, p. 162.

1. The United States feels that it has an interest in the stability and economic development of the countries in the region. It believes that instability, conflicts between regional Powers, and a major change in the local balance of power would serve the interests of the Soviet Union or China and therefore would tilt the world military balance in its disfavor. In other words, Washington considers that it is, generally speaking, in its interest to maintain the status quo; of course, a change of the status quo which would favor allies or friends of the United States would not be unwelcome.

2. In the decades following World War II, the United States has provided billions of dollars in economic and military assistance to countries of the region. Apart from this political-military "investment," the United States economy has over $10 billion of commercial investments in the area, including about $3.5 billion in oil. Exports to and imports from this area each amount to over $3 billion. While the United States imports only about 10 percent of its oil requirements from the Persian Gulf, Western Europe imports over 60 percent of its oil and Japan nearly 90 percent of its oil from the Gulf. Naturally, Washington cannot disregard this vital interest of its allies.

3. The United States has a historic interest in the maintenance of the freedom of the seas, the freedom to keep open for navigation not only the high seas but also international straits. The peculiar character of the Indian Ocean, with its funnel-shaped entry areas and choke-points, demands special attention in this respect. While passage through the Indian Ocean is less vital to the United States than to Europeans, Japanese, or Australians, it should be remembered that 20 percent of world shipping takes place in the Indian Ocean.

4. For strictly strategic reasons, the northern parts of the Indian Ocean may be important to the United States as launching areas for its ballistic missiles. If, as a result of the Soviet-American nuclear arms agreements, the relative strength of United States submarine-based missiles is to be increased, it is most likely that their partial deployment in the Indian Ocean will be considered inevitable.

There is no doubt that the Indian Ocean has a low-priority interest if compared with the Atlantic and Pacific Oceans or the Mediterranean Sea.[31] If we could define the United States interest on a scale from 0 to 10, the Indian Ocean would lie in the 2-3 interest range, while the Mediterranean would be in the 7-8 and the North Atlantic and eastern Pacific in the 8-9 range.[32] As a result of the Vietnam War and the so-called Nixon Doctrine, Washington has officially lowered its ranking of interest in Asia and, consequently, in the Indian Ocean as well. But the western Pacific, East Asia, and even Southeast Asia must still rank higher than the Indian Ocean, in general.

Under the Nixon Doctrine, which was announced in Guam in the summer of 1969, the conventional defense in the Asian theater is the responsibility of the

[31] See Howard Wriggins, "U.S. Interests in the Indian Ocean," in *The Indian Ocean*, ed. A. J. Cottrell and R. M. Burrell (New York, 1972), pp. 360-362.

[32] On the scale of Soviet interest, the Indian Ocean would rank higher than on the American, possibly 5-6.

country directly concerned, with the United States assisting its allies where "United States interests are involved." Insurgencies are best handled by the threatened governments by means of police, paramilitary action, and economic and social reforms. "New commitments by the United States will be viewed in the light of careful assessment of U.S. national interests, specific threats to those interests, and U.S. capacity to contain those threats at an acceptable risk and cost."[33]

While the United States is intent upon showing a modest profile in the Indian Ocean, its activity there reflects a contingency planning which recognizes the present low-ranking interests of the region but seeks to be potentially ready to meet possible crises which require a higher degree of American attention. Even if the relative degree of concern may differ, Soviet activities largely demonstrate a similar determination: to prepare for potential future developments.

This raises the question of whether there exists between the two superpowers an acute rivalry for influence and domination in that part of the world, as is oftentimes alleged, or whether their reciprocal presence in the region is compatible with a mutual recognition of coexistence and with the much-heralded détente which is said to guide and contain their political aims and endeavors.

Rivalry or Coexistence

There can be no doubt that at least some of the Soviet and American objectives for their naval presence in the Indian Ocean are competitive and therefore antagonistic, while others are not. Some of these activities, while potentially harmful to each other's interests, cannot be challenged or objected to either under international law or from the political view as hostile or unfriendly acts.

An evident area of common interest for Moscow and Washington is the demand for free navigation. This includes free and unimpeded passage through the straits leading to the Indian Ocean for both merchant and naval vessels. It is mainly for this reason that neither the United States nor the Soviet Union were ready to endorse the Zone of Peace proposal pending before the General Assembly of the United Nations. They also object to attempts by littoral states to establish control over navigation in straits (e.g., the Malacca Strait), to extend excessively the width of territorial waters and exclusive fishing zones, and to have the archipelago concept accepted.

Neither Washington nor Moscow could take exception of the presence of each other's warships on the high sea, whether it be the Atlantic or the Pacific or the Indian Ocean. Nor can littoral states of these oceans complain against such moves. Visits by foreign warships, upon the invitation of the host governments, cannot be construed as hostile acts against other countries. An appearance of an excessively strong fleet before the coast or harbors of a foreign country could be considered to be a threat and therefore a hostile act. But in time of war such a

[33]U.S. Department of State, *Background Notes, Thailand* (Washington, D.C., January 1973). This is an official interpretation of the Nixon Doctrine.

move may be justified as a precautionary measure or as a pressure toward ending hostilities.[34] The periodic visits of the relatively modest American and Soviet forces in the Indian Ocean can hardly *per se* be interpreted as a menace, either to the littoral countries or to each other's basic interests, nor do they violate even in a remote manner any rule of international law. Objections by some littoral governments have been mostly directed against the American and not so much against Soviet naval presence, an attitude rightly characterized as "double standard."

It is in the nature of the contemporary (and also past) international system that its member states are keen to increase their influence or prestige and that they do not like their influence or prestige diminished. This is true not only in the Indian Ocean region but also anywhere in the world. And such sensitivity to their power status is particularly characteristic of the superpowers, since the global balance of power relies to a great extent on the credibility of the assistance these countries may provide to their allies and friends. Because of the need to maintain their international credibility, the urge to maintain a status quo of friends and allies is not a reflection of national pride or vanity alone; rather it is an objective element of the superpowers' national interests. From this point of view, attempts at changing the status quo—as often appears to be the objective of the Soviet Union or China—are opposed by the United States and compel Washington to resort to countervailing measures. Washington has on various occasions emphasized that the American presence was "emphatically not a threat to any nation or nations in the area."[35]

Political stability and economic development in the region and the avoidance of dangerous conflicts are in the ultimate interest of both superpowers. This view may not be fully shared by Moscow, which at least theoretically favors the spread of the victory of socialism over capitalism and feels free to support "national liberation movements."

It also appears to be in the interest of both superpowers to avoid an arms race—a competitive build-up in the Indian Ocean which would be extremely costly in financial terms, would antagonize many if not all of the coastal nations, and would have no rational purpose, especially in a period when arms limitations talks are being conducted both on the global, nuclear level and in Europe in regard to conventional build-ups.

In their naval presence in the Indian Ocean, both the Soviet Union and the United States possess certain "congenital" advantages or disadvantages which help or harm their respective deployment and contingency planning.

The Soviet Union possesses certain intangible ascendancy by being regarded as neither a former colonial nation (the domination over millions of Asians in

---

[34]The entry into the Bay of Bengal of a United States task force headed by the carrier *Enterprise* at the time of the Bangladesh War in early 1973 was regarded by New Delhi as a hostile action. See pp. 93n and 175.

[35]From a statement of Jowen Zurhellen, Jr., Deputy Director of the U.S. Arms Control and Disarmament Agency, on Feb. 22, 1974, before the House Foreign Affairs Committee, as reported by *The Times of India*, Feb. 23, 1974.

Soviet Asia is consistently overlooked) nor a friend or ally of former colonialists such as the United States. Furthermore, to be the flag bearer of socialism also endows Moscow with the halo of "progressiveness" and the image of the champion of the underprivileged and oppressed. The reputation of the Soviet state as one which has risen, by its own devices, from an underdeveloped country to a modern industrialized superpower also enhances its presige among the countries of the Indian Ocean. On the other hand, the fact that communism is associated with atheism detracts from this prestige in the eyes of believers, especially conservative Muslims.

As a more tangible advantage, the Soviet Union possesses a territorial proximity to the Asian rimland of the Indian Ocean, while the United States lies on the other side of the globe. In the nineteenth century British Russophobes feared that Russia would push its Asian advance to the doorsteps of India or to the shore of the Persian Gulf. And even during Stalin's time the traditional Russian principle of contiguity, that is, that influence and domination could only be secured by the contiguous presence of its military might, was fully upheld. It was Khrushchev who ventured beyond such proximity and into countries beyond the seas. With the naval expansion and deployment of the Soviet Navy into all the oceans, it appears that this traditional strategy is being abandoned. Nevertheless, the simultaneous territorial proximity and naval presence in the Indian Ocean provide an evident advantage to Soviet military planners; the Asian rimland of the Indian Ocean has thus—figuratively speaking— been placed in a Soviet vise.

Except for this strategic advantage, Moscow suffers—compared to the more favorable situation enjoyed by Washington—from impediments imposed on its maritime outreach into the Indian Ocean. Geography does not favor Soviet naval deployment on the high seas. The Soviet Arctic Ocean coast, except for Murmansk and its environs, is icebound through a considerable part of the year. The Baltic and Black Seas—those nearest to Soviet population and industrial centers—are connected only by narrow straits with the high seas. The Pacific coast of the Soviet Union is far distant from the main demographic and economic areas of the country. Communication by sea between these Soviet coastlines is hindered by geographic and climatic factors. For the present, most of the Soviet warships entering the Indian Ocean start on their mission from their Pacific bases; to reach Singapore, the entrance to the Indian Ocean, from Vladivostok, a distance of 4,000 miles has to be covered, and the Korea and Formosa Strait have to be passed—narrows between potentially hostile coastlines.

From a Soviet Black Sea port to the Red Sea is only 2,000 miles, but to get there the Turkish Straits (the Bosporus and the Dardanelles) and the Suez Canal must be transited. Passage of warships through the Turkish Straits is restricted by the Montreux Convention in various ways: notification (eight days in advance) is required; submarines are not permitted; and larger surface ships have to pass singly (escorted by two small craft) and another larger vessel can only pass when the former has exited. All this slows down movements and excludes their confidentiality. In time of war or when Turkey considers itself threatened, it may even close the straits to belligerent or potentially hostile warships.[36] When the Suez Canal is closed to shipping, Soviet warships—from the Black Sea, the Baltic, or the Murmansk coast—have to circumnavigate Africa, a distance to the Indian Ocean of about 12,000 miles. Warships based in the Baltic have to pass the Sound, a narrow passage between Denmark and Sweden, the Kattegat and the Skagerrak, the English Channel or the waters between the Danish Faeroe Islands and Scotland, or those south or north of Iceland; those from the Black Sea, in addition to the Turkish Straits, have to transit the Strait of Gibraltar before reaching the Atlantic. To get to the Indian Ocean, they have to round the Cape of Good Hope under the electronic surveillance of the South African Republic, an utterly hostile power.

It should also be remembered that Soviet warships from the Pacific, Baltic, Arctic, or Black Sea coasts on the way to the Indian Ocean do not possess any naval base of their own, no sovereign or leased base, and along long stretches would find no friendly port which would offer them base facilities.

The United States is considerably more distant from the Indian Ocean than the Soviet Union. Still, the approach from America to those waters is both geographically and strategically easier. From San Diego to Subic Bay is over 6,000 miles, but at Subic Bay the United States runs a semisovereign naval base under a lease by the Philippine government. The long sea route from the American mainland to the Philippines is strewn with United States-controlled islands and bases: Pearl Harbor, Guam and the many islands of the United States Trust Territory in the Pacific. From Subic Bay it is 1,400 miles to Singapore.[37] From the Atlantic side, American warships can also sail without having to pass potentially hostile narrows and round the Cape in friendly waters. Or, when coming via the Mediterranean and the Suez Canal, ports of allied nations (e.g., Gibraltar, Naples, Greek and Turkish harbors) are open for purposes of fueling, repairs, or crew recreation.

Even within the Indian Ocean, the United States Navy enjoys better and more permanent base facilities than the Soviet Union. The latter, as we have seen, uses a number of port facilities, amounting at places to full-fledged "base facilities," but it does not have long-term treaty rights to this effect, or any official treaty rights at all.

On the other hand, under treaty the United States uses a restricted harbor area in Bahrain (whose permanence is, however, doubtful) and has user's rights of further forty years duration on the island of Diego Garcia, which is a communication facility with an airstrip and fuel storage conveniences. The

[36]For details see Váli, especially pp. 40-57 and 108-163.

[37]On Jan. 1, 1972, the "chop line," or jurisdictional boundary, of the Pacific Fleet Command was extended to include almost the entire Indian Ocean; the longitude extending due south from the western border of Pakistan divides the jurisdiction of the Pacific and Atlantic naval commands. Hanson W. Baldwin, "The Indian Ocean Contest, III," *New York Times*, Mar. 22, 1972.

lagoon of Diego Garcia will be deepened so that it will be able to handle a dozen ships rather than the two or three at present.[38]

American warships will also be allowed to use the Australian Cockburn naval base when it is completed in 1978. The various communication facilities in Australia have already been mentioned.

In such manner, the United States enjoys priorities over the Soviet Union, advantages which stem from geography, cooperation with Britain (which retained for strategic reasons fragments of its former colonial empire), and an alliance with a regional power (Australia) which is ready to offer reliable and permanent uses of its territory for naval-air facilities. The Russians have no such allies who would expose themselves to accusations of having under treaty surrendered harbors or areas for the permanent or semipermanent use of Moscow.

It is not that Moscow does not aspire to obtain secure and long-term leases for base facilities; it has approached India in this matter but was given a polite refusal.[39] We can assume that other littoral states, among them Somalia, were also contacted for the same purpose without avail.

It would be unreasonable to accuse Washington of readiness to utilize to its advantage favorable geographic factors or political situations as long as its presence is not a threat to littoral nations and cannot be interpreted as a competitive build-up against the Soviet presence in that region. Nor can the United States be reproached for having naval craft which the Soviet Union—for lack of time to construct or because of differing strategic concepts—does not possess. It has been pointed out that aircraft carriers are equivalent (although more vulnerable) to land-based airfields except for the advantage that carriers have the capability to move into any sea as political situations require.[40] It is now assumed that Moscow is hastening to obtain similar capabilities, which it has now accepted as important.[41]

There are also disparities in regard to the servicing of submarines in the Indian Ocean region. It is not known whether Soviet submarines can obtain facilities for this in such ports as Berbera, Vishakapatnam, and Umm Qasr. Even if they can, these facilities cannot be relied on like the services American submarines may receive in Subic Bay or, should Diego Garcia be prepared for such a task, at this base. The servicing of submarines figured in the Vladivostok summit conference

[38]There are about 400 American servicemen in Diego Garcia; under present plans, quarters are to be improved so that an increase of personnel will be possible. The increased length of the airfield will allow landing of the largest aircraft. Britain has, under the treaty, equal rights of access to the facilities of the base.

[39]Private information obtained by this writer.

[40]See the interview with Admiral Elmo R. Zumwalt, Jr., then U.S. Chief of Naval Operations, Reader's Digest, January 1972, pp. 127-128.

[41]The Soviet Navy has two helicopter carriers, the Moskva and the Leningrad. According to newspaper reports, two carriers are being constructed (one, the Kiev, is supposed to be ready) in Black Sea shipyards. However, if these are declared full-fledged aircraft carriers, their passage through the Turkish Straits would not be permissible under the Montreux Convention.

on nuclear arms limitations in November 1974; the better servicing possibilities of American submarines which allowed them additional time on patrol was pointed out by the Soviets, who claimed that their submarines must return to their home ports to be serviced.[42]

Whether the reopening in 1975 of the Suez Canal, which had been closed since the Six-Day War in June 1967, will meaningfully alter the naval balance in the Indian Ocean depends on the Soviet's determination to expand their naval presence. Passage through the 100-mile-long canal—instead of around the Cape— shortens the route from the Black Sea to the Persian Gulf by somewhat more than 6,000 miles. Soviet naval units, having mostly entered the Indian Ocean from the Pacific, may now be joined by those in the Mediterranean which were based on Soviet Black Sea harbors.

Nevertheless, United States policy supported the clearing of the canal and its opening for international shipping; American experts and ships participated in the dredging operations. Washington believed that the Suez Canal in operation would greatly contribute to peace in the Middle East and minimize another outbreak of Egyptian-Israeli hostilities. American warships, belonging to the Sixth Fleet in the Mediterranean, might also be able to reach the Indian Ocean via the Suez Canal. In any case, American policy, which gave high priority to the resolution of the Arab-Israeli conflict, was ready to ignore the Soviet strategic advantage which could result from the opening of Suez's direct passage from the Mediterranean to the Indian Ocean.[43]

It should not be overlooked that the more frequent regular visits of United States naval forces were prompted by the renewed hostilities between Israelis and Arabs in October 1973, when, after the global alert of American military forces, the carrier *Hancock* with four destroyers was sent into the Indian Ocean.[44] The appearance of these forces in the Arabian Sea gave rise to speculation that this was a contingency move in case air support was to be provided to Israel. It also demonstrated the potential use of an aircraft carrier as a movable "base" that could be placed on the far eastern flank of the crucial Middle East, distant from the Mediterranean but still close enough for the deployment of air power.

Apart from some sporadic crises, both the United States and Soviet naval presences serve essentially contingency purposes if considered from the military point of view. The long-range objectives of both countries are to maintain or win influence. However, in this respect diplomatic efforts and economic and military

[42]This bargaining point was, however, dropped. *New York Times,* Dec. 3, 1974.

[43]See Drew Middleton's report in the *New York Times,* Nov. 19, 1974. According to an Indian spokesman, General Harbakhsh Singh, (retired), the United States would gain by the opening of the Suez Canal by "luring" the bulk of the Russian Navy, particularly the nuclear submarine force, into the Indian Ocean, which would place American and West European targets out of its range. "U.S. Strategy in the Indian Ocean," in *Indian Ocean Power Rivalry,* ed. T. T. Poulose (New Delhi, 1974), pp. 5-6.

[44]This task force was subsequently replaced by the more modern carrier *Oriskany. New York Times,* Dec. 1, 1973.

aid programs may be even more important and effective than movements of warships. In any case, a restrained or intensive competition to gain influence in countries where such a move is appropriate or useful is being pursued by Washington and Moscow in the Indian Ocean region and elsewhere among countries of the Third World, irrespective of the presence of their navies in that ocean or in others. Such attempts to increase one's ascendancy in one or another country are a natural political process in today's international environment and need not be considered as a "confrontation" or threat of opposition to another's intents. Such policies do not affect vital interests of the competitors and are customary even between friendly and allied powers. They are by no means incompatible or inconsistent with "coexistence" or a détente between Washington and Moscow.

To prevent a competitive build-up of their surface navies in the Indian Ocean, should such a development take place, an understanding to limit such an expansion would, in the absence of essential interests at stake, easily be possible. Such a competition cannot be compared in terms of prime national interests with the nuclear arms race. Evidently, the situation is not viewed, either in Washington or in Moscow, as sufficiently advanced to warrant negotiations on the merits of such an understanding.[45]

The rivalry—mostly more acute and venomous than that with the United States—between the Soviet Union and China around the periphery of the Indian Ocean is political rather than military. For this reason, it is hardly suitable to adjustment and restraint as the Soviet-American relationship in that area.

China and the Indian Ocean

The catalyst which induced China to enter into a relation of seminormalcy with the United States was the Soviet military threat along 4,000 miles of common border (including the border with Mongolia) where Soviet divisions are stationed. This triangular relationship between China, the Soviet Union, and the United States created an equilibrium which can rightly be considered as the mainstay of peace in East and South Asia.[46]

China's primary interest, as that of other countries, is the defense and security of its homeland. Its navy is the third largest after the United States and the Soviet Union, in terms of manpower (otherwise behind the navies of Britain and France), but it is geared for coastal defense and has so far refrained from showing the flag in the Indian Ocean.

[45]In mid-1971 the United States did approach the Soviet Union on the subject of mutual naval restraint in the Indian Ocean, but after initial discussions the matter was not taken up at the talks on limitations of strategic weapons. See the testimony of U. Alexis Johnson, Under Secretary of State, before the Senate Foreign Relations Committee, as reported in *New York Times*, Feb. 3, 1972. A Congressional plea in April 1976 for an attempt to negotiate with Moscow for restraint in naval developments in the Indian Ocean was rejected by the State Department because it could be interpreted as an acquiescence in the Soviet-Cuban intervention in Angola. *New York Times*, April 22, 1976.

[46]See Eugene V. Rostow, "Triangular Power," *New York Times*, Dec. 6, 1972.

The momentous event in China's relations with the countries of South Asia which influenced subsequent developments was the 1963 border war with India.[47] The Sino-Indian hostility determined Peking's stand in the Pakistani-Indian conflict; it persuaded neutralist India to conclude the Treaty of Peace, Friendship, and Cooperation with Moscow. This, in turn, provided to the Chinese the perception that they were "encircled" and motivated them to regard Soviet presence in the Indian Ocean as a follow-up of "British imperialism." They stated that Soviet social imperialism wished to open up an arc-shaped maritime route, stretching from the Black Sea across the Mediterranean, the Red Sea, the Indian Ocean, and the western Pacific to the Sea of Japan.[48]

Of course, their accusations are not restricted to Moscow; the United States is also blamed for scrambling for strategic bases and threatening the security of the Third World countries. But the principal target of these charges is the Soviet Union, which, among others, is accused of robbing the resources of the coastal nations and violating their sovereignty.[49]

As mentioned earlier, China's presence is mostly political; it has no bases and no arrangements for her warships in Indian Ocean ports. Its commercial shipping enjoys facilities in Dar es Salaam, in Tanzania; it runs, according to some sources, a tracking station in Zanzibar.[50]

Its political impact in some countries is substantial. In these countries it is in sometimes arduous competition with Soviet influences. Thus Sri Lanka, Pakistan, Ethiopia, Tanzania, and Zambia are countries where its position is stronger than that of the Soviet Union. Peking is the main arms supplier to Pakistan, Tanzania, and Zambia. In Somalia, it has largely reduced its arms deliveries, which, in contrast with those provided by Moscow, were of a defensive kind.

Generally speaking, Peking opposes what Moscow proposes. Where Soviet military support prevailed over China's, the latter slowly is withdrawing. In such a way Peking stopped supporting Arab guerrilla movements around the Persian Gulf, in Oman, in Eritrea, and within other areas of Ethiopia. It established cordial relations with Iran, Sri Lanka, Mauritius, and Ethiopia. It has close contacts with Pakistan and also with Tanzania. But China supports liberation movements in southern Africa, where its aid is often more considerable than that of the Soviets.

While India considers its friendship treaty with Moscow a form of insurance against Chinese aggression, Peking sees it as an expression of hostility. To counter the potential danger from the south, China showed great determination to protect Pakistan from dismemberment. It regarded the uprising in East Pakistan

[47]N. Maxwell, "China and South Asia. A Survey," *Collected Papers of the Study Conference on the Indian Ocean in International Politics*, p. 79.

[48]*Peking Review*, June 27, 1969, pp. 16-18.

[49]J. P. Jain, "Indian Ocean as a Zone of Peace. An Appraisal of the Chinese Attitude," in *Indian Ocean Power Rivalry*, ed. T. T. Poulose (New Delhi, 1974), pp. 43-45.

[50]See UN report (original) of the three experts on the military presence in the Indian Ocean of May 3, 1974, p. 19. The revised report omitted this information.

(Bangladesh) as fomented by India and supported by the Soviet Union. However, threatened by the Soviet Union's concentration of troops, its assistance remained limited. Except for some sporadic fighting on the border between Tibet and Sikkim and official condemnation of both India and the Soviet Union, it could not prevent the loss of Pakistan's eastern part.

Good relations with Pakistan date back to the early 1960s; in 1963 China and Pakistan signed a boundary treaty—a treaty which India was unwilling at that time to sign—in which Pakistan gave up some of the claims upheld by the British. During the 1965 Kashmir War (when the Soviet danger was considered less imminent) Peking concentrated forces at the Nathu La Pass (opposite the Sikkimese border) but without meaningfully influencing the outcome of the fighting.

Pakistan showed great interest in the rapprochement between the United States and China. Henry Kissinger's first secret visit in 1970 to Peking was prepared with the help of the Pakistani Foreign Ministry. His mysterious disappearance from Rawalpindi and flight to Peking on a Pakistani International Airlines plane was managed under the good offices of the Pakistanis. By establishing direct and friendly links between Washington and Peking, Pakistan contributed to the building of the triangular power relations which served to restrain Soviet and, indirectly, Indian ambitions in the Indian Ocean region. But it could not prevent the disintegration of Pakistan.

Peking is strongly aware of Afghanistan's dependence on Soviet assistance and support. Their short common boundary, at the head of Afghanistan's panhandle, the Wakham Strip, divides the Soviet Union from Pakistan, and its integrity is therefore an important asset both for that country and its protector, China. This borderline of fifty miles had been demarcated in the mid-1960s to exclude possible conflicts.

The Himalayan states, sandwiched between China and India, remain a neuralgic area. Nepal's shuttle politics between India and China have been described earlier. Bhutan has, so far, refrained from entering into direct diplomatic relations with Peking; if it should do so, it would imitate the politics of Nepal. On the other hand, Sikkim (the danger spot for a much-dreaded Chinese invasion) has been incorporated into India and powerfully garrisoned by Indian armed forces.

Although Burma settled its boundary question with China, its relations with its powerful northern neighbor remain ambivalent. Secessionist guerrillas in Burma are supported by Peking, and the Maoist Communist Party is active in the country. New Delhi, considering Burma to be another buffer between itself and China, was ready to oblige the government of Rangoon by sending military instructors and military equipment to Burma, a move which has been duly noted in Peking.

China has for a long time been reluctant to establish diplomatic relations with Bangladesh (which Peking insisted on calling "East Bengal"). After the August 1975 coup the new leaders of the country were eager to approach China in order to somewhat counteract the one-sided dependence on India.

The looming shadow of China extends over the Indian subcontinent and even far out into the Indian Ocean. In Sri Lanka, Peking's sympathies are sought to counteract Indian pressures; in East Africa, Chinese prestige has risen because of the construction of the TanZam railway, which plays a role there similar to the dramatic display of the Aswan Dam in Egypt. In Australia, China is regarded as a factor in the policies of Southeast Asia. Despite their apprehensions and antipathies, the ASEAN countries realize that sooner or later they will have to come to talking terms with Peking. Malaysia and Thailand have already established diplomatic relations with China.

Peking already has stretched its hands out toward the Malacca Strait, the gateway to the Indian Ocean. In January 1974 Chinese warships sank a South Vietnamese patrol boat off the Paracel Islands 250 miles south of the island of Hainan. The Paracel Islands were claimed by China and by both South and North Vietnam. Peking's forces have now taken possession of these outposts in the South China Sea. The Spratly Islands, 600 miles further south (and the same distance from Singapore) are also claimed by Peking. While these moves are just the expression of China's traditional insistence on claiming territories once Chinese, they can also be regarded as a demonstration of China's naval power in the seas near its national territory. In fact, the islands in question lie along the maritime route toward the Malacca Strait; oil also may be found in the sea bed around these islets.

China is also ready to support regional powers in the Indian Ocean region in their endeavor to "exclude great power rivalries." Thus Peking backed the Zone of Peace proposal in the United Nations. It is, on principle, in favor of associations of regional powers as long as nonregional great powers (meaning generally the Soviet Union) are excluded. Thus China has shown no enmity against the Association of South East Asian Nations or against the Regional Cooperation for Development.

On questions of the law of th sea, Peking has also favored attempts by local powers to extend their jurisdiction over territorial waters even beyond the six- or twelve-mile limit; it approved, at least on principle, Malaysian and Indonesian efforts to exercise jurisdiction over the Malacca Strait, and had no word against the archipelago concept as upheld by Indonesia or the Philippines. All this may give rise to the assumption that, at least in the near future, the Chinese have no plans to enter the Indian Ocean with their navy. One may also assume that they would support any plan which would exclude navies of the superpowers from that ocean but, at the same time, they would not be enthusiastic if the Americans should abandon these waters while the Russians stayed. In this they share the opinion of almost all the littoral states.

There is no doubt that Chinese opposition and criticism weaken the Soviet impact in the area under scrutiny. Leftist elements are persuaded to compare the Soviet and the Chinese approaches to socialism, and the latter have the advantage that they are Asians and not Europeans. Also the "peasant communism" adopted and propagated by Peking has a greater appeal than the Stalinist type of "crash industrialization."

The fact that China is also a nuclear power has increased its prestige among many nations of the area. India's plans to develop nuclear arms, if true, would be aimed at raising its own prestige rather than creating a threat against China.

The triangular power relationship in the Indian Ocean region benefits China partly because it permits it to inveigh against "the superpowers," thus throwing the Soviets and Americans into the same basket but hurting Moscow much more than Washington. This relationship also helps provide a certain guarantee that the Russians will not establish a naval monopoly as well as a monopoly of influence in the area. Washington has no reason to complain of the Chinese political presence; except for the guerrilla movements, supported by Peking in certain restricted areas, China does not appear to be a serious menace to the peace and stability of the region.

However, the superpowers and China are not the only major nations which have, as it appears, a stake in the development of the Indian Ocean region. Former colonial powers, with a residue of influence and interest, also play a not inconsiderable role in the life and development of the area. Aside from Britain and France (and to a very minor extent Portugal), Japan is another outsider which, in terms of its interest (navigation, economics, and especially the oil of the region) is definitely an "insider" whose attitudes cannot be ignored when discussing the politics of that part of the world.

Selected Bibliography

Australian Federal Parliament, Joint Committee on Foreign Affairs. *Report on the Indian Ocean Region.* Canberra: Australian Government Publishing Service, 1972.

Braun, Dieter. *Internationale Interessenprofile in der Region "Indischer Ozean."* Ebenhausen-Isar: Stiftung Wissenschaft und Politik, 1972.

Budhray, Vijay Sen. *Soviet Russia and the Hindustan Subcontinent.* Bombay: Somaiya Publications, 1973.

Davidov, V. F., and Kremenyuk, V. A. "Strategiya SshA v Zone Indiyskovo Okeana" (United States Strategy in the Indian Ocean). *USA, Economics, Politics, Ideology* (Moscow), No. 5 (May 1973), 6-17.

Fairhall, David. *Russian Sea Power.* Boston: Gambit, Inc., 1971.

Imam, Zafar. "The Soviet Union and the Indian Ocean." In *Indian Ocean Power Rivalry,* pp. 13-19. Edited by T. T. Poulose. New Delhi: Young Asia Publications, 1974.

Jain, J. P. "Indian Ocean as a Zone of Peace. An Appraisal of the Chinese Attitude." In *Indian Ocean Power Rivalry,* pp. 38-49. Edited by T. T. Poulose. New Delhi: Young Asia Publications, 1974.

Jukes, Geoffrey. *The Indian Ocean in Soviet Naval Policy.* London: International Institute for Strategic Studies, (Adelphi Papers No. 87), 1972.

Jukes, Geoffrey. *The Soviet Union in Asia.* Berkeley: University of California Press, 1973.

Kudryavtsev, V. "The Indian Ocean in the Plans of Imperialism." *International Affairs* (Moscow), No. 11 (Nov. 1974), 114-118.

Labrousse, Henri. *Le golfe et le canal.* Paris: Presses Universitaires de France, 1973.

McConnell, James M. *The Soviet Navy in the Indian Ocean.* Arlington, Va.: Center for Naval Analyses, 1971.

Maxwell, N. "China and South Asia. A Survey." In *Collected Papers of the Study Conference on the Indian Ocean in International Politics,* pp. 79-92. Southampton (England): University of Southampton, 1973.

Millar, T. B. *Soviet Policies in the Indian Ocean Area.* Canberra: Australian National University Press, 1970.

Millar, T. B. "Soviet Policies South and East of Suez." *Foreign Affairs* 49 (October 1970), 70-80.

Ogunsanwo, Alaba. *China's Politics in Africa, 1958-71.* London: Cambridge University Press, 1974.

Polmar, Norman. *Soviet Naval Power.* New York: National Strategy Information Center, 1972.

Singh, (General) Harbakhsh. "U.S. Strategy in the Indian Ocean." In *Indian Ocean Power Rivalry,* pp. 3-6. Edited by T. T. Poulose. New Delhi: Young Asia Publications, 1974.

Sjaastad, Anders C. "The Indian Ocean and the Soviet Navy." *Norsk Militaert Tidskrift* (Oslo), October 1971 (as translated in the U.S. *Congressional Record,* Mar. 30, 1972, pp. E3143-E3148).

Smolansky, Oles M. "Soviet Entry into the Indian Ocean." In *The Indian Ocean. Its Political, Economic, and Military Importance,* pp. 337-355. Edited by Alvin J. Cottrell and R. M. Burrell. New York: Praeger, 1972.

Subrahmanyam, K. "Ebb and Flow of Power in the Indian Ocean Area." *USI* (United Service Institution) *Journal* (New Delhi), January-March 1968, 3-16.

United Nations. *Report* of the Secretary General pursuant to the General Assembly Resolution 3080 (XXVIII) on the Indian Ocean as a Zone of Peace, transmitting statement by three experts on the great powers' military presence in the Indian Ocean, dated May 3, 1974.

United Nations. *Statement* of the Secretary-General pursuant to the General Assembly Resolution 3080 (XXVIII) on the Indian Ocean as a Zone of Peace, transmitting the revised report by three experts on the great powers' military presence in the Indian Ocean, dated July 11, 1974.

United States, House of Representatives. *The Indian Ocean. Political and Strategic Future.* Hearings before the Subcommittee on National Security Policy and Scientific Developments of the Committee on Foreign Affairs. 92d Cong., 1st sess. July 20, 22, 27, and 28, 1971. Washington, D.C.: Government Printing Office, 1971.

Váli, Ferenc A. *The Turkish Straits and NATO.* Stanford, Calif.: Hoover Institution Press, 1972.

Wheeler, G.. "The Indian Ocean Area. Soviet Aims and Interests." In *Collected Papers of the Study Conference on the Indian Ocean in International Politics,* pp. 69-77. Southampton (England): University of Southampton, 1973. (Mimeographed.)

Wriggins, Howard. "U.S. Interests in the Indian Ocean." In *The Indian Ocean. Its Political Economic, and Military Importance.* Edited by Alvin J. Cottrell and R. M. Burrell. New York: Praeger, 1972.

Chapter 10

Residual Colonials and the Principal Outsider: Britain, France, Portugal, and Japan

O mighty Caesar! does thou lie so low?
Are all thy conquests, glories, triumphs, spoils,
Shrunk to this little measure?

Shakespeare, *Julius Caesar*

The Indian Ocean region has been "decolonized" but not totally. Britain, France, and, at the time of this writing, nominally even Portugal still hold territorial possessions under their sovereignty around the periphery of these waters. Decolonization is not a process which can apply automatically, without the consideration of factors other than self-determination. And even the latter basic argument for independence may be reversed: the population of a territory may decide to remain under the control of its colonial ruler. Under the principle of self-determination, no people can be forced to become "independent."

However, the principle motives for colonial powers to retain at least a residue of their possessions are often different. Having had to abandon the major colonial areas to hold onto the residuum may not be attractive; having lost the cake, what reason is there to preserve the crumbs? Generally speaking, the

motives are sentimental, strategic, or economic. There is also a feeling of
responsibility for persons who have laid their trust in their masters, or for
institutions and political entities which were created under their guidance.
National pride (you may call it vanity) and the desire not to give up what does
not have to be given up, also play a role in these attitudes.

But in the last analysis, decisions to maintain sovereignty over certain areas
are based on a rationale of their usefulness to the national interest of the
countries in question and on the price to be paid for such a policy.

The countries of Western Europe are, naturally, vitally interested in the
shipping of the Atlantic Ocean, particularly the sea traffic with North America;
and so are the United States and Canada. But European powers have much less
interest in the navigation of the waters of the Pacific Ocean, where Britain and
France hold possessions of minor interest. The control which is exercised by the
United States over shipping in the Pacific has relieved Europeans of anxiety
concerning these waters. With the Indian Ocean, however, the situation differs.
Washington has no such vital interest at stake there, whereas the countries of
Western Europe do. An embargo on the flow of oil from the Persian Gulf may
bring about a total collapse of Western Europe's economy.

Japan, in addition to other major economic interests which it has in the
Indian Ocean region, is absolutely dependent on the oil which has to be
transported across those waters.

Speaking generally, the power relations in the Indian Ocean region are more a
European than American concern. But the interested European powers are much
less able, if able at all, to interfere in developments in the area and, in case of
need, to secure by force the freedom of ship movements in those seas. For this
purpose they have to rely on the United States although its interests, while
parallel, are not equally intense.

The NATO treaty has limited its own sphere of application to the area north
of the Tropic of Cancer. Such an artificial division of the Atlantic into the
northern section where the territories and shipping of the signatory powers are
guaranteed against hostile attack and a southern section where they are not may
not be expressive of the real interests of the nations involved. Hence the
occasional attempts to extend NATO's attention to the South Atlantic and the
Indian Ocean—waters across which the oil lifeline of the European NATO
members leads while the Suez Canal is closed to shipping.[1]

Barring unforeseen events, it seems still unlikely that members of the North
Atlantic alliance would resort to some collective precautionary measures in those
distant areas. Among its European members, only Britain and France (and until
recently, Portugal) have territorial assets at stake which would warrant consid-

[1]In November 1972 the North Atlantic Assembly called on the NATO Council to authorize
plans for the protection of Western European shipping in the Indian Ocean and the South
Atlantic; *The Economist* (London), Dec. 16, 1972. On June 19, 1974, the NATO Council
meeting in Ottawa reminded the member states that "their interests can be affected by
events in other areas of the world." This was a reference to the Soviet naval presence in the
Indian Ocean; *New York Times,* June 20, 1974.

ering the peacetime defense of their Indian Ocean interests (and especially justifying it to their people). And only two Western European powers have the capability to take such measures. Britain has, to some extent, assured the assistance of the United States by operating common installations in that region, and by having prepared joint contingency plans for the eventuality that common action would be required.

British Interest in the Indian Ocean

When the United Kingdom extended its sovereignty over most of the coastal territories of the Indian Ocean, it secured safety for the shipping of all nations in the waters of that ocean, including those which, like the Persian Gulf or Malayan seas, were infested by piracy. It was the British Navy which, after arduous efforts, swept the African slave trade off the seas. *Pax Britannica* meant freedom of navigation and also the extinction of tribal warfare in the areas under the control of London.

When the countries around the Indian Ocean successfully achieved their independence (except for some of the island possessions), Whitehall considered any major defense forces in those regions superfluous and as exceeding the resources of Britain, which rather should be concentrated in the NATO area. By the end of 1967 Britain still controlled the sheikdoms in the Persian Gulf, and still maintained considerable forces in Malaysia and Singapore. The decision to withdraw from east of Suez by 1971 meant the abandonment of the Persian Gulf protectorates and the departure of most of the forces from the Southeast Asian theater. Only limited naval deployments would thereafter be undertaken from time to time.

With this move, Britain abdicated any claim to naval supremacy in the Indian Ocean (as it has abandoned territorial sovereignty over almost all the lands of the region), but it has by no means declared itself disinterested in the area. And it continues to exert diplomatic influence as well as limited but still significant military influence in the region. Both in the diplomatic field and in its military-naval presence, London prefers to maintain a rather restrained, low-key attitude. However, in parts of the region, in many countries formerly under British control, London's "background" influence remains considerable.

The British island possessions which London wished to retain were gathered together by an Order of Council in 1965 and named the British Indian Ocean Territory (BIOT). BIOT consists of the Chagos Archipelago (detached from Mauritius in return for a payment of 3 million pounds) and of the islands of Aldabra, Farquhar, and Desroches (detached from the Seychelles in return for the international airport constructed on Mahé Island).

The Chagos Archipelago is composed of groups of circular atolls covering a shoal area of about 21,000 square miles. The archipelago lies about 1,000 miles southwest of Ceylon and the same distance due east from the Seychelles. The Diego Garcia atoll is situated in the southwestern corner of the shoal area.

Desroches Island is some fifty miles south, and Farquhar 130 miles southwest of Mahé. Aldabra, the largest island of the territory, lies at the northern entrance of the Mozambique Channel, north of the Comoro Islands.

The purpose of the formation of the BIOT was strategic: to enable Britain (and the United States) to establish defense facilities. The islands' and attolls' main attraction, apart from their location in the western and central areas of the Indian Ocean, was their lack of population. Those few inhabitants were non-permanent—fishermen or guano collectors—from the Seychelles, Mauritius, and other islands.

The United Kingdom also maintained some staging posts on leased territories. Those used by the Royal Air Force at Salalah (in the Dhofar Province) and on the island of Masirah, under an agreement concluded in 1958 with the Sultanate of Muscat and Oman (now Oman), are to be given up by Britain in March 1977. Before attaining independence, the government of the Maldives consented to lease facilities on Addu Atoll, the southernmost group of the Maldives, up to December 1986. These facilities include an airfield on Gan Island and a radio communication station on Hithadoo Island. The lagoon in the Addu Atoll may be used as a natural harbor.

Britain may also use airfields, harbors, and a naval communication station (to expire on one year's notice) on the island of Mauritius. It still maintains small forces (both land and air) in Malaysia and Singapore; it could also use facilities in the harbors of these countries.

On December 3, 1974, the British government announced further reductions in the number of its overseas forces, including those stationed in the Indian Ocean region. The garrison placed in Singapore was to be withdrawn, and the troops in Gan were to be reduced. On the other hand, London agreed to the American plan for a "modest extension" of the facilities on Diego Garcia. Roy Manson, Defense Minister, announced, "We and the United States Government have also agreed to pursue consultations with the aim of developing realistic progress toward arms limitations in the Indian Ocean."[2]

The reasons of the British interest in the Indian Ocean may be summed up as follows:

1. Although the United Kingdom has given up almost all of its possessions in the Indian Ocean region, it has not abandoned London's Far Eastern outpost, namely, Hongkong. Britain does not plan to relinquish this Crown colony. Furthermore, Britain also has other commitments in South and Southeast Asia (membership in CENTO, the Five Power Defense Pact). The nondescript commitments stemming from membership in the Commonwealth may also require action or the possibility of action.

London wished to maintain a line of communication with the Indian Ocean region and across that ocean to Southeast Asia and the Far East. Strategic mobility demands staging bases all along the route so as to make possible the dispatch of transport planes and fighter-bombers to the places of danger. Since

[2]*New York Times*, Dec. 4, 1974.

Britain has abandoned the construction of aircraft carriers, British warships operating in the Indian Ocean must receive air protection from airfields in the area.

There are three air routes to reach the Indian Ocean, Southeast Asia, Australia, and Hongkong from Britain. The shortest link to the Indian Ocean is via Cyprus, then across Turkey and Iran to Masirah–Gan–Singapore, and further to Hongkong. The second would lead to the South Atlantic (with possible stops at St. Helena or Ascension Island) and thence via Mauritius to Singapore and further east. The third is the west-about route across the North American continent, American islands in the Pacific, to Hongkong or to Australia, and points in the Indian Ocean. There is a time difference of at least fourteen hours between the eastern and western routes. London intends to rely primarily on the eastern route via Cyprus and has built up the stepping-stones for air transportation in that direction.

2. The second reason—which is closely allied with the first—is political. The fact that Britain has a naval, air, and military capability in the Indian Ocean area renders British commitments credible. Without such a potential to intervene in force, defense pacts, guarantees, and diplomatic representations or protests would be worthless or even ludicrous.

The relative strength of British influence in the region, which no doubt has a stabilizing impact, is due primarily to the diplomatic skill, personal contacts, and traditional expertise in and knowledge of affairs of the countries there. There is an attitude of trust toward Britain and its representatives which is held by many leaders of the new nations once formerly within the British Empire, with many still remaining members of the Commonwealth. Some of these leaders received their education in England; many of the military officers were trained in Sandhurst or fought with the British in World War II. These ties—intangible as they are—add strength to British advice, initiatives, and representations. But diplomatic-political pressures often need "teeth" to become acceptable or persuasive. Cooperation with the United States adds to the force and credibility of London's political activity; joint contingency planning with Washington provides a more serious aspect to provisional or established projections.

3. The British interest in protecting trade routes and maintaining freedom of navigation in the Indian Ocean is even greater than that of the United States. British trade with the countries of that ocean (including the Persian Gulf) amounts to 22 percent of Britain's oversea transactions. Forty percent of British overseas investments are based in the region.

At any given time, about one-fifth of the British merchant fleet is sailing in the Indian Ocean. British experience, dating back many centuries, seems to prescribe that commercial shipping should be protected by the navy. While the relatively modest presence of the Royal Navy in those waters might be inadequate in the unlikely event of interference by a hostile power, the British rightly believe that a limited potential is better that no potential at all.

The British attitude toward the Zone of Peace plan for the Indian Ocean was rather negative; the plan was considered "unrealistic." The project of "arms limitation" is evidently one which is to be taken up with the Soviet government, rather than with the littoral countries.

To sum up, despite the contraction of forces for economic reasons, Britain has by no means lost interest in the Indian Ocean area, which, though secondary in comparison to the European theater, continues to concern the British.

French Interest in the Indian Ocean

During the last hundred years, France's attention has been focused on the western section of the Indian Ocean area, particularly the Horn of Africa and the islands along the East African coast where Madagascar, the third largest island of the world, formed the most precious French colonial possession.

Since the end of World War II, the control exercised by Paris over its Indian Ocean possessions has undergone radical changes.[3] The French Somali coast has grown into the self-governing overseas territory known as the French Territory of the Afars and Issas. The Comoro Islands (except for Mayotte Island) became independent in 1975. The island of Réunion has been an overseas *département* of France since 1946. Madagascar, independent since 1960 under the name of the Malagasy Republic, was tied financially, militarily, and politically to the former colonial master until it severed these strings and declared itself "uncommitted."

The agreement of June 1973 that forced Paris to withdraw its forces from Madagascar, including the highly important naval base of Diego Suarez, was a blow to France's military presence in the area—a blow which that country accepted with apparent equanimity. The loss of Diego Suarez was especially difficult to sustain; Djibouti has an excellent harbor but is exposed both landward and seaward; Réunion lacks a good harbor. France, however, retained under an annually renewable agreement berthing and repair rights in Diego Suarez, and French military planes have landing rights at Ivato Airfield.

France's determination to hold onto its position in the Indian Ocean was expressed by the establishment of a new naval command to extend over the entire Indian Ocean and the Cape route leading to it—from West Africa to Sumatra, and from Djibouti in the north to the Kerguelen Islands in the Antarctic seas.[4] At the same time it was also announced that France wished to strengthen its naval presence in the Indian Ocean. The operation headquarters of the commander-in-chief have been placed on the 26,000-ton fleet tanker *La Charente,* converted for this purpose to carry helicopters and short-take-off-and-landing aircraft. When not on a cruise, the flagship *La Charente* is anchored at Djibouti.

[3]The small French settlements in India, Chandernagor, Karikal, Pondicherry, Yanaon, and Mahé were given up shortly after India's independence and incorporated by the latter.

[4]*Christian Science Monitor,* Feb. 27, 1974. France formed in 1955 into an administrative unit its "Southern and Antarctic Lands," which include the Kerguelen Archipelago, the islands of St. Paul and Amsterdam, the Crozet Islands, and Adelie Land on Antarctica.

A force of about 2,000 infantry, three frigates with commando units, and a squadron of the air force are stationed in the Territory of Afars and Issas. Parts of an infantry battalion, one destroyer, and three minesweepers are stationed on Réunion. France's military communication with its Indian Ocean outposts is assured by the staging posts which it operates in its former colonies in West and Central Africa. For the *Force d'Intervention* (airborne and airportable motorized units), it is thus possible to dispatch reinforcements without delay to the Indian Ocean region.

In contrast to the British endeavor to maintain a credible military-political presence in the Indian Ocean area by combining efforts with those of the United States, France is resolved "to do it alone." The reasons why Paris has continued to regard its presence of considerable importance may be stated as follows:

1. France's foreign policy in regard to the Indian Ocean region does not differ from French foreign policy elsewhere: it is based on the assumption that France is a great power, one which even in the era of superpowers continues to have a say in affairs of the world. It denies any justification for what Michel Jobert, Foreign Minister under Pompidou, called the "condominium of the two superpowers."

Paris finds it natural that the Soviet Union established a naval presence in the Indian Ocean, because it is a "Great Power." But for the very same reason, France claims the same right. As Michel Debré, in 1970 Minister of State in charge of defense (who is also deputy for Réunion), declared:

The Great Powers wish to be everywhere. The U.S.S.R. established its presence in the Indian Ocean for economic as well as political reasons: one should not draw different conclusions from this presence than those from its presence elsewhere. One should not have particular fears because of this, nor should one be surprised. One should not be astonished because of a situation which is an inevitable development [*dans l'ordre de fatalité*]: global political balance will from now on not allow zones of twilight and zones of security.[5]

Accordingly, as long as France possesses a foothold in the region, it will continue to act in the manner required by an Indian Ocean Power. Of course, impulses of national prestige would not alone justify the economic burden involved in this policy; Paris is able to point to more tangible and pragmatic motives for its Indian Ocean involvement.

2. France's Indian Ocean possessions lie along the sea lanes leading from and toward the Suez Canal and those from and toward the Cape route. Its main oil supplies come from the Persian Gulf and pass those shores. France wants to be in the position to protect "her" sea routes should such a necessity arise.

3. France is a nuclear power and is engaged in nuclear testing. It is interested in tests of other powers, both relating to detonation of nuclear devices and to firing and collecting of missiles. Its communication facilities in the Indian Ocean area serve the purpose of monitoring any such activity.

[5]*Le Monde* (Paris), Aug. 27, 1970.

4. Paris is most conscious of the advantages which naval power can earn through its presence and occasional visits to places of its own control and to foreign harbors. This *politique du pavillon* (show-the-flag policy) is being used to impress those peoples who historically have had contacts with France or continue to speak the French language. Both the population of the Seychelles Islands and that of Mauritius are francophone. Although these countries adopted English as their "official" language, they remain open and receptive to French cultural influences. By various means—by the dispatch of teachers and of books, by radio, and also by promoting French tourism—Paris has undertaken a "cultural reconquest" of these islands which it has politically lost to Britain.

Although the French naval and military presence is modest in comparison with what Moscow usually displays or Washington occasionally musters in the Indian Ocean, it is certainly not a negligible factor in the power balance of the western half of that ocean area.

The End of Portugal's Indian Ocean Empire

The Portuguese presence in the Indian Ocean has become historical in the last years. Until the military coup at the end of April 1974, Lisbon attempted to preserve its African colonial empire against the onslaught of anticolonialist forces. Among these possessions was Mozambique on the Indian Ocean. Salazar's authoritarian regime was imbued with the ideology of Portugal's civilizing mission, its Christian heritage, and its historic proprietary claims to its Indian Oceanic and African possessions. But with the overthrow of the authoritarian government this ideological stance and the fiction of a unitary Portuguese Empire had to be abandoned. Thereby the 450 years of Portuguese presence in the Indian Ocean, dating back centuries longer than that of the British or French, came to an end.

Still, after the attainment of independence by Mozambique, the fate of a small Portuguese possession at the outskirts of the Indian Ocean region remained in suspense. This was the eastern half of the island of Timor, with a population of 650,000: the other half of the island belongs to Indonesia. Portuguese Timor was saved from being swallowed up by Indonesia by the strange reluctance of President Sukarno to lay hands on a territory which never belonged to the Dutch. Although Jakarta had severed diplomatic relations with Lisbon, the governors of Indonesian and Portuguese Timor maintained friendly contacts.

In August 1975 fighting broke out between the political parties of Portuguese Timor, and the Portuguese governor fled to the nearby island of Atauro. In November 1975 the victorious Timorese Liberation Front proclaimed the People's Republic of East Timor. Thereupon Indonesia sent a small force to East Timor which helped to restore the rule of the pro-Jakarta forces over most of the area. On May 31, 1976, the Timorese People's Assembly formally approved the integration of East Timor with Indonesia. These developments on that island are not without interest to Australia some 350 miles across the Timor Sea.

Japan's Interest in the Indian Ocean

With the relinquishing of its overseas empire, Portugal has ceased to be a weight in the balance of power of the Indian Ocean region. Japan, without any territorial sovereignty in the area but with its economic weight, is a major factor in the power relations of the region. But as matters stand, its interests are even higher than its capability to influence developments.

Japan imports 99.5 percent of its current requirement of crude oil. Over 85 percent of this import originates in the Persian Gulf area and has to be shipped across the Indian Ocean; over 10 percent of the remaining requirement is imported from Indonesia, mostly from Sumatra. Among countries of the Persian Gulf area, Iran's share in Japanese oil imports is the largest, over 42 percent of the total; Saudi Arabia's, 17 percent; the Neutral Territory's (between Saudi Arabia and Kuwait), about 12 percent; Kuwait 9 percent; and the rest is divided between Abu Dhabi, Oman, and others.

Japan has to import 95 percent of the iron ore indispensable for its industry. Over 28 percent of Japan's iron ore imports emanate from Western Australia and are shipped across the eastern Indian Ocean to the Java Sea and the Pacific. Another 16 percent of Japan's iron ore is supplied by India, while 31 percent of the coal needed by Japan is provided by Australia.

Nearly 10 percent of Japan's total exports are directed to countries of the Indian Ocean; 21 percent of Japan's total imports proceed from that area (mainly because of oil, imports exceed exports). It may also be mentioned that Japan has now surpassed the United Kingdom as Australia's number one trading partner. For Australia this partnership is more significant than for Japan: 98 percent of Australia's coal exports are directed to Japan, plus 85 percent of its iron ore exports and 60 percent of all its other mineral exports.

The importance of Japan in the Indian Ocean may also be demonstrated by the fact that about 50 percent of Japan's seaborne trade passes through those waters, whether directed to Europe or to the countries of the Indian Ocean region.

Japan has invested heavily in the Persian Gulf area; Japanese oil companies operate, explore, and transport oil from that area and also from the Indonesian islands. Other Japanese investments have been made in practically all countries of the region but are particularly heavy in Indonesia, in Iran, and also in India. For some countries in the region, Japan is the first trading partner; half of Iran's exports are directed to that country.

It may be evident from the above survey that the Indian Ocean region, especially in respect to fuel importations, is not only important but indispensable, indeed irreplaceable, for Japan. In reverse, Japanese economy supplies many indispensable articles to the countries of the Indian Ocean, and therefore these countries are also dependent on Japanese production but to a lesser extent.

Japan's influence in the area under scrutiny relies on its enormous economic power, which through various channels makes itself felt: Japan has power as a purchaser or supplier of commodities, as an investor, as an adviser for industrialization and development, as a source of financial assistance, and as the main shipper of goods in those waters.

The Japanese Constitution of May 1947 adopted the principle which rejects war and the threat or the use of force as instruments of national policy. Therefore, it has no "armed forces," only a Self-Defense Force whose members are civil servants with arms. Although Tokyo has a Maritime Self-Defense Force with a limited capability to carry out distant operations, the constitutional restriction and the lack of enthusiasm for any such undertaking would prevent it from using this force in the waters leading to the Indian Ocean or the ocean itself. Under present Japanese contingency planning, the dispatch of forces overseas is not foreseen, even if vital Japanese interests were endangered.[6]

Japan may hope to obtain assistance from the United States under the Mutual Security Treaty of 1960 (extended in 1970), but it appears improbable that the promise to assist can be applied to contingencies other than an attack against Japan's national territory or its territorial waters. However, it also seems unlikely that any measure denying passage to commercial vessels in the straits leading to the Indian Ocean or in the ocean itself will be introduced selectively against Japan only.

The reluctance or inability to defend its interests by military measures induces Japan to broaden its options to employ political and economic leverage when its important interests are in peril. In other words, while Japan remains dependent on imports (especially oil) from the Indian Ocean region, the countries of that area should be made, as much as possible, dependent on the Japanese economy.

Whenever it is not inconsistent with its clear interests, Japan supports the political proposals of the regional governments within the United Nations and outside of it. Thus Japan voted for the proposals for the establishment of a Zone of Peace in the Indian Ocean when most of the countries interested in international navigation failed to do so. Yet freedom of the seas and unhindered seaborne traffic are vital for a Japan whose ships and tankers are teeming in the ports and waters of the Indian Ocean. There are at any time no fewer than 110 tankers at sea between Japan and the Persian Gulf.

For Japan, more than for any other nation, the free use of the critical narrows leading from and to the Indian Ocean is crucial. Japan will certainly have its weight felt when attempts are made to establish new rules of the law of the sea and when old tenets of this body of law undergo meaningful modifications.

Selected Bibliography

Freymond, Jacques. "Western Europe and the Indian Ocean." In *The Indian Ocean: Its Political, Economic, and Military Importance*, pp. 419-431. Edited by Alvin J. Cottrell and R. M. Burrell. New York: Praeger, 1972.

[6]It appears that even if Japan's oil lifeline should be cut by a closure of the Malacca Strait or the Strait of Lombok, it would not attempt to open the strait by force. *New York Times*, Mar. 4, 1973.

Gangal, S. C. "Britain and the Indian Ocean." In *Indian Ocean Power Rivalry,* pp. 20-23. Edited by T. T. Poulose. New Delhi: Young Asia Publications, 1974.

Narashimha, P. A. "Japan and the Indian Ocean." In *Indian Ocean Power Rivalry,* pp. 50-59. Edited by T. T. Poulose. New Delhi: Young Asia Publications, 1974.

Okita, Saburo. "Natural Resource Dependency and Japanese Foreign Policy." *Foreign Affairs* 52 (July 1974), 714-724.

Sargent, J. "Japan and the Indian Ocean." *Collected Papers of the Study Conference on the Indian Ocean in International Politics,* pp. 93-104. Southampton (England): University of Southampton, 1973. (Mimeographed.)

Tippet, A. S. "British Naval Interests in the Indian Ocean." In *Collected Papers of the Study Conference on the Indian Ocean in International Politics,* pp. 55-67. Southampton (England): University of Southampton, 1973. (Mimeographed.)

Vivekanandan, B. "Britain and the Indian Ocean." In *Indian Ocean Power Rivalry,* pp. 24-31. Edited by T. T. Poulose. New Delhi: Young Asia Publications, 1974.

Chapter 11

Oil, Shipping, and the Law of the Sea

> *The use of the sea and air is common to all; neither can a title to the ocean belong to any people or private persons, for as much as neither nature nor public use and custom permit any possession thereof.*
>
> Queen Elizabeth I of England
> to the Spanish ambassador, 1580

The power balances in the Indian Ocean region, as elsewhere, rest on a complexity of forces and factors; military capability is only one of them. Geographic location, size, and population, as well as economic strength, are all elements of national power. Wealth can buy arms and exert political influence. If wealth is based on the monopolistic marketing and pricing of essential products, it can be synonymous with power.

The cartelization of fossil fuel raised the power status of the oil-producing Persian Gulf powers to an unprecedented height, this area being the source of over 60 percent of the oil moving in world trade. The standing of other members of the Organization of Petroleum Exporting Countries (OPEC), as the oil cartel calls itself, has equally increased (including that of Indonesia, another Indian Ocean country). But the monopoly of oil power is largely controlled by the giants of the "liquid gold"—Saudi Arabia, Iran, Kuwait, Iraq, and Abu Dhabi.

This is not the first time in history that trade and finance between Europe and the Indian Ocean countries have exercised an important influence on their economies and, therefore, on their power relations.

It might be recalled that the importation of Oriental luxury articles to the Roman Empire during the first three centuries of the Christian era drained the Mediterranean countries of much of their gold and silver, especially the former. Precious stones, pearls, aromatics, ebony, carpets, and silk were brought into Rome from India and beyond, across the Indian Ocean and the Red Sea. As to price levels, we read that one pound of silk was valued equally with one pound of gold. Historians differ on whether or not this gold drain pauperized the empire and contributed to its internal decay.[1]

During the Crusades the prosperous classes of Western Europe became acquainted with the products of the Indies, primarily spices and luxury items of various sorts. Through the intermediary of the Arab merchant sailors and the Italian merchant cities of Venice, Genoa, Pisa, and others, these articles reached France, England, the Low Countries, and Germany at costs inflated by each and all of these middlemen. Again, Europe had nothing but metalic currency to offer in return. The Western world was saved from another gold drain partly by the inflow of gold and silver from the New World and partly by the Portuguese breakthrough to India. Finally, British and Dutch colonial control of the areas beyond the Levant, enabling these countries to become tax collectors themselves, ended this imbalance in payments; the British also began exporting their industrial goods to the Orient, the Dutch introduced a system of forced agriculture.[2]

Thus the "exploitation of Europe" came to an end, but the "exploitation of the East" began. Raw materials, sugar, coffee, tea, rubber, and indigo were exacted against articles of industry. While slave labor was abolished, indentured laborers were employed until the early twentieth century, when harsh methods, where they existed, were gradually abandoned.

With the oil price hike and the oil embargo, as practiced against the United States and other countries since late 1973, a new era of East-West exploitation opened, this time to the detriment of the West and revolving around a commodity more vital than the articles produced and exported before.

Just as in Roman times or during the Middle Ages and thereafter, East-West trade today depends on shipping. Navigation in the Indian Ocean and in the narrow waters leading to and from it requires safety and order, just as it did in the past. The security of shipping is conditioned on the respect of the law of the sea. Questions of international law, such as the width of the territorial waters, the status of international straits, the archipelago concept supported by the insular powers, and lastly the parceling and demarcating of the continental shelf, are all replete with political significance, probably even much more in the Indian Ocean region than in other parts of the world.

[1] See Edward Gibbon, *The Decline and Fall of the Roman Empire,* abridgement by D. M. Low (New York, 1960), p. 29.

[2] See M. de Pradt, *Les Trois Âges des colonies* (Paris, 1802), Vol. II, pp. 452-453; Holden Furber, *John Company at Work. A Study of European Expansion in India in the Late Eighteenth Century* (Cambridge, Mass., 1951), 16-20.

The Oil-rich and the Oil-poor Countries

For several decades fossil fuel was explored, produced, and marketed by the big oil companies of America and Western Europe.[3] They provided the investment capital that served to develop the oil empire of the Middle East, mainly in the area around the Persian Gulf. However, since the late 1960s the position of these companies has completely changed. Gradually, under the constant threat of nationalization or because of nationalization itself, actual decision making on all important questions, such as production levels, investment, exports, and pricing, has passed under the control of the host governments. As long as sales were competitive, the companies still possessed some bargaining leverage; but with the increase in demand for oil, this leverage was lost.

Where they still operate on the local scene, these companies have been reduced to the provision of technical services and the refining, transportation, and distribution of the product. They were forced to comply with the directives of various host governments under the threat of further unilateral cancellations of existing agreements.[4] In most respects the companies have been reduced to the status of contractors or agents operating under the instructions of the local governments; in other places, the operations have been completely Arabized or Persianized. The foreign companies continue to make profits, but the host countries interfere even in their pricing mechanisms, their profits, and how and where oil is to be delivered. Some governments operated through their own state-owned companies and have begun acquiring tanker fleets. Their absolute control over the production and flow of oil was demonstrated in the second half of 1973 by two major developments. The first was the "supply shock" administered by Arab producers, an embargo imposed on some consumer nations, classed as "friends of Israel," and a simultaneous cutback in production to create a scarcity. The second was the "price shock" when the OPEC doubled the price of oil on October 16, 1973, and further doubled it on December 23. Thus within ten weeks the oil cost its consumers over four times more than in September of that year.

The timing and suddenness of these monstrous price hikes was "more than a crime, it was a mistake," to use Talleyrand's words. It was in its effect worse than the increase of the price itself. The timing and speed prevented the termination or reduction of the inflationary process under which the entire world suffered at that time and created an instantaneous imbalance in the trade and payment relations of all nations except those of the Soviet bloc and China. There was no reason for such precipitate action; the production costs were minimal compared to the $3 per barrel price in September 1973 (raised to this

[3]The principal companies were five Americans (Standard Oil of New Jersey, Mobil Oil, Texaco, Standard Oil of California, and Gulf Oil), the British-Dutch Royal Dutch-Shell Group, the British Petroleum Company and the French Compagnie Française des Pétroles.

[4]See Walter J. Levy, "World Oil Cooperation or International Chaos," *Foreign Affairs,* 52 (July 1974), 693-694.

level from 90 cents in 1970), which skyrocketed to about \$10 per barrel by December. A hike, if thought to be necessary, could have come gradually, stretched over several years. But the sudden realization of power—the delirium of power and greed, indeed—prevented a rational and considered action.

It seems hardly fruitful to discuss here the justification for the decision of the oil producers. Evidently, production costs played no role whatsoever. Oil brought a relative affluence to the producing countries; even before the price hike, their per capita income was higher than that of the non-oil-producing countries of the region. Employees of the oil companies earned higher wages than those paid by the local employers or the governments. Exploitation of the oil-producing countries or of local labor can thus hardly be adduced as an excuse. Exploitation in earlier colonial or precolonial periods seems no valid argument. Should there be any validity in looking back into the pages of history, it will be—as we have seen—difficult to ascertain whether the East has been exploited more by the West or vice versa.

Arguments concerning the higher cost of other sources of energy, such as coal, can easily be refuted by reference to their much higher costs of production. That the oil reserves of at least some of the oil producers will be exhausted before the end of this century or even earlier is certainly true; but to industrialize their countries before their oil wells dry out would demand a rational and well-planned investment policy, one which would not harm those countries wherefrom the know-how for industrialization is to be obtained and in which much of the accumulated wealth of the oil producers is to be invested. It is doubtful whether the advantages of the sudden bonanza for the oil countries will be commensurate with the damage they have done to the economy and power status of other nations, many of them allies, and the damage which they have thereby inflicted to themselves.

It seems highly questionable whether the gargantuan surplus of petrodollars can be usefully absorbed by any of the Persian Gulf oil exporters. While more populated countries, such as Iran (32 million), which are near or at the take-off stage of development, may be able to take in at least the major part of their inflated oil income (with expenditure on armaments), Saudi Arabia, with a population of about 8 million and a higher oil income than that of Iran, will find it more difficult to do so. An even more extreme case is Abu Dhabi, with a population of 100,000 (that is, 1.25 percent of Saudi Arabia's population) but with an oil production one-fifth as great as that of her much larger neighbor. Oil states are unlikely to guarantee themselves prosperity in the lean years to come through investments in often useless construction projects or armaments which, if they rust away in the sand and become unserviceable, will end like the navy Moscow once delivered to Sukarno's Indonesia. Nor will dubious short-term investments in the West significantly improve their economic plight or provide a long-term home for the ever-accumulating petrodollars. The unilateral and arbitrary actions of the recent past omitted taking account of the evident community of interest between the oil-producing countries and their customers in the West. To damage the industrial nations and then make them the beneficiaries of such investments seems hardly a judicious *modus procedendi*.[5]

The "price shock" has hit those developing nations which have no or only insignificant oil resources of their own much harder than the industrial nations of the West or Japan. The ill-considered, hasty decision was not intended to penalize fellow Third World countries. Of course, no attempt was made to set differential prices in favor of these "innocent sufferers" (futile in any case).

The steep oil price hike drove a wedge between the oil-rich and the oil-poor nations of the Indian Ocean region. India, Pakistan, Bangladesh, Sri Lanka, and Ethiopia head the long list of these countries, victims of exploitation by their fellow ex-colonials and alleged earlier martyrs of Western exploitations both.[6]

For many of these countries which have to pay the exorbitant oil prices, the steep climb of costs meant, at least for the time being, an end to their difficult growth process. For some—India and Bangladesh, for example—it also added to their problem of feeding and preventing the starvation of their fast-growing populations.

Strangely enough, these countries were generally reluctant to stand up openly against this exploitative rise in oil prices (if so, they have done it most discreetly), partly because of a sense of solidarity they still profess to share with those nations which have just emerged from "economic oppression" and partly because they hoped to enter into individual agreements with the oil lords which would alleviate their plight. Indira Gandhi, Prime Minister of India, even defended the Arab oil producers because the Persian Gulf nations were "exploited" in the past.[7]

The oil-rich countries have undertaken certain palliative measures for assisting the developing countries whose economies have been severely drained by their oil bills. For instance, one-third of India's oil imports from Iran are to be sold to New Delhi on a low-interest concessional basis to be paid for in six to ten years. Other loans are channeled through the Kuwait Fund for Economic Development to all developing countries or through the International Monetary Fund.[8] However, in OPEC circles it is still believed that primary responsibility for

---

[5]This community of interest was recognized in 1972 by Sheik Ahmed Zaki Yamani, the Saudi Arabian Minister of Oils and Minerals, as an "indissoluble catholic marriage of the interests of producing nations, consuming nations and the oil companies" (*New York Times*, Oct. 8, 1972). Subsequent developments rather revealed that OPEC disregarded this community of interest which had all the characteristics of a "shotgun wedding."

[6]Others are Burma, Egypt, Kenya, the Malagasy Republic, Mauritius, Somalia, the Sudan, Tanzania, Thailand, the two Yemens, and Zambia. Malaysia is likely to produce sufficient oil for its own use within a few years. Singapore is no longer in a "developing" stage. Smaller countries, such as Nepal or Malawi, are equal sufferers.

[7]*New York Times*, Oct. 5, 1974. In 1974 India spent $1.2 billion on oil imports compared with $483 million in 1973.

[8]See Elizabeth Monroe and Robert Mabro, eds., *Oil Producers and Consumers: Conflict or Cooperation* (New York, 1974), pp. 34-35 and 55-60; Khodadad Farmanfarmaian et al., "How Can the World Afford OPEC Oil?" *Foreign Affairs*, 53(January 1975), 214-218.

economic assistance to the less developed countries rests with the "rich" industrial nations.

The oil-rich governments also advised their less fortunate brethren in Asia and Africa to follow their example and form cartels to increase the prices of certain raw products required by the West and Japan. In the wake of inflation, these prices have gone up, but often still fluctuate according to the law of supply and demand. For instance, natural rubber, a product of the Indian Ocean nations of Malaysia (the principal producer), Indonesia, and Thailand (plus smaller amounts by India and Sri Lanka), has to compete with synthetic rubber manufactured in the large industrial nations—the United States, Britain, West Germany, and Canada.[9] Because oil is required for the manufacture of synthetic rubber, the price of artificial rubber might increase and allow a more constant rise in that of natural rubber. Still, there cannot be established such monopolistic production and delivery of this commodity as happened with oil.

The loans and other concessions made by the OPEC countries to the developing nations are likely to be temporary expedients only. Eventually these will exhaust their creditworthiness, and their expected and much-hoped-for developmental process is likely to come to a standstill. The economic recession into which the industrial world has slumped, partly due to the "oil shock" and concomitant balance-of-trade difficulties, will boomerang into the Third World including the less developed nations of the Indian Ocean region, except, of course, for those which were permitted by geography to lift themselves into an Eldorado, at least for the next decade or so.

The peremptory hike of oil prices turned a handful of oil-rich countries of the Persian Gulf into super-Croesuses and placed them in the position of being able to amass a surplus of perhaps $600 billion within the next ten years[10] and thereby effected a radical shift in the balance of power, in both the global and the regional meaning of the term.

Oil and the Balance of Power

According to estimates the oil revenue of the OPEC countries in the five years from 1975 through to 1979 will amount to $600 billion (in 1974 dollars); the share of the Persian Gulf countries will be roughly $400 billion.[11]

[9]*New York Times,* Jan. 9, 1975. Phosphate appears to be the only raw material where cartelization might prove successful; but phosphate is used to produce fertilizers, and an immoderate increase of its price will harm countries like India much more than developed nations.

[10]Monroe and Mabro, p. 73. It should be remembered, in this respect, that at the time of this writing United States foreign investments amount to about $90 billion.

[11]Farmanfarmaian et al., p. 201. Other estimates are either higher or lower; see Thomas O. Enders, "OPEC and the Industrial Countries. The Next Ten Years," *Foreign Affairs,* (July 1975), 625-637.

The surplus funds of the Persian Gulf governments, that is, the amounts available for domestic expenditure above normal needs (for investments, armaments, possible regional aid), as well as investments abroad, in the decade from 1974 to 1983 may amount to $955 billion.[12] These possible accurate estimates reflect the enormous financial power which the governments of the northwest corner of the Indian Ocean region could wield in the near future. A faster than originally expected recycling of the oil revenue surpluses into Western economies would somewhat reduce the plutocratic strength of the major oil producers and increase an "interpenetration" of consumer and producer economies.

Here we are less concerned with the economic repercussions of this anomalistic and brusque concentration of wealth in the hands of a few countries, none of them very powerful in terms of their overall economy or their military capability; some of them are "fragile entities, without substantial strategic and military strength in the world."[13] Only Iran and, in lesser degree, Saudi Arabia and Iraq can be considered medium powers; Kuwait, Abu Dhabi, Qatar, Bahrain, Dubai, and Oman are ministates. The two giant oil producers, Iran and Saudi Arabia, especially the former, are attempting to turn themselves into military powers by crash programs, but in any case their military capabilities will not be proportionate to the financial status they have attained.

The economic dependence of the Western powers and of Japan has reduced their relative power status not only in relation to the oil-producing countries, over which they have lost much of their leverage, but also in absolute terms. In other words, the so-called free world, now economically weakened and disunited, has lost a great deal of its ascendancy over the socialist camp, which has so far remained largely unaffected by this upheaval created by the oil-exporting powers.

A strange situation has arisen in which, for instance, Iran, an ally of the United States, has contributed to the undermining of the economy of its ally, in disregard of the fact that its security depends ultimately on a power balance whose principal pivot is that very same United States.

Saudi Arabia, like Iran, is highly apprehensive of Soviet advances and the potential dangers emanating from Moscow. Still, with the unrestrained use of its oil power, it went along to weaken a friend and thereby strengthen the arch foe.

The oil squeeze contributed to the inflationary and recessional process in the Western world and in Japan, which might easily result in internal unrest and unstable governments, and could exercise a debilitating influence on the conduct of foreign affairs of these countries. Of course, these countries may rightly blame themselves for their lack of unity in the face of the impending oil threat, a confusion which has not ended at the time of this writing.

The situation created by the oil embargo and oil price avalanche is complicated by the Arab-Israeli conflict, over which the Atlantic allies are equally out of harmony. The relations between the Arab countries and the United States are

[12]Monroe and Mabro, p. 73.

[13]Levy, p. 705.

also asymmetric: some of them are openly pro-Soviet (e.g., Syria and Iraq); others wish to keep an equal distance from both Washington and Moscow (e.g., Egypt); and still others are formal or informal allies of the United States (e.g., Jordan or Saudi Arabia) but are opposed to the American policy toward Israel.

The "unholy alliance" of pro-Soviet and anti-Soviet Arab governments united against Israel prompted the oil boycott of late 1973 and early 1974. This boycott, or embargo, was intended to force the United States and other "friends of Israel" to change their Middle Eastern policies—to reduce or abandon their assistance to Israel; it was a highly hostile act (one may call it "oil imperialism"), although not inconsistent with international law.

The open discord between nations which, apart from the oil crisis and the Arab-Israeli feud, recognize the need for collaboration in the face of Communist or leftist revolutionary dangers does not fail to be felt in the power balances of the Indian Ocean region. The confrontation between the powers which dictate extortionist oil prices but are militarily weak and those which cringe under the weight of the oil price avalanche but are militarily strong is particularly anomalous and replete with dangers. Characteristic of the confusion created is the thought that armed force should be employed in retaliation and defense against another oil boycott.[14] There is no doubt that in this confrontation between the oil exporters and the oil consumers of the West and of Japan, as well as between the oil-rich and oil-poor less developed nations, the *tertius gaudens* (the third party who rejoices) is the Soviet Union.

At present, the Soviet Union and China are the only major powers which are not directly dependent on the oil supplies of the Middle East. However, this is not equally true for the Eastern European client states of Moscow; since the Soviet Union is not in a position to satisfy their full needs for energy, they are compelled to import quantities of Middle Eastern oil at the price set by OPEC. Furthermore, it appears that in a not too distant future Moscow may be required to resort to these same sources unless it can substitute East Siberian production for its own dwindling oil resources or restrict the demand of its own consumers.[15] While the Soviet Union is not able to benefit directly from the oil price hike, nor influence directly the future developments in pricing or restricting the oil flow, it can exploit politically, diplomatically, and propagandistically the rift between the oil producers and consumers as well as that within the divided world of "oil-hungry capitalists."

In the Indian Ocean, Moscow principally has to face the United States, a country less deeply hurt by the oil squeeze than its European partners and Japan. However, the diminution of influence and prestige of America, the leading capitalist and military power of the West, can be exploited in various ways. Moscow, of course, supports the "emancipation" of the oil-producing

[14]On Jan. 2, 1975, Secretary of State Henry Kissinger said in an interview that he could not rule out completely the use of force against oil-producing countries, but·as a last resort to save the Western world, not as a way to lower oil prices. *New York Times*, Jan. 3, 1975.

[15]See Arnold L. Horelick, *The Soviet Union, the Middle East, and the Evolving World Energy Situation* (Santa Monica, Calif., 1973).

countries from the yoke of "blood-sucking" companies and welcomes the price rise which ends the colonial-type exploitation of developing nations. As the possible cleavage between the United States and the oil-producing governments widens, Moscow might try to extend its own protective arm over the countries "threatened" by Western imperialism. On the one hand, the Soviet leadership would enjoy the sight of a—most unlikely—United States military intervention in the Persian Gulf to secure oil supplies but, on the other hand, would be frightened by the prospect of the American-Soviet conflagration which might thus ensue.

The scenario which Moscow would most welcome would be a further erosion of American, British, and French influence in the Indian Ocean area—an open split and disruption of ties of alliance between the West and Middle Eastern countries—and a further strengthening of its position in those nations which so far have been rather antagonistic to any Soviet presence in the region. However, as long as Iran, Saudi Arabia, and others are recipients of American, British, and French arms—arms which constitute a counterdependence, one by no means so tense as that created by the demand for oil—and as long as there is a hope that a form of cooperation between the West and OPEC can be belatedly established, the Soviet Union can only watch developments and hope for the best.

Moscow will probably not be too happy to observe the increasing power and influence which the Persian Gulf powers could exert over the oil-poor countries of the Indian Ocean. For instance, India's dependence on the goodwill of these oil producers, as displayed by Iran, Saudi Arabia, and Iraq, would create a quasi client-and-master relation which would in some respects substitute for a similar actual or hoped-for relationship between New Delhi and Moscow. If only the Soviets could step in and offer their oil assistance (as they have delivered wheat on occasion to India), it would immensely strengthen their hold over India and other countries thus benefited. Similarly, if Moscow could substitute for Japan's dependence on Middle Eastern oil the latter's dependence on the so far chimerical oil of East Siberia, the political advantage would be sky-high. As things stand, Moscow can profit only by the chaotic situation indirectly and by watching further developments and mistakes which either the oil producers or the oil consumers might commit.[16]

The oil situation has certainly added to the already existing uncertainties and instabilities of the Indian Ocean region. The questions and crises created by the precipitate and inconsiderate action of the oil producers will have to be solved or settled on a level beyond the confines of the ocean. Crises might erupt in this

[16] A lack of moderation by the oil producers, as would be manifest in another boycott of oil, or another steep price increase would be such a mistake. A precipitate reaction or overreaction by the United States would be another. A military seizure of the oil wells, as suggested by Robert W. Tucker ("Oil. The Issue of American Intervention," *Commentary* 51 [January 1975], 21-31), along the Arabian coast of the Persian Gulf, from Kuwait to Qatar (400 miles in length), could be supported only as a last-ditch measure to prevent "strangulation" would be bound to have most vehement repercussions among the Arabs and the Soviets, and could trigger unforeseeable events, even a clash between the superpowers. See *New York Times,* Jan. 10, 1975.

region because of oil; but the basic questions of finance, the recycling of surplus profits, the approach toward self-sufficiency in the United States, and the eventual balancing out of trade and payments, which will also affect the regional oil-poor nations—these and other problems will have to be dealt with by the industrial powers of the West and Japan, on the one hand, and OPEC, on the other. The rather doubtful results of the meetings of UNCTAD (United Nations Conference on Trade and Development) might, to some extent, improve the status of the poorer nations located along the shores of the Indian Ocean.

The delivery of the masses of oil, as well as other important commodities which are shipped across the Indian Ocean, is just as vital as the production of these materials. And smooth and uninterrupted surface and air transit is a question which concerns not only the producing and purchasing parties but practically all the nations around the Indian Ocean as well.

Shipping and Its Protection

The Indian Ocean region is the source of large percentages of the world's production of various mineral and agricultural products. The importance of the region as the principal producer of crude oil has been described earlier. It should also be remembered that over 16 percent of the world's output of copper originates in that area (Zambia and South Africa), 20 percent of manganese (mostly India and South Africa), 20 percent of antimony (South Africa), 17 percent of vanadium (South Africa), 77 percent of gold (South Africa), and 15 percent of diamonds (South Africa).

Among agricultural products, 60 percent of the world's tea output comes from the Indian Ocean region (mostly India and Ceylon), 67 percent of jute (mostly Bangladesh), and 25 percent of hemp.[17]

A considerable amount of these raw products is required by the countries of Europe, North America, and Japan. In reverse, mostly manufactured articles of these countries are being shipped in large quantities to the nations of the Indian Ocean region. Furthermore, transports from Europe and South America pass the ocean en route to Japan and China, and Japanese and Chinese goods also are shipped across these waters to Europe and the Americas. Compared to these movements of ships, the trade relations and transports between the littoral countries of that Ocean are minimal.[18]

Among all the ships entering the Indian Ocean from any direction in 1971, 2,385 were dry-cargo vessels (including the "tramp" ships) and passenger liners, and 1,355 were tankers. Among the former, those carrying the British flag were

[17]See Charles Issawi, "The Politics and Economics of Natural Resources," in *The Indian Ocean. Its Political, Economic, and Military Importance,* ed. Alvin J. Cottrell and R. M. Burrell (New York, 1972), pp. 18-34.

[18]Keith Trace, "International Trade and Commercial Relations," in *The Indian Ocean,* ed. Alvin Cottrell and R. M. Burrell (New York, 1972), pp. 50-51.

the most numerous (435), followed by Greek (241), Japanese (189), and Indian (147) ships. The destination of these ships, entering from around the Cape, varied principally between Japan (456), India (402), Australia (206), China (203), Mozambique (146), and the Persian Gulf (124).[19]

Among the 1,355 tankers, 1,090 belonged to Western countries, 178 to Japan, and only 41 to countries of the Soviet bloc and China. The remainder (224) belonged to various Asian, African, or South American countries. Of all tankers, 1,050 transported oil from the Persian Gulf; the destination of 578 tankers was Europe (around the Cape); the destination of 280 tankers leaving the Persian Gulf was Japan; the destination of 74 was East and West Africa; and 40 sailed to the east coast of the United States. The remainder were destined for South America.[20]

All the tankers originating from or heading toward the Persian Gulf en route to or from Europe or North America pass the Mozambique Channel before or after rounding the Cape. However, other commercial vessels frequently use the route east of Madagascar (when heading for Ceylon or the Bay of Bengal or the Malacca Straits). Ships moving to and from Australia use the direct maritime route from the Cape, generally south of Mauritius.

Since the reopening of the Suez Canal on June 5, 1975, maritime routes and their frequencies have somewhat changed. However, it is not believed that the significance of the canal will be the same as in the past. Ships with a draught beyond thirty-five feet cannot pass it; thus larger tankers and supertankers continue to take the Cape route when heading for Europe or North America.[21]

Geography compels maritime traffic to converge in certain channels or straits, called "focal sea areas." In the Indian Ocean such places are the Cape of Good Hope area, the Mozambique Channel, the Bab el Mandeb Strait, the Hormuz Strait, the Malacca and Singapore Straits, and also several straits between Indonesian islands, in particular the Lombok and Sunda Straits. According to the data compiled by Henri Labrousse, 18 tankers and 28 other commercial vessels passed the Cape each day in 1971, that is, one ship every half hour. Through the Mozambique Channel an average of 20 tankers and 13 cargo vessels passed daily in both directions. Through the Malacca and Singapore Straits 23 tankers and 13 cargo ships passed daily, through the Hormuz Strait 3 cargo ships and 38 tankers. During the closure of the Suez Canal, the Strait of Bab el Mandeb lost most of its traffic; only 2 cargoes passed there daily in 1971 and only 3 tankers, instead of the 50 ships of all categories which crossed it daily in June 1967.

An interdiction or partial interdiction of the maritime traffic on the principal international routes of the Indian Ocean would have far-reaching economic and

[19]These figures were compiled by Henri Labrousse in his notable book *Le golfe et le canal* (Paris, 1973), pp. 149-156.

[20]*Ibid.*

[21]After the opening of the Suez Canal half as many ships used it before it was closed in 1967; *New York Times*, Sep. 14, 1975.

political significance. It would deprive the industrial countries of Europe and America, as well as Japan, not only of oil but also of other indispensable raw materials. It appears almost futile to speculate on the circumstances in which maritime traffic may be interrupted or cut. Any government which would explicitly undertake such a step would have to face violent reactions from those nations whose ships were blocked, seized, endangered, or sunk. In the United States, as well as in NATO military circles, the contingent event which is being examined is an undeclared war by hostile (e.g., Soviet) submarines against Western shipping.

Moscow is much less vulnerable in the Indian Ocean than in many other theaters; the dry or liquid cargo that Soviet ships carry is generally less essential for Soviet requirements than that carried by Western and Japanese vessels. The Soviet units operating in the Indian Ocean may, for lack of reconnaissance or fighter-bomber aircraft, provide only limited protection to Soviet shipping unless some of the littoral countries make available their airfields for Soviet use. On the other hand, the Western powers, particularly the United States, are well equipped to carry out reconnaissance or other air action in any portion of the Indian Ocean. Washington may be able to concentrate a number of its carriers, and its land-based aircraft may operate from Diego Garcia. Western warships would, however, be vulnerable to Soviet submarine attacks.

In critical situations littoral states are likely to lay mines in some of the focal areas in their vicinity, in narrow waters, such as the Bab el Mandeb, Hormuz, or Malacca Straits, or in areas of the high sea which they claim as their territorial waters. Such operations, in time of peace, are naturally dependent on the interpretation of the law of the sea, which generally prohibits interference with shipping on the high seas and in international straits.

Territorial Waters and Straits

The question of the width of territorial waters affects both the littoral nations of the ocean and those outsiders which have navigational interests in the region. Just as is true with other waters, the Indian Ocean is afflicted with the incertitudes stemming from controversies in regard to the span of the territorial sea. However, in the region under our scrutiny, this question is related more than in any other part of the world with the navigational rights through narrow waters; important straits which serve international ship routes are more numerous here, and impediments to shipping placed in these maritime gateways would more seriously affect the international community than elsewhere.

The Third Law of the Sea Conference is likely to accept an extension of the territorial sea up to twelve miles provided the participating nations agree on other important issues. Among these, unimpeded transit through international straits figures prominently.[22] Freedom of navigation through straits should turn

[22]See John R. Stevenson and Bernard H. Oxman, "The Preparations for the Law of the Sea Conference," *American Journal of International Law,* 68 (January 1974), 8-9.

into a more precise and broader concept than the present controversial "innocent passage" provision which has been incorporated into Article 24 of the 1958 Convention on the Territorial Sea and the Contiguous Zone. This article defines "innocent passage" as one which does not prejudice the peace, good order, or security of the coastal state or states. Under this definition of "innocent passage" coastal states could, by giving an extensive interpretation to the concept, control and interfere with shipping in their territorial waters in a rather arbitrary manner, by excluding warships, for instance, forcing submarines to pass on the surface, and refusing passage selectively to certain flags or certain cargoes.

On the other hand, the increase of the span of the territorial sea to twelve miles would place many of the important international straits (that is, straits which connect two parts of the high seas) in the Indian Ocean under the jurisdiction of coastal states and subject transit through them to their subjective interpretation of "innocent passage." It should also be remembered that "innocent passage" means passage for ships and does not permit free overflight by warplanes and, in many instances, civilian aircraft.

Among the international straits affected by the twelve-mile territorial waters, the Malacca and Singapore Straits should be listed first. Indonesia and Malaysia, in a declaration dated November 16, 1971, denied that the Strait of Malacca is an "international strait" and rather ambiguously asserted that navigation in it "was the responsibility of the coastal states concerned." Singapore only took notice of the denial of the "international" character of this strait but agreed on the necessity of tripartite cooperation to ensure the safety of shipping in these narrows.[23]

With the twelve-mile width, the territorial waters of Indonesia and Malaysia would overlap in the Malacca Strait, and those of Singapore and Indonesia in the Singapore Strait. Similarly in the wider channel of the Bab el Mandeb Strait, the jurisdiction of France and South Yemen would meet along the median line should France follow South Yemen's example in extending its marginal sea to twelve miles (the small channel, between Perim Island and the coast of Yemen, is already under the territorial jurisdiction of Aden).

Also in the Strait of Hormuz the territorial waters of Iran and of Oman would overlap.[24] With twelve miles from both sides, the Zanzibar Channel (between Zanzibar Island and the Tanzanian mainland) would be placed under Tanzanian jurisdiction eliminating the belt of the high sea which at present divides the marginal sea extending east and west.

Similarly, many important straits between the Indonesian islands (e.g., the Sunda, Lombok, and Wetar Straits) would be included in their entirety in the Indonesian territorial sea.

[23]This declaration was prompted by Japan's insistence upon providing for greater safety of navigation, which would permit secure passage to their 200,000-ton tankers. The declaration sought to exclude Japan from interference in the affairs of the Malacca and Singapore Straits. See K. E. Shaw and G. G. Thomson, *The Straits of Malacca* (Singapore, 1973), pp. 67-72.

[24]See Chap. 6, pp. 125-26.

The Gulf of Aqaba would totally be embraced in the territorial waters of Saudi Arabia and Egypt (provided this country regains control over the Sinai Peninsula) except for the head of the gulf adjacent to the Israeli and Jordanian coast where these two countries have their territorial sea. With a broad interpretation of "innocent passage," Israeli shipping to and from the Red Sea (and the Indian Ocean) might be legally interdicted on this legal argument should Israel lose military control.[25]

The major shipping nations—the United States, Britain, the Soviet Union, as well as Japan to some extent—are strongly opposed to any curtailment of free navigation through international straits. While Japan is more ready to compromise, the other major powers oppose any extension of territorial waters into the strait areas unless "free passage" (to replace the concept of innocent passage) is simultaneously agreed upon. They would, however, agree that "innocent passage" be continued for passage through territorial waters, in general, but insist that special provisions be created for international straits. But even the major shipping powers differ on how to formulate the idea of "free transit"; Moscow, possibly to please some of the interested Third World nations, would also include in the provisions relating to straits certain obligations for the flag states. Some of the Indian Ocean littoral states share the anxieties and views of the outside shipping nations; for instance, Ethiopia has proposed to establish a corridor within the straits (thinking of Bab el Mandeb) which would have the status of the high seas. And the Organization of African Unity has suggested that the principle of innocent passage be made more precise.[26] Australia has also proposed a detailed definition of "innocent passage," considering certain claims reasonable (such as the requirement that submarines should pass surfaced through strait) while rejecting others.

The extension of territorial waters to twelve miles would, in any case, considerably reduce the area of the high seas. But the width of the territorial sea will remain controversial. For example, some Indian Ocean littoral states, such as the Malagasy Republic and India, pose excessive claims to territorial waters of up to a breadth of 100 miles. Much also depends on the protrusion of the territorial seabelt into the high seas—that is, on where the so-called baselines are set, lines wherefrom the width of the territorial sea is measured. Under the rules of international law, states with indented, rugged coasts are entitled to draw their baselines direct from promontory to promontory, cutting through the short and deep sinuosities of the coast. The shore of Burma is of such a character, and so is the Indonesian side of the Malacca Strait.

In the Malacca Strait, Indonesia has laid its baselines in such a manner as to cut through many of the indentations. On the Malaysian side, however, the coast is straight, and therefore the baseline has to follow the shoreline. The median

[25]Mordechai Abir, *Sharm al-Sheikh—Bab al-Mandeb. The Strategic Balance and Israel's Southern Approaches* (Jerusalem, 1974); Majid Khadduri, *Major Middle Eastern Problems in International Law* (Washington, D.C., 1972), pp. 78-86.

[26]Stevenson and Oxman, p. 11.

line in the strait which divides Malaysian from Indonesian territorial waters is the line equidistant from the two baselines on each side. Because Indonesia is using the "straight" baseline system, the median line is generally closer to the Malaysian shore and leaves a much larger water surface under the sovereignty of Indonesia than vice versa.

However, the drawing of baselines by island states in such a manner as to include distant parts of an archipelago led to the construction of the "archipelago theory," which is yet another controversial feature of the Indian Ocean scenery.

The Archipelago Concept

The island states of Indonesia, Mauritius, the Philippines, and Fiji, calling themselves "archipelagic" nations, claimed the right to draw straight lines joining their outermost islands; waters within these lines are to be either territorial waters or, according to Indonesia, internal waters,[27] and entry into or passage through those waters is to be considered an "innocent passage" of a kind subject to the regulations and controls of the "archipelagic state." Overflight by aircraft would also depend on the permission of the territorial state and be confined to certain "corridors" indicated by it.

In addition to Indonesia and Mauritius, it can be expected that another island state of the Indian Ocean, namely the Republic of the Maldives, will claim "archipelagic" status; the Seychelles and the Comoros, achieving independence, are most likely to raise similar claims.

These claims have prompted strong opposition on behalf of the major maritime powers. Indonesia extends for over 3,000 miles from Sumatra to Irian; should the archipelagic concept apply, not only could no ship pass without permission of Indonesia through its many straits and other waters, but overflight across this space would depend on the discretionary ruling of the Indonesian government. Similarly, in case of the Maldives, their island chain extends for over 1,000 miles from north to south; it would form, should the archipelagic theory apply, a barrier harmful to shipping and aviation under rules and conditions set by the government in question.

Evidently, the unreasonableness of such claims has been recognized by the Mauritian government, which would refrain from including distant possessions in the archipelagic complex (such as Rodrigues Island, which lies 200 miles from Mauritius) provided its claims for an extended contental shelf were recognized.

Britain, an island state itself, suggested a more modest type of archipelagic principle when proposing that the baselines connecting outermost points of the outermost islands should not be longer than forty-eight nautical miles and that the ratio of the area of the sea to the area of land territory within the perimeter

[27]Internal waters are estuaries, harbors, and certain bays (situated landward from the baseline), waters where even the "innocent passage" principle does not apply and where entry of foreign ships depends on permission by the territorial authority.

in question should not exceed five to one. Even so, the freedom of transit required in straits would apply to the straits within the archipelago through which international shipping routes led at the time when the agreement was reached. In other waters of the archipelago, the principle of innocent passage is to apply. Unrestricted overflight would be permitted through certain international defined corridors. It appears that Australia, much affected by the status of Indonesia, would more or less support the British proposition.

On the issue of archipelagic waters, as in the case of international straits and territorial waters, the security interests, exercise of sovereign rights, and national pride of the littoral nations oppose the navigational, commercial, and strategic interests of exogenous powers. But not exclusively: geographic location and other circumstances often divide Indian Ocean nations on these issues. For instance, Singapore, so much dependent on international trade and shipping, opposes obstacles to navigation; Ethiopia, because of its dependence on free traffic through the Bab el Mandeb Strait (over which it exercises no control), also promotes "freedom of movement." Generally speaking, each nation considers the interpretation of and future legislation on rules of the law of the sea from its own, often very narrow, angle of interest. This creates strange alliances, which cut across the usual divisions between friends and foes, and renders agreement more difficult.

Attitudes of coastal states are also divergent on the problem of resource jurisdiction beyond the territorial sea, a topic which in recent years has drawn even greater attention than the questions of straits and the width of territorial waters. The economic exploitation of the continental shelf and the length of its extension into the ocean floor created acute controversies which the Conference on the Law of the Sea will find hard to resolve.

The Continental Shelf and Resource Jurisdiction

Coastal nations in the Indian Ocean region, as elsewhere, claim the right of exclusive exploitation of the resources of the sea in the spaces adjacent to their territorial waters. This includes jurisdiction over the sea bed and its subsoil and over the economic uses of superjacent waters, that is, the exclusive right to catch fish. The relative provisions of the 1958 Convention on the Continental Shelf are considered outdated and superseded by developments. Claims and proposals on these questions vary from country to country. Many suggest a 200-mile exclusive "economic zone"; but even among the proponents of this plan (which includes the African coastal states of the Indian Ocean), there are differences as to whether the 200 miles should extend in any case or only if the outer edge of the continental shelf is less than these 200 miles.

These questions are complicated by the fact that many land-locked or shelf-locked countries (the latter are those which for geographic reasons are deprived of a continental shelf) wish to participate in the gains to be derived from the exploitation of sea resources. Iraq, for example, is a state which, because of its location, is barred from staking out continental shelf claims. Land-locked hinterland states of Tanzania, Uganda, and Zambia wish to participate in the profits to be derived from the continental shelf off Tanzania's coast. The plan to make the bed of the high seas into a "common heritage" of mankind where exploitation would be controlled by an international agency for the benefit of the world community would also suffer if large tracts of the ocean floor should fall under the exclusive jurisdiction of the coastal states. [28]

Oil ranks foremost among the mineral resources which coastal nations hope to exploit. Spurred by the rise of the price of oil and in order to improve their shattered trade balances and also hoping that by the windfall of a rich oil deposit they may emerge as one of the oil-rich nations, governments around the periphery of the Indian Ocean have issued permits to explore for oil. Some discoveries have already raised expectations; oil-poor India is searching for oil in the Gulf of Cambay and in certain parts of the Gulf of Bengal.[29] Oil is also being prospected for around the west coast of Australia and in the Timor and Arafura Seas. South Africa has also issued permits for exploration along its coast. The oil-rich countries, Indonesia and those of the Persian Gulf, are extending their search for further oil finds. Mauritius hopes that within its islands and shoals the discovery of "fluid gold" will end the economic problems of its increasing population. In many areas of the Indian Ocean there are high expectations of finding other mineral products in the sea bed, such as manganese, nickel, copper, zirconium, cobalt, and molybdenum.

The question of fishing sets against each other the "long distance" fishing nations (for example, the Soviets or the Japanese) and the coastal nations of the Indian Ocean, which wish to reserve the catch in large areas adjacent to their shore for themselves. India, Sri Lanka, Kenya, and the Malagasy Republic wish to make the suggested 200-mile economic zone coterminous with the exclusive fishery zone. On the other hand, the Soviet proposal wishes to restrict coastal states to the area adjacent to their twelve-mile-wide territorial waters and to impose regulation by international fisheries organizations. Where there is lack of such regulations, agreements are to be concluded with other fishing nations. Similarly, the Japanese are willing to give some preferential treatment to coastal states, to be conditioned on agreements to be reached with "long distance" fishing nations concerned.

Land-locked countries of the region, as in the case of sea bed resources, ask for regional solutions whereby they could also profit from the advantages gained by the fishing of the coastal states. The fisheries problem particularly calls for international if not regional solutions; conservation, equitable allocation, and reasonable harvesting demand cooperation by both the littoral and the nonregional fishing nations.

---

[28]See Seyom Brown and Larry L. Fabian, "Diplomats at Sea," *Foreign Affairs,* 52 (January 1974), 301-321.

[29]*New York Times,* Jan. 18, 1975.

Pollution of the ocean is another problem which faces the nations of the region. In view of the enormous quantities of oil shipped across its waters, greater quantities than anywhere else in the world, countries along the shores of which oil tankers pass, such as Malaysia, Indonesia, Singapore, and also South Africa, are particularly alert to the immediacy of these questions.

As we have been able to observe, issues of oil and navigation and questions of the law of the sea also create tensions between the regional countries of the Indian Ocean area. These issues establish solidarities between some of them which are opposed to the community of interests which bring others together. These questions also foment conflicts between some of the regional states and the great powers outside the area. It is characteristic of the Sino-Soviet tension that on the issue of the territorial waters (and the allied question of navigation through straits), Moscow and Peking are more virulently opposed than any other power.

China supports the coastal powers which wish to extend the territorial sea beyond the twelve-mile width; Moscow views any "unilateral extension of territorial waters beyond the twelve-mile limit as illegal."[30] Whereas Peking approves of the "nationalization" of the Malacca Strait by Indonesia and Malaysia, the Soviet attitude is highly critical. Moscow insists that this strait is an "international waterway" and that the high seas cannot be narrowed by claims to territorial waters in excess of the twelve miles (which Moscow unilaterally decreed to be its territorial sea limit more than twenty years ago).

In practically every respect, the Indian Ocean region is the major diplomatic playground for the Sino-Soviet feud. But the region, although of secondary interest to Washington and Moscow, forms an arena of superpower rivalry and of encounters by local nations among themselves and also with nonregional powers. As for the industrialized and developed nations, the sudden emergence of the oil-rich countries as a new power center has created problems which are of a more vital character than they have witnessed since World War II and which have caused a power imbalance between the West and the oil-producing states of the Third World in which struggle the oil-poor countries of the Third World are the major sufferers.

Selected Bibliography

Abir, Mordechai. *Oil, Power, and Politics. Conflict in Arabia, the Red Sea and the Gulf.* London: Frank Cass, 1974.

Abir, Mordechai. *Sharm al-Sheikh—Bab al-Mandeb. The Strategic Balance and Israel's Southern Approaches.* Jerusalem: Hebrew University of Jerusalem, 1974.

Brown, Seyom, and Fabian, Larry L. "Diplomats at Sea." *Foreign Affairs* 52 (January 1974), 301-321.

[30] O. Khlestov, "The Problems of the Pacific Ocean in International Law," *Mezhdunarodnaya Zhizn* (Moscow, February 1973).

Butler, William E. *The Soviet Union and the Law of the Sea.* Baltimore: John Hopkins University Press, 1971.

Enders, Thomas O. "OPEC and Industrial Countries. The Next Ten Years." *Foreign Affairs* 53 (July 1975), 625-637.

Evensen, Jens. *Certain Legal Aspects Concerning the Delimitation of the Territorial Waters of Archipelagos.* United Nations Document A/Conf. 13/18, 1957.

Farmanfarmaian, Khodadad, et al. "How Can the World Afford OPEC Oil?" *Foreign Affairs* 53 (January 1975), 201-222.

Friedmann, Wolfgang. *The Future of the Oceans.* New York: George Braziller, 1971.

Furber, Holden. *John Company at Work. A Study of European Expansion in India in the Late Eighteenth Century.* Cambridge, Mass.: Harvard University Press, 1951.

Gibbon, Edward. *The Decline and Fall of the Roman Empire.* Abridgement by D. M. Low. New York: Harcourt, Brace & Co., 1960.

Graham, Gerald S. *Great Britain in the Indian Ocean. A Study of Maritime Enterprise, 1810-1850.* Oxford: Clarendon Press, 1967.

Horelick, Arnold L. *The Soviet Union, the Middle East, and the Evolving World Energy Situation.* Santa Monica, Calif.: Rand Corporation, 1973.

Hunter, Alex. *Oil Supply in Australia's Defence Strategy.* Canberra: Australian National University Press, 1973.

Issawi, Charles. "The Politics and Economics of Natural Resources." In *The Indian Ocean. Its Political, Economic, and Military Importance.* Edited by Alvin J. Cottrell and R. M. Burrell. New York: Praeger, 1972.

Khadduri, Majid. *Major Middle Eastern Problems in International Law.* Washington, D.C.: American Enterprise Institute for Public Policy Research, 1972.

Labrousse, Henri. *Le golfe et le canal.* Paris: Presses Universitaires de France, 1973.

Levy, Walter J. "World Oil Cooperation or International Chaos." *Foreign Affairs* 52 (July 1974), 690-713.

Monroe, Elizabeth, and Mabro, Robert. *Oil Producers and Consumers. Conflict or Cooperation.* New York: Center for Mediterranean Studies, 1974.

Pradt, (Abbé) M. de. *Les Trois Âges des colonies.* Vol. II. Paris: Giguet et Cie., 1802.

Sargent, J. "Japan and the Indian Ocean." In *Collected Papers of the Study Conference on the Indian Ocean in International Politics,* pp. 93-104. Southampton (England): University of Southampton, 1973. (Mimeographed.)

Shaw, K. E., and Thomson, G. G. *The Straits of Malacca.* Singapore: University Education Press, 1973.

Stevenson, John R., and Oxman, Bernard H. "The Preparations for the Law of the Sea Conference." *American Journal of International Law* 68 (January 1974), 1-32.

Trace, Keith. "International Trade and Commercial Relations." In *The Indian Ocean. Its Political, Economic and Military Importance,* pp. 35-61. Edited by Alvin Cottrell and R. M. Burrell. New York: Praeger, 1972.

Tucker, Robert W. "Oil. The Issue of American Intervention." *Commentary* 51 (January 1975), 21-31.

Wenk, Edward, Jr. *The Politics of the Ocean.* Seattle: University of Washington Press, 1972.

Chapter 12

The Weight of Balances

> *Weight is the degree of control in the making of decisions or the shaping of policies.*
>
> Harold D. Lasswell, *Power and Society,* 1950

The Cold War which followed World War II entailed a global cleavage between members of the world community. Nations which wished to evade being drawn into the antagonistic camps were considered dispensable, or in any case too feeble to carry weight. When the Cold War ended, the opposing battle lines broke up and the superpowers—the major antagonists—endured a fragmentation among their ranks. The erstwhile bipolarized world gave way to a multipolarized spectrum of forces. Nonalignment not only acquired legitimacy but also brought leverage to many governments. The number of medium powers increased, and they began to perform a function in the balance of forces in their region or subregion and even beyond it.

The Indian Ocean region, an area of mostly newly independent nations, is geographically more distant from the superpowers than Europe or East Asia, the major fields of their confrontation, and has benefited from the process of emancipation and realignment. Even during the most acute tensions of the Cold War, Washington and Moscow never faced each other in this region as they did in other parts of the world. In the areas where the two camps had come into collision, a "dissociation" was required to restore more normal relations; in contrast, the Indian Ocean region never needed to become a "region of dissociation."

Although neither the United States nor the Soviet Union (nor for that matter Britain, France, China, or Japan) could remain disinterested in the affairs of the

Indian Ocean, it would still appear that all these "outside" great powers ultimately shared a common interest: that the Indian Ocean region, speaking generally, should not become an area of contest or conflagration between them. Nevertheless, it is inevitable that, at the present stage of superpower and great power relations, any "offensive" or "expansionist" move by one of these leading powers would be followed by a countermove by others. But there is a difference between the two superpowers and the other great powers: both Washington and Moscow are capable of carrying out a countermove, while the other great powers are more limited in their capabilities to respond by really meaningful riposte gestures.

If no major attempts are made to shift the weight of the central balance of power by an action implemented in the Indian Ocean region, the area is likely to continue to be a place of superpower dissociation. For instance, a massive increase in the Soviet naval presence following the opening of the Suez Canal would be considered as an attempt to tilt the balance of power between the United States and the Soviet Union.

However, there are some further hazards which should be avoided lest the region turn into an area of aggressive confrontation between the "outsiders." There is always a possibility that regional rivalries might spark reactions which could involve the superpowers and possibly the other great powers should they believe that certain developments would affect their stake in the balance of power of that area.

The Role of Superpowers

The national leaders of the Indian Ocean countries are divided on the issue of whether the presence of exogenous great powers in the region is desirable or not. Only a few favor the complete removal of all outsiders and demand to be "left alone." Others, while possibly paying lip service to a demand for withdrawal of all outside forces and influences, are rather apprehensive lest their removal would lead to increased tensions among the regional powers. Therefore, these would prefer a balanced presence and a balanced display of weight by the superpowers. And again other nations of the region, especially those which consider themselves to be "encircled" by hostile forces, conceive that their security requires protection by one of the superpowers and possibly other outside great powers.[1] But practically all countries of the region are in need of some form or another of outside aid, whether it be economic or military aid or simply military supplies (for which some are able and ready to pay).

[1]The prevailing attitude of regional leaders toward exogenous great powers was thus characterized by Norman D. Palmer: "We want you when we want you but we don't want you when we don't want you." United States House of Representatives, *The Indian Ocean,* hearings before the Subcommittee on National Security Policy of the Committee on Foreign Affairs, House of Representatives, 92d Cong., 1st sess., July 20-28, 1971 (Washington, D.C., 1971), p. 149.

As noted earlier, the Indian Ocean region, as a whole, is not pivotal for the security of the United States. Still, shifts in the power relations of the area would, at least marginally, affect American security interests. Shock re-actions of any such adverse developments might be felt in parts of the world more vital to the United States. For instance, a disintegration of Pak-istan or of Ethiopia would create the hazards of conflagration which could have far-reaching consequences. It must therefore remain an objective of American foreign policy to prevent such destabilizing developments any-where in the region.

No serious observer could doubt that American objectives in the Indian Ocean region are neither offensive nor expansionist, but rather aim at sustaining the status quo in the area. The build-up of the Diego Garcia communication station, or "base," has been given a grossly exaggerated interpretation by people within and outside the United States; it has been represented as the establish-ment of an American Gibraltar or Vladivostok in the Indian Ocean. By them-selves, the modesty of the amounts asked for Diego Garcia from Congress refutes any such inflated ideas about its purpose and dimensions.

Diego Garcia and other American communication stations assist Washington in monitoring, tracking, and directing ship, airplane, missile, and satellite move-ments—both American and non-American. They therefore serve peaceful or nonaggressive purposes. But Diego Garcia and the Bahrain base are also useful as elements of contingency planning should the eventuality of increased armed presence be required. They also provide credibility to any "latent" or "active" suasion in support of American policy aims.[2]

It is to be remembered that in the northwest and northeast corners of the Indian Ocean the intensity of direct American concern is considerably higher than in the central or southern sections of the ocean. The Persian Gulf is a "hot" area because of its oil production, which is vital not so much to the United States as to its European allies and Japan. Following London's decision to withdraw from the gulf, Washington, in agreement with its British ally and with friendly governments of the area, supported Iran's (and also Saudi Arabia's) massive armament program in order to secure local stability, a stability not directly dependent on outside help. The American Navy would hardly be able to protect both the lifeline of Japan (the oil route across the Indian Ocean) and the vitally important routes across the Atlantic against Soviet submarine hazards. In such a manner is the stability of the Northeast Asian status quo intertwined with the peace in the Indian Ocean region.

The northeast corner of the Indian Ocean has already passed through neu-ralgic shocks because of the Vietnam conflict. With the withdrawal of American military personnel from Vietnam and the phasing out of bases in Thailand, Washington's involvement was gradually reduced. Nevertheless, the take-over by revolutionary forces of Cambodia and of South Vietnam greatly impinges on the security perceptions of the countries along the southeastern shore of the Indian Ocean. The "domino theory," rightly or wrongly discredited in political circles

[2]See Edward N. Luttwak, *The Political Uses of Sea Power* (Baltimore, 1974), pp. 3-38.

of the United States, is by no means disbelieved by the leaders of the nations concerned. Still, although China looms large over these parts of the region, the danger of direct or indirect Chinese intervention is not considered realistic or imminent.

However, an unbiased observer cannot fail to recognize Soviet activities in the Indian Ocean region as reminiscent of classic Russian imperial policies in the pre-World War I period. Soviet endeavors do not pursue one particular objective, nor are they directed to control any one country or piece of territory. What Moscow pursues is the chance to exploit any weakness, any possibility that offers itself to increase its influence, to bring adversaries into disarray, and to create a clientèle among the regional countries. Like Napoleon's strategy, Moscow's political strategy and much of its success are based on the mistakes and errors committed by others.

Washington is often reluctant or refuses to supply arms to countries engaged in or threatened by foreign aggression or states which are pursuing some counter-insurgency campaign; it reacts thus because it does not wish to raise further expectations or to get deeply involved, even at the price of risking its popularity or its friendship with the nations concerned. The Soviets, on the contrary, are ready to provide arms—with no ideological discrimination—to many but wish "to measure their arms shipments by the yardstick of the docility of their clients."[3]

There are, moreover, certain specific strategic areas in which greater Soviet interest is concentrated than in the region at large. Such areas are the Persian Gulf and the area around the Bab el Mandeb Strait, which includes Southeast Arabia and the Horn of Africa. One can presume that the interest in the latter subregion is due to the strategic value of this strait as the outlet to the Indian Ocean especially since the Suez Canal was opened again. As to the Persian Gulf, naturally the wealth of oil and the geostrategic importance of the area cannot fail to attract Moscow's attention. It is also through influence gained in these subregions that the Soviet Union may hope to exert additional pressures or to gain additional influence in the Middle East at large. These areas are the most likely ones in the region for a possible confrontation between Moscow and Washington. It is here that the United States and its European allies cannot be expected to remain idle should Soviet influence or domination jeopardize their vital interests.

It is not suggested that Moscow would be willing to risk an open conflict with the United States and sacrifice détente for ephemeral results in the region. Most of the Soviet moves are gradual, and taken individually they are not too significant; but their overall effect may cause the tilting of local balances in favor of Moscow's clients and thus secure palpable advantages to Soviet Power.

More pervasive than the American-Soviet competition in the Indian Ocean region is the unremitting contest between Moscow and Peking. While rivalry between Washington and the Kremlin is more or less open, though lacking in venom and fanaticism, the projection of the Sino-Soviet conflict into the Indian Ocean is mostly covert, stealthy, and imbued with ideological bigotry.

[3] André Fontaine in *New York Times,* Feb. 23, 1974.

Speaking in general terms, both the United States and the Soviet Union (and even more so the Chinese) lack the power to control much of what happens in the Indian Ocean region (and, for that matter, in many other parts of the world). They can make their influence felt and mostly are listened to by those governments over which they have a certain leverage. But if any of the regional countries is dead set on embarking upon some action or policy, neither Washington nor Moscow will find it worthwhile to use drastic steps to attempt a change of mind. Regional governments are generally more willing to follow suggestions, advice, or warnings given to them by sister regional countries than by either of the superpowers.

The least successful approach to problems of the regional nations is to handle them according to some general or universal pattern, formula, or principle. It is a not-infrequent shortcoming of Washington's approach, especially toward more distant countries (for which Capitol Hill is more responsible than the Department of State), to operate with universalist formulas and to apply broad determinants of foreign policy to individual issues.

In a way, Soviet policies in the Indian Ocean area are generally even less flexible than those of the United States. Although Moscow's earlier distinction between "progressive" and "reactionary" regimes has mostly been jettisoned, ideological selections still hamper Soviet diplomacy, especially if countered by Chinese moves which pose unavoidable Marxist-Leninist categories. As mentioned before, Soviet successes in the area are due to a skillful exploitation of situations (the Arab-Israeli conflict being the prime example) rather than a result of cautious and discrete diplomatic spadework or laborious uphill struggle. The Soviet approach to many delicate situations is often characterized by an obvious lack of pliancy and accommodation to circumstances. The insistence on having an "army" of experts and advisers accompany the supply of sophisticated weapons proved to be a fiasco in Egypt and elsewhere.

Surprisingly, China has shown greater flexibility and adaptability in many places. It gave up support of "national liberation" guerrilla movements when these proved to be incompatible with the maintenance of cordial relations with governments whose stance in the balance of power coincided with Peking's interests.

However, the "presence" or influence of the United States, the Soviet Union, or China—as pointed out earlier—is not the principal reason for the instabilities and crises which prevail in the region. The superpowers and other great powers are not, as it is claimed in some quarters, the *fons et origo* of these evils endemic in the region, although they are occasionally exploited by one or another of the exogenous great powers for their own benefit. More often the regional powers are responsible for a great power intrusion; one or the other of them induces or provokes one of the outside powers to intervene in its favor to maintain a balance of strength or to change the existing balance in its favor.

Regional Powers, Great and Small

The instabilities and infirmities of the countries around the periphery of the Indian Ocean stem from various causes. First of all stands the very fact that all but a few of these political entities are freshly independent states, new nations (if nations at all) which are still in search of their identity, their place in the world, and in need of confirmation of the legitimacy of their existence. Other reasons for their debilities vary from country to country—frailties which the new states share with the older ones. These reasons are internal and external. Among the former we may list the lack of national, ethnic, or religious cohesion, an explosive growth of population, social or economic stratification and backwardness, and inept democratic or exploitative autocratic or arbitrary systems of government. Among the external reasons for instabilities we may refer to a state of insecurity among their neighbors, realistic or unrealistic "encirclement" complexes, fear of hegemonial ambitions by other states or existing unsatisfied hegemonial ambitions by others, territorial disputes, and lastly widespread traditional-historic antagonisms.

The east and west, the north as well as the island states of the ocean region, must be recognized as having different problems and as differing in structure, tradition, and also in elements of statehood. There exists, however, a geopolitical linkage between the subregions of the area; the dividing lines between them being largely artificial, adjacency creates political, social, and ideological "bridges." Longer distances between the countries weaken the impact of the linkage but do not entirely efface its impulses. Instabilities and unbalanced situations which prevail in one subregion not only radiate into the neighboring countries but also may reach out into more distant parts of the region. There is, therefore, a "linkage of instabilities" which extends throughout the area. Hence the desire by certain nations of the Indian Ocean to secure greater stability by the removal of the "outsiders," blamed for the precariousness of the region. It is easier to blame "outsiders" than to eliminate causes of crises—the fears of the small nations or ambitions of the big ones.

In the southeastern corner of the ocean, the role of Australia is special. It is a white continent connected by a cluster of islands with the Asian mainland and thus adjacent to Malay-Melanesian peoples. Until recently, it considered itself and was considered a political annex of the Anglo-Saxon world, while geographically juxtaposed to the Asian world north of its shores. Now, while not abandoning its security relations with the United States and Britain, it is attempting to identify with its geographical partners around the Indian Ocean and with other nations of Asia.

Among the other states which extend along the southeastern coast of the Ocean, Indonesia stands out as a colossus that, no longer in Sukarno's aggressive fashion, but in a circumspect diplomatic manner, seeks to gain hegemonial status within the group of southeast Asian countries. Suspicion is thereby created between itself and its neighbors—Malaysia, Singapore, and others.

On the Indian subcontinent, India lays claim to predominance over its neighbors. With the partition of Pakistan, its strategic superiority has clearly been established. While defending its receipt of massive arms support from Moscow, New Delhi opposes the maintenance of defensive ties or the shipment of military supplies by "outsiders" to other countries of the subcontinent, especially Pakistan.[4] Such an ambition is naturally a disturbing factor in its relations, not only with Pakistan but also with Sri Lanka and other neighboring states.

While India is vitally dependent on the importation of oil and of fertilizers (the oil price increase has upset its foreign trade balance), the counries of the Persian Gulf area witnessed a quantum jump in their economic and military weight due to their successful wielding of the oil weapon. Particularly Iran, which managed to establish a *de facto* supremacy in the gulf, and Saudi Arabia have become the guardians of the oil treasures of the gulf, thus succeeding the British lion. Iran is also keen to project its power out into the Indian Ocean, the route of the essential fossil fuel.

In and around the Horn of Africa and the Red Sea, the turmoil centers (but not exclusively) in the Ethiopian realm. Vulnerable because of the inclusion within its boundaries of alien ethnic populations which harbor traditional centrifugal tendencies, Ethiopia appears like a crumbling historical monument. Eritrean guerrillas fight to sever that province; Somali irridentism threatens the east and southeast. Ethiopia's problems, at the same time, epitomize antagonism between Muslims and Christians and between Arabs and Africans, all of whom are there in a kaleidoscopic array. These antagonisms have also created crises in the past, from which Ethiopia managed to emerge and may once again.

In southern Africa, the white supremacist South Africa, surrounded by reluctant clients and a tottering Rhodesia, has so far been unable, because of its internal structure, to copy the Australian policy of seeking alignment with the non-European African environment. As an alien body, it has to struggle, relying on its strength and dominant status in that part of the world.

In Africa, the present national borders were inherited from colonial times. They are not based on ethnic or tribal divisions, but are imposed by decisions, themselves the results of insensitive bargaining between the chancelleries of London, Paris, Berlin, Brussels, and Lisbon. But at the present juncture, any attempt at altering the present boundary lines would create a *bellum ominium contra omnes,* a chaotic situation which would intensify rather than decrease mutual claims and recriminations.[5]

Existing conflicts between the regional powers are oftentimes augmented by the impact of confrontations or crises which occur between powers outside the Indian Ocean region. The unsettling emanations of the Sino-Soviet feud into the area have already been mentioned. India's acute Sinophobia has a bearing on Pakistani-Indian relations; similar antipathies influence the policies and attitudes of countries in Southeast Asia. American-Soviet rivalry in the Middle East also

---

[4]Prime Minister Gandhi's speech before the Upper Chamber, condemning the lifting of the arms embargo by the United States was particularly revealing. She stated, "The decision of the United States to resume arming Pakistan shows that the policymakers of that great country continue to subscribe to *the fallacy of equating Pakistan and India." New York Times,* Feb. 27, 1975. (Italics added.)

[5]See C. L. Sulzberger in *New York Times,* Feb. 23, 1975.

radiates into the riparian areas of the Indian Ocean. Many African states were induced in 1973 by the Arabs to join the anti-Israeli front; but many of them have now found that no Arab quid pro quo was forthcoming. Members of the Arab League had raised expectations that, in return for African alignment against Israel, financial support would be available to poor African nations which had to face the hardship of increased oil costs.

Indeed, another new cleavage among littoral powers of the Ocean has been created by the adversary relationship between oil-producing and oil-importing countries. This dissension did not reveal itself at once, because many leaders of the oil-poor developing nations approved the OPEC actions and refused to make common cause in public with the United States, the West European powers, and Japan. In this they were also encouraged by the members of the oil cartel, which promised to find ways to help their Third World Asian and African colleagues pay the new price of oil without going bankrupt.

Certain such supporting devices were initiated, mostly in the form of credits or grants-in-aid. Among Asian powers, India and Pakistan did receive such assistance, but they may ask themselves whether this is a long-range solution. Credits will eventually have to be repaid; otherwise, new ones will not be available. Interest, even if at low rates, has to be paid as well.

Development loans and grants provided by Arab states to their African partners in the Organization of African Unity were in the magnitude of millions when billions were required to fill the trade gaps. Rifts have unfolded, not only between the Arab League and the OAU but also between oil-producing and oil-importing members of the African organization. Two African-Arab states— Libya and Algeria—as well as the African states of Nigeria, Gabon, and Angola are oil exporters, but none of the African littoral nations of the Indian Ocean is producing oil.[6]

The yearning to become an oil-producing country and thus reach the nirvana of opulence led many countries in the Indian Ocean region into a scramble for the control of the sea bed adjacent to their shores and even for participation in resources of the sea far out on the high seas. The confines of these sea-bed areas are controversial and give rise to additional altercations. Excessive extensions of territorial waters or economic zones are bringing littoral countries into collision with the major seafaring nations interested in unhindered navigation in the waters of the ocean. Controls to be exercised over narrow waters, the various gateways to the Indian Ocean, are opposed by those nations which insist on free navigation for their warships and merchant vessels (including vital oil tankers) and also claim freedom of overflights for their civilian and military airplanes.

Facing all these problems and dissensions, the quest for a Zone of Peace in the Indian Ocean region must appear somewhat anomalous or visionary. And still this idea attracted large numbers of the immediately concerned nations and others outside the region itself. But it has so far failed to receive support from the superpowers and great powers, excepting China.

[6]*New York Times,* Mar. 2, 1975.

Neutralization and Denuclearization

The original Zone of Peace declaration for the Indian Ocean called upon the great powers to enter into immediate consultations with the littoral states with a view toward halting the further escalation and expansion of their military presence in the ocean and toward eliminating from that area "all bases, military installations and logistical supply facilities, the disposition of nuclear weapons and weapons of mass destruction and any manifestation of great power military presence in the Indian Ocean conceived in the context of great Power rivalry."[7]

No such consultations took place, for the United States, the Soviet Union, Britain, and France abstained from voting for the declaration. Nor had any steps been taken for the establishment of a "system of universal collective security" between the littoral and hinterland states of the Indian Ocean, on the one hand, and the permanent members of the Security Council and other major maritime users of the ocean, on the other, as also was suggested by the declaration.

It appears from this declaration and subsequent declarations and the report of the Ad Hoc Committee on the Indian Ocean[8] that what is essentially envisaged by the promoters of the Zone of Peace plan is a neutralization (demilitarization) and denuclearization of the region, but it remains ambiguous whether these measures are to apply to the ocean area only or also to the land territory surrounding the ocean, which would include the littoral and hinterland states themselves. There seems to be a basic dissension among the more powerful and less powerful nations in this respect: India is reluctant to assume the obligation of renouncing nuclear armaments (it has not signed the convention banning nuclear proliferation), and so is South Africa. Major littoral powers in addition to India—such as Iran, Saudi Arabia, Pakistan, and Indonesia (and probably Somalia and Ethiopia)—would refuse to reduce their military expansion and to eliminate their military, naval, and air bases and installations, while smaller Indian Ocean powers,—for instance, Sri Lanka, Singapore, the Himalayan states, and some African states—would welcome such moves, which would solve some of their most urgent security problems. Furthermore, nations which have concluded defense or friendship treaties with outside powers—as India and Iraq with the Soviet Union, Pakistan and Iran with the United States, Malaysia and Singapore with Britain, or Australia with the United States—would hardly welcome an abrogation of these agreements.

This manifest antinomy in the meaning of the Zone of Peace would become the Achilles heel in any negotiations which would attempt to draft a formal treaty endorsing the principles of the proposal.

It seems hardly practical to expect that an agreement could be reached between the littoral powers for the neutralization (demilitarization) and denuclearization of the water surface and subjacent waters (outside the territorial

[7]United Nations General Assembly Resolution 2832 (XXVI) of Dec. 16, 1971.

[8]United Nations General Assembly, Official Records. Twenty-Eighth Session, Supplement 19 (A/9029), New York, 1973.

waters) of the Indian Ocean which would involve the permanent withdrawal of warships and of military aircraft of nonregional powers. The prohibition against the use of the ocean by warships and military aircraft of outside powers "for any threat or use of force against the sovereignty, territorial integrity and independence" of any regional nation, as was also suggested by the 1971 declaration, is redundant because such actions have already been proscribed by the Charter of the United Nations.

For the neutralization of a maritime area, history provides us with the precedent of 1856, when, after the conclusion of the Crimean War, the participants in the Paris Peace Conference agreed that the Black Sea be neutralized and its waters "formally and in perpetuity interdicted to the flag of war of the Powers possessing its coasts, or of any other Power."[9] However, the neutralization extended also to the Black Sea coastline, where the maintenance of military-naval establishments was also prohibited. The neutralization of the Black Sea was, upon the insistence of Russia, ended in 1871.

The Treaty for Prohibition of Nuclear Weapons in Latin America of 1967 (also known as the Tlatelolco Treaty) declared the entire Latin American continent (the land territory and territorial waters) a nuclear-free zone. The United States, Britain (both with certain reservations), and also France have acceded to this treaty, but not the Soviet Union. This convention was made possible by the fact that none of the Latin American countries has developed nuclear weapons.[10]

How would the residual colonial possessions of Britain and France be affected if the Zone of Peace proposal should be converted into a regular international treaty? It appears that, in the minds of many promoters of the plan, the Zone of Peace concept would be incompatible with the continued colonial regimes in the region. But it is unlikely that either Britain or France would be willing to renounce its possessions just to please the anticolonialist regional powers. And as long as these countries maintain sovereignty over certain limited territories, they will not give up their right to maintain defense installations in these areas; actually, in some cases, as with the BIOT, the purpose of holding onto the islands in question is to use them for the maintenance of staging areas, communication and monitoring stations, and naval bases.

The weight of the Zone of Peace proposal is evidently directed against the superpowers. Both the United States and the Soviet Union keep—even if not on a permanent basis—naval units in the Indian Ocean; they have either official or inofficial (admitted or nonadmitted) air and naval bases in the area. Furthermore, they are suspected of maintaining nuclear weaponry, both on their surface and on their underwater warships. The presence of American and Soviet naval and air forces seems to be incompatible with the concept of neutralization or denuclearization of the Indian Ocean. But the ocean is not only an area of

[9]Treaty of Paris between Great Britain, France, Austria, Prussia, Sardinia, the Ottoman Empire, and Russia dated Mar. 30, 1856; United States, Department of State, *The Problem of the Turkish Straits* (Washington, D.C., 1947), pp. 17-18.

[10]T. T. Poulose, "Nuclear Strategy and the Indian Ocean as a Zone of Peace," in *Indian Ocean Power Rivalry*, ed. T. T. Poulose (New Delhi, 1974), pp. 190-205.

deployment of these forces; it is also a transit area where both naval and air units are moved from the Atlantic to the Pacific and vice versa. Prohibition of both presence and transit (and how to distinguish between these two types of entry into the area) affects the global or central balance of power existing between these superpowers as this balance has been laid down in agreements or has evolved in the past decade.

The Indian Ocean and the Central Balance of Power

The state of mutual and stabilized nuclear deterrence existing between the United States and the Soviet Union—on which the ultimate global balance of power has to lean—is built on a triad of strategic weapons: the intercontinental bomber force, the land-based intercontinental ballistic missiles, and the fleets of nuclear-powered submarines carrying nuclear missiles. Due to recent developments of technology and the results of the SALT I and SALT II agreements, it appears that the weight of the nuclear equation between the two superpowers is gradually shifting toward the sea-based nuclear deterrents. The relative invulnerability of the underwater missile carrier submarines secured for them a more indispensable role as components of the second-strike capability, the most essential element of deterrence.

As reported earlier (Chapter 9), the potential presence of American Polaris-Poseidon missile submarines in the Indian Ocean, capable of hitting targets in the central parts of the Soviet Union, may have been one of the reasons for the Soviet Navy's entry in force into that ocean. A further expansion of the United States underwater fleet by 1978, with the addition of submarines equipped with the Trident I missile, would extend the target range to 4,000 miles (and, subsequently, with the Trident II the range would be extended to 6,000 miles). The entire territory of the U.S.S.R. would thus be exposed to these missiles, and the widened range would also allow these submarines to withdraw to the wide areas of the Indian Ocean around and south of the Equator, while still being able to hit Soviet targets. The much greater difficulties of hunting down these submarines in the vastnesses of the ocean by Soviet antisubmarine submarines or surface craft would be an additional guarantee of their invulnerability.

The significance for both the Soviet and American surface warships of being able to move unhindered into or out of the Indian Ocean and across its narrow gateways has already been discussed. For Moscow, over and above the political urge to "show the flag," the Indian Ocean must serve as the transit route which connects its Europe-based navy (the Black Sea, the Baltic, and Arctic fleets) with that in the Soviet East Asia. For Washington, apart from the political and geostrategic uses of its vessels, the free use of Indian Ocean waters serves to protect the shipment of indispensable oil and other raw material originating in that region.

These are weighty reasons for both Washington and Moscow to be interested in the Indian Ocean, although their vital national security and survival are not directly involved. However, the present and more so the future use of the waters of this ocean by missile submarines and, consequently, by antisubmarine craft affects the nuclear deterrent capability of both superpowers, a matter which is of vital interest and which affects the survival of both nations.

Should the Indian Ocean develop, if it has not done so already, into a major area of confrontation between American missile-carrying submarines and their underwater or surface Soviet hunters, both the free entry into this ocean and the use of monitoring and detecting devices in its waters and on its sea bed would be matters of paramount importance. Such a trend is bound to influence the evolution of the rules of the law of the sea, at least to the extent to which the two superpowers and their allies may impose their weight on the negotiations leading to new agreements concerning these issues.

The successful operation of submarines, both American and Soviet, requires secrecy, and it would be jeopardized if they were forced to pass surfaced into the ocean through the narrow entrances. No such problems exist for those submarines which move around the Cape or around Australia where nobody can even demand that they surface. But American and Soviet underwater craft would prefer the much shorter routes from the Pacific into the Indian Ocean across the Malacca, Sunda, Lombok, or Wetar and Ombai Straits. Under the present interpretation given to the concept of "innocent passage" by the littoral states, their safety would require submarines to pass surfaced through territorial waters. And with the extension of these waters to twelve miles, all the crucial straits would be converted into territorial waters of the adjacent states. It is thus unlikely that, for the above-mentioned reasons, either Moscow or Washington will renounce their claim to "free passage" across these gateways, that is, passage which can be made submerged and unannounced. Especially in the Indian Ocean region, any developments concerning the law of straits and of territorial waters will have to take account of the nuclear balance in regard to sea-based deterrents.

The law of the sea as it relates to the sea bed outside territorial waters, that is, the continental shelf and the ocean floor beyond the continental shelf, also affects the equation of sea-based deterrent systems. The latest technological advances have greatly improved underwater monitoring and detecting devices. Hydrophones have to be hooked up to shore stations and therefore require permission of coastal states. But the SOSUS (sound surveillance under sea) antisubmarine warfare listening devices are placed below the 200-meter depth and part way down the slope of the shelf. Under currently valid international law, these latter instruments may be emplaced without the consent of any Indian Ocean government. But if the width of the sea bed reserved for the exclusive resource jurisdiction of an adjacent state is extended beyond the continental shelf, the use of such devices will again become dependent on the approval (unlikely to be obtained) of this state and the confidentiality of the process will be lost.[11]

[11] See Ann L. Hollick and Robert E. Osgood, *New Era of Ocean Politics* Baltimore, 1974), pp. 90-134.

In order to forestall competition and escalation, Moscow and Washington may possibly agree on a mutual limitation of their navies in the Indian Ocean.[12] However, geographic restrictions on the deployment of nuclear submarines would necessarily fall within the competence of talks (SALT). Numerical ceilings on different types of nuclear deterrents have been agreed on, but so far no initiatives have been taken in regard to geographic distribution and limitation of missile submarines and their area of operation.

The Soviet memorandum of December 7, 1964, presented in the United Nations proposed the establishment of nuclear-free zones which included two maritime areas, the Mediterranean and the Indian Ocean.[13] This suggestion was not followed up by negotiations between Washington and Moscow, and it is doubtful whether the Soviet Union would presently entertain such ideas. Should, however, the two superpowers decide on some spatial-geographic limitation or division of their sea-based deterrents, the Indian Ocean area might create particular difficulties.

The nuclear forces of the two adversaries have often been characterized as "asymmetric" because of their divergent quantitative emphasis on qualitatively different types of nuclear weaponry. Should it come to a desire to establish geographic limitations, the Indian Ocean would prove to be geographically "asymmetric" and difficult to trade off as against other spatial concessions. While both United States and Soviet sea-based missiles can be targeted against their respective homelands from the Atlantic and the Pacific Oceans, from the Indian Ocean only American seaborne missiles can threaten Soviet targets, and there Soviet submarines could perform no offensive function. Therefore, any restriction of the use of the waters of the Indian Ocean by missile-launching American submarines would one-sidedly affect American deterrent capabilities and benefit Soviet antinuclear defenses.

It may be significant to note that Moscow's refusal to sign the Tlatelolco Treaty was explained by the Soviet reluctance to renounce the right to transport nuclear weapons through the nuclear-free zone of Latin America and its territorial waters. One may conjecture that the Soviet Union wished to keep its hands free for the potential use of the Caribbean as a launching area against the United States. We should also be reminded of the Soviet naval base at Cienfuegos in Cuba and of the frequently recurring rumors concerning the visit to that harbor of Soviet nuclear missile-carrying submarines.

The Caribbean would, however, hardly be a quid pro quo against the Indian Ocean should Moscow propose a denuclearization of the former and the latter. The Caribbean is a relatively small maritime area interspersed with islands and, therefore, does not offer the safety of concealment that the huge area of the Indian Ocean offers. Should there be any attempt at a trade-off for the

[12]See, among others, the statement of Professor Howard Wriggins in United States, House of Representatives, *The Indian Ocean,* hearings before the Subcommittee on National Security Policy and Scientific Developments of the Committee on Foreign Affairs, House of Representatives, 92d Cong., 1st sess., July 20-28, 1971, pp. 63-69.

[13]See Geoffrey Jukes, *The Indian Ocean in Soviet Naval Policy* (London, 1972), pp. 7-8.

withdrawal of United States submarines from the Indian Ocean, compensation should be sought elsewhere than in the Caribbean.

The Indian Ocean, in the context of strategic parity, again reminds us of its "asymmetric" and therefore special character. While the Atlantic and Pacific clearly divide continents, three continents confront each other around the semicircular Indian Ocean. The Atlantic and Pacific embrace Eurasia and the Americas, but the Indian Ocean is hugged by Asia, Africa, and Australia. One-third of humanity lives around its shores. For centuries these nations were ruled by outsiders. Now they have attained independence, but live in overt or covert contest. Some of them strive to gain weight over the others or to create an imbalance of forces. And the exogenous superpowers and other great powers still carry weight in the area.

The Indian Ocean is an old stage of power politics; it has been ruled by the Portuguese and the British. As a home of many independent nations, large and small, it has become the stage of new and dramatic rivalries. Whether the weight in the power balances will be held by the indigenous nations or some of them, or whether once again the weight will fall in to the hands of the exogenous nations or one of them, will largely influence the power relations on both sides of the Atlantic and Pacific.

Selected Bibliography

Adie, W. A. C. *Oil, Politics and Seapower. The Indian Ocean Vortex.* New York: Crane, Russak & Co. (for the National Strategy Information Center), 1975.

Hollick, Ann L., and Osgood, Robert E. *New Era of Ocean Politics.* Baltimore: Johns Hopkins University Press, 1974.

Jukes, Geoffrey. *The Indian Ocean in Soviet Naval Policy.* London: International Institute for Strategic Studies (Adelphi Papers No. 87), 1972.

Lewis, Bernard. "The Great Powers, the Arabs and the Israelis." *Foreign Affairs* 47 (July 1969), 642-652.

Luttwak, Edward N. *The Political Uses of Sea Power.* Baltimore: Johns Hopkins University Press, 1974.

United States, House of Representatives. *The Indian Ocean. Political and Strategic Future.* Hearings before the Subcommittee on National Security Policy and Scientific Developments of the Committee on Foreign Affairs. 92d Cong., 1st sess. July 20, 200, 27, and 28, 1971. Washington, D.C.: Government Printing Office, 1971.

Appendixes

Appendix 1

Littoral and Hinterland States of the Indian Ocean Region

The Southeast

The Commonwealth of AUSTRALIA

Capital: Canberra

Area: 2,967,741 square miles

Population: 13,100,000

Gross National Product: $73.5 billion ($5,610 per capita)

Annual Military Expenditures: $2.3 billion (3.12% of GNP)

Total Active Armed Forces: 69,100 (0.52% of population)

Steel and Iron Production: 13.1 million metric tons

Coal Production: 72.4 million metric tons

Oil Production: 15.40 million metric tons

Electric Power Output: 58 billion kwh

Merchant Marine: 136 ships (1,444,114 gross tons)

Civil Air Fleet: 64 jet, 63 turboprop, 47 piston transports

SOURCES: United States, Department of State, *Background Notes* (Washington, D.C.: Government Printing Office); published every two years on individual countries; *The Almanac of World Military Power*, 3d ed., Trevor N. Dupuy, Grace P. Hayes, and John A. C. Andrews (New York: R. R. Bowker Co., 1974); and *The Military Balance, 1974-75* (London: International Institute for Strategic Studies, 1974).

Republic of INDONESIA

Capital: Jakarta

Area: 779,675 square miles (13,500 islands)

Population: 132 million

Gross National Product: $15 billion ($113 per capita)

Annual Military Expenditures: $1,108 million (7.38% of GNP)

Total Active Armed Forces: 286,000 including 20,000 in Mobile Police Brigade (0.22% of population)

Coal Production: 173,000 metric tons

Oil Production: 53.8 million metric tons

Electric Power Output: 1.87 billion kwh

Merchant Marine: 513 ships (618,589 gross tons)

Civil Air Fleet: 15 jet, 32 turboprop, 14 piston transports

Federation of MALAYSIA

Capital: Kuala Lumpur

Area: 128,727 square miles

Population: 11.8 million

Gross National Product: $4.63 billion ($392 per capita)

Annual Military Expenditures: $243 million (5.25% of GNP)

Total Active Armed Forces: 62,600, including security police (0.53% of population)

Oil Production: 4.4 million metric tons

Rubber Production: 1,325 million metric tons (60% of world supply)

Tin Production: 75,000 metric tons (20% of world supply)

Electric Power Output: 3.7 billion kwh

Merchant Marine: 99 ships (149,504 gross tons)

Civil Air Fleet: 7 jet, 9 turboprop, 12 piston transports

Republic of SINGAPORE

Capital: Singapore

Area: 225.6 square miles

Population: 2 million

Gross National Product: $5.1 billion ($2,217 per capita)

Annual Military Expenditures: $269 million (5.27% of GNP)

Total Active Armed Forces: 30,000 (1.3% of population)

Electric Power Output: 1.64 billion kwh

Merchant Marine: 281 ships (870,513 gross tons)

Civil Air Fleet: 14 jet, 21 turboprop

Kingdom of THAILAND

Capital: Bangkok

Area: 198,500 square miles

Population: 40 million

Gross National Product: $11.4 billion ($285 per capita)

Annual Military Expenditures: $371 million (3.25% of GNP)

Total Active Armed Forces: 217,400, including security forces (0.54% of population)

Electric Power Output: 3.73 billion kwh

Merchant Marine: 69 ships (108,271 gross tons)

Civil Air Fleet: 10 jet, 9 turboprop, 8 piston transports

Subcontinent India and Its Neighbors

Republic of AFGHANISTAN

Capital: Kabul

Area: 253,861 square miles

Population: 18 million

Gross National Product: $1.6 billion ($87 per capita)

Annual Military Expenditures: $45 million (2.81% of GNP)

Total Active Armed Forces: 86,000 (0.47% of population)

Coal Production: 136,000 metric tons

Electric Power Output: 325 million kwh

Civil Air Fleet: 2 jet, 6 piston transports

BANGLADESH

Capital: Dacca

Area: 55,126 square miles

Population: 83 million

Gross National Product: $5 billion ($60 per capita)

Annual Military Expenditures: $81 million (1.6% of GNP)

Total Active Armed Forces: 33,000 (0.04% of population)

Steel Production: 177,000 metric tons
Electric Power Output: 1.43 billion kwh

Kingdom of BHUTAN

Capital: Thimthu

Area: 18,147 square miles
Population: 854,000
Gross National Product: $64 million ($75 per capita)
Annual Military Expenditures: not available
Total Active Armed Forces: 4,000 (0.47% of population)

Socialist Republic of the Union of BURMA

Capital: Rangoon

Area: 261,789 square miles
Population: 31 million
Gross National Product: $2.9 billion ($93 per capita)
Annual Military Expenditures: $120 million (4.14% of GNP)
Total Active Armed Forces: 167,000 (0.54% of population)
Oil Production: 1 million metric tons
Electric Power Output: 474 million kwh
Merchant Marine: 40 ships (54,877 gross tons)
Civil Air Fleet: 1 jet, 8 turboprop, 6 piston transports

Republic (Union) of INDIA

Capital: New Delhi

Area: 1,266,596 square miles
Population: 602 million
Gross National Product: $86.7 billion ($144 per capita)
Annual Military Expenditures: $2.6 billion (3% of GNP)
Total Active Armed Forces: 1,074,000, including Border Security Force (0.18% of population)
Coal Production: 69.01 million metric tons
Oil Production: 7.07 million metric tons
Electric Power Output: 58.9 billion kwh
Merchant Marine: 412 ships (2.65 million gross tons)
Civil Air Fleet: 27 jet, 31 turboprop, 13 piston transports

Republic of MALDIVES

Capital: Male

Area: 115 square miles (19 atolls, ca. 2,000 coral islands)
Population: 123,000
Gross National Product: not available

Kingdom of NEPAL

Capital: Kathmandu

Area: 54,362 square miles
Population: 12 million
Gross National Product: $920 million ($77 per capita)
Annual Military Expenditures: $7 million (0.77% of GNP)
Total Active Armed Forces: 20,000 (0.16% of population)
Electric Power Output: 31 million kwh
Civil Air Fleet: 5 turboprop, 7 piston transports

Islamic Republic of PAKISTAN

Capital: Islamabad

Area: 310,403 square miles
Population: 60.17 million
Gross National Product: $7.6 billion ($126 per capita)
Annual Military Expenditures: $722 million (9.5% of GNP)
Total Active Armed Forces: 423,000, including frontier corps (0.7% of population)
Coal Production: 1.25 million metric tons
Oil Production: 450,740 metric tons
Gas Production: 3.05 billion cubic meters
Electric Power Output: 2 billion kwh
Merchant Marine: 131 ships (532,607 gross tons)
Civil Air Fleet: 1 jet, 7 turboprop transports

State of SIKKIM (incorporated into India)

Capital: Gangtok

Area: 2,818 square miles
Population: 204,760
Gross National Product: $25.2 million ($123 per capita)

Annual Military Expenditures: not available
Total Active Armed Forces: 300 (0.15% of population)

Republic of SRI LANKA (Ceylon)

Capital: Colombo

Area: 25,332 square miles
Population: 14 million
Gross National Product: $2.6 billion ($186 per capita)
Annual Military Expenditures: $24 million (0.92% of GNP)
Total Active Armed Forces: 13,600 (0.09% of population)
Electric Power Output: 816 million kwh
Merchant Marine: 28 ships (13,107 gross tons)
Civil Air Fleet: 2 jet, 1 turboprop, 2 piston transports

Persian Gulf Countries

State of BAHRAIN

Capital: Manama

Area: 240 square miles
Population: 250,000
Gross National Product: $180 million ($720 per capita)
Annual Military Expenditures: not available
Total Active Armed Forces: 1,100 (0.44% of population)
Oil Production: 3.5 million metric tons
Civil Air Fleet: 2 jet, 3 turboprop, 7 piston transports

Empire of IRAN (Persia)

Capital: Tehran

Area: 636,291 square miles
Population: 32 million
Gross National Product: 35.6 billion ($1078 per capita)
Annual Military Expenditures: $10 billion (28% of GNP)[1]
Total Active Armed Forces: 250,000 (0.76% of population)
Coal Production: 323,000 metric tons

[1]Including orders for arms deliveries pending in 1975.

Oil Production: 250 million metric tons
Electric Power Output: 7 billion kwh
Merchant Marine: 77 ships (181,000 gross tons)
Civil Air Fleet: 10 jet, 3 piston transports

Republic of IRAQ

Capital: Baghdad

Area: 169,925 square miles
Population: 11 million
Gross National Product: $5.6 billion ($509 per capita)
Annual Military Expenditures: $803 million (14.3% of GNP)
Total Active Armed Forces: 135,000, including security police (1.22% of population)
Oil Production: 71.05 million metric tons
Electric Power Output: 2.1 billion kwh
Merchant Marine: 45 ships (121,000 gross tons)
Civil Air Fleet: 3 jet, 3 turboprop, 15 piston transports

State of KUWAIT

Capital: Kuwait

Area: 6,880 square miles
Population: 1.21 million
Gross National Product: $5.4 billion ($4463 per capita)
Annual Military Expenditures: $162 million (3% of GNP)
Total Active Armed Forces: 10,500 (0.86% of population)
Oil Production: 151.2 million metric tons
Merchant Marine: 164 ships (656,403 gross tons)
Civil Air Fleet: 7 jet

Sultanate of OMAN

Capital: Muscat

Area: 82,000 square miles
Population: 760,000
Gross National Product: not available
Annual Military Expenditures: $359 million
Total Active Armed Forces: 12,900 (1.69% of population)

Oil Production: 14 million metric tons
Electric Power Output: not available
Merchant Marine: 3 ships (2,013 gross tons)

State of QATAR

Capital: Doha

Area: 6,000 square miles
Population: 115,000
Gross National Product: $280 million ($2,434 per capita)
Annual Military Expenditures: not available
Total Active Armed Forces: 2,200 (1.9% of population)
Oil Production: 22.9 million metric tons

Kingdom of SAUDI ARABIA

Capital: Riyadh

Area: 873,972 square miles
Population: 8 million
Gross National Product: $12 billion ($1,348 per capita)
Annual Military Expenditures: $6.34 billion (52% of GNP)[2]
Total Active Armed Forces: 71,000, including National Guard (0.85% of
    population)
Oil Production: 286 million metric tons
Electric Power Output: 770 million kwh
Merchant Marine: 3 ships (50,369 gross tons)
Civil Air Fleet: 7 jet, 5 turboprop, 20 piston transports

UNITED ARAB EMIRATES

Capital (provisional): Abu Dhabi

Area: 32,000 square miles
Population (estimated): 242,000
    Population of Member States (estimated):

Abu Dhabi	100,000
Dubai	69,000
Sharjah	31,500
Ras-al-Khaimah	24,500

[2]Including orders for arms deliveries pending in 1975.

Fujairah	9,700
Ajman	4,200
Umm-al-Quaiwain	3,700

Gross National Product: $530 million ($2,409 per capita)

Annual Military Expenditures: not available

Total Active Armed Forces: 11,500 (6.4% of population)

Oil Production: 58.3 million metric tons

Electric Power Output: not available

Civil Air Fleet: 2 jet, 6 turboprop, 5 piston transports

The Horn of Africa and the Red Sea Countries

ARAB REPUBLIC OF EGYPT

Capital: Cairo

Area: 386,900 square miles

Population: 37.5 million

Gross National Product: $17.9 billion ($477 per capita)

Annual Military Expenditures: $6.1 billion (34% of GNP)

Total Active Armed Forces: 322,000, excluding security forces (0.86% of population)

Oil Production: 11.02 million metric tons (excluding Israeli production from fields of occupied Sinai)

Electric Power Output: 7.13 billion kwh

Merchant Marine: 127 ships (241,429 gross tons)

Civil Air Fleet: 11 jet, 6 turboprop, 2 piston transports

ETHIOPIA

Capital: Addis Ababa

Area: 471,776 square miles

Population: 27.5 million

Gross National Product: $2.7 billion ($98 per capita)

Annual Military Expenditures: $80 million (2.96% of GNP)

Total Active Armed Forces: 53,000, including security forces and border guard (0.19% of population)

Electric Power Output: 455 million kwh

Merchant Marine: 23 ships (45,903 gross tons)

Civil Air Fleet: 4 jet, 19 piston transports

French Territory of AFARS AND ISSAS

Capital: Djibouti

Area: 8,880 square miles
Population: 125,000
Gross National Product: $80 million ($640 per capita)
Annual Military Expenditures: not available
Total Active Armed Forces: 6,000 (7.5% of population)

State of ISRAEL

Capital: Jerusalem

Area: 8,017 square miles (excluding occupied territories)
Population: 3.36 million
Gross National Product: $11.7 billion ($3,482 per capita)
Annual Military Expenditures: $3.5 billion (29% of GNP)
Total Active Armed Forces: 166,000, not including mobilized reserves (4.9% of population)
Oil Production: 6.1 million metric tons (including production from occupied Sinai)
Electric Power Output: 7.7 billion kwh
Merchant Marine: 102 ships (645,585 gross tons)
Civil Air Fleet: 13 jet, 9 turboprop transports

Hashemite Kingdom of JORDAN

Capital: Amman

Area: 37,737 square miles (including area occupied by Israel)
Population: 2.73 million
Gross National Product: $1 billion ($366 per capita)
Annual Military Expenditures: $155 million (15% of GNP)
Total Active Armed Forces: 80,000, including gendarmerie (2.9% of population)
Electric Power Output: 165 million kwh
Civil Air Fleet: 7 jet transports

Republic of KENYA

Capital: Nairobi

Area: 224,960 square miles
Population: 13.37 million

Gross National Product: $2.5 billion ($187 per capita)

Annual Military Expenditures: $2.5 million (0.1% of GNP)

Total Active Armed Forces: 9,020, including internal security forces (0.07% of population)

Electric Power Output: 556 million kwh

Merchant Marine: 23 ships (21,857 gross tons)

Civil Air Fleet: 4 jet, 8 turboprop, 37 piston transports

SAUDI ARABIA

(See Persian Gulf Countries)

SOMALI Democratic Republic

Capital: Mogadishu

Area: 246,155 square miles

Population: 3 million

Gross National Product: $300 million ($100 per capita)

Annual Military Expenditures: $15 million (5% of GNP)

Total Active Armed Forces: 23,000, including security troops (0.76% of population)

Electric Power Output: 70 million kwh

Merchant Marine: 148 ships (873,209 gross tons)

Civil Air Fleet: 2 turboprops, 5 piston transports

Democratic Republic of the SUDAN

Capital: Khartoum

Area: 967,491 square miles

Population: 17.9 million

Gross National Product: $2.8 billion ($156 per capita)

Annual Military Expenditures: $97 million (3.6% of GNP)

Electric Power Output: 392 million kwh

Merchant Marine: 14 ships (35,502 gross tons)

Civil Air Fleet: 2 jet, 8 turboprop, 1 piston transport

Republic of UGANDA

Capital: Kampala

Area: 91,134 square miles

Population: 11.36 million

Gross National Product: $2 billion ($176 per capita)

Annual Military Expenditures: $49 million (2.45% of GNP)

Total Active Armed Forces: 21,000, including security police (0.18% of population)

Electric Power Output: 817 million kwh

Merchant Marine: 1 ship (5,510 gross tons)

Civil Air Fleet: 7 piston transports

YEMEN Arab Republic

Capital: Sanaa

Area: 75,000 square miles

Population: 6 million

Gross National Product: $600 million ($92 per capita)

Annual Military Expenditures: $58 million (9.6% of GNP)

Total Active Armed Forces: 40,000, including tribal levies (0.61% of population)

Merchant Marine: 4 ships (2,844 gross tons)

Civil Air Fleet: Yemen Airlines (numbers not available)

People's Democratic Republic of YEMEN

Capital: Aden

Area: 112,000 square miles

Population: 1.66 million

Gross National Product: $500 million ($301 per capita)

Annual Military Expenditures: $26 million (5.2% of GNP)

Total Active Armed Forces: 18,000 (1.08% of population)

Electric Power Output: 194 million kwh

Merchant Marine: 5 ships (1,417 gross tons)

The Southwest

Republic of the COMORO ISLANDS

Capital: Moroni

Area: 800 square miles (4 islands; the Island of Mayotte decided to maintain links with France)

Population: 270,000
Gross National Product: not available

Republic of BOTSWANA

Capital: Gaberones

Area: 220,000 square miles
Population: 669,000
Gross National Product: $70 million ($105 per capita)
Annual Police Expenditures: $1.2 million (1.7% of GNP)
Total Active Armed Forces (Police): 1,100 (0.16% of population)
Civil Air Fleet: 1 turboprop transport

Kingdom of LESOTHO

Capital: Maseru

Area: 11,719 square miles
Population: 1 million
Gross National Product: $80 million ($73 per capita)
Annual Police Expenditures: $1.2 million (1.5% of GNP)
Total Active (Police) Forces: 900 (0.96% of population)
Civil Air Fleet: 6 piston transports

Democratic MALAGASY Republic (Madagascar)

Capital: Tananarive

Area: 228,000 square miles
Population: 7 million
Gross National Product: $1.3 billion ($173 per capita)
Annual Military Expenditures: $13.8 million (1.06% of GNP)
Total Active Armed Forces: 8,700, including gendarmerie (0.11% of population)
Electric Power Output: 152 million kwh
Merchant Marine: 48 ships (52,162 gross tons)
Civil Air Fleet: 3 jet, 6 turboprop

Republic of MALAWI

Capital: Zomba (Capital-designate: Lilongwe)

Area: 45,747 square miles
Population: 5 million

Gross National Product: $636 million ($127 per capita)
Annual Military Expenditures: $1.5 million (0.23% of GNP)
Total Active Armed Forces: 1,600 (0.03% of population)
Electric Power Output: 144 million kwh
Civil Air Fleet: 1 jet, 4 turboprop, 2 piston transports

MAURITIUS

Capital: Port Louis

Area: 720 square miles
Population: 810,000
Gross National Product: $159 million ($190 per capita)

MOZAMBIQUE

Capital: Maputo (Lourenço Marques)

Area: 303,769 square miles
Population: 9 million
Gross National Product: $2 billion ($230 per capita)
Annual Military Expenditures: $25 million (2.5% of GNP)
Total Active Armed Forces: 45,000 (0.50% of population)
Coal Production: 300,000 metric tons
Electric Power Output: 558 million kwh
Civil Air Fleet: 3 jet, 3 turboprop transports

(La) RÉUNION

Capital: St. Denis

Area: 970 square miles
Population: 380,000

RHODESIA

Capital: Salisbury

Area: 150,820 square miles
Population: 6.27 million (273,000 whites)
Gross National Product: $3.1 billion ($494 per capita)
Annual Military Expenditures: $102 million (3.29% of GNP)
Total Active Armed Forces: 11,000, including security policy (1.7% of population)

Coal Production: 3.33 million metric tons
Electric Power Output: 6.41 billion kwh
Civil Air Fleet: 7 turboprop, 6 piston transports

SEYCHELLES Islands

Capital: Victoria (on Mahé Island)

Area: 100 square miles (85 islands)
Population: 53,000

Republic of SOUTH AFRICA

Capitals: Pretoria (administrative)
Cape Town (legislative)

Area: 472,494 square miles (without South West Africa)
Population: 24.9 million
Gross National Product: $32.5 billion ($1305 per capita)
Annual Military Expenditures: $1.3 billion (4% of GNP)
Total Active Armed Forces: 50,500, including paramilitary police (0.20% of population)
Coal Production: 58.4 million metric tons
Iron and Steel Production: 21.6 million metric tons
Electric Power Output: 52.9 billion kwh
Merchant Marine: 255 ships (511,190 gross tons)
Civil Air Fleet: 34 jet, 3 turboprop, 64 piston transports

Kingdom of SWAZILAND

Capitals: Mbabane (administrative)
Lobamba (legislative)

Area: 6,704 square miles
Population: 500,000
Gross National Product: $110 million ($247 per capita)
Annual Active Police Expenditures: $1.9 million (1.72% of GNP)
Coal Production: 130,000 metric tons
Iron Ore Production: 3.1 million metric tons
Electric Power Output: 90 million kwh
Civil Air Fleet: 4 piston transports

United Republic of TANZANIA

Capital: Dar es Salaam

Area: 364,900 square miles
Population: 15.1 million
Gross National Product: $1.9 billion ($126 per capita)
Annual Military Expenditures: $42 million (2.21% of GNP)
Total Active Armed Forces: 14,600 (0.96% of population)
Electric Power Output: 396 million kwh
Merchant Marine: 11 ships (18,218 gross tons)
Civil Air Fleet: 5 piston transports

Republic of ZAMBIA

Capital: Lusaka

Area: 290,724 square miles
Population: 4 million
Gross National Product: $2.5 billion ($532 per capita)
Annual Military Expenditures: $78 million (3.12% of GNP)
Total Active Armed Forces: 7,600, including internal security forces (0.16% of population)
Coal Production: 623,000 metric tons
Electric Power Output: 1.2 billion kwh
Civil Air Fleet: 3 jet, 4 turboprop transports

Appendix 2

Coastline Measurements of the Indian Ocean Littoral States

Country (Political Division)[1]	Nautical Miles
Australia (continent)	13,971[2]
Indonesia (13,500 islands)	19,889
Portuguese Timor	33
Singapore	28
Malaysia (Malaya's west coast)	440
Thailand (west coast on Andaman Sea)	324
Burma	1,230
Bangladesh	230
India	2,759
Sri Lanka (Ceylon)	650
Maldive Islands	not available
Pakistan	440
Iran	990
Iraq	10
Kuwait	115
Saudi Arabia (on Persian Gulf)	296
Bahrain	68

SOURCE: United States, Department of State, *Sovereignty of the Sea* (Washington, D.C.: Bureau of Intelligence and Research, 1965).

[1]The states are listed counterclockwise.

[2]Indian Ocean coastline about two-thirds of this.

Country (Political Division)	Nautical Miles
Qatar	204
United Arab Emirates	420
Oman	1,005
People's Republic of Yemen	654
Arab Republic of Yemen	244
Saudi Arabia (on Red Sea)	1,020
Jordan	5
Israel (on Gulf of Aqaba)	4
Egypt (on Red Sea)	769
Sudan	387
Ethiopia	546
French Territory of Afars and Issas	123
Somalia	1,596
Kenya	247
Tanzania (including Zanzibar)	669
Mozambique	1,352
Malagasy Republic (Madagascar)	2,155
Mauritius	87
Reunion	100
South Africa	1,430

Appendix 3

Principal Straits and Channels in the Indian Ocean Region

Strait or Channel[1]	Geographic Location	Width of Narrowest Section (Nautical Miles)
Bass Strait	Between the Australian continent and Tasmania	80
Torres Strait	Between Australia and New Guinea (Papua)	100
Wetar Strait	Between Portuguese Timor and Wetar Island (Indonesia)	50
Ombai Strait	Between Portuguese Timor and Alor Island (Indonesia)	16
Sape Strait	Between Komodo and Sumbawa Islands (Indonesia)	8
Alas Strait	Between Lombok and Sumbawa Islands (Indonesia)	5
Lombok Strait	Between Bali and Lombok Islands (Indonesia)	11

SOURCES: United States, Department of State, *Sovereignty of the Sea* (Washington, D.C.: Bureau of Intelligence and Research, 1965); and United Nations, *A Brief Geographical and Hydrographical Study of Straits* (by Commander R. H. Kennedy), Document A/Conf. 13/6 and Add. 1, 1957.

[1] The straits and channels are listed counterclockwise.

Strait or Channel	Geographic Location	Width of Narrowest Section (Nautical Miles)
Bali Strait	Between Bali and Java Islands (Indonesia)	2
Sunda Strait	Between Java and Sumatra (Indonesia)	12
Singapore Strait	Between Singapore and the Riau Islands (Indonesia)	8
Malacca Strait	Between Malaysia and Indonesia (Sumatra)	20
Palk Strait	Between India and Sri Lanka (Ceylon)	3
Hormuz Strait	Between Iran and Oman (Musandam Peninsula)	21
Bab el Mandeb	Between South Yemen and the French Territory of Afars and Issas	14
Tiran Strait	Between the Sinai Peninsula (Egypt, now Israeli-occupied) and Saudi Arabia	950 yards
Zanzibar Channel	Between Zanzibar and the Tanzanian Mainland	16
Mozambique Channel	Between Mozambique and Madagascar (Malagasy Republic)	250

Index

Abd al Kuri Island, 137
Abdul Razak, Prime Minister Tun, 79
Abu Dhabi, 122–24, 210, 213, 216
Abu Musa, 114, 123
Addu Atoll: *see* Gan Island
Aden, 5, 8, 15, 21, 57, 138, 178; *see also* Yemen, People's Republic of
Aden, Gulf of, 27
Adulis, 4
Aduwa, Battle of (1895), 15, 135
Afars, 133, 135–36
Afghanistan, 108–109
 foreign relations of, 88, 109, 175, 194
 geographic location of, 108
Agalega Islands, 168
Agulhas Current, 26
Ajman, 123–24
Albuquerque, Affonso de, 8, 111, 137
Aldabra Island, 201–202
Alexander VI, Pope, 8
Alexander the Great, 3, 29, 111
Algiers Summit Conference (1975), 116
Almeida, Francisco de, 8
Alula, 134
Amiens, Treaty of (1802), 12
Andaman Islands, 20, 27, 95
Andaman Sea, 27
Andriamahazo, General, 164

Anglo-Persian Oil Company, 17
Angola, 51, 155
ANZUS Treaty, 66
Apartheid, 146, 148
Aqaba, Gulf of, 137, 139, 223
Arab Israeli Wars, 137, 190, 191, 237
Arab League, 51, 131, 137*n*
Arabian Sea, 27
Arafura Sea, 25, 27, 71
Archipelago concept, 74–75, 168, 224–25;
 see also Law of the sea
Asmara, 132, 134*n*, 174
Assab, 130
Association of South East Asian Nations
 (ASEAN), 66, 71, 74–77, 79, 85–86,
 195
Australia, 15, 65–72
 foreign policy of, 52, 66–72, 174, 195,
 207
 geopolitical status of, 68–69
 an Indian Ocean power, 31, 66-72, 177*n*,
 235
 and the law of the sea, 223, 225
Austro-Hungarian monarchy, 46

Bab el Mandeb Strait, 15, 27, 126, 128, 131,
 136–38, 140, 181, 210, 222
Bahrain, 21, 121–23, 173–74

Balance of power, 45–46, 49–53, 210, 240–43
Baluchistan, 88, 109
Banda, Dr. Hastings Kamuzu, 159
Bandanaraike, Prime Minister Sirimavo, 60, 102
Bandung Conference (1955), 50, 90
Bangladesh, 34, 50, 89, 101–102, 177, 194, 214
Barnaby, Dr. Frank, 61
Bases, 56–58
Basra, 17, 118
Beira, 155–56, 158
Bender Abbas, 114, 126
Bengal, Gulf of, 27, 226
Berbera, 134, 178n, 190
Bhutan, 88, 91, 106–107, 194
Bhutto, Zulfikar Ali, 28–29, 98, 100n, 115
BIOT (British Indian Ocean Territory), 21, 168, 174, 201–206, 239
Boer Wars, 147
Botswana, 152–53, 160
Bourdonnais, Bertrand Francois Mahé de la, 11
Britain
  in control of the region, 12–16, 36–37, 44, 88, 112, 147, 182
  its interest in the Indian Ocean, 17, 53–54, 171, 201–204
  and the law of the sea, 223–25, 238–39
  relations with regional powers, 52, 67–72, 104–107, 109, 125, 147–51, 154, 161
  withdraws from the region, 21, 46–49, 112–13, 117, 152–53, 167, 173
British High Commission territories: see Botswana, Lesotho, Swaziland
Bubiyan Island, 119, 178
Buddhism in the Indian Ocean region, 31–32
Burma, 20, 88, 107–108, 194
Bushire, 114

Cabora Bassa, 157
Cape Leeuwin, 24
Cape of Good Hope, 6–7, 8, 24, 35, 149–50, 181, 189, 205, 210
Caprivi Strip, 148
Central Treaty Organization (CENTRO), 53–54, 114–16, 173, 202
Ceylon: see Sri Lanka
Chagos Archipelago, 168, 173, 179, 201
Chah Bahar, 113, 126

Chandernagor, 13, 204n
Cheng Ho, Admiral, 6
China
  and the law of the sea, 127, 195
  relations with regional powers, 50–57, 72, 91, 98, 104, 106, 132–33, 145, 158–59
  rivalry with the Soviet Union, 176, 182–83, 193–96, 233–34
  role in Indian Ocean, 5–6, 171–72, 192–96
Chittagong, 178–79
Chola Empire, 5
Christians in the Indian Ocean region, 31–32
Christmas Island, 69
Clive, Robert, 12
Cockburn Sound naval base, 69, 190
Cocos (Keeling) Islands, 69
Comoro Islands, 15, 21, 44, 53, 145, 165, 204, 224
Compage, 30, 30n
Continental shelf, 225–61; see also Law of the sea
Coral Sea, Battle of the, 20
Côtiers, 162
Covilham, Pero de, 7
Cuba, 51, 155–56

Dammam, 120
Danakils, 129
Daud Khan, General Mohammad, 98, 109
Debré, Michel, 166, 205
Desroches Island, 201
Dharan, 120, 173
Dhofar rebellion, 51, 125
Dias, Bartolomeu, 6
Diego Garcia, 173–74, 174n, 184
  expansion of, 57, 67, 74, 77, 93–94, 99, 104, 115, 132, 142, 161, 163, 167, 189–90, 190n
  strategic location of, 134n, 201–202, 232
Diego Suarez, 15, 20, 53, 163, 166, 204
Djibouti, 21, 130–31, 135, 166; see also French Territory of Afars and Issas
Douglas-Home, Sir Alec, 94
Dubai, 122–27
Dupleix, Joseph François, 11
Duval, Gaétan, 167

Egypt, 3–4, 56, 128, 137n, 139–40
Eilat, 140
Enterprise, aircraft carrier, 93n, 175, 187n
Eritrea, 132, 142, 236
Erythrean Sea, 27

Ethiopia
earlier history of, 4, 7, 9, 15, 18, 135
foreign relations of, 129-33, 135, 173, 193
geographic location and instability of, 51, 129-30, 142

Farquhar Island, 201
Five Power Defense Pact, 53, 76-77, 202
Force d'intervention, 205
France: see also French Territory of Afars and Issas; Comoro Islands; Réunion Island
colonial involvement of, 10-13, 15-16, 21, 36-37, 51-53, 136-37, 204-206
relations with regional powers, 51-52, 130-31, 162-63, 165-68, 171, 204n, 238-39
Fraser, Prime Minister Malcolm, 67, 69, 71
FRELIMO (Mozambique Liberation Front), 56, 156
French Territory of Afars and Issas, 21, 51, 53, 131, 135-37
Fujairah, 122-24
Funan Empire, 5

Gama, Vasco da, 7, 7n, 30, 156
Gan Island, 57, 105, 202
Gandhi, Prime Minister Indira, 71, 91, 115, 214, 236n
Geopolitics, 29, 38
Germany, 17-18, 20
Ghurkas, 106
Gibraltar, Strait of, 189
Goa, 8, 11, 96
Great Britain: see Britain
Great Rift Valley, 33, 159
Gunboat diplomacy, 58-59, 94, 181
Gupta kingdom, 94

Haile Selassie, Emperor, 130, 141
Hanferi, Ali Mirrah, 133, 136
Henry, Prince (the Navigator), 6
Himalayan States: see Nepal; Bhutan; Sikkim
Hinduism in Indian Ocean region, 31-32
Hitler-Stalin Pact, 47
Hodeida, 178
Holland: see Netherlands
Hongkong, 202
Hormuz Strait, 7, 10, 111-14, 117, 123, 125-26, 181, 210, 222

Horn of Africa, 51, 128-29, 142
Houtman, Cornelius de, 10
Hughes, Sir Edward, 12

Idi Amin, 141
India, 89-95
foreign relations of, 49-50, 56, 90-94, 105-107, 115, 176, 193, 214-15
hegemonial aspirations of, 89, 94-96, 107, 235-36
under British rule, 17-21, 36-37, 88-89, 96
Indian Ocean: see also Malacca Strait; Hormuz Strait; Bab el Mandeb Strait; Law of the sea
history and geopolitics of, 1-22, 24-29, 33-35
shipping in and straits of, 35, 39, 175-79, 207, 210, 190-91, 219-21, 233, 240-43
Indian Ocean region: see also Zone of Peace
economic significance of, 32, 34, 210-19
geopolitics of, 29-35, 38-41, 241-42
history of, 1-22, 35-38, 44, 65-66, 171-72, 200-206
instabilities and balances of power of, 39-41, 45-46, 52-59, 210, 231-37
Indonesia, 73-76
foreign relations of, 73-76, 80, 195, 206, 222-24, 235
history of, 20, 50, 66
Iran: see also Persia; Persian Gulf
foreign relations of, 19, 99, 113-17, 125-26, 173, 175
hegemonial aspirations of, 51, 113-15, 232, 236
oil wealth of, 210, 213-18
Iraq, 19, 21, 117-18, 178, 210
Islam, 4-6, 7n, 27n, 30-32
Islamic Summit Conference (1974), 100, 105
Israel, 71, 116-17, 131-32, 139-40, 212
Issas, 133, 135-36
Italy, 15, 18, 130
Ivato Airfield, 204

Japan
its interest in the region, 72, 112, 207-208, 222-23
in World War II, 19-20, 65, 105, 171
Java Sea, Battle of the, 19
Jidda, 140
Jinnah, Mohammed Ali, 96

João II, King, 6-7
Johore Strait, 84
Jordan, 21, 139-40
Jubaland, 17
Jufair Naval Base, 122

Kachchaitivu Island, 103n
Kagnew Station, 132, 134n, 174
Kariba Dam, 155
Kashmir, 89, 96, 194
Kaunda, President Kenneth, 158-59
Kenya, 15, 134, 141-42
Kenyatta, President Jomo, 141-42
Kerguelen Islands, 204
Kharg Island, 114, 125
Khor Abdullah Channel, 118, 178
Khrushchev, 91, 176, 188
Khurramshahr, 114
Kissinger, Henry A., 95n, 101, 151n, 194, 217n
Kra Peninsula, 85, 86
Kuala Lumpur Declaration (1971), 66, 77, 83
Kuwait, 21, 119-20, 173, 178, 207, 210, 216
KwaZulu, 149

La Charente flagship, 204
Lancaster, Captain James, 10
Law of the sea, 221-27, 241
League of Nations, 18, 59, 130
Lee Kuan Yew, Prime Minister, 81-82
Lenin, 176
Lesotho, 152-53, 159
Linschoten, Jan Huyghen van, 10
Lombok Strait, 84, 222, 241
Lourenço Marques: see Maputo

Machel, Samora M., 156
Madagascar, 21, 26, 145; see also Malagasy Republic
Mahé Island, 165, 202
Malacca Strait, 8, 10, 74, 82-86, 195, 220, 222-23, 241
Malagasy Republic, 21, 52-53, 75, 162-64, 204, 223, 227
Malawi, 21, 149, 159-60
Malay races, 75
Malaysia, 20, 22-24, 50-51, 76-80, 195
Maldives, Republic of the, 21, 88, 105, 202, 224
Malik, Foreign Minister Adam, 74
Mancham, President James R., 165

Manoel I, King, 7
MAPHILINDO, 75
Maputo, 155-56
Mascarene Islands, 166, 168
Masirah Island, 57, 202
Massawa, 130
Mauritius, 10, 13, 21, 145, 166-69, 173, 178, 201-202, 224
Maurya kingdom, 94
Mayotte Island, 165, 165n, 204
Menelik II, Emperor, 129-30, 135
Merinas, 162
MIDEASTFOR (U.S. Middle East Task Force), 123, 173-74
Mogul Empire, 11, 14, 94
Mohamed Siad Barre, 133
Mohammad Riza Shah, 63n, 113-17
Monsoon winds, 26, 26n, 29
Moynihan, Daniel P., 93n
Mozambique, 15, 21, 53, 156-58, 206, 210
Mozambique Channel, 164
Musandam Peninsula, 123, 126
Muscat: see Oman

Naga guerrillas, 91
Nagumo, Vice Admiral, 19
Namibia: see South West Africa
Napoleon I, 13, 29
Napoleonic Wars, 12-13, 166
Nehru, Prime Minister Jawaharlar, 89, 91, 95
Nepal, 88, 106-107, 194
Netherlands, 10-12, 13, 19-20, 36, 210
Nicobar Islands, 20, 27, 95
Nimeri, President Jafar Muhammad, 139
Nixon Doctrine, 185-86
North Atlantic Treaty Organization (NATO), 40, 200-201, 221
Nyerere, President Julius, 160

Oil
  affecting balance of power, 214-19, 220-21
  deposits in the region, 112, 212, 226, 237
  transportation of, 151-52, 219-21
Oman, 10-11, 21, 51, 115, 117, 124-25, 160, 202
Oman, Gulf of, 27, 126
Ombai Strait, 84, 241
Organization of African Unity (OAU), 40, 51, 130, 150, 155, 159-63, 236-37
Organization of Petroleum Exporting Coun-

tries (OPEC), 116, 210, 212-19, 237
Oriental trade, 6, 8-9, 210
Ottoman Empire, 7, 9, 15, 46, 142, 176

Pakistan
  creation and composition of, 20, 30, 50-
    51, 88-89, 96-97, 100-101
  foreign relations of, 96-97, 89, 92, 109,
    173, 193-94, 235-36
Papua-New Guinea, 70
Paracel Islands, 195
Paris, Treaty of (1763 and 1783), 12
Paris, Treaty of (1814 and 1815), 13, 166
Paris, Treaty of (1856), 239, 239n
Pax Britannica: see Britain
Payva, Affonso de, 7
Perim Island 137, 137n
Periplus of the Erythrean Sea, 4
Persia, 3, 17, 111; for period after 1935,
    see Iran
Persian Gulf
  political role of, 16, 30, 51, 112, 173-76,
    232-33
  as source of oil, 39, 207, 210, 212-18
Philippines, 65, 224
Plassey, Battle of (1757), 12
Politique du pavillon, 206
Pondichéry, 11, 13, 204n
Portugal, 6-11, 21, 35-36, 53, 124, 155-57,
    199, 206
Prester John, 6, 9
Pushtunistan, 97, 109

Qabus, Sultan, 125
Qatar, 21, 121-22
Qishm Island, 126
Qoins Islands, 126

Raffles, Sir Stamford, 14
Ramanantsoa, President, 163-64
Ramgoolan, Sir Seewoosagur, 167
Ras-al-Khaimah, 122-24
Ratsiraka, President Didier, 164
Red Sea, 27, 128-29, 137, 139
René, Albert, 165
Réunion Island, 166, 204
Reza Shah, 19
Rhodesia, 40, 51, 150-56, 236
Rodriques Island, 168, 224
Roman Empire, 3-4, 211
Russia, 12, 114, 175-76; for period after
    1918, see Soviet Union

Russo-Japanese War, 12

Sabah, 76
Saddam Hussein, 116
Safavi, Admiral Shams, 61
Said bin Tamur, Sultan, 124
Salalah Airfield, 202
Sarawak, 76
Saudi Arabia
  foreign relations of, 17, 99-100, 120-21,
    173
  oil wealth of, 207, 210, 213-18, 236
Seif-bin-Sultan, 11
Seychelles Islands, 21, 44, 145, 164-65,
    179, 201-202, 224
Seyyid Said, 13, 160
Sharjah, 122-24
Shatt-el-Arab, 17, 114-18
Sheba, Queen of, 132
Shri Vijaya, 5
Sikkim, 88, 91, 107, 194
Simonstown base, 150
Singapore
  foreign relations of, 34, 50-51, 57, 69-71,
    78-82, 202, 225
  origin and ethnic composition of, 14, 76,
    79-81
Singapore Strait, 81, 83-84, 210, 222-23
Singh, Sardar Swaran, 93n
Smith, Ian, 154
Socotra, 8, 15, 137, 178-79
Solomon, King, 132
Somalia, 21, 51, 130-33, 140, 178, 236
Somerville, Admiral Sir James, 19
SOSUS (sound surveillance under sea), 241
South Africa
  foreign relations of, 145-53, 226
  origin and geopolitical status of, 15, 34,
    40, 51-52, 236
South East Asian Treaty Organization
    (SEATO), 54, 66, 66n
South West Africa, 144, 148-49
Soviet Union
  and the law of the sea, 223, 226-27
  naval presence of, 33-39, 48-49, 53-55,
    57-58, 60, 134, 157-58, 175-79, 180n,
    231-34
  political interest in the region, 172, 176,
    217-18, 233-34, 238-43
  relations with regional powers, 51, 56,
    97-99, 109, 114-15, 132-33, 145, 148,
    150, 167, 176

rivalry with China, 182–83, 191–96, 233–34
strategic interest of, 40–41, 179–84
Spices, trade in, 6, 8–9
Spratly Islands, 195
Sri Lanka, 13–14, 20, 50, 53, 60, 88, 102–105, 193, 226
Straits: see Malacca Strait; Hormuz Strait; Bab el Mandeb Strait; Law of the sea
Subic Bay naval base, 57, 189
Subrahmanyan, K., 61
Sudan, 21, 131, 138–39
Suez Canal
  reopening of, 191, 231, 233
  shipping route, 15, 18, 99, 139–40, 188, 205, 210
Suffren, Pierre André de, 12
Suharto, 74
Sukarno, 50, 55–56, 73, 206, 213
Sunda Strait, 84, 222, 241
Swaziland, 152–53, 160

Tanganyika: see Tanzania
TanZam Railway, 158–59, 161, 195
Tanzania, 17–18, 21, 51–52, 141, 160–62, 193, 225–26
Territorial waters: see Law of the sea
Thailand, 15, 84–86
Tibet, 16, 91, 175
Timor Island, 75, 206
Timor Sea, 25, 27, 71
Tiran, Strait of, 140
Tlatelolco Treaty (1967), 239, 242
Tordesillas, Treaty of (1495), 9
Torres Strait, 27, 84
Transkei, 149
Trincomalee, 12, 53, 57, 173
Tromelin Island, 168
Trucial States: see United Arab Emirates
Tsiranana, President Philibert, 162, 164
Turkey, 114, 118
Turkish Straits, 188–89

Uganda, 21, 141, 161
Ugaz, 133
Umm Qasr, 118, 178, 190
Umm-al-Qaiwain, 122–24
Union of Soviet Socialist Republics: see Soviet Union
United Arab Emirates, 21, 122–24
United Kingdom: see Britain
United Nations, 59–62, 154, 172, 186, 219,

237, 238n; see also Zone of Peace proposal
United States of America: see also Diego Garcia
  bases and naval presence of, 39, 57, 60, 67–68, 122, 165, 173–75, 190–91, 232
  economic interests of, 112, 185, 215n, 217–18
  and the law of the sea, 223, 227
  political interest of, 172, 184–86, 200–201, 232–34, 238–39, 240–45
  relations with regional powers, 52–53, 67, 69, 72, 98–99, 104, 120, 132, 173, 232–33
  and the strategic balance, 184–86, 192n, 240–43
  submarines of, 175–76, 191, 240–43

Vacuum of power, 37, 47–48
Verwoerd, Hendrik F., 146
Victoria, Queen, 14
Vietnam War, 85, 177
Vishakapatnam, 178–79, 190
Vladivostok Summit Conference, 190–91
Voortrekkers, 147
Vorster, Prime Minister John, 159

Wakham Strip, 194
Waldheim, Dr. Kurt, 61
Warba Island, 119, 178
Wetar Strait, 84, 222
Whitlam, Prime Minister Gough, 67, 70–71
World Wars I and II, 17–20

Yamani, Sheik Ahmed Zaki, 214n
Yemen, People's Republic of, 126, 131, 137n, 138, 179n
Yemen Arab Republic, 131, 138

Zafer, King Mohammad, 109
Zambesi River, 148, 155, 157
Zambia, 21, 158–59, 193
Zanzibar, 11, 15, 124, 160–62
Zanzibar Channel, 222
Zone of Peace proposal
  before the United Nations, 40–41, 50, 59–63
  endorsed by regional powers, 74, 77–78, 85, 104, 115, 141, 161–63, 167, 195
  opposed by some nonregional powers, 186, 203–204, 237–40
Zulus, 146–47